THE INTERNATIONAL HANDBOOK OF FINANCIAL REPORTING

INTERNATIONAL

CHAPMAN & HALL

University and Professional Division

London · Glasgow · New York · Tokyo · Melbourne · Madras

Published by Chapman & Hall, 2-6 Boundary Row, London SE1 8HN

Chapman & Hall, 2-6 Boundary Row, London SE1 8HN, UK

Blackie Academic & Professional, Wester Cleddens Road,
Bishopbriggs, Glasgow G64 2NZ, UK

Chapman & Hall Inc., 29 West 35th Street, New York NY10001, USA

Chapman & Hall Japan, Thomson Publishing Japan, Hirakawacho
Nemoto Building, 6F, 1-7-11 Hirakawa-cho, Chiyoda-ku, Tokyo 102, Japan

Chapman & Hall Australia, Thomas Nelson Australia, 102 Dodds Street,
South Melbourne, Victoria 3205, Australia

Chapman & Hall India, R. Seshadri, 32 Second Main Road, CIT East,
Madras 600 035, India

First edition 1993

© 1993 Nexia International

Printed in England by Clays Ltd, St Ives plc

ISBN 0 412 55690 1

A catalogue record for this book is available from the British Library

Library of Congress Cataloging-in-Publication data available

∞ Printed on permanent acid-free text paper, manufactured in accordance with the
proposed ANSI/NISO Z 39.48-1992 and ANSI Z 39.48-1984

Contents

Preface

The growth in the number of cross-border mergers and acquisitions and the globalisation of the world's securities markets mean that investors, analysts, business executives and financial advisors have an increasing need to look at financial reports issued in countries other than their own. As discussed in the Introduction to this book, there are major pitfalls for the unwary, as differing history, cultures, and commercial environments of nations around the world have evolved a variety of approaches to reporting financial information to the public at large.

This guide has been prepared to give a brief description and explanation of the accounting and reporting practices in selected countries. Its layout, by country and then by subject matter, is intended to:

● portray the financial reporting procedures in each country; and

● facilitate the comparison of the procedures by using, for the most part, the same subject headings for each country selected.

Although this book covers many of the important matters to be considered in looking at financial statements, it is not intended to be a comprehensive survey of all differences in accounting methods among countries. It aims to provide general guidance and does not seek to provide answers to all the questions that may arise in any given situation.

The financial statements of unincorporated business concerns such as partnerships are not dealt with specifically, though many of the accounting principles and practices described in each chapter will be relevant to them.

Users of this guide are strongly advised to read the overview of the main systems of accounting in use and the background against which those systems can be assessed, as presented in the Introduction.

Whilst all reasonable care has been taken in the preparation of this book no responsibility or liability is accepted by the authors for any omissions or

Preface

misstatements it may contain or for any loss or damage howsoever occasioned to any person relying on any statement or omission in this book. Professional advice should be sought before any decisions are taken.

The scope of experience reflected in this book is the result of time, effort, and co-operation from many partners and staff of Nexia International which is an international organisation with 280 offices in more than 60 countries employing over 7,500 individuals. Member firms provide clients with a comprehensive range of accounting, auditing, tax and consulting services on both a national and international basis.

Nexia International professionals have spent hundreds of hours working on this book. Besides the partners identified in the Appendix, Patrick Wright in London deserves special thanks for his contribution to the preparation, research, and co-ordination of this book.

Should further information or advice be required whether generally or on specific issues raised in this book, readers should contact their local Nexia Technical Contact partner, a full list of which is found at the end of this book.

Introduction

Objectives

Those faced with the task of understanding a set of foreign financial statements will naturally tend to base their judgement on their knowledge and experience of the way in which financial statements are prepared in their own country. It can, however, be very misleading to attempt to apply this knowledge and experience to financial statements prepared in another country without first having a basic understanding of the accounting and reporting practices of that country.

Financial statements are produced in response to the varying needs of users. The answers to the questions – "Whom are they meant for?" and "What do those people need them for?" and other related questions – have shaped the development of accounting and reporting practices worldwide. There are various factors that help provide the background against which a company's financial statements can be viewed:

● What class of users are the financial statements intended for? Does the government's need for accounting information take precedence over that of investors/creditors? How active is the capital market/stock exchange? Are users more interested in performance and profitability or balance sheet strength?

● How much emphasis is placed on creditor protection and conservatism? Is the prudence concept tempered by the need for fair presentation or is heavy conservatism applied in valuing assets and making provisions?

● To what extent does the company dictate the form of the financial statements? Are the detailed requirements formulated by the accounting profession or by law? How good is the general quality of financial statement disclosure? Requirements established largely by the professional bodies are usually published in the form of "Accounting Standards". For example, in the United States there are virtually no legal requirements but the pronouncements of the Financial Accounting Standards Board (FASB) are binding for companies producing financial statements that are prepared in accordance with generally

3

Introduction

accepted accounting principles.

● How strongly have tax laws influenced the measurement of items in the financial statements?

● What is the aim of the financial statements? Are they intended to show a fair commercial view or a legal one?

The answers to these questions have resulted in a spectrum of accounting systems. At one extreme is what might be called the "legalistic" framework, where financial statements are drawn up in accordance with a rigid set of rules, irrespective of whether adherence to those rules contradicts the commercial realities. At the other extreme is the "commercial" framework where the only inviolable rule is that the financial statements must give a clear and realistic picture of the performance and financial position of the reporting company.

Historically, with the notable exception of Japan, those countries with larger securities markets, where the emphasis has been on raising business finance through equity rather than debt, have tended to fall in the commercial half of the spectrum; the interests of the investor or potential investor are paramount. Correspondingly, countries in the other half of the spectrum are those where, in the past, securities markets have been less strong and banks have played a more dominant finance role in the economy.

However, the distinction between the two is being blurred by the trend toward international harmonisation, a trend that is being driven by macroeconomic factors such as the arrival of the single European market, the globalisation of securities trading and indeed the increase in the size of securities markets throughout the world.

It should be remembered that current practices in many countries are interlinked through historical and economic connections. Indeed, there have been relatively few generators of accounting philosophy and many of the new industrialised nations with younger professions have either adopted procedures of a particular country or group of countries, or have opted to follow international standards in total.

Legalistic Framework

Under these systems the emphasis is directed more to:

● safeguarding the interests of creditors and providers of loan finance above those of the shareholders, creating a tendency to conservatism in valuation principles and the creation of hidden reserves.

● determining tax liabilities, which give rise to very detailed rules for income measurement and asset valuation and the way in which items must be charged in the financial statements. This can mean that the financial statements may be drawn up more for the benefit of the fiscal authorities than for other users, and overdepreciation and undervaluation of assets (for example) are not uncommon.

There tends to be great emphasis on uniformity of presentation. In countries such as France a General Accounting Plan is created so that the accounting system can serve as a tool for the furtherance of national economic objectives. The plan is established by the government to provide information on which policy making can be based, and the financial statements must comply with it in order to facilitate the extraction and comparison of financial information.

These systems require the auditor to report whether or not the financial statements have been drawn up correctly in accordance with the law rather than reporting on a "true and fair view". Many countries however which have historically followed a legalistic approach now also require reporting in terms of the truth and fairness of the financial statements. Less regard is paid to presenting a fair commercial view of a company's affairs to the investor. Consequently, in some countries, the auditor has little scope for exercising independent judgment.

Fair Commercial View

Here, the emphasis is placed on providing information to investors who are regarded as the prime users of the financial statements. The financial statements are intended to give a fair commercial view of a company's affairs and operations. Thus, there is less rigidity in the legal framework, and taxation requirements do not determine the format of the financial statements. By and large, standard setting tends to be the responsibility of the professional bodies, and the system is more flexible in response to changing circumstances as a result.

This flexibility also shows through at the individual entity level, and the auditor may exercise greater judgement in giving his opinion, which is directed to "fair presentation".

In some cases, this principle of truth and fairness, which in itself may be a legal requirement (for example, as in the United Kingdom), overrules other legal requirements if the fair commercial picture would be distorted by strict compliance with those other requirements.

Often referred to as the "Anglo-Saxon" approach, the main adherents to this philosophy include the United States, Canada, the United Kingdom, Australia, Hong Kong, Ireland, New Zealand, South Africa and the Netherlands.

Harmonisation of Practice

The variations in financial statements drawn up under existing practices have led to attempts at harmonisation of accounting procedures and disclosure.

There are two affiliated international organisations of the accounting profession with a common membership, the International Accounting Standards Committee (IASC) and the International Federation of Accountants (IFAC). IASC has issued a series of International Accounting Standards (IAS) to define a set of accounting principles that can be adopted internationally, aiming to make financial statements comparable on a worldwide basis.

In addition, certain considerations should govern the selection and application of the accounting policies. These are:

● Prudence – Transactions are often subject to uncertainties. This should be recognised by exercising prudence.

● Substance over form – Transactions should be dealt with according to financial reality (substance), not merely legal form.

● Materiality – Items should be disclosed if they are material enough to affect evaluations or decisions.

Depending on the amount and quality of the disclosure, the reader can then ask, "How has that item been measured?" In other words, "What methods have been used to fix its value at a particular point in time?" For example, replacement cost is often used in the Netherlands; in Brazil, financial statements are, for some companies, adjusted for inflation in accordance with government requirements; the last-in-first-out method (LIFO) of valuing inventory is rarely permitted – one notable exception being the United States.

Format for this Book

The book has been prepared to give an overall view for each country of the framework within which the financial statements are prepared (eg, the first four topics in the list that follows). The detailed subjects that follow cover the major elements of financial reporting, and items of topical interest.

The first chapter in this book describes the international pronouncements under these headings as a yardstick against which countries' actual practices can be compared. The second chapter looks more closely at the requirements of European Community Directives, which, although not all yet taken up by member states, clearly show the "Anglo-Saxon" drift of the Community toward reporting practice followed in the United States. Subsequently, the book is divided into chapters covering each country's accounting and reporting practices, and for each country most of the following subjects are covered, in the order shown here:

Form and Content of Financial Statements

Public Filing Requirements

Audit Requirements

Valuation Principles

Group Financial Statements

Depreciation

Introduction

Leasing

Research and Development

Inventories

Capital and Reserves

Foreign Currency Translation

Taxation

Unusual and Prior Period Items

Retirement Benefits

Treatment of Government Grants

Related Party Transactions

Segmental Information

Commitments and Contingencies

Price Level Changes

Future Developments

In Conclusion

Because of the diversity of practice, be warned against taking apparent harmonisation at face value. In particular, an audit report that mentions the words presents fairly or the phrase true and fair view may actually be referring to a fair legalistic view (that is, a correct, legal view) and not a commercial view. Translation of stock phrases from one language into another may not succeed in translating conventional (but unspoken) interpretations of their meaning.

It is hoped that this book will be of help in giving a clearer picture of the similarities and differences where they exist.

International Standards and Guidelines

This chapter summarises some of the requirements included in the International Accounting Standards (IAS) published by The International Accounting Standards Committee (IASC) and in the International Standards on Auditing (ISA) published by the International Auditing Practices Committee (IAPC) of the International Federation of Accountants (IFAC).

The IASC has published a statement of intent entitled "Comparability of Financial Statements" which will ultimately lead to a reduction in the number of alternatives which are available to companies when choosing appropriate policies/disclosures for their financial statements. Many of the IAS are therefore likely to be revised in the short to medium term.

Form and Content of Financial Statements

The preface to IAS explains that financial statements cover balance sheets, income statements, statements of changes in financial position, and notes and other explanatory material. Statements of changes in financial position are required by IAS7.

Three fundamental accounting assumptions – going concern, consistency and accruals – underlie financial statements that are presented in accordance with IAS. The concepts of prudence, substance over form, and materiality should govern the selection of accounting policies. IAS are not intended to apply to immaterial items. IASC has also issued a "Framework for the Preparation and Presentation of Financial Statements" which deals with the objectives and qualitative characteristics of financial statements, the definition, recognition and measurement of the elements of financial statements and concepts of capital and capital maintenance. It also identifies the users of financial statements and their needs.

IASC has not so far prescribed formats for the presentation of information in financial statements, but IAS5 includes a detailed list of items required to be disclosed, whether on the face of the income statement or balance sheet, or in the notes. These basic disclosure requirements are augmented by the requirements of other IAS.

International Standards and Guidelines

IAS5 includes the overall requirement that "all material information should be disclosed that is necessary to make the financial statements clear and understandable," and it also requires financial statements to show comparative figures for the preceding period.

Audit Requirements

In cases where national laws or conventions require an audit report, guidance to auditors is provided by an IAPC Standard (ISA 13) that covers the form and content of the auditor's report issued after an independent audit of the financial statements. The audit report should contain a "clear written expression of opinion on the financial information" and should represent the auditor's overall conclusion as to whether:

● the financial information has been prepared using acceptable accounting policies, which have been consistently applied;

● the financial information complies with relevant regulations and statutory requirements;

● the view presented by the financial information as a whole is consistent with the auditor's knowledge of the business of the entity; and

● there is adequate disclosure of all material matters relevant to the proper presentation of the financial statements.

Four categories of audit opinion are recognised: unqualified, qualified, and adverse opinions, and a disclaimer of opinion. Where a qualified opinion is given the reasons should be stated in the audit report in a clear and informative manner.

Valuation Principles

IAS generally are based on the historical cost basis of accounting but IAS16 allows the revaluation of property, plant, and equipment and IAS25 allows the revaluation of investments. IAS2 permits the valuation of inventory on a LIFO basis. IAS28 requires investments to be valued using the equity method in consolidated financial statements and either at cost, equity or revalued amount in the investors individual financial statements.

Financial statements are required by IAS1 to include clear and concise disclosure of all significant accounting policies.

In hyperinflationary economies IAS29 requires financial statements to be adjusted and stated in terms of the measuring unit current at the balance sheet date.

Group Financial Statements

Consolidated financial statements are required, under IAS27, to be prepared by enterprises (parents) that control one or more other enterprises (subsidiaries). Control is defined as the "power to govern the financial and operating policies of the management" of the subsidiary so as to obtain benefit from its activities. Both foreign and domestic subsidiaries are required to be consolidated but subsidiaries should be excluded from the consolidation if control is intended to be temporary or if they operate under severe long-term restrictions that impair control by the parent. Such subsidiaries are accounted for as investments (IAS25).

Parents do not require consolidated financial statements if they themselves are wholly owned, or if they are "virtually" wholly owned and the minority shareholders do not object. In such cases, the name and registered office of the ultimate parent should be disclosed.

The members of the group should have uniform accounting reference dates, and consolidated financial statements should be prepared using uniform accounting policies unless it is impracticable to do so.

IAS28, "Accounting for Investments in Associates" requires that such investments be accounted for by the equity method in consolidated financial statements, unless it was purchased for resale in which case it should be valued at cost. Under the equity method the investor's share of the investee's results of operations are included in the consolidated income statement and the carrying amount of the investment is adjusted for any change in the net assets of the investee. Associates are defined as enterprises in respect of which the investor has no intention of disposing of its interest and over which the investor has significant influence, ie, the power to participate in (but not control) the financial and operating policy decisions. Significant influence is presumed when 20% or more of the voting power of the investee is held, unless it can clearly be demonstrated otherwise; equally it is presumed that significant influence is not exercised where less than 20% is held, again, unless demonstrated otherwise.

IAS31 deals with the treatment of joint ventures, which are contractual arrangements between two or more parties who share in the control of an activity in such a way that joint managerial decisions are required. Those enterprises that conduct a proportion of their activities as joint ventures, or whose joint ventures are an extension of their other activities, may account for them using the proportionate consolidation method. Under this method the investor's pro-rata share of the assets, liabilities, revenues, and expenses of each joint venture are aggregated with those in its own financial statements. The equity method of accounting is however an allowed alternative.

IAS22 describes two ways of accounting for business combinations:

● The purchase method, under which fair values are attributed to the assets and liabilities of a subsidiary acquired and any balance of the purchase price remaining is accounted for as goodwill. Positive goodwill may either be written off to reserves on acquisition or be amortised over its useful life. Negative goodwill may be treated in a similar way or may be allocated to nonmonetary depreciable assets.

● The pooling of interests method, under which the assets, liabilities, income, and expenses of the combining enterprises are included in the financial statements for the period in which the combination occurs and for any comparative period as if the enterprises had been combined from the start of those periods.

The pooling of interests method may only be used where there is a uniting of interests, that is, when the shareholders of the enterprises combine in one entity the whole of the net assets and operations of the enterprises in such a way as to achieve a continuing mutual sharing in the risks and benefits of the combined entity. A uniting of interests results from an exchange of voting common shares between the enterprises involved and there is normally continuing participation by the management of both enterprises in the management of the combined enterprise.

Disclosure

Consolidated financial statements should include an appropriate listing of all significant subsidiaries, associates, and joint ventures. Other disclosure requirements are numerous, particularly in respect of changes in the composition of the group or exclusion of subsidiaries from consolidation.

Depreciation

Assets that are expected to be used during more than one accounting period but have a limited useful life and are held for use in the production or supply of services, for rental, or for internal administrative purposes should be depreciated (IAS4). Their cost (or revalued amount) should be allocated on a systematic basis to accounting periods over their useful life. Under IAS4, land would not normally be depreciated, since it has an indefinite life, but buildings would be depreciated.

For each major class of asset, disclosure should be made of:

● the depreciation methods used;

● the useful lives or depreciation rates used;

● total depreciation allocated for the period; and

● accumulated depreciation.

The depreciation method selected should be applied consistently and if changed, the reason for and the effect of the change should be disclosed.

Leasing

IAS17 distinguishes between "finance leases" under which substantially all the risks and rewards of ownership of an asset are transferred from the lessor to the lessee and "operating leases" where such a transfer does not take place.

Finance Leases
Lessees should account for finance leases as the acquisition of an asset and the assumption of an obligation. The amount included as an asset is the fair value of the item acquired at the inception of the lease (or the present value of the lease payments if lower) and this amount is then depreciated in the same way as other purchased assets. Lease payments are divided between the finance charge, which is an expense, and the reduction of the outstanding capital liability to the lessor.

In the balance sheet of a lessor, an asset subject to a finance lease is shown as a deferred receivable and not as property, plant, and equipment. Lease receipts are then divided between interest income (on a basis that gives a constant return on the investment outstanding) and a reduction of the receivable.

Operating Leases
A lessee should charge operating lease payments to income as they are incurred and should not include the underlying assets in the balance sheet.

The lessor includes the asset in the balance sheet as property, plant, and equipment.

Disclosure
Lessees should disclose:

● the amount of assets subject to finance leases;

● liabilities relating to those assets; and

● commitments for minimum lease payments under both types of leases.

Lessors should disclose:

● the gross investment in finance leases and related unearned finance income;

● the basis for allocating income from finance leases; and

● the cost and depreciation of assets subject to operating leases.

Research and Development
Under IAS9, research and development costs include salaries and wages of research and development personnel, materials and services consumed, depreciation or amortisation of equipment, patents or licenses used, and general overhead expenses. All such costs should be charged as an expense in the period in which they are incurred unless they are development costs for a specific project which meets all the following conditions: the project is clearly defined and the related costs can be identified; the project has been proved to be technically feasible and management intends to produce and market or use the product; there is a clear indication that a market exists for the product; and adequate resources exist to complete the project.

13

If these conditions prevail, development costs may be carried forward and should be amortised over the period in which the product is expected to be sold or an underlying process used. The net carrying amount for development costs carried forward should not exceed the amount that can be recovered from future revenues. Development costs, once written off, should not be reinstated.

Disclosure should be made of research and development expenses for the period (including amortisation of development costs carried forward) and of the movement in and balance of unamortised development costs, together with the method of amortisation.

Inventories

According to IAS2, inventories should be carried at the lower of cost and net realisable value. Cost is the aggregate of costs of purchase (including import duties, purchase taxes, and transport costs), costs of conversion, and a systematic allocation of overheads, so far as they relate to putting the inventory into its present location and condition. IAS2 indicates that historical cost is usually calculated using the FIFO or weighted average cost formula, but LIFO and base stock are permitted if there is disclosure of the effect of using them. Net realisable value may be calculated item by item or by groups of similar items.

IAS11 deals with accounting for long-term contracts, being those which begin and end in different accounting periods, whether of the fixed price or cost plus types. The standard allows the use of either the percentage of completion method or the completed contract method, though the chosen method should be applied consistently.

Disclosure should be made of the accounting policy used to value inventories, including the cost formula, and inventories should be subclassified to show the values held in each of the main categories appropriate to the business. For long term contracts the work in progress and payments received/receivable should also be disclosed.

Foreign Currency Translation

ISA21 requires different treatment of foreign currency transactions and balances for:

- an entity itself (including overseas branches or subsidiaries whose operations are an integral part of those of the parent); or

- overseas branches or subsidiaries that are not an integral part of the operations of the parent.

For the former category, foreign currency transactions are recorded at the rates of exchange in force at the time of the transaction. At each balance sheet date, monetary assets and liabilities are restated at the closing exchange rate but non-monetary items (such as property, plant, and equipment) are not restated and are maintained at historical rates. Exchange differences on monetary items are recognised in the income statement for the period, unless they relate to long-term items, in which case they may be deferred and recognised in future periods over the remaining life of the item concerned.

For the latter category, at each balance sheet date, all assets and liabilities are translated at the closing rate, and the exchange difference on translating the parent's opening net investment at the closing rate is taken direct to shareholders' interest. Any such difference may be offset by a difference on a long-term liability designated as a hedge against the investment in the overseas branch or subsidiary. Income statement items are translated at either the average rate for the period or the closing rate.

Disclosure should be made of:

● the amount of exchange differences on long-term monetary items that has been deferred;

● any exchange difference on investments in overseas entities taken direct to shareholders' interests; and

● the exchange difference taken to income on the translation of the monetary items of an overseas entity integral to the operations of the parent, together with the methods of translation of overseas entities.

Taxation

Under IAS12, the tax expenses for a period should be determined by reference to the income and expenditure included in the income statement for the period, and tax effect accounting should be adopted, using either the deferral or the liability method. Provision is normally made on both short and long-term timing differences, though tax on the latter need not be provided if there is reasonable evidence that the timing differences will not reverse for a considerable period – at least 3 years ahead. Timing differences not provided (both for the current period and the cumulative total) should be disclosed. Deferred tax assets should not be carried forward unless there is reasonable expectation of realisation.

Disclosure should be made of:

● tax on income from ordinary activities;

● tax on unusual and prior period items;

● the tax effect of the revaluation of assets; and

● the reason for any difference between actual tax expense and tax, at statutory rates, on accounting income.

Unusual and Prior Period Items

Unusual items are defined in IAS8 as gains or losses deriving from events or transactions outside an enterprise's ordinary activities and, therefore, not expected to recur frequently or regularly. The nature and amount of each unusual item should be separately disclosed. In either case sufficient information must be disclosed to enable comparisons to be made of the figures for the period presented.

Prior period items, being items arising from errors and omissions in previous financial statements and adjustments arising from changes in accounting policy, should either be reported by adjusting opening retained earnings and amending the comparative figures in the income statement or be separately disclosed in the income statement as part of net income for the current year. The effect of changes in accounting estimates (such as bad debt provisions or estimates of the useful lives of fixed assets) should be included as part of income from ordinary activities.

Retirement Benefits

The treatment of the cost of providing retirement benefits to employees is described in IAS19 which distinguishes retirement benefit plans having fixed benefits from those where the benefits are defined by the level of contributions.

For the former, IAS19 requires that the cost should be provided in the income statement by consistently using an actuarial accrued benefit or projected benefit valuation method. Costs should not be accrued only on a cash basis or be provided only the retirement of employees. Retirement benefit costs relating to current service of employees should be charged systematically over the remaining working life of the employees. Past service costs may be treated in the same way or may be charged to income as they arise.

For a retirement benefit plan with benefits defined by the level of contributions, the employer's contributions required under the plan are charged to income in the relevant period.

Disclosure

The financial statements of an employer should disclose:

- the accounting policies adopted for retirement benefit plan costs;

- any difference between the amounts transferred to a retirement benefit plan and the contributions charged against income; and

- for a plan with fixed benefits, a statement of the funding approach adopted, the amount of any shortfall of plan assets over the actuarially determined value of future benefits which are not conditional on continued employment and the date of the latest actuarial valuation.

Related Party Transactions

IAS24 considers parties to be related if one has the ability to control the other or exercise significant influence over the other in making financial and operating decisions. Related parties, therefore, include the members of a group, associated enterprises, owners of sufficient voting power to have significant influence, or key management personnel, such as directors.

Disclosure

Since a related party connection may have an effect on the financial position and operating results of an enterprise, the following disclosures are required:

● If one party has the ability to control the other, the relationship should be disclosed regardless of whether there have been transactions.

● If there have been transactions between the parties, the nature of the relationship, the types of transactions, and the elements of the transactions (such as an indication of the volume, amounts outstanding and pricing policies) are disclosed.

Segmental Reporting

Publicly traded and other economically significant entities must disclose the following information for each industry and geographical segment which is considered to be significant to the enterprise:

● description of the activities of each industry segment and the composition of each geographical segment;

● sales, or other revenue, identifying separately that which is inter-segment and that which is external;

● segment result;

● segment assets employed; and

● basis of inter-segment pricing.

A reconciliation should be provided between the sum of the information provided on individual segments and the aggregated information in the financial statements.

Where a change in the identification of segments, or accounting practices followed, takes place the nature and reason for the change must be disclosed, together with, where practicable, its financial effect.

Treatment of Grants

Government grants should not be recognised until there is reasonable certainty that:

● conditions attaching to the grant can be complied with; and

● the grant will be received.

The treatment of grants, as outlined in IAS 20, depends upon whether the grant is a contribution to revenue items or to assets.

Where the grant is given as compensation for revenue expenses it should be matched with those costs in the income statement as they arise. Where the costs (or losses) have already been incurred the grants should be taken to income immediately and if appropriate disclosed as an unusual item.

Grants contributing to the cost of an asset should either be deducted from cost or treated as deferred income.

Where a grant becomes repayable the repayment should first be offset against any unamortised deferred credit and any excess charged to income immediately as a revision of an accounting estimate. If the grant was deducted from the cost of an asset the repayment should be recorded by increasing the carrying value of the asset. Any additional cumulative depreciation then required should be charged immediately to income.

The accounting policy for grants should be disclosed in the financial statements together with a note showing the nature and extent of grants and other assistance received. If there are any outstanding conditions relating to grants already recognised these must be disclosed.

Contingencies

IAS10 deals with the accounting treatment of contingencies and events occurring after the balance sheet date. It requires an accrual to be made for a contingent loss where it is probable that the value of an asset has been impaired and a reasonable estimate of the loss can be made. Contingent gains should not be accrued. If provision is not made, and unless the possibility of the loss is remote, disclosure is required of:

● the nature of the contingency;

● the uncertain factors that might affect the future outcome; and

● an estimate of the financial effect or a statement that such an estimate cannot be made.

Price Level Changes

IAS15 requires enterprises whose "levels of revenues, profit, assets, or employment are significant in the economic environment in which they operate" to provide information reflecting the effects of changing prices. The information may be presented in the primary financial statements or on a supplementary basis. Disclosure is required of:

- the adjustment to depreciation;

- the adjustment to cost of sales;

- the adjustments relating to monetary items and the effect of borrowing and equity interest, when those adjustments are made; and

- the overall effect on results of the adjustments made.

The method used to compute the information should be disclosed. If a current cost method is adopted, the current cost at the balance sheet date of property, plant and equipment, and inventories should also be provided.

Where an enterprise reports in the currency of a hyperinflationary economy IAS 29 requires that their financial statements should be stated in terms of the measuring unit current at the balance sheet date. The corresponding figures for the previous year should also be restated.

The gain or loss on the net monetary position should be included in net income and separately disclosed.

The following should be disclosed:

- the fact that the figures have been restated;

- whether the financial statements are based on the historical or current cost basis; and

- the identity and the level of the price index used and the movement in that index for the current and previous periods.

International Standards and Guidelines

Definitive Statements Issued by IASC

Preface to statements on International Accounting standards

Framework for the Preparation and Presentation of Financial Statements

IAS1   Disclosure of Accounting Policies

IAS2   Valuation and Presentation of Inventories in the Context of the Historical Cost System

IAS3   Superseded by IAS 27 and 28

IAS4   Depreciation Accounting

IAS5   Information to Be Disclosed in Financial Statements

IAS6   Superseded by IAS15

IAS7   Statement of Changes in Financial Positions

IAS8   Unusual and Prior Period Items and Changes in Accounting Policies

IAS9   Accounting for Research and Development Activities

IAS10   Contingencies and Events Occurring after the Balance Sheet Date

IAS11   Accounting for Construction Contracts

IAS12   Accounting for Taxes on Income

IAS13   Presentation of Current Assets and Current Liabilities

IAS14   Reporting Financial Information by Segment

IAS15   Information Reflecting the Effects of Changing Prices

IAS16   Accounting for Property, Plant, and Equipment

IAS17   Accounting for Leases

IAS18   Revenue Recognition

IAS19   Accounting for Retirement Benefits in the Financial Statements of Employers

IAS20   Accounting for Government Grants and Disclosure of Government Assistance

IAS21   Accounting for the Effects of Changes in Foreign Exchange Rates

IAS22   Accounting for Business Combinations

IAS23   Capitalisation of Borrowing Costs

IAS24   Related Party Disclosures

IAS25   Accounting for Investments

IAS26   Accounting and Reporting by Retirement Benefit Plans

IAS27   Consolidated Financial Statements and Accounting for Investments in Subsidiaries

IAS28   Accounting for Investments in Associates

IAS29   Financial Reporting in Hyperinflationary Economies

IAS30   Disclosures in the Financial Statements of Banks and Similar Financial Institutions

IAS31   Financial Reporting of Interests in Joint Ventures

European Community Directives

The Council of the European Communities (CEC) has adopted a number of Directives on company law. The Directives do not have direct legal effect on the members of the European Community (EC) but member states are legally bound to incorporate the content of each Directive into their national law in accordance with the timetable included within the Directive.

 In addition to the mandatory requirements which all member states are required to incorporate into national law, the Directives include many member state options that may be included in national law at the option of each member state.

Membership of European Community
on 1 April 1993

	Date Admitted to Full Membership
Belgium	April 1965
Denmark	January 1973
France	April 1965
Germany	April 1965
Greece	January 1981
Ireland	January 1973
Italy	April 1965
Luxembourg	April 1965
Netherlands	April 1965
Portugal	January 1986
Spain	January 1986
United Kingdom	January 1973

European Community Directives

Company Law Directives Adopted or Proposed

Number	Date of Adoption	Descriptive Title
First	9 March 1968	Public filing of such items as constitutions, financial statements, boards of directors by companies; validity of obligations entered into by companies
Second	13 December 1975	Formation of public companies, minimum capital requirements and rules for maintaining, increasing and reducing capital of public companies
Third	9 October 1978	Regulation of merger by fusion between public companies in the same member state
Fourth	25 July 1978	Form and content of annual financial statements of companies
Fifth	Not yet adopted	Regulation of structure of public companies and boards of directors Employee participation
Sixth	17 December 1982	Regulation of demerger by scission of public companies
Seventh	13 June 1983	Requirement to prepare consolidated financial statements and method of preparation
Eighth	10 April 1984	The approval of persons responsible for carrying out statutory audits
Ninth	Draft withdrawn	The conduct of Groups containing a public company as a subsidiary
Tenth	Not yet adopted	Mergers between public companies not in the same member state
Eleventh	Not yet adopted	Disclosures to be made by branches of companies registered in another member state or non-EEC country
Twelfth	Not yet adopted	Single member private limited companies
Thirteenth	Not yet adopted	Takeovers

Form and Content of Financial Statements

The Fourth Directive requires that financial statements include a balance sheet, income statement, and notes. The Directive also contains alternative formats for the layout of the balance sheet and income statement, one of which is required to be adopted in detail as to layout, order of items, nomenclature, and terminology. There are reduced disclosure requirements for small and medium-sized enterprises. (See Public Filing Requirements below).

Corresponding amounts for the previous year must be shown for each balance sheet and income statement item. Financial statements are required to "give a true and fair view of the company's assets, liabilities, financial position, and profit or loss".

Public Filing Requirements

The First Directive requires each member state to maintain a file in a central, commercial, or companies' register for each of the companies registered therein. The annual financial statements are required to be deposited in this file, together with the auditors' report. A member state option allows small and medium-sized enterprises to file abbreviated financial statements.

Small and medium-sized companies are companies which, on their balance sheet date, do not exceed the limits of two of the following three criteria:

	Small	Medium-sized
Balance sheet total	2 million ECU	8 million ECU
Net turnover	4 million ECU	16 million ECU
Average number of employees during the year	50	250

These limits are, of course, subject to change by further Council Directive. As a rough guide there is approximately $1.2 US dollars to the ECU.

Audit Requirements

The Fourth Directive requires all companies to have their financial statements audited, though member states may exempt small companies from the requirement. In addition to auditing the financial statements, the auditor must ensure that the annual report is consistent with those statements. The qualifications required for auditors are detailed in the Eighth Directive. Auditors are required to carry out their work with "professional integrity", and are also required to be independent.

Valuation Principles

The Fourth Directive includes general valuation principles, which are to be followed in the preparation of financial statements. Any exceptional departures must be disclosed, together with the reasons for such departures and their financial effect.

European Community Directives

These general valuation principles include:

- Presumption that the company is a going concern

- Consistency from year to year

- Prudence

- Inclusion of income and charges relating to the financial year irrespective of the date of receipt or payment (ie accruals)

The prudence principle provides that "only profits made at the balance sheet date may be included" and "account must be taken of all foreseeable liabilities and potential losses" at the balance sheet date. The detailed valuation rules for individual assets "are based on the principle of purchase price or production cost" but a member state option allows for the use of certain other valuation methods (including the revaluation of tangible and financial fixed assets and methods of inflation accounting) as long as full disclosure is made of historical cost or the difference between historical cost and the valuation method used.

Disclosure of the valuation methods applied to the various items in the financial statements is required.

Group Financial Statements

The Seventh Directive requires the preparation of consolidated financial statements by any enterprise (a parent) having one or more subsidiaries. Financial holding companies may be exempted from the requirement by member states, as may groups meeting the medium-size criteria (see Public Filing Requirements above). Parents that are themselves 90% or more owned by another enterprise in a member state need not prepare consolidated financial statements, provided that any minority shareholders agree and provided that the other enterprise does itself prepare consolidated financial statements. By member state option, this exemption may be extended.

Subsidiaries over which the parent's control is severely restricted and subsidiaries held for resale need not be consolidated. Subsidiaries with activities very different from those of the rest of the group should not be consolidated if the resulting financial statements would not give a true and fair view of the group.

Merger accounting may be used at the option of member states under certain conditions.

Minority interests are required to be separately disclosed in the balance sheet and income statement.

Consolidated financial statements should be prepared as if the separate members of the group were a single undertaking, by eliminating intra-group balances and transactions. Uniform accounting policies should be used in the financial statements of each of the members of the group to be consolidated.

A positive consolidation difference, or goodwill, may either be depreciated over a period not exceeding its useful economic life (a five-year life being suggested), or (under a member state's option) be deducted from reserves.

If a member of the group exercises significant influence over the financial and operating policy of another undertaking (not itself a member of the group), the interest in the "associated" undertaking should be separately shown in the balance sheet. Significant influence is presumed when 20% or more of the voting rights are held. The group's share of the profit or loss of the associated undertaking is shown as a separate item in the income statement and the goodwill in the investment must be separately disclosed in the balance sheet or the notes.

Depreciation

The cost of fixed assets with "limited useful economic lives" is required to be reduced by "value adjustments" calculated to write off the value of such assets systematically over their useful economic lives. The cumulative amount of such value adjustments is required to be disclosed, together with corrections to the value adjustments of previous years. Two of the possible income statement formats require the disclosure of the total value adjustments for the year. In the other two formats, the value adjustments are included within other headings, such as cost of sales and administrative expenses.

Leasing

The Directives contain no specific requirements in relation to accounting for leases.

Research and Development

Costs of research and development are required to be separately disclosed as a category of intangible fixed assets, so far as member states allow such costs to be deferred and carried forward as assets. The cost of research and development should normally be written off over a maximum period of five years, though in exceptional circumstances, member states may allow a longer period, as long as the reason is explained in the notes. Distribution of profits is not normally allowed unless distributable reserves and retained profits after any such distribution are at least equal to any research and development expenses not written off.

Inventories

Four items are required to be disclosed, either in the balance sheet or in a note:

- Raw materials and consumables

- Work in progress

- Finished goods and goods for resale

- Payments on account

European Community Directives

Inventories are required to be valued at purchase price or production cost. For goods of the same category and all fungible items, this amount may be calculated using weighted average prices, FIFO, LIFO, or some similar method.

Any material difference between the value included in the balance sheet and the last known market value, prior to the balance sheet date, must be disclosed.

Intangible Assets

The Fourth Directive specifically allows the recognition of intangible assets in the financial statements. These include research and development, patents, licences and trademarks and goodwill.

Goodwill and research and development should normally be written off over a period not exceeding five years unless a longer period is justified in which case disclosure should be made of the reason for adopting a longer period.

Other intangible assets should be written off over their estimated useful lives.

Capital and Reserves

The following items are separately disclosed in the balance sheet:

- Subscribed capital

- Share premium account

- Revaluation reserve

- Profit or loss brought forward

- Profit or loss for the year

The notes should include:

- the number and nominal value (or accounting par value) of shares subscribed during the year;

- the number and nominal value (or accounting par value) of each class of share in issue; and

- a description of any participation certificates, convertible debentures, or similar securities or rights, with an indication of their number and the rights they confer.

Foreign Currency Translation

The Directives do not contain any specific rules concerning foreign currency translation, but the general rules concerning the valuation of items in the financial statements apply. The basis of conversion of items in foreign currency are, however, required to be disclosed.

Taxation

The tax on the profit on ordinary activities should be separately disclosed in the income statement, as should be the tax on extraordinary profits or losses. Member states may allow the two items to be combined on the face of the income statement, but separate disclosure is then required in the notes.

Where the amount of tax charged for a financial year and for earlier years is materially different from the amounts of tax payable for those years, the difference must be disclosed. Disclosure may be made by way of a note to the financial statements. It can also be achieved by separately identifying current and deferred elements of tax on the face of the balance sheet.

If fixed assets are the subject of exceptional value adjustments (or depreciation) for tax purposes, the amount of the adjustments and the reason for making them must be indicated. In addition, the cumulative effect of such adjustments on the income statement must be disclosed, together with the influence of the adjustments on future tax charges.

Unusual and Prior Period Items

Extraordinary income and charges are separately disclosed in the income statement together with related taxes and are defined as income and charges that arise other than in the course of the company's ordinary activities. An explanation of the amount and nature of extraordinary items must be given in the notes.

Income and charges relating to a prior financial year must be quantified and explained in the notes.

Retirement Benefits

Pension costs charged in the income statement are required to be disclosed as a component of social security costs.

Financial commitments concerning pensions that are not included in the balance sheet must be separately disclosed if the information is of assistance in assessing the financial position.

Commitments arising from or entered into with respect to retirement benefits for former directors are also required to be disclosed.

Related Party Transactions

There are no specific requirements with respect to related party transactions.

Commitments and Contingencies

The total amount of any financial commitments not included in the balance sheet must be disclosed if the information would assist in assessing the financial position. Commitments concerning affiliated undertakings must be separately disclosed. Commitments by way of guarantee of any kind must, if they are not shown as liabilities, be clearly set out at the foot of the balance sheet or in the notes. Disclosure of any valuable security provided should also be made, and guarantees in respect of affiliates must be separately identified. Provisions for liabilities and charges should cover losses or debts that are either likely or certain to be incurred but uncertain as to the amount, or as to the date on which they will arise. A member state may also authorise such provisions to cover charges, but no such provisions should "exceed in amount the sums that are necessary".

Price Level Changes

There is no requirement to disclose information about the effects of price level changes, but member states may permit or require the use of valuation methods "designed to take account of inflation for the items shown in annual financial statements, including capital and reserves". Replacement values may also be used for tangible fixed assets with limited useful lives and for stocks as well as for revaluations of tangible and financial fixed assets.

Australia

Duesburys

Australia, as a member of the Commonwealth, has traditionally tended to follow the accounting principles and practices adopted in the United Kingdom. However, the Australian accounting profession has more recently looked to the United States and International Standards to provide guidance.

Australian taxation laws have little influence on Australian accounting as companies are allowed to record different values in their accounting records from those required for tax purposes. However, many companies use 30 June as their balance sheet date because this is the normal tax year end.

The accounting profession has developed generally accepted accounting principles that aim to show a true and fair view of a company's financial affairs and performance; thus the commercial view takes precedence over legal requirements. There is generally a good quality of disclosure and full explanatory notes.

Until 1984, accounting standards had no legislative backing but since 1985 the Australian Accounting Standards Board (AASB) has been prescribing standards that are legally binding on companies under the Corporations Law.

Form and Content of Financial Statements

The form and content of a company's financial statements are prescribed by law embodied in the Corporations Law and the accompanying Corporations Regulations. The Corporations Law and Corporations Regulations were passed by the Commonwealth Parliament in December 1990 and became effective on 1 January 1991. The Corporations Law replaced the various Companies Acts which operated in the States under the former national co-operative scheme which came into existence in 1981.

In addition, a company which is a reporting entity is required to comply with legally enforceable "Applicable Accounting Standards" in its financial statements. A

Australia

"reporting entity" is essentially an entity in respect of which it is reasonable to expect the existence of users dependent upon the entity's financial statements for the purpose of making and evaluating economic decisions. Applicable Accounting Standards, indicated by the abbreviation AASB, are issued by the Australian Accounting Standards Board and are given legislative backing by the Corporations Law. Thus, the directors and auditors of a company which is a reporting entity are required to ensure such a company's financial statements comply with AASB standards and the directors face penalties where such standards are not complied with.

In contrast, a company which is not a reporting entity is only required to comply with those AASB standards that the directors deem necessary to comply with in order for the company's financial statements to present a true and fair view. The overriding concern is that a company's financial statements show a true and fair view of its state of affairs and its results for the financial period in accordance with the reporting framework adopted and disclosed in the financial statements.

The Australian accounting bodies (the Institute of Chartered Accountants in Australia and the Australian Society of Certified Practising Accountants) have also issued accounting standards called "Australian Accounting Standards" (AAS) and other accounting guidance statements, including Statements of Accounting Concepts (SAC). The principles contained in AAS's and SAC's are not mandatory in law, but are binding on members of the accounting bodies involved in the preparation or audit of financial statements for a reporting entity. Whilst the AASB standards apply to companies, the AAS (which are almost identical to the AASB standards) only apply to non-corporate entities such as trusts and partnerships.

A company's financial statements are prepared by the directors to give a true and fair view of the company's financial state of affairs and to present an historical record to the shareholders, annually, of the use of resources and performance of the company in the period being reported on.

The financial statements must contain:

- Directors' report
- Directors' statement
- Profit and loss account
- Balance sheet
- Notes to the financial statements, including the accounting policies adopted
- Statement of cash flows
- Auditors' report

Comparative figures are required to be shown.

The directors are required by the Corporations Law to make a statement as to whether, in their opinion, the profit and loss account and the balance sheet give a true and fair view of the results for the period and the state of affairs of the company at the balance sheet date; and at the date when the statement is made whether the company is able to pay its debts as and when they fall due.

Additionally, where a company has entities under its control, consolidated accounts must be prepared and presented to the shareholders. The consolidated accounts are required to take the form of a single set of financial statements covering the parent company and all the entities it controlled during all or part of the financial period.

Companies listed on the Australian Stock Exchange also publish a chairman's statement and are obliged to provide information about their major shareholders. They must comply with the Listing Rules of the Australian Stock Exchange Limited (ASX).

Public Filing Requirements

All companies, both private (unless exempt) and public, must file financial statements, with an annual return, each year with the Australian Securities Commission. These documents are available for public inspection through any office of the Commission.

The annual return contains details of:

- The registered office of the company
- The authorised share capital and issued share capital
- The amount of mortgages and charges on the company's assets
- Shareholders and their shareholdings
- Directors, secretaries, and (if applicable) auditors

The directors of the company are responsible for the preparation and filing of the financial statements and the annual return.

In addition, public companies are required by the ASX to file an interim unaudited report with the stock exchange every six months (mining companies – every three months).

A distinction is made between a public and a private or proprietary company. A public company is empowered to offer its shares to the public and must state in its memorandum that it is a public company and have the words "Limited" (Ltd) or "No Liability" (NL) (used for oil and mining companies) as the last part of its name. Such a company may be listed on the stock exchange, in which case it must have a minimum issued share capital of A$1,000,000 (at least 500 shareholders each with a parcel of shares having a value of at least $2,000).

A private or proprietary company may not offer its shares to the public, must have the words "Proprietary Limited" or "Pty Ltd" as the last part of its name and must have not more than 50 shareholders.

A proprietary company achieves "exempt" status if no shareholding is held directly or indirectly by a public or foreign company. Exempt proprietary companies do not have to file their financial statements with the annual return provided that those financial statements are audited and the auditor signs the annual return. If the financial statements are not audited then the company must include key financial data in its annual return.

Australia

Audit Requirements

The financial statements of a company must be audited unless the company is an exempt proprietary company and all the shareholders have agreed to dispense with the audit.

The auditor is appointed by the shareholders and reports to them each year giving his opinion as to whether the financial statements:

● show a true and fair view of the state of affairs of the company and of the operating results for the year;

● have been prepared in accordance with the requirements of the Corporations Law; and

● have been prepared in accordance with Statements of Accounting Concepts and applicable Accounting Standards.

The audit report must be signed by a registered company auditor. The Corporations Law requires that an auditor must not be an officer of the company and must:

● be a member of The Institute of Chartered Accountants in Australia, the Australian Society of Certified Practising Accountants or a similar overseas body; or

● in rare cases, hold a prescribed degree or have an acceptable level of experience in auditing.

These requirements are designed to ensure that the auditor is independent and sufficiently skilled to carry out an audit. In practice, a firm of accountants is usually appointed rather than an individual.

The auditor is required by the Corporations Law and the accounting bodies to refer in his report to any departure of material consequence from an applicable Accounting Standard and must forward a copy of a qualified audit report containing such a departure to the Australian Accounting Standards Board within seven days.

Valuation Principles

Australian companies almost invariably adopt the historical cost convention. Certain fixed assets, in particular real estate, may be revalued to market value and any unrealised gain arising transferred to a separate asset revaluation reserve shown in the balance sheet. The gain should not be reflected in the profit and loss account, unless it reverses an unrealised loss previously charged to the profit and loss account. An unrealised loss will be charged to the profit and loss account unless it reverses a previous revaluation increment still reflected in the asset revaluation reserve.

Australia

Depreciation

AASB 1021 (AAS 4) requires depreciation to be charged on all non-current assets with a limited useful life. It is considered that most physical assets, except for land but including buildings, have a limited useful life and are therefore depreciable.

Depreciation will be charged on the historical cost of the assets (or substituted valuation) less the net amount expected to be recovered on disposal of the asset at the end of its useful life. To calculate depreciation, the straight line method and reducing balance method are both commonly used. Disclosure of the method of depreciation is usually made in the notes to the financial statements.

The financial statements of the company are required by law to show the:

● amount charged or provided for depreciation during the year;
● aggregate cost (or valuation) of each class of asset;
● aggregate amount written off in respect of each class of asset since acquisition (or revaluation); and
● net amount after deducting the accumulated depreciation since the date of acquisition (or revaluation) from the cost (or valuation).

Leasing

The required methods of accounting for leases are contained in AASB 1008 (AAS 17) which is similar in application to IAS 17 and depend upon whether the lease is classified as a finance lease or an operating lease.

Under a finance lease the liability should be introduced at an amount equal to the present value of the minimum lease payments using the interest rate implicit in the lease as the discount rate (or an estimate of this rate). The liability will be reduced by the lease payments after allowing for interest at the implicit interest rate. The asset to which the lease relates should be brought into the books at an amount equal to the opening amount of the liability and amortised over its useful life.

Under an operating lease, lease payments should be written off in the accounting periods in which they fall due.

Research and Development

These costs may be capitalised in certain circumstances. The Corporations Law does not define these circumstances, but AASB 1011 (AAS 13) requires research and development costs to be carried forward on a project, provided that future benefits are expected, beyond reasonable doubt, to equal or exceed the costs carried forward.

Costs written off cannot later be reinstated. The total charge to the profit and loss account must be disclosed if material. The costs deferred in the year, the total deferred costs and the accumulated amortisation at the end of the year must also be disclosed, together with the basis of amortisation.

The amounts capitalised should be amortised on a systematic basis from the start of commercial production of the product.

Mining, Oil and Gas Industries

AASB 1022 (AAS 7) "Accounting for the Extractive Industries" requires exploration and evaluation costs to be accumulated by area of interest and written off unless either the costs are expected to be recouped by sale or development and exploitation, or continuing exploration and evaluation is required before an assessment can be made.

Restoration costs should be provided for during the production period.

Exploration and evaluation costs carried forward should be amortised over the expected life of the economically recoverable reserves.

Inventories

AASB 1019 (AAS 2) deals with inventory valuations and is consistent with, but more restrictive than, IAS 2 in that LIFO and base stock methods are unacceptable methods of valuation.

Inventories are divided into three categories:

- Raw materials
- Work in progress
- Finished goods

AASB 1009 (AAS 11) requires that profit on long-term construction contracts, where the work extends for more than one year, be brought to account using the percentage of completion method when the contract is at a stage such that the outcome can be estimated reliably. Provision should be made for possible future losses as soon as such losses are foreseeable.

Capital and Reserves

There is no requirement to set aside amounts out of the profits each year to special reserves. The only restriction on the payment of dividends is that they can only be paid out of profits and may not be paid out of share capital.

Foreign Currency Translation

AASB 1012 (AAS 20) deals with foreign currency translation and is consistent with IAS 21 with the following exceptions:

- AASB 1012 (AAS 20) requires disclosure of the net foreign currency gain or loss for the period whereas IAS 21 requires disclosure of that part of the gain or loss resulting from integrated foreign operations.

Australia

- IAS 21 allows exchange differences "resulting from a severe devaluation or from depreciation of a currency against which there is no practical means of hedging and that affects liabilities arising directly on the acquisition of assets invoiced in a foreign currency" to be capitalised with the related assets. AASB 1012 (AAS 20) only permits this in specific instances.

- AASB 1012 (AAS 20) provides that monetary items be translated at the rates applicable at the balance sheet date and non-monetary items at the rates applicable at the dates of the relevant transactions. Financial statements of foreign subsidiaries are translated at the current exchange rate at the balance sheet date where the subsidiary is self-sustaining, and using the "temporal" method where the subsidiary is integrated with the parent company.

Taxation

Company tax is payable at the rate of 39% on the taxable income of a company. The taxable income is arrived at after adjustments are made to the operating profit of the company. Taxable income comprises income and capital profits derived by the company.

The most common adjustments are:

- Depreciation: This is only a deduction to the extent that depreciation rates used for accounting purposes agree with income tax guidelines on depreciation rates.

- Provisions: Increases in provisions debited to the profit and loss account are generally not deductible, nor are decreases in provisions assessable. Only when amounts are actually incurred can they be claimed as deductions.

- Tax losses brought forward: Income tax losses of previous years may be carried forward indefinitely and offset against taxable income until they are absorbed. Losses incurred in pre 1989/90 years are only allowed to be carried forward for a maximum of seven years. In addition, groups of companies which have a 100% common ownership can transfer losses from "loss companies" to companies with taxable income.

- Capital gains tax: For all assets acquired after 19 September 1985, capital gains tax is payable on the difference between the sale proceeds and the indexed cost base of the asset upon its disposal.

- Dividend imputation: Dividends paid by a company, provided the profits from which they are paid have borne tax, will be free from tax in the hands of the recipients. The company is required to maintain a "Qualifying Dividend Account" that identifies profits from which tax free dividends can be paid. AASB 1020 (AAS 3) requires the profit and loss account for a period to show the income tax expense attributable to the pre-tax accounting profit for that period using tax-effect accounting. AASB 1020 (AAS 3) is similar to IAS 12, but AASB 1020 has the further requirement that only the liability method be used and not the deferral method.

Additionally, where the prima facie income tax expense varies by more that 15% from the income tax expense provided in the profit and loss account, Schedule 5 to the Corporations Regulations requires a note to be included in the financial statements reconciling the two amounts by showing permanent differences and over/under provisions of income tax in previous years.

Where the provision for current income tax differs from income tax expense the difference may be analysed into items which give rise to:

● Provision for deferred income tax: where the tax expense in respect of timing differences will be paid more than 12 months after the balance date.

● Future income tax benefit: where tax is currently payable in respect of timing differences that relate to a later accounting period or where a tax benefit has been recognised in respect of tax losses of the company. Whilst a future income tax benefit in respect of timing differences can only be carried forward as an asset where realisation of the benefit is assured beyond reasonable doubt, a tax loss can only be recognised as an asset where realisation of the benefit is virtually certain. It is considered that the test of virtual certainty will only be met in rare and exceptional cases.

Where part of the future income tax benefit is attributable to tax losses, this should be disclosed in the notes. In addition, where the benefit of tax losses has not been brought to account, the amount of the potential benefit should be shown as a note.

The balances of the deferred provision/future benefit accounts may only be netted off where the related timing differences will reverse in the same period otherwise the balances are to be shown separately in the balance sheet.

Unusual and Prior Period Items

The profit and loss account should show extraordinary and abnormal items arising in the year. AASB 1018 (AAS 1) defines an extraordinary item as one that is derived from events or transactions outside the company's ordinary activities and not of a recurring nature. It is expected that only on rare occasions will items fall within the definition of extraordinary items. An abnormal item is described as an event or transaction attributable to the ordinary operations which is considered abnormal by reason of its size and its effect on the results for the period.

Amounts relating to prior periods should be included in the results for the current year with no adjustments being made to prior years' figures. If the amount is material it should be disclosed in the profit and loss account as either an abnormal or extraordinary item. A prior period item may only be adjusted directly against opening retained earnings/accumulated losses when this is required as part of the initial implementation of an accounting standard or concepts statement or is necessary to comply with a statutory requirement.

Australia

Retirement Benefits

Employees are entitled to long service leave after a period of continuous employment with a company that varies between 5 and 15 years depending upon conditions of employment and the State in which an employee is employed. Provision is usually made in the financial statements for the cost of long service leave.

Under Commonwealth Government legislation, employers are required to provide retirement or pension benefits for employees. Such benefits are usually provided by the employer setting funds aside to a superannuation fund which is established under a deed of trust.

Contributions to the fund are expensed in the period in which they are made and details of the company's superannuation commitments (including details of the fund and basis of contributions) are required to be disclosed by certain companies, including listed corporations.

Even where the company is the trustee of the fund, the superannuation fund is treated as a separate entity for accounting purposes and the assets of the fund are not included in those of the company.

Related Party Transactions

AASB 1017 (AAS 22) requires disclosure in the financial statements of information relating to the company's relationship with related parties and details of material transactions with related parties. Related parties include entities which have control or significant influence over the company, entities controlled or significantly influenced by the company, directors and their director-related entities (i.e. a director's spouse, a relative of a director or spouse, or an entity under the control or significant influence of a director, the director's spouse or a relative of the director or spouse).

The standard deems disclosures relating to directors to be material regardless of the amounts involved. These disclosures include directors' names, directors' remuneration, directors' retirement benefits and loans to directors. Other transactions involving directors or their director-related entities, that occur within a normal employee or customer relationship on terms and conditions no more favourable than those available on similar transactions to other employees or customers, are only required to be disclosed by general description.

Details of transactions between entities in the wholly-owned group are not required to be disclosed in the consolidated accounts where such transactions are eliminated on consolidation.

Statement of Cash Flows

AASB 1026 (AAS 28) requires all companies that are reporting entities to include a statement of cash flows in their financial statements for financial years ending on or after 30 June 1992. The statement of cash flows, which replaces the former statement of sources and applications of funds/statement of changes in financial position, requires cash flows to be classified and disclosed according to whether they relate to operating activities or other activities, with other activities normally being analysed between financing and investing activities.

Cash flows are defined as cash movements resulting from transactions with parties external to the company. Cash inflows and outflows are required to be disclosed separately, however, a net basis of reporting can be adopted in respect of companies handling cash on behalf of its customers or in the case of investments and loans where turnover is rapid and the volume of transactions is large.

Price Level Changes

There is no statutory requirement to account for price level changes. The accounting bodies recommend in their statement of accounting practice SAP 1, that as a measure to account for the effects of changing prices, all entities should publish current cost accounting (CCA) financial statements as a supplement to their conventional financial statements. However, SAP 1's recommendations are widely disregarded in practice and few entities publish additional CCA financial information.

The CCA method recommended involves:

● calculating the cost of goods sold at the current cost of the goods at the time of sale;
● recognising gains or losses on holding monetary liabilities and assets (except for gains or losses on loan capital); and
● restating non-monetary assets at written down current cost or recoverable amount (whichever is less).

Austria

Hamerle – Reinold
Ewb Revisions- Und Treuhandgesellschaft M.B.H.

Austria, bordering on Germany, is often viewed as sharing similar national characteristics and indeed its accounting principles and practices tend to follow those of Germany quite closely.

Financial statements are prepared with the primary objective of protecting creditors and third parties against questionable business practices. This often means that, in practice, companies create hidden reserves by understating the value of assets and by making excessive provisions. The Commercial Code governs the keeping of the company's records and the preparation of financial statements and also forces some degree of comparability between the financial statements of similar companies.

The other major influence on accounting practices in Austria is tax law. This tends to distort the commercial view and emphasizes the tendency to conservatism in valuing assets because, as a rule, amounts can only be claimed as deductions for tax purposes if they are recorded in the books of the company.

As far as the financial statements are concerned, public companies' statements usually give a fair amount of detail and comparative figures are shown. There is generally less disclosure in private companies' statements. It is becoming standard practice for accounting policies to be applied consistently and disclosed in the business report of the Executive Board, though this is not universally the case.

The accounting profession, though very small, is quite strong and issues recommendations to its members, although these are not binding. It is also involved in the development of new laws on accounting and auditing matters.

Form and Content of Financial Statements

The Commercial Code (Handelsgesetzbuch), which is the basic legislation applying to all companies, and tax law provide that every business enterprise which has a registered firm name, including a branch of a foreign enterprise, is required to keep books in accordance with generally accepted accounting principles (Grundsätze ordnungsmäßiger Buchführung) and to draw up annual financial statements based on physical inventories of the assets.

The main types of company are, as in Germany, The Aktiengesellschaft (AG), the stock corporation, and the Gesellschaft m.b.H. (Ges.m.b.H.), the private limited company.

Until the end of 1991 the form and content of financial statements of AG's and Ges.m.b.H.'s were prescribed by the Aktiengesetz and by the Gesetz für Gesellschaften m.b.H.

The new Financial Reporting Act (RLG) was prepared with a view to attaining international standards in accounting, and adapting Austrian accounting and financial reporting to EC directives. The Act impinges upon several Austrian statutes, in particular on the Austrian Commercial Code. The new Act also amends and updates several provisions of the Austrian Commercial Code which relate to the obligation of entities to keep proper books of account.

The new Financial Reporting Act/Commercial Code applies to most business entities, only small businesses (some proprietorships and partnerships) being exempt. The provisions of the Act relate specifically to:

- the duty of entities to keep commercial books of account;
- inventory;
- valuation;
- the duty to have financial statements audited; and
- the appointment of auditors.

According to the Financial Reporting Act the financial statements of AGs and Ges.m.b.H.s must contain:

- the balance sheet at the end of the financial year;
- the income statement for the financial year; and
- notes to the financial statements (a new part of the financial statements).

The "notes" are generally intended to amplify or explain the items presented in the main body of the financial statements. If the financial statements give an incomplete picture of the performance and the financial position of the enterprise, according to the full disclosure principle, additional information that is needed to complete the picture must be included in the notes: e.g., description of the accounting policies and methods used in measuring the elements reported in the statements, explanation of uncertainties and contingencies, and statistics and details which are too lengthy for inclusion in the statements.

The financial statements are prepared by the Executive Board and have to be presented to the shareholders within 5 months after the end of the year. Other companies (partnerships, sole proprietors) have to prepare the financial statements within 9 months after the end of the year. The financial year for Austrian companies is often the calendar year, which is also the fiscal year. Other year ends are permitted if there are economic reasons.

Furthermore, the managers of the corporations have to produce a business report which shows the development and the economic situation of the entity. Moreover, the annual report has to deliver further information, such as the future outlook, research and development costs and other important events after the balance sheet date.

The management system in Austria, as in Germany, is a two-board system (and not a single board system as in the United Kingdom and France) consisting of:

- The Executive Board (Vorstand)

- The Supervisory Board (Aufsichtsrat), which must consist of at least three individuals. One third of the members must be representatives of the Betriebsart (an employee committee). No member can also be on the Executive Board.

An AG must have a Supervisory Board. A Ges.m.b.H. is required to have a Supervisory Board when capital stock exceeds one million schillings, or the number of stockholders exceeds 50, or where the annual average number of employees is more than 300. It may however appoint one voluntarily.

Public Filing Requirements

Generally public and some private corporations publish and publicise their financial statements and business reports.

The following corporations have to publish and publicize their annual financial statements:

- AGs
- Ges.m.b.Hs which are obliged to have a Supervisory Board.
- large Ges.m.b.H's (with a balance sheet total of more than ATS 200.000.000, balance sheet total, with sales of more than ATS 300.000.000, or more than 300 employees).

A copy of their financial statements and business report has to be filed with the commercial register.

Such companies are also obliged to publish their financial statements, together with the names of the members of the Executive and Supervisory Boards and the auditor's certificate, in the official section (Amtsblatt) of a federal state-owned daily newspaper (Wiener Zeitung). As proof that it has done so, the Executive Board of such a company is obliged to file a copy of the relevant newspaper with the commercial court.

Austria

So called small Ges.m.b.H's (balance sheet total of less than ATS 200.000.000 or sales less than ATS 300.000.000 or less than 300 employees), which are not obliged to have a Supervisory Board do not have to publish their financial statements and business reports.

Audit Requirements

The financial statements and business reports of the following types of corporation have to be audited:

- AGs
- large Ges.m.b.H's
- Ges.m.b.s.H's which are obliged to have a Supervisory Board

Statutory audits of AGs must be carried out by a Wirtschaftsprüfer. Ges.m.b.H.s may be audited by a Buchprüfer. After having examined the books and financial statements together with the business report, the auditor must express his opinion. This states whether or not the financial statements and the business report, based on the books, are in accordance with legal provisions. The auditor must report any departures from the law. Where there are departures this can have a strong influence on the future credibility of the company as well as (in many cases) on the position of management.

As well as the auditor's opinion, the auditor must prepare a report (the "long form report") on the financial statements showing all the assets, liabilities, reserves, and provisions, their composition and development during the period under audit, and the reasons why they were found correct with regard to generally accepted accounting principles, legal provisions, and the statutes.

When the audit is complete, the Executive Board must ask the Supervisory Board to approve the financial statements and the business report. If the Supervisory Board approves, the financial statements are fixed (festgestellt) which means they cannot be altered by the stockholder's meeting. In cases where the Supervisory Board refuses to give its approval, the Executive Board has to ask the stockholders' meeting for its approval. This may result in some amendments within the bounds of the legal and accounting framework.

The audit report has to express an opinion as to whether the financial statements give a true and fair view of the financial position of the company.

The auditor also has to report if, while carrying out his normal audit work, he became aware of any facts that seriously endanger the existence of the company or its development, or if the Executive Board has acted against the laws or statutes.

Valuation Principles

Generally, assets must be stated at original cost subject to depreciation. Current assets must be stated at original cost or market value, whichever is the lower. Liabilities must be stated at their original value or their market value, whichever is the higher. Losses arising out of transactions or operations up to the end of the fiscal year must be anticipated by making adequate provisions which are debited against the income statement.

Group Financial Statements

The new Financial Reporting Act (RLG) contains regulations concerning consolidated financial statements and group reports. Special requirements for the audit, disclosure, publication and examination by the commercial courts of consolidated financial statements are also set out in the new Code. Obligatory consolidation provisions are contained in Sections 244-267.

The new regulation concerning consolidated financial statements becomes effective for all statements with fiscal years ending on or after 1 January 1994.

Section 253 (1) of the Commercial Code requires "full" consolidation generally for investments of more than 50% of the stock. Sections 254 to 257 regulate the consolidation process. Section 156 deals with intercompany profits and losses and does not require their elimination under certain circumstances.

In Austria the lower limit for the mandatory use of the equity method is ownership of 25% of the shares. The equity method is only applicable to consolidated financial statements and cannot be applied to individual financial statements as a valuation method for investments.

Disclosure in the group notes are required in the case of material intercompany profits and losses and their elimination.

In the individual financial statements investments are shown separately at cost. Amounts receivable from, or payable to, group companies must be separately disclosed in the balance sheet. Additionally, the business report of the Executive Board must disclose connections with other group companies.

Depreciation

Fixed assets that have a limited economic useful life are subject to systematic depreciation. Normally the straight line method is applied at rates which are commercially reasonable and approved by the Tax Board. If market value becomes lower than the book value, then in the case of investment properties the company has to make an extraordinary depreciation charge. This is also true in the case of other fixed assets if the value is reduced significantly. Accelerated depreciation (see Taxation) must be entered in the records to be deductible for tax purposes and has to be disclosed separately in the financial statements.

Registers must be kept that record all financial details of each asset.

Austria

Leasing

Generally speaking, finance leases are accounted for as purchases, and operating leases are accounted for as rental contracts.

Research and Development

These costs may be capitalised in specific circumstances, in which case the amount has to be written off systematically. Tax incentives are available in certain cases. In any case the nature and the amount of research and development costs have to be shown in the business report.

Inventories

Inventories are divided into five categories:

- Raw materials/supplies and production material
- Work in progress
- Finished goods/products
- Services not yet invoiced
- Payments in advance

Raw materials are valued at the lower of purchase price and market value. Other inventories are valued at production cost of each individual item unless the net realisable value is lower, in which case the lower value must be substituted. Production cost includes purchase price and operating costs such as wages, direct overheads, and depreciation, but excludes selling costs. Purchase price or production cost can be computed according to either the FIFO, LIFO, or average price methods. LIFO may not be used for tax purposes.

By law, a physical count of inventory must be made once a year, either on the balance sheet date or within a perpetual inventory system.

Capital and Reserves

Austrian companies must issue all their share capital, but only 25% need be paid up. Apart from share capital and retained earnings, public companies must also maintain a legal reserve by transferring 5% of the net profits each year to a separate account until the balance on the account reaches 10% of the share capital.

There are also legal requirements in the event of a serious fall in the total of shareholders' funds. If the accumulated losses exceed 50% of the share capital, a shareholders' meeting must be called to consider the company's future. If they exceed 100%, or the company cannot pay its bills, management must apply for a winding up order.

Provisions are not made for proposed dividends. They are recorded as appropriations of profit when paid.

Foreign Currency Translation

All balance sheet items must be stated in the Austrian currency (Schillings). Transactions must be recorded at the exchange rate in force on the day of the transaction. At the end of the financial year, foreign currency balances have to be translated using the exchange rate at the balance sheet date and revalued according to the valuation principles of lower of cost or market values. Exchange gains and losses are part of the profit or loss for the year.

Taxation

Companies pay taxes (corporation tax and business tax) calculated on a net worth basis, based on the difference between net assets at the beginning and end of the financial year. Thus, taxable profits differ from trading profits only insofar as "differences" caused by "disallowables" such as corporation tax itself, tax on net worth, and tax on remuneration of members of the Supervisory Board.

Thus, in practice financial statement income is computed broadly in accordance with the tax laws.

The tax year is the calendar year. Businesses are assessed to tax on the income of the financial year ending in the tax year. The approval of the tax authorities is required if the financial year is not the calendar year. The company has to make adequate provisions in its financial statements for taxes on its profit.

Substantial tax incentives are granted for investment, notably a tax allowance of 20% on the cost of fixed assets, and for export business.

No provisions are made for deferred tax.

Unusual and Prior Period Items

According to section 233 of the Commercial Code extraordinary items are material events and transactions that are distinguished by their unusual nature and by the infrequency of their occurrence. In determining whether an item is an extraordinary expense or revenue, the environment in which the entity operates is of primary importance.

Prior period items, however, are not part of the extraordinary items. Examples of events that may be classified as extraordinary items are gains and losses resulting from accidents, expropriation or prohibition of a firm's activity by a government, or acts of God.

Retirement Benefits

According to the Austrian Income Tax Act of 1988, pension arrangements which are in writing and binding on the employer have to be accounted for. Certain restrictions, such as a maximum pension benefit of 80% of the active employee's salary and a fixed discount rate of 6%, apply. Funding with marketable securities cannot be considered to be funding in the U.S. sense, since the securities are not set aside.

The Business Pension Plan Act of 1990 (Betriebspensionsgesetz) also makes it possible to have vested plans.

The pension accrual is calculated by actuaries according to the individual level premium method or the entry age normal method. Both methods are acceptable under the Commercial Code, whereas for tax purposes only the individual level premium method may be used. Future salary levels and employee turnover are not taken into account in Austria.

Severance payments (Abfertigungszahlungen) are calculated like pension benefits according to the Commercial Code, which means that actuarial computations have to take place. For tax purposes the restrictive regulations of the Income Tax Act of 1988 must be followed.

Price Level Changes

There is no legal requirement or practice to provide for the effects of inflation in financial statements.

Belgium

André Hoste & Partners

In the past, Belgian accounting and reporting procedures were significantly influenced by tax and commercial considerations. Since the publication of the accounting law in 1975, the Royal Decree of 8 October 1976 and other subsequent Royal Decrees and finally the adoption of the EC Fourth Directive in 1983, little is left to the discretion of companies when preparing financial statements because this legislation defines the accounting and valuation principles which are applicable.

The accounting law, passed in July 1975, was regarded as an innovation since no clear and uniform body of law on accountancy matters existed until then. Previously, the law of accountancy was part of company law and was concerned basically with creditors. As a result, the emphasis was on the balance sheet and the net worth of the company. The effect of the legislation of July 1975 was to broaden the perspective to take into account the economic and social dimension of companies and their function in society.

The Commission for Accounting Principles (CAP), a government body, was established to interpret the law by studying the accounting concepts and principles involved. The Institut des Reviseurs d'Entreprises, the Belgian professional body, issues recommendations that tend to follow those of IASC. However, these are not mandatory so their adoption is inconsistent.

Belgian financial statements are closest in philosophy to those produced in France, Italy and Spain. The quality of disclosure in public companies' financial statements is reasonable but disclosure by private companies can be very limited and their financial statements should be interpreted with care.

Form and Content of Financial Statements

The form and content of a company's financial statements are laid down in the law of July 1975, and in various Royal Decrees since October 1976. The financial statements of all companies must comply with a General Accounting Plan, which is drawn up by

51

the CAP in order to facilitate the extraction and comparison of statistical information. The Plan details the principles laid down by law.

The directors of a company are responsible for the preparation and filing of its financial statements. By law, the financial statements should contain :

- Commentary by the directors

- Balance sheet

- Income statement (profit and loss account), often abridged but showing profit from commercial, financial, and exceptional sources less taxation

- Disclosure notes, including the accounting policies adopted by the company

- General information, such as the names of the directors and the commissaire (statutory auditor), the registered office, the authorised and issued share capital, and the conclusion of the commissaire's report

Accounting and valuation principles must be consistently applied. Changes must be explained and justified in the notes to the financial statements. Comparative figures must be shown.

As far as non-resident or foreign companies are concerned, only their Belgian branches must comply with these requirements but all the Belgian establishments of a foreign company are treated as one business. The business records must be kept in Belgium.

The requirements of the EC Fourth Directive have been incorporated into Belgian law.

Public Filing Requirements

All business enterprises must deposit their financial statements with the Registrar of the Commercial Court which must be announced in the Official Gazette.

The level of detail in these financial statements depends on the size of the business; a distinction is made between large companies and other companies. A large company is one which:

- either has more than 100 employees;

- or exceeds more than one of the following three criteria
  - more than 50 employees
  - turnover exceeding 170 million BF
  - balance sheet total exceeding 85 million BF;

- or is a member of a group that exceeds, on a consolidated level, more than one of the three criteria.

Companies not classified as large are permitted to deposit less detailed (schéma abrégé) financial statements. The financial statements of all companies are available for public inspection.

These requirements apply also to Belgian branches of foreign companies and to foreign enterprises that intend to issue their shares in Belgium or wish to be listed on the stock exchange.

Audit Requirements

All large companies (as defined above) must appoint a commissaire selected from the list of members of the Institut des Reviseurs d'Entreprises – a commissaire-reviseur. The ethics and requirements of the Institut des Reviseurs d'Entreprises ensure that the commissaire is independent and is sufficiently skilled to carry out an audit.

The commissaire reports to the shareholders whether in his opinion the financial statements show a true and fair view of the financial position and of the results of the company in conformity with Belgian accounting regulations. The commissaire-reviseur must also refer to deficiencies in internal control, if any.

Valuation Principles

Within the limits of the law, the valuation rules are to be determined by the management of the company and summarised in the notes to the financial statements.

By law, valuation at cost price is the basic principle. However, the cost of the inventory may be determined on the basis of the LIFO and tangible fixed assets, with a limited useful life, may be valued by the replacement value method.

Fixed assets (tangibles, investments, and other financial fixed assets) may be revalued if there is a permanent rise in the value of the asset over its acquisition cost. The depreciation on revalued fixed assets is not deductible by the tax authorities. The surplus must be credited to a separate account until it is realised. Such a surplus can, however, be incorporated into the capital of the company without attracting tax.

Normally the valuation rules must correspond to those used in the previous accounting year. They must be changed, however, if this is necessary to give a true view of the company. Valuation principles must be determined according to the norms of prudence, sincerity, and good faith.

Group Financial Statements

The law of 17 July 1975 authorizes the government to impose an obligation on companies to draw up and publish consolidated financial statements, and to establish rules related thereto. The EC Seventh Directive has been incorporated into Belgian law.

Depreciation

Tangible and intangible fixed assets with a limited economic useful life are depreciated according to the method determined by the directors of the company and laid down in the notes to the financial statements.

The depreciation of fixed assets is based on the purchase or investment value. This is interpreted as the price actually paid including related costs (import duties, cost of transport, installation, assembly, etc.) and the costs of any subsequent additions or improvements. The company may, however, elect to write-off these related costs in the year in which they were incurred, or in the first year of use.

Two methods of depreciation are normally used :

● the straight line method; and
● the reducing balance method.

Provided such amounts have been recorded in the books of the company, under special tax laws, accelerated depreciation is available for:

● investment in industrial buildings, machinery and equipment in development areas;

● equipment used for scientific research that may be depreciated over a three-year period;

● buildings for banks. The purchase price of real property acquired to be demolished and rebuilt may be fully written off. The value of the land and recoverable materials must be deducted from the purchase price; and

● ships may be depreciated over 8 years.

Leasing

The law requires that those leases (finance leases) which in effect constitute a purchase of fixed assets should be capitalised.

The tangible fixed asset must be recorded at an amount equal to the purchase price representing the total repayment of capital under the contract. The fixed asset is depreciated using the company's normal method. The respective liability of instalments not yet due must be presented in the balance sheet as "Debts in respect of long lease, leasing contracts, and similar debts" split between debts due after more than one year and debts due in less than one year.

Finance charges related to the above borrowings are recorded as business expenses.

Research and Development

Research and development costs may only be capitalised to the extent that the costs carried forward do not exceed their future use value or profitability. All other expenditure is expensed in the period in which it is incurred. Amounts carried forward are presented in the balance sheet as intangible fixed assets. Those assets with a limited useful life are depreciated according to the method determined by the company.

Accelerated depreciation in accordance with tax law is permitted for scientific research. Furthermore, supplementary, or exceptional, depreciation is allowed if the book value exceeds its economic value to the company as a result of obsolescence or changes in technological or economic circumstances.

Inventories

Inventories are divided into six categories:

- Commodities, consumable goods, and supplies
- Goods in the course of manufacture, work in progress, and waste
- Finished goods
- Bought-in trade goods
- Prepayments on purchases for inventories
- Real estate held for resale

Inventories are valued at either cost or acquisition price, market value or replacement price at the date of the balance sheet, whichever is the lowest.

By law the acquisition value is either:

- The acquisition price, being the purchase price plus related costs such as nonrecoverable taxes and transport costs; or

- The cost of manufacturing, being the costs of acquisition of raw materials, consumable supplies and other supplies, the production costs directly attributable to the individual product or group of products, and a proportional part of the production costs that can only indirectly be attributed to the product, to the extent that these costs relate to the period of manufacture. However, the company may choose not to include the whole or part of the direct costs of production. If so, this should be mentioned in the commentary on the annual financial statements.

Allowable valuation methods are actual individual price, weighted average price, LIFO, and FIFO.

Capital and Reserves

It is a legal requirement for a company to transfer 5% of its annual net profit to a non-distributable legal reserve until the balance on the reserve account reaches 10% of the share capital. There is a non-distributable tax reserve (see Taxation section).

The appropriation section of the income statements shows the transfer to reserves and the proposed dividends for the year.

If the net worth of a company falls to 50% of the share capital then the company can only continue if the shareholders vote accordingly in a general meeting.

Foreign Currency Translation

The general principles established by law do not deal with specific areas such as foreign currency translation. However, the following generally accepted accounting principles have been established by the accounting profession:

- The transaction is recorded at the exchange rate ruling on the date of the transaction. Any resulting exchange gain or loss is dealt with through the income statement.

- At the balance sheet date, monetary assets or liabilities (e.g. bank balances) denominated in a foreign currency are normally retranslated using the closing exchange rate and any exchange gain or loss again reported as part of the financial results in the income statement. Non-monetary assets (e.g fixed assets) are not retranslated.

Taxation

A company's financial statements, as approved by the general meeting of shareholders, are the starting point for the computation of the company's taxable income which is based on the difference between the net worth of the company at the beginning and at the end of the taxable period. The computation of taxable income requires fiscal adjustments to the profit as reported in the financial statements of the company. The major adjustments are:

- Certain business expenses are deemed not to be deductible for tax purposes. For example, excessive and luxury expenses, interest payments which exceed a certain limit, expenses (interest, royalties, fees, etc.) which amount to profit shifting and international tax avoidance, 50% on restaurant expenses, 50% on gifts, 25% on all car expenses (including depreciation, tax and insurance,) excluding benzine.

- Certain remuneration of company directors.

- Dividends paid.

- Depreciation, reductions in value and other valuations in excess of what is fiscally permitted.

The rules on valuations, depreciation, reductions of value and general provisions for contingencies, as laid down by the Royal Decree of 8 October 1976, are accepted by the tax administration for the determination of the taxable basis, except to the extent that the tax law explicitly deviates from those rules.

The income statement is charged with the tax due for the year based on the corporate income tax assessment. Furthermore, the income statement should show separately "Tax on results for the financial year" and "Tax on results for previous financial years".

Although there is no tax effect accounting as such, the tax savings arising from special investment incentives are credited to a non-distributable reserve on the balance sheet.

Unusual and Prior Period Items

By law, a material amount relating to a prior year item or to an extraordinary item (one which is derived from events or transactions outside the company's ordinary activities) should be shown in the income statement as "Extraordinary Income" or "Extraordinary Charges".

Thus, the figure brought forward for distributable reserves is rarely, if ever, changed, partly because it has been approved by the shareholders.

Retirement Benefits

If an additional pension scheme is provided for employees or directors, by law a succinct description thereof and an indication of the measures taken by the company to cover the cost should be set out in the notes to the financial statements.

Price Level Changes

The Belgian government does not consider it desirable to permit inflation accounting before it can be judged as to its merits, risks, and disadvantages on the basis of experience in other countries. However, nothing prevents a company from indicating in its report what the effect of implementing inflation accounting would be on the capital or profits.

In order to allow for price fluctuations, several provisions were introduced by the Royal Decree of 8 October 1976 :

● The cost of acquisition of inventories may be determined using LIFO.

● Tangible fixed assets may be revalued, within the limits of prudence, to a more realistic value.

Bermuda

Neville Russell

Bermuda's international reputation is based on two major industries: tourism and offshore finance, both of which are large contributors to the country's foreign exchange earnings. Its attractions as a tourist resort are obvious. With its economic and political stability and virtually no direct taxation, its position as a centre for international business is well established. As a result the overall standard of living in Bermuda is one of the highest in the world.

There are no taxes on income, profits, or capital gains in Bermuda. The government has enacted legislation under which the Minister of Finance is authorised to give an undertaking to exempted companies that future legislation imposing income, profits, or capital gains taxes shall not apply to such companies. This undertaking is currently extended for a period ending in March 2016. The legislation setting up this facility has, to date, been supported by both government and opposition parties.

Apart from the absence of taxes on the island, Bermuda is also attractive to overseas investors wishing to preserve their anonymity as there are no filing requirements. The only document relating to a company that is available to the public is its Memorandum of Association which merely shows the head office, capital structure, objectives of the company and its register of members. However, as shareholdings may be in the names of nominees, confidentiality as to beneficial ownership can be preserved. Limited liability companies may be either "local", which means they must be at least 60% Bermuda-owned, or "exempt". Exempt companies are owned by non-Bermudians who conduct business outside Bermuda from an office in the country.

Bermuda is also well known for its insurance and reinsurance companies (1,323 at 31 December 1991). Because of their size and influence, they are specially regulated by the Insurance Act 1978 and must be properly administered by qualified personnel. The Institute of Chartered Accountants in Bermuda (ICAB) is formally affiliated with the Canadian Institute of Chartered Accountants and therefore the generally accepted accounting principals in Bermuda are those promulgated by the Canadian Institute. Accounting firms, however, recognizing the needs of their clients in respect of a variety of other jurisdictions, ensure they have sufficient knowledge and resources, either locally or through their affiliations, to prepare and examine financial information in conformity with accounting principles and auditing standards recognised in other countries.

Form and Content of Financial Statements

The Companies Act of 1981 stipulates that, except in certain circumstances, audited financial statements, signed by two directors, shall be presented to the shareholders in general meeting. These financial statements, prepared in accordance with generally accepted accounting principles (GAAP) should include:

- Statement of the results of operations
- Statement of retained earnings or deficit
- Balance sheet
- Auditors' report stating whether in the opinion of the auditor the financial statements fairly present the financial position of the company and the results of its operations.

Other than as described above, the form and content of each of the above statements is not prescribed by law, but instead follows GAAP.

The Insurance Act of 1978 requires all insurance and reinsurance companies to prepare audited statutory financial statements in a prescribed form and in accordance with the requirements of the Insurance Act rather than GAAP. These include:

- Balance sheet
- Statement of income
- Statement of capital and surplus
- Notes to the statutory financial statements

The fundamental difference between the Insurance Act accounting policies and GAAP relates to the treatment of "non-admitted assets". For Insurance Act purposes, items such as fixed assets, goodwill and deferred acquisition costs cannot be recorded as assets.

Filing Requirements

There are no filing requirements for companies, other than those requirements for insurance companies set out below. The financial statements of companies are not available for inspection by the public.

The Insurance Act requires an annual Insurance Return to be submitted to the Registrar of Companies but this is not available for inspection by the general public. Although statutory financial statements must be prepared, they need not be submitted with the Insurance Return. However, they must be maintained at the registered office of the company for five years for review by the Registrar if he should so require.

The Insurance Return includes:

- a solvency certificate giving key figures in the statutory financial statements and a statement of whether the minimum solvency margin and the minimum liquidity ratio have been met;

- a declaration of statutory ratios, disclosing certain operating ratios; and

- an auditor's report.

Audit Requirements

The Byelaws of every company must include a requirement for an audit of the company at least annually by "an independent representative" of the shareholders appointed by them. He reports to them whether, in his opinion, the financial statements fairly present the financial position of the company and the results of its operations and change in its financial position on a consistent basis and in accordance with GAAP. The jurisdiction of the GAAP adopted is also disclosed.

The auditor must also refer in his report to any instances where:

- the financial statements are affected by a departure from GAAP;

- it has not been possible to obtain sufficient appropriate audit evidence to determine whether there has been a departure from GAAP (a scope limitation); and

- the comparability of the financial statements between periods has been materially affected by changes in accounting policies or in their application.

The auditor is also required to:

- identify specifically the financial statements reported on; and

- state that the examination has been made in accordance with generally accepted auditing standards of a specified country.

In the case of insurance and reinsurance companies, the firm of auditors selected by the shareholders must be approved by the Minister of Finance. This requirement generally results in only resident firms being approved. For other companies, the auditor is not required to be a member of ICAB but in practice will usually be one. It is worth noting that individuals cannot identify themselves as public accountants unless they are members of ICAB.

Accounting Issues

As previously mentioned, the Companies Act of 1981 requires financial statements to be prepared in accordance with GAAP, without specifying the jurisdiction of the

Bermuda

GAAP. Canadian GAAP is the most widely used in Bermuda, followed by US GAAP. The reader should refer to those chapters in this book to determine the specific accounting principles and disclosure requirements followed for the main elements of financial statements.

Brazil

Trevisan Auditories Independentes

Brazil has a mixed economy supported by many natural resources, though oil still accounts for most of its imports. Over the last 40 years the trend has been away from cattle raising and farming into manufacturing. Only certain sectors such as telecommunications and public utilities are under government control.

The United States has a significant influence on the Brazilian economy, mainly because of the large volume of activities carried out by US companies. This extends to accounting literature in Brazil, with US audit firms increasingly influencing Brazilian accounting and auditing standards. In general terms, accounting and reporting practices in Brazil also follow international standards.

Financial statements of all Brazilian companies are adjusted for inflation through indexation. This has been the practice since the enactment of Law 6404, in 1976, which simplified "monetary correction" procedures. However, with the aggravation of inflation, publicly-held companies are now required to produce indexed, constant currency financial statements using an official index, the IGPM (General Consumer Price Index), as a basis.

The current format of financial statements, including the explanatory notes, is regulated in detail by law, as are the methods of valuing assets and liabilities. Open capital and audited companies follow more comprehensive rules set out by Instituto Brasileiro de Contadores (IBRACON – the Brazilian Institute of Accountants) and Comissao de Valores Mobiliários (CVM – the Brazilian Securities and Exchange Commission). The audited financial statements presented to shareholders are intended to give a true and a fair view of the company's financial state of affairs.

Tax laws affect the preparation of financial statements, particularly where provisions are concerned. For example, depreciation is charged at the rates set by the government and excess amounts are not tax deductible. Since, in practice, these are similar to realistic, conservative depreciation rates in terms of trade, there is no conflict with the truth and fairness of the financial statements.

Brazil

The accounting profession is well-established and the services provided by independent accountants are similar to those provided by a US certified public accountant.

Form and Content of Financial Statements

All the practices here refer to a corporation or Sociedade Anônima (SA), though most of them are followed by the other types of companies permitted by Brazilian law, such as the Sociedade por Quotas de Responsabilidade Limitada (LTDA) which is part-company and part-partnership. In both cases, the directors or partners and the certified accountant (see below) are jointly responsible for the preparation of a company's financial statements.

The type, form and content of a corporation's financial statements are prescribed by the Corporation Act (Law no 6.404/76). They must also comply with the standards adopted by the Conselho Federal de Contabilidade (Federal Council of Accounting) and, for publicly-held companies, of the Securities and Exchange Commission (CVM).

The financial statements of a business enterprise must be signed by a certified accountant, as well as the directors. The accountant must be legally qualified and registered with the Conselho Federal de Contabilidade and cannot be the independent auditor.

The financial statements should by law, contain:

- Director's report (Relatório da Administração)
- Balance sheet (Balanço Patrimonial)
- Income statement (Demonstração do Resultado do Exercício)
- Statement of changes in shareholder's equity (Demonstração das Mutações do Patrimônio Líquido)
- Statement of changes in financial position (Demonstração das Origens e Aplicações de Recursos)
- Notes to the financial statements including the accounting policies adopted by the company

It should be accompanied by the auditors' report where required. Comparative figures must be shown in each statement.

A publicly-held holding corporation must publish consolidated financial statements dealing with the group as a whole, together with its own financial statements, if the conditions described under "Group financial statements" are met.

Public Filing Requirements

All SAs, or public and private corporations must file their bylaws with the Junta Comercial (Commercial Registry) and publish annual financial statements in the Diário Oficial (Official Gazette) at least five days before the date of the annual shareholders' meeting. They must also publish summarized minutes of that meeting and file a full copy of this publication with the Junta Comercial. Publicly-held corporations must also file some of the above and certain quarterly information with the CVM. A publicly-held corporation is one whose shares are publicly traded, whether in the stock exchange or over the counter, and it should be registered as such with the CVM.

The Brazilian law provides for the use of the word limited or Ltd only at the end of the name of a company that has limited liability under its articles, and whose capital is divided into nominative quotas, rather than shares. These enterprises, the LTDAs, do not need to meet any of the filing requirements of an SA.

Audit Requirements

Audited financial statements are mandatory by law in the case of publicly-held companies, financial institutions, public utilities, and government controlled companies, as well as for certain other organizations. In practice, many of the larger private companies' financial statements are also audited.

The audit report on the financial statements of a corporation must be signed either by an individual auditor, or by a firm of independent auditors registered with the Conselho Federal de Contabilidade. To be an auditor of a publicly-held corporation the auditor must also be registered with the CVM.

The IBRACON, in conjunction with the Conselho Federal de Contabilidade issues ethical rules and requirements to be complied with by auditors and accountants in their professional practices. This ensures that an auditor is independent, has no personal interest in the audited company, and is technically and legally able to carry out an audit. In practice, a firm of auditors rather than an individual is appointed by either the directors or the shareholders of the company.

In his report the auditor must state:

- which financial statements have been analysed and when;

- that the responsibility for issuing the financial statements lies with the management, and that the auditors are responsible for expressing an opinion thereon;

- that the examination was conducted in accordance with auditing standards and describe the main accounting procedures prescribed thereunder;

- in the opinion paragraph that the financial statements examined conform with generally accepted accounting principles and if the effects of inflation have been fully recognized (statements in constant currency). Should any simplified "monetary correction" procedures, as permitted in Law 6404/76, have been used, compliance with this law must be disclosed.

If such an opinion cannot be given, the auditor should clearly state the reasons in his report.

Valuation Principles

Since 1986, financial statements have been drawn up under a system of monetary correction, laid down in Law 6404/76 which is an indexation-based form of accounting for inflation, affecting only permanent investments, fixed assets, deferred assets and equity accounts, with the net effect being taken to income.

This continues to be required for closely-held companies and LTDAs. Whilst in contrast, following a recent decision of the CVM, publicly-held companies must now publish "constant currency" financial statements.

Under the monetary correction system, the basis for indexation is a monthly adjustment, given in par value, of UFIR, (a fiscal reference daily adjustable unit computed daily and monthly) which in turn is based on the variation of the IGPM.

Generally, the differences arising from the application of monetary correction are added to the related balances, except for corrections to paid-in capital, which are recorded in a special reserve. This may be capitalised, if so decided at the shareholder's meeting. The various monetary correction adjustments are accumulated and entered into a special account, the net balance of which is included in the income for the year and which is also taxable.

Under Law 6404/76, assets and rights acquired must be stated at the purchasing cost in current currency; likewise, manufactured goods must be shown at manufacturing cost. These concepts, however, had to be tailored to hyperinflationary conditions, lest accounting information be impaired. For example: cash would be stated at its present value, whereas credit sales revenues would be shown at their future discounted value and the cost of goods and inventories would reflect past values.

It should be noted that, in highly inflationary conditions such as those prevailing in Brazil, accounting as prescribed by Law 6404/76, leads to serious distortions, in that it aggregates monetary amounts derived from different bases (current, past and future) as though they were shown under a single monetary denominator.

The generally accepted accounting principles approved by the Conselho Federal de Contabilidade in 1991 take into consideration all these concepts, and require the financial statements to be presented based on prices prevailing at the balance sheet date. This information must be included in the Note on Accounting Practices and in the independent auditors' opinion.

Fixed assets may be revalued periodically to market prices, by legally empowered professionals. Any excess arising from such a revaluation is treated as taxable revenue in the year of revaluation, unless the respective amount is transferred to a revaluation reserve, in which case a portion thereof may be taxed annually in succeeding years, to compensate for the increase in depreciation caused by the revaluation of assets. This reserve is distributable to the stockholders only when the related assets are sold or fully depreciated.

Group Financial Statements

Under the Corporation Acts, a publicly-held corporation must prepare and publish consolidated financial statements, where:

- it has the power to elect the board of administration of the investee company (a controlling interest), whatever the percentage of interests held;

- more than 30% of its shareholders' equity (apart from the controlling interest) is invested in voting shares or quotas issued by affiliates and subsidiaries. Elimination of this limit is currently being considered, providing the company is a controlled company.

Other companies may prepare consolidated financial statements, although they are not legally required to do so.

CVM is the authority that decides whether companies should be included in or excluded from consolidation. Where the business of corporations within a group are so different that they cannot reasonably be treated as a single undertaking they are excluded from consolidation.

Investments in subsidiaries are monetarily corrected and stated using the equity method based on the shareholders' equity of the subsidiary as shown in its balance sheet. Cash dividends received by the investor and paid by the investee are deducted from the stated investment, and thus not included in the computation of the investor's income.

The financial year ends of subsidiaries should coincide with those of the holding company, although consolidating statements closed not earlier than 60 days before the holding company's statement date is accepted.

The consolidation procedures follow generally accepted standards, such as the elimination of intercompany balances, investment in subsidiaries, intercompany profits on goods sold by the holding company but still retained in stock by the subsidiary and disclosure of the participation of the holding company and minority interests in stockholders' equity and in profits.

In acquiring control of a subsidiary, the holding company should show in its accounting records the amount of the subsidiary's assets at a fair market value, any cost excess or shortfall being shown as positive or negative goodwill on acquisition.

The equity method is also adopted for valuing an investment in shares or partnerships in other companies, provided that the investment is at least 10% of the capital of the investee company but less than a controlling interest. If so, there is no consolidation of financial statements (as in the case of holding companies). The value of relevant investments is adjusted each year to the investor's share in the stockholder's equity shown in the balance sheet of the investee company, with the resulting increase or decrease being included in the income statement of the investor.

Depreciation

Depreciation rates are determined by the tax authorities. Present rates are:

- Buildings – 4%
- Vehicles – 20%
- All other fixed assets – 10%

In certain circumstances, other rates may be used if supported by a specialised report from the Instituto Brasileiro de Tecnologia (National Institute of Technology) or a similar body.

The accumulated depreciation is shown on the face of the balance sheet as a deduction from gross fixed assets. Both original cost and accumulated depreciation are monetarily corrected each year.

Leasing

There is no legal requirement regarding the method of accounting for leases. Generally, the periodic rental is charged against income in the year it is due, and disclosure made in a note. If the company exercises the right to buy the goods at the residual value at the end of term, the transaction is treated as an ordinary acquisition at that time.

In the case of a sale and leaseback, the accounting treatment may be different, with mandatory disclosure of the policy adopted and the amounts involved.

Research and Development

These costs may either be written off when incurred or carried forward for future amortisation, over the period of anticipated economic return, at the company's discretion.

Inventories

These include:

- Finished goods
- Work in progress
- Raw materials

They are stated at purchasing or manufacturing cost (subject to monetary correction, in the case of financial statements in constant currency), net of such valuation reserves as are necessary to adjust their value to market. Cost is determined to be the actual cost, average cost or FIFO. LIFO is not accepted for income tax purposes.

If the company has no cost accounting system, it is required to value its inventories for tax purposes, as follows:

- work in progress either at 150% of the raw material content cost, or at 80% of the value of the equivalent finished goods; and
- finished goods: at 70% of highest sales price ruling in the base-period.

Capital and Reserves

Financial statements will normally show capital stock, capital reserves, revaluation reserves and other reserves, and retained earnings. The following points deserve particular attention.

- **Legal reserve** – This must be maintained by transferring to it 5% of the net profits each year until the balance on the account reaches 20% of the paid-up share capital. The legal reserve needs not be identified separately on the face of the balance sheet, but will be analysed in the statement of changes in shareholders' equity.

- **Dividends** – A minimum dividend of 25% of the annual net profit after income tax, and net of accumulated losses and transfer to the legal reserve is required by the Corporation Acts. Dividends may not be paid if the company cannot afford them, in which case the reasons should be disclosed by the management and approved by the general shareholders' meeting.

- **Accumulated losses** – In the event of losses, it is the directors' responsibility to explain the situation to the shareholders in a management report. Any loss must be absorbed by retained earnings, revenue and legal reserves and, should any balance exist, by capital reserves.

Foreign Currency Translation

Transactions denominated in foreign currencies are recorded at the exchange rate ruling on the date of the transaction, including investments, receivables and payables. Gains or losses on translation are dealt with through the income statement.

At the balance sheet date, monetary assets or liabilities denominated in a foreign currency should be translated using the closing exchange rate and any exchange gain or loss should be treated as part of the ordinary profit or loss for the year.

When a foreign subsidiary's financial statements are consolidated, the income statement may be translated at either the closing or the average rate, but the method used must be consistent from year to year.

Brazil

Taxation

Corporations pay income tax based on their trading profit as reported in the financial statements for the fiscal year, which ends on 31 December. There is a distinction between the accounting net profit shown in the income statement and the taxable (so called) real profit. The latter is the basis for income tax and is arrived at after adjustments (which are registered in a special fiscal book) are made to the profits shown in the income statement. These adjustments result from accrual of non-deductible expenses and inclusion of non-taxable revenues. Allowances for depreciation, amortisation and depletion of fixed assets are made at annual rates fixed by law.

A provision for income tax is calculated and recorded at the end of each year as a charge against profits in the income statement. Adjustments to prior year's provisions are treated as prior period items.

There is no tax-effect accounting

Unusual and Prior Period Items

The treatment of unusual items follows US practice.

The law requires that any gain or loss related to prior periods shall be recorded as "adjustments to prior years" and set off against retained earnings, and not included in the current year's profit and loss account, provided that it relates either to an estimate or accounting error, or a change in accounting criteria. In either case an explanatory note should be included in the financial statements.

Retirement Benefits

Payments to public and private pension plans are charged against income when due to be paid. The employer's contributions are made at fixed rate. No other provisions or disclosures are made except for private pension plans.

Canada

Lyle, Tillie, Davidson
Friedman & Friedman
Mintz & Partners
Lazer Grant & Company
Orr & Company
Hudson & Company
Campbell, Saunders & Co.

Although UK ideas influenced the Canadian profession's practice, it is probably fair to say that current practices lie closer to that of the United States. Even so, Canada has retained her independence from US accounting and auditing standards and the profession works out its own solutions to current technical problems.

As a rule, US requirements are more detailed and specific than their Canadian counterparts. Canadian requirements are normally set in the context of broad principles with some latitude for the use of professional judgement. Following this theme, there is also less codification of principles in Canada, which leaves Canadian accountants freer to decide what they think is needed for "fair" presentation.

There is a strong independent accounting profession that develops its own regulations covering ethics and training requirements as well as technical standards. In fact, it is so strong that the legal requirement for the form and content of most financial statements are simply that they should be prepared in accordance with the profession's handbook – the primary source of generally accepted accounting principles (GAAP).

Overall, high standards of financial reporting are achieved aimed at producing a fair presentation of the financial position of the organisation.

Form and Content of Financial Statements

A company may be incorporated, at its option, under the corporate legislation of the province in which it primarily operates or under the federal legislation, being the Canada Business Corporations Act (CBCA). Legislation of each of the provinces is relatively similar in its approach to the financial reporting of companies.

Under the CBCA, the form and content of a company's financial statements are prepared in accordance with the requirements of the Handbook of the Canadian Institute of Chartered Accountants (CICA).

The directors are responsible for the preparation of a company's financial statements. Financial statements are prepared in order to provide shareholders and other users with sufficient information to assess the company's financial position, results of operations and the sources and uses of its cash resources. The CICA Handbook requires the following to be included in financial statements:

- Balance sheet
- Income statement
- Statement of retained earnings
- Statement of changes in financial position
- Notes to the financial statements, including the accounting policies adopted by the company.

The financial statements are to be accompanied by the auditors' report (if necessary) and comparative figures are required. Consolidated financial statements must be prepared if the company holds more than 50% of the issued voting capital stock of other companies.

Public Filing Requirements

All companies with revenues of more the C$15 million and gross assets of more than C$10 million must file financial statements (including the auditors' report) and an annual return under the Corporations and Labour Unions Returns Act. For companies incorporated under the CBCA, these documents are available for public inspection at a Federal Government Office, though there is no national register of company names. Thus, it is essential to know the province of incorporation in order to locate the financial statements and annual return.

The annual return contains details of:

- Head office address
- Nature of business
- Province of incorporation
- Directors and officers
- Authorised and issued equity (share) capital
- Major corporate shareholders;
- Major shareholdings of other corporations
- Capital debt
- Payments to non-residents

In addition, all public companies listed on a stock exchange are obliged to provide quarterly unaudited financial information to their respective securities commissions. Failure to do so, will result in a suspension of trading, and ultimately delisting from the exchange.

Canada has two official languages, English and French. Financial statements may be published in either or both languages, although English is the predominant language of commerce in Canada. Almost all financial statements are denominated in Canadian dollars. Where a currency other than Canadian dollars is used, that fact must be clearly disclosed.

The length of accounting periods is dictated by taxation authorities. A fiscal year cannot exceed 53 weeks. In order for an entity to change its year-end, it must request approval from the tax department(s). Approval is routinely granted where the entity has a valid business reason for making the change.

Audit Requirements

Public companies (those whose securities are traded in the public market) as well as private companies over a certain size (C$10 million of gross revenues or C$5 million of gross assets under CBCA) are required to present audited financial statements annually to their shareholders though they need not file them unless they meet the size criteria (referred to in the Public Filing Requirements section above). Other companies may elect, provided there is unanimous shareholder approval, not to have their financial statements audited.

The statutory requirements of the various Corporations Acts and the profession's code of ethics ensure that the auditor is independent. Generally accepted auditing standards, as set out in the CICA Handbook, dictate the overall basis for conducting an audit examination and reporting upon the financial statements.

The auditor is appointed annually by the shareholders. The auditor reports to the shareholders whether in his opinion the financial statements present fairly, in accordance with generally accepted accounting principles, consistently applied, the financial position, results of operations, and changes in financial position of the company.

Under generally accepted auditing standards, the auditors' report must also refer to any:

- significant departures from GAAP including disagreements as to valuation, appropriateness of accounting treatment, or adequate disclosure; and

- limitations in the scope of the audit.

A "subject to" qualification is not permitted. Material contingencies and going concern considerations do not require a qualified audit report in Canada if such uncertainties are appropriately disclosed in the notes to the financial statements.

Canada

The regulation of professions is a provincial not federal responsibility. As such, there is some divergence, over such things as what qualifications an auditor must have. Some provinces require auditors to be licensed. There is ongoing rivalry between the three "recognised" professional accounting bodies; Canadian Institute of Chartered Accountants (CICA), Society of Management Accountants (SMA) and Certified General Accountant's Association (CGA).

Valuation Principles

Financial statement in Canada are prepared on the historical cost basis, whereby assets and liabilities are stated at original acquisition cost, less accumulated depreciation and amortisation. As a general rule, assets are not restated to market value.

Current assets are carried on the balance sheet at the lower of cost and market value. Non-current assets are written down to market value if there is evidence that the decline in value is of a permanent nature.

GAAP requires the disclosure of significant accounting policies followed in the preparation of the financial statement. The fundamental concepts outlined in the general introduction to this book underly Canadian accounting principles.

Group Financial Statements

Consolidated financial statements are required to be prepared when the reporting entity holds over 50% of the voting shares of another company. A company is not required to prepare consolidated financial statements if it is itself a wholly owned subsidiary.

In addition, a subsidiary may be excluded from the consolidated financial statements if:

● the parent company is not likely to share in the subsidiary company's increases in equity or if the parent's control over the subsidiary is seriously limited;

● control by the parent company is temporary and a formal plan exists to dispose of the investment in the subsidiary; or

● the components of the subsidiary's financial statements are such that consolidation would not provide the most informative information to the parent company's shareholders.

Where the financial year ends of the subsidiaries do not coincide with that of the parent company, disclosure of this fact is required.

The interest of minority shareholders is separately disclosed.

Where it is possible to identify one of the combining companies as the acquirer (the majority of situations), the consolidated financial statements are prepared using the purchase method. Under this method, the assets and liabilities of the acquired business are recorded at their fair values at the date of acquisition. Any excess of consideration paid over net fair values so obtained is recorded as goodwill. It is not permissible to record negative goodwill. In situations where negative goodwill would otherwise arise, the values attributed to assets are reduced correspondingly. Goodwill must be amortised on the straight line basis over its estimated useful life, not to exceed 40 years.

In those rare instances where it is not possible to identify an acquirer, the consolidated financial statements are prepared under the uniting (pooling) of interests methods. Under this method, the consolidation reflects the assets and liabilities of the combining companies at the value recorded in the individual companies' financial statements, adjusted where necessary to make the accounting policies uniform.

Where a company does not hold over 50% of the voting shares of another company but has the ability to exert significant influence over the operations of the other company (assumed to be a 20% or more interest in the voting shares), the investment in that company is required to be accounted for by the equity method.

Under the equity method, the investor company records as income its proportionate share of the investee's net earnings or loss.

Depreciation
GAAP requires the cost of fixed assets, less their estimated residual value, to be depreciated or amortised on a systematic basis over their estimated useful lives.

The company is free to select any reasonable depreciation policy. In practice, the straight line or reducing balance methods are generally used. Income-producing real estate properties are frequently depreciated on the sinking fund basis (increasing annual depreciation charges).

Financial statements must disclose:

● the accumulated allowance for depreciation and depletion for each fixed asset category;

● the total amount of the charge for depreciation, depletion, and amortisation (this information is often presented on a category by category basis); and

● the effects of any changes in the estimated useful lives of fixed assets.

Leasing
The CICA Handbook contains the requirements for accounting for leases. Leases, which in substance represent the purchase of fixed assets must be capitalised and the corresponding obligation recorded as a liability.

Canada

Guidelines established by the CICA in assessing whether a lessee should capitalise a lease include:

- Transfer of ownership of property by the end of the lease term
- Existence of a bargain purchase option
- Lease term equalling 75% or more of the estimated useful life of the asset
- Present value of the minimum lease payments equalling 90% or more of the fair value (at the inception of the lease) of the leased asset

Should any of the preceding guidelines be met, generally the lease will be capitalised.

There are also detailed disclosure requirements associated with leases.

Research and Development

The CICA Handbook requires that research costs be expensed as incurred. Development costs may be capitalised only if certain criteria are satisfied.

Development costs not previously capitalised cannot be reinstated even if new circumstances would satisfy the requirements for capitalisation. Capitalised development costs are to be amortised to income on a systematic basis commencing with commercial production or use of the product or process.

Financial statements must disclose:

- unamortised deferred development costs;
- development costs deferred during the year;
- research and development costs charged as an expense; and
- the basis on which the amortisation of deferred development costs is calculated.

Inventories

Inventories are divided into four categories:

- Raw materials
- Work in process
- Finished goods
- Goods purchased for resale

Inventories are valued at the lower of cost and market value. Acceptable methods of determining cost include FIFO, LIFO, average and actual prices for specific items. The method used will depend on the circumstances.

The cost of raw materials and goods purchased for resale is "laid-down" cost, which includes costs such as freight, duty and brokerage.

For work in process and finished goods, cost will include laid-down cost plus direct labour and the applicable share of manufacturing overhead expenses. Distribution, selling and administrative costs are excluded. Market value is either replacement cost or net realisable value, depending on the circumstances.

Capital and Reserves

As a general rule for trading and profit-oriented enterprises, there are no legal requirements to maintain special reserves and, in fact, transfers to such reserves are not allowed for income tax purposes. There are generally no restrictions on the payment of dividends other than such payment cannot endanger a company's ability to pay its creditors. Corporations may repurchase their own outstanding shares for cancellation.

Foreign Currency Translation

The CICA Handbook identifies three distinct sources of foreign currency denominated transactions:

- Those undertaken directly by the reporting enterprise itself.
- Those undertaken by an "integrated" foreign operation of the reporting enterprise.
- Those undertaken by a "self-sustaining" foreign operation of the reporting enterprise.

An "integrated" foreign operation is one whose activities are heavily dependent upon the reporting entity for financing, source of supply or other significant operating aspects. It is considered that the activities of such an operation will have a direct impact on the cash flows of the reporting enterprise.

A "self-sustaining" foreign operation is one whose activities are essentially independent of the reporting enterprise, both financially and operationally. It is considered, therefore, that the activities of such an operation do not have a direct impact on the cash flows of the reporting enterprise. However, a self-sustaining foreign operation in a country with a high rate of inflation is deemed to be "integrated" on the basis that the currency of a high-inflation economy is not a stable measuring base.

The activities in a foreign currency undertaken directly by the reporting enterprise (unless hedged) or by an "integrated" foreign operation are translated under the "temporal" method. Under this method, transactions are recorded at the rate prevailing at the transaction date. Monetary assets and liabilities are translated at the year-end rate; non-monetary items (including related income statement items) are translated at the historic transaction date rate except in circumstances when such items are carried at market value. In these circumstances, they should be translated at the year-end rate. With the exception of gains on long-term monetary assets and liabilities, translation gains and losses are reflected in the income statement. Gains or losses on fixed term, non-current monetary items are deferred and amortised over the remaining term of the related assets or liability.

Canada

For "self-sustaining" foreign operations, the current rate method of translation is used. Under this method, all assets and liabilities (whether or not monetary) are translated at year-end rates. Income statement items are translated at the rate prevailing at the date the transactions were recorded in the foreign currency statements (normally done by use of weighted averages). Any resultant gain or loss is deferred and included as a separately disclosed section of shareholders' equity.

Taxation

Companies compute their liability for corporate income taxes based upon earnings reported in their financial statements. Adjustments to reported earnings are made in order to compute taxable income.

Significant adjustments include:

- Depreciation and amortisation expenses recorded in the financial statements are not deductible. Instead, capital cost allowances, at varying maximum fixed rates, are substituted for tax purposes.

- Certain types of interest expense may not be tax deductible if they were not incurred to earn income.

- As a general rule, provisions are not deductible in computing taxable income. A reasonable provision for bad debt losses on accounts receivable is, however, permitted.

- The tax deduction for charitable donations is limited to 20% of net income for tax purposes.

Where timing differences exist between accounting income and taxable income, the CICA Handbook requires that the tax effect (based on current rates for build-ups and accumulated rates for drawdowns) be reflected in the financial statements under the caption "Deferred Income Taxes". These provisions apply to both short-term and long-term timing differences.

The future benefit of losses carried forward for income tax purposes may be recognised if there is virtual certainty that they will be used within the prescribed time period or to the extent that they will be reversed within the prescribed time period by not claiming, for income tax purposes, items such as capital cost allowances (depreciation) on which deferred income taxes have already been provided.

Unusual and Prior Period Items

Extraordinary items are defined as gains, losses, and provisions for losses, the underlying nature of which is not typical of the normal business activities of the enterprise, are not expected to occur regularly over a period of years and are not considered as recurring factors in any evaluation of the ordinary operations of the enterprise.

Such items must be explained in the financial statements, and are shown net of tax after "Earnings from Operations".

Prior period items must:

● be specifically identified with and directly related to the business activities of particular prior periods;
● not be attributable to subsequent economic events;
● depend primarily on decisions or determinations by persons other than management or owners; and
● could not be reasonably estimated prior to such decision or determinations.

Items meeting these criteria are excluded from current earnings and are shown net of tax as an adjustment to opening retained earnings.

Changes that are made in estimates are treated on a current and prospective basis, not retroactively as is required by changes in accounting policies. Examples of changes in estimates included determination of:

● doubtful accounts receivable;
● inventory obsolescence;
● estimated useful lives of fixed assets; and
● period to amortise deferred costs.

The distinguishing feature between changes in estimates and changes in accounting policies is that the former is a result of obtaining new information. The latter is a result of new handbook recommendations, legislative requirements, or the belief that a change provides more appropriate accounting and/or presentation of events or transactions in the financial statements.

Interest Capitalisation

The amount of any interest capitalised in the period should be disclosed. This information assists users to assess the impact of a company's capitalisation policy on its results.

Long Term Debt

The title of the issue, the interest rate, the maturity date, the amount outstanding, and any redemption, conversion, or other features should be disclosed in the financial statements. Payments required in each of the next five years to retire long-term debt should also be presented. The portion of long-term debt payable in the next year out of current funds should be classified as a current liability. In addition, if the debt is payable in a currency different from that in which the balance sheet is stated, the currency should be indicated.

Interest expense on long-term debt should be stated separately in the income statement.

Canada

Any secured liabilities should be stated separately and the related security should also be indicated.

Financial statements should also indicate when a company has defaulted with respect to any provision in a long-term debt obligation, particularly if the default remains outstanding at the balance sheet date.

Retirement Benefits

The CICA Handbook deals with accounting for, and disclosure of, pension costs and obligations in the financial statements of an enterprise that has established a pension plan to provide retirement income benefits to its employees.

The CICA Handbook discusses two different types of pension plans;

- Benefit-Based Plan where the employee pension benefits payable are a function of numerous factors, such as the number of employees qualifying for retirement benefits and the amount of salaries on which the benefits will be based.

- Cost-Based Plan (money purchase plan or defined contribution plan) where the employee pension benefits payable are directly related to the contributions made to the plan by the employer, as determined by a formula stated in the plan.

Accounting for Benefit-Based Plans

Actuarial assumptions used must be realistic and internally compatible. For accounting measurement purposes, a specific actuarial valuation method must be used. The accrued benefit method is required to compute the full cost of pension benefits provided in exchange for employees' services rendered in the period.

Market-related values should be used for valuing pension fund assets. The valuation of pension fund assets has an impact on the pension expense recognised in each period because it affects the amount of experience gains and losses. In addition, assumed earnings on pension fund assets reduce the cost of pension benefits.

The following cost components are normally amortised over the expected average remaining service life of the employee group covered by the plan:

- past service costs arising from the introduction or modification of a plan;
- adjustments arising from changes in assumptions; and
- experience gains and losses resulting from short-term variations from assumptions.

Any gains or losses on plan settlements, partial settlements, or curtailments should be recognised in income immediately.

The pension expense for a reporting period includes:

- the cost of pension benefits provided in exchange for employees' services rendered in the period;

- the amortisation of past service costs, adjustments arising from changes in assumptions and experience gains and losses; and

- gains or losses on plan settlements, partial settlements or curtailments.

The financial statements must disclose separately the actuarial present value of accrued pension benefits attributed to services rendered up to the reporting date and the market value of pension fund assets.

The following disclosures in financial statements are desirable:

- the pension expense for the period;
- the amount of the deferred charge or accrual for pension costs;
- the basis of valuing pension fund assets;
- assumptions used in determining the pension expense and the actuarial present value of accrued pension benefits;
- the method and period used to amortise past service costs, changes in assumptions, experience gains and losses and the net pension asset or net pension obligation;
- a general description of the pension plan;
- the date of the most recent actuarial valuation performed for accounting purposes; and
- the nature and effect of significant matters affecting the comparability of information presented.

Accounting for Cost-Based Plans

The cost of pension benefits is the employer's required contribution provided in exchange for employees' services rendered in the period.

Costs relating to past services normally should be amortised over the expected average remaining service life of the employee group covered by the plan.
The pension expense for the period includes the cost of pension benefits provided in exchange for services rendered in the period and the amortisation of past service costs.

Financial statement disclosure includes the present value of required contributions in respect of past service. The following disclosures in financial statements are desirable:

- the pension expense for the period;
- a general description of the pension plan(s); and
- the nature and effect of significant matters affecting the comparability of information presented.

Treatment of Government Grants

Government assistance towards current expenses or revenues should be included in the determination of net income for the period. Where government assistance relates to expenses of future accounting periods, the appropriate amounts should be deferred and amortised to income as related expenses are incurred. The amount of government assistance deferred, the period and the basis of amortisation of the deferral should be disclosed.

Government assistance towards the acquisition of fixed assets should be either:

- deducted from the related fixed assets with any depreciation calculated on the net amount; or
- deferred and amortised to income on the same basis as the related depreciable fixed assets are depreciated. The amounts of the deferral and the basis of amortisation should be disclosed.

The appropriate portion of the estimated total of government assistance to be received should be accrued in the accounts, provided there is reasonable assurance that the enterprise has complied, and will continue to comply, with all the conditions.

The liability to repay government assistance should be accounted for in the period in which conditions arise that will cause government assistance to be repayable. It should not be accounted for as a prior period adjustment.

Related Party Transactions

Parties are considered to be related when one party has the ability to exercise, directly or indirectly, control or significant influence over the operating and financial decisions of the other. Two or more parties are also considered to be related when they are subject to common control or significant influence.

When a reporting entity has participated in transactions with related parties during a financial reporting period, disclosure of those transactions should be made.

When the ongoing operations of a reporting entity depend on a significant volume of business with another party, the economic dependence on that party should be disclosed and explained.

Segmental Information

The financial statements of enterprises, the securities of which are traded in a public market or that are required to file financial statements annually with a securities commission, and all life insurance enterprises should disclose information which segments their total operations first by industry and second by geographic area. In addition, such enterprises should disclose the amount of their export sales.

An industry segment is a distinguishable component of an enterprise engaged in providing a product or service, or a group of related products or services, primarily to customers outside the enterprise.

A geographic segment is a single operation or a group of operations located in a particular geographic area. Such operations are those that generate revenue, incur costs and have assets employed in or associated with generating such revenue. An enterprise's domestic operations are considered to be a separate geographic segment.

The accounting principles underlying the segmented information should be the same as those followed in the preparation of the financial statements of the enterprise.

Intersegment transactions that have been eliminated in the financial statements should be reinstated and included in the segmented information. Particulars of any contractual obligations that are significant in relation to the current financial position or future operations should be disclosed.

Commitments and Contingencies

The amount of a contingent loss should be accrued in the financial statements when:

- it is likely that a future event will confirm that an asset had been impaired or a liability incurred at the date of the financial statements; and
- the amount of the loss can reasonably be estimated.

The existence of a contingent loss at the date of the financial statements should be disclosed in the notes to the financial statements when the occurrence of:

- the confirming future event is likely but the amount of the loss cannot be reasonably estimated; or
- the confirming future event is likely and an accrual has been made but there exists an exposure to loss in excess of the amount accrued; or
- the confirming future event is not determinable.

Contingent gains should not be accrued in financial statements; however, if a gain is likely it should be disclosed in a note to the financial statements.

Subsequent Events

In general, there are two types of subsequent events:

- those that provide further evidence of conditions which existed at the financial statements date; and
- those that are indicative of conditions which arose subsequent to the financial statements date.

Financial statements should be adjusted when events occurring between the date of the financial statements and the date of their completion provide additional evidence relating to conditions that existed at the date of the financial statements.

Financial statements should not be adjusted for, but disclosure should be made, of those events occurring between the date of the financial statements and the date of their completion that do not relate to conditions that existed at the date of the financial statements but:

- caused significant changes to assets or liabilities in the subsequent period; or
- will, or may, have a significant effect on the future operations of the enterprise.

Price Level Changes

There is currently no requirement to report the effects of changing prices.

Future Developments

Financial reporting in Canada is kept under constant review and as at the beginning of 1993 the profession has issued thirty four abstracts on a wide range emerging issues including pension surplus recognition, reverse takeover accounting and revenue and expenditures during the pre-operating period.

Denmark

Revisionsfirmaet Preben Larsen

In Denmark, financial statements were historically orientated towards producing information for the tax authorities, particularly in the case of smaller companies. Allied to this was the tendency to protect the position of the creditor at the expense of commercial reality. However, in 1973, the law began a trend towards improved disclosure in financial statements and this was continued by the implementation of the EC Fourth Directive in the Company Accounts Act of June 1981. Denmark was the first EC member to implement these requirements. Financial statements now give a true and fair view of the affairs of the company within the context of the legal requirements.

In a way this relatively rapid increase in the quality of financial statements' disclosure has been caused by Denmark's own development, from an essentially agricultural economy pre-1950s to an industrial one where overseas capital was needed. The earlier emphasis on producing financial statements as a basis for taxation has changed to a system where the commercial view takes precedence. Accounting and taxable income will differ and there is no need for certain items to be recorded in the records of the company before they can be claimed for tax purposes.

The accounting profession in Denmark is well-established. Having previously restricted guidance issued to comments on government proposals for legislation, the profession has now started making pronouncements of its own in the form of accounting guidelines. International Accounting Standards remain an integral part of what is considered "good accounting practice" in Denmark.

Form and Content of Financial Statements

The form and content of a company's financial statements are prescribed in the Danish Company Accounts Act. This act is based on the requirements of the EC Fourth Directive.

The directors are responsible for the preparation of a company's financial statements,

Denmark

which are audited and presented to the shareholders to give a true and fair view of the company's financial state of affairs. By law, the audited financial statements should contain:

- Income statement (resultatopgorelse)

- Balance sheet (balance)

- Notes to the financial statements (noter til regnskabet) including the accounting principles adopted by the company. Accounting principles can be disclosed in notes or be shown as separate items in the balance sheet and income statement

- Annual report (aarsberetning) covering items such as any important events that have occurred since the end of the financial year, the company's likely future development and activities in research and development.

These statements must constitute a composite whole. Comparative figures for the preceding year must be shown.

Parent companies must publish group financial statements, normally in the form of consolidated financial statements, dealing with the group as a whole. It is standard practice to include a statement of changes in financial position.

Public Filing Requirements

All limited companies, both public and private, must file audited financial statements including the Annual Report and Auditor's Report each year with the Danish Commerce and Companies Agency (Erhvervs & Selskabsstyrelsen). These reports are available for public inspection.

Smaller private companies are permitted to file "modified" (less detailed) financial statements in that, if the gross assets are less than DKK 2 million then only a balance sheet is required.

A legal distinction is made between:

- a public limited company which must have a minimum allotted share capital of DKK 500,000 (and 50% of that allotted share capital or DKK 500,000 whichever is the greater must be paid up), and must state that it is a public company and have the word Aktieselskab or A/S as part of its name: and

- a private limited company (Anpartsselskab or ApS), which must not offer shares to the public.

Listed companies are required by the stock exchange to publish an interim half year unaudited report. They must also announce to the stock exchange the results for the year and the dividend proposed, when the financial statements have been approved by the directors.

Audit Requirements

Each company requires an audit report on its financial statements which must be signed by a State Authorised Public Accountant (SAPA) (statsautoriseret revisor) or a Registered Accountant (RA) (registreret revisor). Generally speaking, the SAPA is the higher qualification and audits the larger firms and listed companies, whereas the RA audits the smaller firms.

The ethical requirements of the accountancy profession and the fact that the auditor must not be an officer of the company ensure that the auditor is independent and is sufficiently skilled to carry out an audit. In practice, a firm of accountants is usually appointed rather than an individual.

The auditor is appointed each year by the shareholders. The auditor must certify that he has audited the annual financial statements and the consolidated financial statements, if any, and state whether they have been drawn up in accordance with the requirements contained in the legislation and the company's statutes.

If the annual financial statements or the annual report do not contain information on the company's assets, liabilities, financial situation and results, the auditor must make a note of this in the audit report and provide the necessary supplementary information.

If the auditor considers that the annual financial statements should not be approved, this must be stated in his report.

If, in his audit, the auditor has found that there are matters that may incur a liability for the members of the board of managers, or if the auditor of a parent company lacks necessary information on a subsidiary's affairs, this must also be disclosed in the audit report.

The auditor may also disclose information which he considers should be brought to the attention of those participating in the company.

For the use of the Board of Directors, the auditor keeps an audit book in which he specifies the audit work that has been carried out and any deficiencies which he may have uncovered in the company's book-keeping and accounting procedures. The audit book is presented to the board and signed by all members of the board. In practice this acts rather like a management letter. Unless there is anything particular to report, the auditor generally writes a short summary of the work he has performed.

Valuation Principles

The Company Accounts Act has adopted the historical cost convention, that is, the assets and liabilities of the company are generally stated at original cost subject to depreciation or provisions. Certain fixed assets, in particular real property, may be revalued to market value. By law, any surplus so arising must be transferred to a separate non-distributable reserve which is shown as such on the balance sheet.

Denmark

By law the items shown in the annual financial statements must be valued in accordance with the general principles stated in the introduction to this book.

Depreciation

The principles are the same as in the United Kingdom.

Leasing

There is no statutory requirement regarding the method of accounting for leases. However, it is required that the total amount which is to be paid during the lease term should be disclosed.

Research and Development

These items may only be included as an asset in the balance sheet if acquired for valuable consideration, and must be written off systematically over a maximum period of 5 years.

Costs written off cannot later be reinstated. There is no requirement to disclose the total charged to the income statement, although movements on amounts capitalised must be shown.

Inventories

The principles are the same as in the United Kingdom.

Capital and Reserves

The amount by which sums received by the company, for shares in a share subscription, exceed their nominal value must, after deduction of expenses incurred in the formation of the company or an increase of the share capital, be allocated to a special reserve.

Reserves may be used for covering losses that are not covered by the distributable profits and for the issue of bonus shares, provided the company does not have an uncovered loss.

The increase in value deriving from the revaluation of tangible and financial fixed assets must be transferred to a separate revaluation reserve under equity capital.

This revaluation reserve must be reduced if the revalued asset is disposed of or taken out of operation, or if the condition for the revaluation has ceased to apply. The revaluation reserve may only be transferred to the profit and loss account if it constitutes a realised profit and must in such a case be entered as a separate item. The revaluation reserve may be capitalised in whole or in part at any time.

Group Financial Statements

Group financial statements, usually in the form of consolidated financial statements, must be prepared when one company owns more than half of the voting power of another enterprise or when one company through a combination of share ownership and agreements controls another enterprise.

These group financial statements need not include subsidiaries where, in the directors' opinion:

- it would be impracticable; or
- the result would be misleading or harmful; or
- the businesses are so different that they cannot reasonably be treated as a single undertaking.

If the composition of the group makes it appropriate to do so, a consolidated report may be prepared instead of consolidated financial statements. The reason why this has been done must be disclosed in the notes. The report contains among other items information on intercompany balances and the total profit or loss for the group for the year.

The form and content of the group financial statements are prescribed by law and are substantially the same as for single companies. Companies belonging to the same group must have the same financial year, unless otherwise dictated by special circumstances.

There are no requirements for accounting for goodwill on the acquisition of businesses and the following methods can be used:

- retention in the balance sheet at original cost;
- immediate or partial write off to reserves; or
- amortisation over a specific period through the profit and loss account.

Purchased goodwill should be written off systematically over a maximum period of 5 years. Non-purchased goodwill cannot be capitalised.

By law, "investments in related companies" must be shown separately on the balance sheet. A related company is one in which the investing company holds shares on a long-term basis for the purpose of securing a contribution to that company's own activities by exerting its influence over the related company. Such influence will be assumed if the holding of equity shares with unrestricted voting rights is more than 20%. These investments are normally accounted for by the equity method, whereby the group financial statements include the group's share of the related companies' profits or losses and reserves since the date of acquisition.

Foreign Currency Translation

The principles are the same as in the United Kingdom.

Denmark

Taxation

Companies pay corporation tax based on their trading profit as reported in their financial statements for the accounting period. The tax rates and allowances are fixed for each year which runs from April 1 to March 31. Corporation tax is normally payable in the November after the end of the company's accounting period.

Various adjustments are made to the profit before tax shown in the financial statements before arriving at taxable profit, mainly because the company, in reporting to the shareholders, is interested in showing a true and fair view of the profit on the usual commercial basis whereas the government has other objectives, for example stimulating investment by generous tax allowances on fixed assets.

The major adjustments are:

- Depreciation charged by the company is not deductible. Instead, capital allowances of 30%, calculated on the reducing balance method can be claimed. There are no allowances on offices or homes, but industrial buildings usually qualify for some allowance as do offices connected with industrial buildings.

- Inventory can be written down by 30%.

- General or contingent provisions are non-deductible.

- Dividends paid are non-deductible.

Where accounting income differs from taxable income it is standard accounting practice to make provision for:

- short-term timing differences that arise on certain items, mainly from the use of the cash basis for tax purposes and the accruals basis for financial statement purposes;

- other timing differences likely to reverse in the future, for example, capital allowances/depreciation; and

- contingent liabilities for tax on surpluses arising from the revaluation of fixed assets.

Losses may be carried forward and set-off against the deferred tax balance, if such a set-off could take place under the tax laws. A deferred tax asset may not be set up by taking future income into account (eg for losses brought forward).

Tax payable more than one year from the balance sheet date is classified as deferred taxation and is included under "Long-Term Liabilities. "Provision for contingent tax is included under "Provision for Liabilities and Charges".

Unusual and Prior Period Items

The financial statements must give particulars of any extraordinary income or charges. An extraordinary item is defined as one that is derived from events or transactions outside the company's ordinary activities.

Material adjustments applicable to prior years are those that arise from changes in accounting principles and from the correction of fundamental errors. Such adjustments may be included in the current year's profit and loss account shown under the items "Extraordinary Income" and "Extraordinary Charges."

Retirement Benefits

Pension obligations that are not covered by insurance policies must either be included in the balance sheet as a liability, based on the capitalised value of future pension obligations, or disclosed in the notes to the financial statements. Best practice is to include these pension obligations in the balance sheet.

Price Level Changes

The Company Accounts Act allows for the possibility of deviating from the historical cost convention in two areas:

● Tangible and financial fixed assets may, in some circumstances, be revalued to market value.

● Stocks may be revalued to a higher value than the purchase price or production cost, but not higher than their replacement value.

Current cost accounts may not replace the statutory annual accounts, but they may be published as supplementary information. There is no tradition for the preparation of annual current cost accounts.

Egypt

Abou Saada & Partners

The Egyptian government establishes law through its financial and economic body in the People's Assembly. These laws are basically intended to protect investors and companies, as well as the country's rights and are established to secure this protection in light of known accounting rules and concepts.

On the other hand, Egyptian Accounting and Auditing organisations are responsible for developing accounting concepts in Egypt. There are several organisations that research new trends in the accounting and auditing fields which include the Egyptian Institute for Accountants and Auditors, the Egyptian Tax Society, the Egyptian Cost Accounting Society and university faculties including the Faculty of Commerce of Ain Shams University.

The Egyptian Institute for Accountants and Auditors has issued auditing guidelines to be implemented by all auditors in Egypt. These guidelines act as standards that must be followed in order to standardise the auditing procedures followed for all companies. These standards represent the most recent development in the accounting profession.

In addition to companies, organisations required to prepare financial statements in accordance with legal and professional pronouncements include non-profit organisations and foreign companies which have a place of business in Egypt. These branches of foreign companies must have an auditor in accordance with the Companies Act No.159.

Form and Content of Financial Statements

The components of financial statements vary according to the nature of the enterprise, eg sole proprietor companies, partnerships, joint venture companies and limited liabilities companies.

Egypt

In the case of partnerships or sole proprietorships, the components of financial statements are not regulated by law. On the other hand joint ventures are required to comply with International Accounting Standards. Currently there are two laws governing joint venture companies: Operations law 159/1981 and law 230/1989 (which modified law 43/1974).

A joint committee, combining the legal affairs committee and the economic affairs committee at the People's Assembly, is responsible for the preparation of these laws. The laws are issued after formal publication in a newspaper and approval by the country's President.

The financial statements of joint venture and stock companies are prepared by the company accountant. The law requires the disclosure of net profits for the financial year, the distribution of reserves, directors bonuses, profits attributable to shareholders, employees profit share and finally retained earnings.

The tax authorities have a limited role in the implementation of laws relating to accounting practices and the form and content of financial statements. In sole proprietorship companies, the tax authority has the right to see all the company files. In joint venture companies, the right to inspect the company's files applies to:

- shareholders;
- the tax authority; and
- the supervising entities represented in the investment organisation or the stock market authority.

Public Filing Requirements

The various accounting bodies in Egypt are currently reviewing the requirements for companies to publicly file their financial statements. It is probable that the new requirements will follow other international requirements.

Audit Requirements

The following companies are required to have auditors:

- Joint Stock Corporation (S A)
- Limited Liability Companies (LTD)
- Foreign branches
- Non-profit making organisations.

In addition, Income Tax Act No.157 for 1981 requires any type of commercial business, sole trader or private company, which has a capital over than LE5000 or sales over LE50000, to maintain proper accounting records and to appoint auditors. However, non-professional businesses are not required to have an auditor.

An auditor who is registered as a public accountant and has five years experience is qualified to be an auditor for any of the companies listed above. Any auditor who has less than five years experience is not qualified to audit joint stock corporations. The reporting requirements for auditors are stipulated in the Companies Act No 159, 1981.

In brief, the auditor is required to state whether:

● all necessary information required to conduct the audit has been obtained;

● the company has maintained proper accounting and costing systems;

● the company's branches have been visited or whether the necessary reports have been received from them;

● a physical count of stocks has been conducted in accordance with best practice;

● the information included in the directors' reports is in agreement with the company's books; and

● the financial statements fairly represent the financial position of the company.

Valuation Principles

Egyptian Accounting Standards are currently being formulated. However, the accounting principles applied in Egypt should be in agreement with International Accounting Standards. Unusual or specific local requirements are not usually applied.

Group Financial Statements

Group financial statements are prepared as if the holding company and its subsidiaries were a single entity without regard to the legal boundaries between them, in order to show the economic capabilities of the whole group.

The holding company has to prepare a consolidated financial statement when:

● the company and its shareholders owns more than 50% of the capital of one or more subsidiary companies; and

● the company and its shareholders have shares in other companies and also have control over the formation of its board of directors.

In general, consolidated financial statements should be prepared in accordance with accepted accounting procedures. In particular:

● all companies included in the consolidated financial statements should adopt the same accounting policies;

● the holding company and its subsidiaries should have the same accounting period;

- the assets and liabilities of subsidiary companies should be recorded at their book value at the time of being acquired by the holding company. Any difference between this book value and the cost of the holding company's investment is recognised separately under capital provisions;

- if the holding company has acquired part or all of the subsidiary's shares during a period, the results of the subsidiary should be consolidated from the date of acquisition;

- where preferred stocks are owned by third parties, the holding company's share of profits is calculated after deducting the preferred stock dividends whether or not the dividends were declared;

- if the total losses of the subsidiary company exceeds its issued capital, the excess is included in the financial statements within creditors. The treatment followed must be explained in the notes to the financial statements;

- unrealised inter-group profits should be eliminated;

- appropriate adjustments should be made on inter-group transactions and balances and eliminated on consolidation; and

- minority interests should be disclosed separately in the consolidated financial statements.

Taxation

When assessing taxable profits the authorities follow different procedures to those used for accounting purposes. Specific areas include:

- Depreciation is allowed for tax purposes only according to the provisions of the unified accounting system.

- Rent is allowed according to a specific formula.

- Publicity and advertising is an allowable expense only if it is relevant to the taxation period.

- Donations to official bodies and exceptional cases such as natural disasters are considered deductible for tax purposes. Donations to other bodies must not exceed 7% of net profit.

- Gifts are considered deductible provided that they do not exceed 30% of turnover and it is proven that they help to generate income.

- Commission paid to company employees is deductible for tax purposes. However, commission paid to the establishment owner or partner are not deductible. Commission paid to unnamed third parties is not tax deductible and in all cases a provision should be made for tax deducted at source.

- Bad debts are considered deductible provided that the corporation has taken the necessary legal steps to try and collect them.

- Interest on capital paid to partners is not considered deductible since they already received a profit for their capital and work, therefore they do not have the right to receive interest for the same capital.

Tax authorities require all types of companies to keep:

- specific accounting books such as a general journal book; and

- an inventory book together with supporting records according to the nature of the companies business and the volume of its activities. In industrial companies it is imperative that costing data is provided as proof of the cost of the product.

France

Groupe Calan Ramolino et Associés

The main feature of French financial statements and their underlying accounting rules is that they are standardised, presented in a uniform format and mainly ruled by governmental bodies.

This is based on the existence of the General Accounting Plan (Plan Comptable Général) which provides an accounting guide containing, amongst other things, definitions of accounting terms, valuation and measurement rules, and structured financial statements.

The General Accounting Plan (the plan) was first issued in 1947 to ensure comparability between nationalised industries. In 1957, the plan was modified to suit different types of industries and became compulsory, mainly for national statistics and tax purposes. The Government created the "Conseil National de la Comptabilité" (CNC), the agency responsible for the definition of accounting policy and practices.

Together with the "Commission des Opérations de Bourse" (COB), the French Securities and Exchange Commission set up in 1967, the CNC has made many recommendations which impose additional reporting requirements. These requirements and the provisions of the fourth EC Directive are included in the 1984 plan.

Since 1983, general accounting principles have been enforced by the Code de Commerce, the general law which introduced the concept of the "true and fair view".

As a consequence, accounting law and practices in France now comply with the EC Fourth and Seventh Directives. However, because of the great influence of tax law on French accounting principles (financial statements are part of the tax returns in France), conservatism and prudence remain very important in French financial statements.

Form and Content of Financial Statements

The financial statements must be prepared in accordance with the following general accounting conventions prescribed by the Code de Commerce:

- the matching of costs and revenues;
- consistency of the method of accounting;
- going concern;
- prudence;
- historical cost;
- intangibility; and
- no set-off between assets and equities.

The plan specifies the form and content of the financial statements. It provides valuation and measurement rules, cost calculation methods and a code of accounts divided into seven classes. Classes 1 to 5 deal with balance sheet accounts and 6 and 7 with operating accounts.

Other professional bodies which are involved in the setting of accounting standards by giving advice or making recommendations are:

- The Compagnie Nationale des Commissaires aux Comptes (CNCC), the auditors' institute;

- The Ordre des Experts-Comptables et des Comptables Agréés (OECCA), which registers all the people who may legally provide accounting services; and

- The Commission des Opérations de Bourse (COB), for listed companies.

The directors are responsible for the preparation of the company's financial statements. These financial statements must give a true and correct view of the company's financial state of affairs. By law, the financial statements should contain:

- Directors' report, including comparative financial data for five years.

- Balance sheet. It is important to note that the equity side must be shown before the deduction of dividends. However, many companies also show the equity after dividends as a comparison.

- Profit and Loss Account. It is usual to present this in a vertical format. Expenses and revenues are grouped according to their nature (eg operating, financial, extraordinary).

- Notes to the financial statements including the accounting policies adopted by the company and the list of holdings and subsidiaries.

- Auditors' report (when required by law).

Comparative figures with the previous financial year must be shown.

Since 1985 there has been a legal requirement for listed and public holding companies to publish group financial statements in the form of consolidated financial statements. This requirement was extended to all private limited companies in 1990.

Public Filing Requirements

Most of the companies in France are S.As. or S.A.R.Ls. (defined below):

- Société Anonyme (S.A.) is a limited company that issues shares. If the shares are listed on the Stock Exchange, the share capital must be at least FF 1,500,000. Otherwise, the minimum capital requirement is FF 250,000.

- Société à Responsabilité Limitée (S.A.R.L.) is a private limited company whose capital, in the form of participations, is at least FF 50,000 minimum.

Both SAs and SARLs must file, within one month after the general meeting, the following documents with the Registrar of Companies :

- the annual accounts (balance sheet, profit and loss account and the notes);
- the consolidated accounts (if applicable);
- the management's report;
- the auditors' reports on the annual and the consolidated accounts (if there are auditors);
- the proposals to the general meeting for the appropriation of profits; and
- an inventory of shares owned in other companies.

Moreover, listed companies must publish certain information in the "Bulletin d'Annonces Légales Obligatoires":

- turnover, every quarter;
- an interim profit and loss account and report, every half year;
- the unaudited financial statements within four months after year end and at least 15 days before the shareholders' general meeting; and
- the approved accounts within 45 days after the shareholders' general meeting.

The published documents, are open to public inspection and the maximum penalty for omission or non-compliance is FF 6,000.

The general meeting of shareholders determines the company's year end. Only the first financial year may be for a period greater than one year. The financial statements must be in French and in French currency.

If financial statements do not comply with legal and professional requirements, they cannot be approved by the shareholders' general meeting. The minutes of the meeting's decision must then be filed with the Registrar of Companies. Prison sentences and fines may be imposed if irregular financial statements are approved.

France

Audit Requirements

Each S.A. is required to have an audit report on its financial statements. An audit report is also compulsory for other types of companies if it meets at least two of three following conditions :

- it has assets of over 10 million francs;
- it has gross revenues (excluding sales tax) of more than 20 million francs; or
- it has over 50 staff.

The audit report must be signed by a state registered auditor (a member of the Compagnie Nationale des Commissaires aux Comptes). The ethics and requirements of this body ensure that the auditor is sufficiently skilled to carry out an audit. The auditor's independence is controlled by a number of measures; he may not be an officer of the company, nor receive any money from the company except for audit work, and he cannot have any family connections with the directors of the company.

The auditor is appointed for six years by the shareholders and is expected to give an opinion regarding the "régularité" (compliance with the legal requirements), the "sincérité" (use in good faith of accepted valuation principles), and the "image fidèle" (the true and fair view of the profit for the year and of the state of affairs of the company). Two auditors have to be appointed if the company issues consolidated accounts.

By law, the auditor must also inform the directors of any difficulties he meets, or of any irregularities which come to his attention in the accounting records. If the auditor does not receive all the information and explanations he requires or if he discovers any fraud, he must inform the Procureur de la République (the public Prosecutor).

Companies whose turnover exceeds FF 120,000,000 or that employ more than 300 staff are required to prepare budgetary statements, which must include:

- a statement of current assets and liabilities;
- a current and budgeted funds flow statement; and
- a budgeted profit and loss account.

The auditor must, by law, check these statements for reasonableness. If this review, or his audit work, indicates that a situation exists which could endanger the future of the company as a going concern, the company chairman must be asked what is going to be done to remedy the situation. If the chairman's reply is not satisfactory, the auditor must repeat the same questions to the directors and then to the shareholders. In the last case, the Comité d'Entreprise (the staff representatives committee) must be informed.

Valuation Principles

According to the plan, only realised income may be recognised at the end of the financial year. Conversely, expenses relating to a financial year must be provided for even if they crystallise after the year end but before the financial statements are issued.

Financial statements are based on the historical cost convention. Certain fixed assets, for example land and buildings may however be revalued to market value but the increase in value is subject to capital gains tax, except when there is a legal revaluation (the last one occurred in 1976). By law, the surplus or deficit arising on revaluation of non-depreciable assets must be transferred to a separate revaluation reserve which is shown as such in the equity part of the balance sheet. The amount by which depreciable assets are revalued must be included in a special revaluation provision.

Legal form remains predominant in the French accounting requirements for the great majority of businesses.

Group Financial Statements

Group financial statements are compulsory for listed holding companies and public companies and the directors are responsible for their preparation. Since 1990, unless they are consolidated by another company, non-listed holding companies have been required to issue consolidated accounts if the group meets at least two of the following conditions :

● total assets of over 100 million francs; or
● total turnover (excluding sales tax) of over 200 million francs; or
● total staff over 500.

Subsidiaries under the control of the holding company or firms in which it has a significant influence (at least 20% of the shares) must be consolidated. If for any reason (for example capital transfer limitations) the control or the influence over the subsidiary is questioned, then the company must be excluded from the consolidation.

The holding company may also decide to exclude a subsidiary from consolidation which is either held with the intention of resale or is not considered to be material.

The form and content of the group financial statements is determined by the plan which incorporates the recommendations of Seventh EC Directive. The plan defines some accounting rules but also allows limited optional accounting practices such as lease capitalisation or different foreign currency translation methods.

Three methods of consolidation are authorised:

● the global or integral method, where all the assets and liabilities of the subsidiary are included in the consolidated balance sheet, with minority interests shown in both the balance sheet and the income statement. This method is used when exclusive control of the company can be achieved (50% of the voting power or 40% of the voting power with nobody else owning more than this amount).

- the equity method, used for associated companies where the holding is at least 20% and for subsidiaries whose activities are substantially different from the activities of the parent.

- the proportional method, where the assets and liabilities of the subsidiary are included proportionally to the interest held. In this case there is no minority interest on the consolidated balance sheet and the income statement. This method is recommended for joint ventures where the management's decisions are taken jointly by the owners.

The difference between the acquisition price and the net value of a subsidiary is allocated first to tangible assets to reflect their fair value at the date of the acquisition of the subsidiary. Any remaining difference, the acquisition difference, often referred to as goodwill, is shown after intangible assets in the consolidated balance sheet.

The acquisition difference is amortised most commonly over a period of 5 to 20 years, according to the expected life of the asset, although it can be offset against retained earnings in some cases.

In the following years, a comparison is made annually between the cost of the investment and the net value of the subsidiary at the beginning of the year. This allows the profit for the year of the subsidiary to be included in the consolidated profit and the retained profits of the subsidiary since acquisition, to be included in the retained profits of the group.

Transactions within the group are eliminated to avoid double-counting of profits and losses.

Moreover, accounting principles followed by associates and subsidiaries must be similar to those used in the holding company, unless they reflect more accurately the economic situation of the subsidiaries' and associates' activities and state of affairs.

The audit report on consolidated accounts must be signed by two registered auditors. They have the same obligations as for individual company accounts and must certify compliance with legal requirements, good faith in the use of accounting principles and the true and fair view.

Depreciation

By law, the cost of any fixed asset, which has a limited economic useful life must be depreciated or amortised systematically over that life.

The usual rates of depreciation are :

	%
Buildings	2 to 5
Plant and equipment	10 to 20
Motor vehicles	20

Depreciation is charged on wasting fixed assets, including buildings but not land using either the straight line or the reducing balance method. This latter method is accepted by French accounting law but it is, in fact, primarily a fiscal incentive to encourage companies to invest in new assets.

The depreciation charge is then divided into two parts. The economic depreciation is deducted from the operating results while the tax-driven excess is part of the extraordinary results and included in the regulated provisions.

Leasing

In France, lease rentals paid during the accounting period are considered as charges for the current year. The lease payments due in future years are reported as commitments in the notes. At the end of the contract, if and when the asset is bought by the company, it will be registered at its final purchase price. There is thus no capitalisation of leased assets at the start of the lease term in individual company accounts.

However, in consolidated accounts, lease capitalisation is allowed and lease payments due in future are shown as part of the group's financial liabilities.

Research and Development

Pure research or research and development costs with no commercial prospects must be written off in the profit and loss account. In some specific circumstances, these expenses may be capitalised and depreciated over a period of up to five years.

Inventories

Inventories are divided into three categories:

- Raw materials and consumables
- Work in progress
- Finished goods

Inventories are valued at the lower of cost or net realisable value. Cost is either purchase price or cost of production.

Purchase price is the actual price paid plus any expenses incidental to acquisition (e.g. freight charges). Production cost is the total of the purchase price of raw materials and consumables used, direct production costs and a reasonable proportion of indirect production costs.

The value of the stock may be determined by using the FIFO or the average cost method. LIFO is not allowed in France.

France

Intangible Assets

Intangible assets are registered, on acquisition, at their purchase price and must be amortised over their economic life.

The usual depreciation periods are 1 to 3 years for software and a maximum of 5 years for goodwill.

Capitalisation of intangible assets produced internally by a company is not recommended and is only permissible under certain limited circumstances. Internally generated goodwill may not be capitalised. In all cases, the value of intangible assets must be reconsidered each year and amortised if necessary.

Capital and Reserves

The equity is shown in the balance sheet as follows :

- Capital
- Share premium
- Revaluation reserve
- Legal reserve
- Reserves
- Retained profits or losses
- Profit or loss of the year.

The legal reserve must be maintained by transferring 5% of the net profits each year until the balance on the account reaches 10% of the share capital.

The surplus of profit and retained earnings after deduction of legal and statutory reserves can be distributed at the discretion of the general meeting.

Some reserves (e.g. share premium) can also be distributed if formation expenses, capitalisation expenses or research and development expenses are completely amortised or if the amount of these expenses does not exceed the distributable reserves.

At the end of the financial year, if the equity amounts to less than 50% of the share capital, an extraordinary general meeting must be called to decide wether or not to continue trading.

If the company continues, there must be a reorganisation of capital if the deficit has not been made up after the second year. If the company does not continue, assets must be liquidated and liabilities reimbursed before there is a repayment of capital.

Foreign Currency Translation

Receivables and liabilities denominated in foreign currencies must be translated at the closing rate at the end of the financial year. The exchange gain or loss arising from the difference between the transaction exchange rate and the closing rate is shown in the balance sheet as "écart de conversion" (exchange difference).

For unrealised losses, a provision must be made in the balance sheet and deducted from the profit and loss account unless the company has forward exchange contracts.

In consolidated accounts, it is common to use the closing rate to convert the balance sheet and the average rate to translate expenses and revenues in the profit and loss account. The difference on translation is usually included as a movement within equity.

Taxation

Companies pay corporate tax on the trading profit reported in their financial statements. Various non deductible items are added back to the profit before tax as shown in the financial statements in order to arrive at the taxable profit. The major adjustments are:

● General or contingent provisions which are not normally deductible for tax purposes

● Provisions for pensions

● A restriction of depreciation on cars whose purchase cost (including sales tax) exceeds FF65,000

As there are rarely material differences between taxable income and accounting income, tax effect accounting is rarely found in France.

The tax rate is 33 1/3% for the financial year starting on 1st January 1993.

Unusual and Prior Period Items

Extraordinary profits or losses are shown separately in the income statement.

Any non-recurrent items or material amounts relating to previous financial years which are included in the profit and loss account must be disclosed in the notes.

Retirement Benefits

Employees and employers contribute to a government fund for pensions and other retirement benefits. Private funds are rare.

Since 1985, accounting law has required companies as a minimum to disclose details of retirement benefits in the notes to the financial statements.

France

Related Party Transactions

Transactions between the company and one of its directors or between two companies having the same director must be previously approved by the other members of the Board of Directors.

Moreover the auditor must issue a special report on these transactions to the general meeting. If the transaction has not been previously approved by the Board of Directors, the auditor must mention this in the report given to shareholders.

Segmental Reporting

Under French accounting law segmental information is only required for turnover. The notes to the financial statements must at least disclose the geographic distribution of sales.

Treatment of Grants

The treatment of grants depends on whether they are operating grants or investment grants :

● Operating grants contribute towards increases in operating expenses or reductions in revenues. As a consequence, these grants are taken to the profit and loss account of the current financial year.

● Investment grants are incentives to encourage companies to invest in new assets or to create new assets. They are virtually part of the shareholders' equity and are released to profits proportionally to the depreciation of the assets they are financing.

Commitments and Contingencies

It is mandatory to disclose to the company's contingencies and commitments in the notes to the financial statements.

Information about guarantees and lease commitments are specifically required but information about unrealised exchange movements or financial transactions are also given.

Price Level Changes

Inflation in France has, at times, been acute and historically public companies have been required to revalue all assets according to a general price index.

Tax deductible provisions for inflation are also permitted if the purchase price of inventories has shown an increase of more than 10% over the last two years. The excess over 10% may be transferred to a "provision pour hausse des prix" for a period of six years.

Germany

BTR Beratung Und Treauhand Ring G.M.B.H.

Financial statements prepared under German laws and practices exhibit the well-known national characteristics of correctness and absolute compliance with those laws The purpose of the financial statements is to report the enterprise's financial position and operating results to the shareholders, creditors and the public. The emphasis is on prudence and protection of capital which may conflict with the Anglo-Saxon "true and fair view," although implementation of the EC Fourth Directive, with its requirement that the financial statements should provide a representation of the company's state of affairs which "correspond to the actual situation" (as the translation from German literally states), does go some way towards reconciling the two objectives.

The reason for this prudence is largely historical. A uniform chart of accounts was developed in the 1930s and made compulsory in 1937. The great depression in the early 1930s prompted the 1931 Companies Act requirement for the financial statements of public companies to be audited. A third factor was the rampant inflation experienced after World War II. This was recognized in the Act passed in 1949 that required companies to revalue their assets at replacement cost after the currency reform. At least that was the intention; the effect was to prevent overstatement of assets and condone their understatement. This remains the tendency today.

Tax plays a major part in shaping the form of the financial statements. The link to the taxation system is much tighter than in other countries. The main point is that expenses and allowances not included in the financial statements often cannot be claimed as deductions for tax purposes.

The accounting profession in Germany is well-established and long respected. It influences the content of financial statements by recommendations and non-mandatory releases. The Institut der Wirtschaftsprüfer (IdW) has only 8,000 or so members – a relatively small number – mainly due to the lengthy and exacting entry requirements and the fact that a member loses his designation as a Wirtschaftsprüfer (WP) when he leaves public practice.

The number of members has increased substantially during the last few years mainly due to the implementation of the EC Fourth Directive with extended audit requirements.

Form and Content of Financial Statements

There are two main types of company:

● Stock corporation (Aktiengesellschaft, AG) which may be public or private and is run by an executive board (Vorstand) overseen by a supervisory board (Aufsichtsrat).

● Limited liability company (Gesellschaft mit beschränkter Haftung, GmbH) run by directors (Geschäftsführer).

In Germany, the limited partnership (Kommanditgesellschaft, KG) is also an important business structure, in particular where it is set up so that the unlimited partner is a limited liability company (GmbH & Co KG).

The form and content of financial statements for a company (GmbH or AG) are laid down in the third book of the Handelsgesetzbuch (business law) which incorporates the EC Directives relating to the preparation and presentation of financial statements for companies and groups of companies. It should be noted that although the basic legal requirements concerning orderly bookkeeping and preparation of annual financial statements also govern business enterprises other than companies, the detailed rules concerning the format and publication of those financial statements apply only to GmbHs and AGs.

Legal requirements specify the standard headings which must be used in the balance sheet and profit and loss account. In addition guidance notes have been developed by the IdW and the auditing profession to ensure they are applied.

The financial statements have to be prepared by the executive directors, who are responsible for the company's activities. They are generally composed of:

● Balance sheet
● Income statement
● Notes to the financial statements
● Business report (Lagebericht) intended to complement and complete the picture provided by the financial statements and to provide a commentary concerning the development of the company during the year and its position at the end of the year
● For AGs only, the report of the supervisory board which explains how the board has supervised management during the year and whether it agrees with the financial statements
● Auditors' report

Comparative figures for the preceding year must be included.

Public Filing Requirements

The basic requirement is that large GmbHs, AGs and other enterprises subject to the Publicity Law (Publizitätsgesetz) must publish their audited financial statements in the Federal Gazette as well as file them with the trade register. Businesses subject to the Publicity Law are all those meeting at least two of the following three requirements:

- Over 5,000 employees
- Over DM 125m total assets
- Over DM 250m turnover

Listed companies must also deliver the required number of printed financial statements and the report of the executive board to the stock exchange and the banks.

Medium-sized corporations must file their audited accounts with the trade register whilst small corporations file unaudited accounts. Companies are categorized as small or medium-sized if, during two consecutive financial years, they do not exceed at least two of the following three limits:

	Small	Medium
Total assets	DM 3.9 m	DM 15.5m
Turnover	DM 8m	DM 32m
Average number of employees	50	250

As well as financial information the trade register also shows:

- The name of the company
- Registered office and branches
- Purpose of the company
- Share capital issued and authorised
- Directors and members of the supervisory board
- Persons who have signatory powers over the company's affairs

Audit Requirements

An audit is required by law for all limited companies other than those qualifying as "small" (see filing requirements) and for other business enterprises which are subject to the Publicity Law. For large companies the auditor must be a qualified WP or Wirtschaftsprüfungsgesellschaft (an auditing corporation in which more than 50 % of the directors are qualified Wirtschaftsprüfer).

The auditor is usually appointed by the shareholders, although the articles of a GmbH may provide otherwise, and he must remain independent. Independence is considered to be threatened not only where, for example, shares in the client company are owned by the auditor, or the client provides an unduly large proportion of the auditor's fee income, but also where the auditor has been involved in carrying out bookkeeping functions or in preparing the financial statements for the client.

Germany

The auditor signs an opinion (using his own name under the auditing firm's name) that is included both in the published financial statements and in a long-form audit report. It states that the accounting records and the financial statements comply with legal requirements, that the financial statements provide an accurate presentation of the company's position and that the business report (Lagebericht) is in accordance with the financial statements.

The long-form audit report provides a great deal of information concerning the financial statements. It basically contains the following:

● details of the audit appointment and the methods and tests employed by the auditor to carry it out;
● a brief comment on the company's economic situation;
● a breakdown of, and commentary on, each individual item in the profit and loss account and balance sheet;
● any facts endangering the company's continued existence and any illegal acts by management; and
● the conclusion given in the audit certificate.

The IdW's published opinions, as well as the statements and guidelines it issues, must be considered by the auditor when issuing a report. If a deviation from generally accepted principles is accepted by the auditor, he should refer to it in his report and state the reasons why. The long-form audit report is strictly confidential and not filed with the trade register although banks, or the tax authorities may ask to see it.

Valuation Principles

The German accounting system is based generally on the historical cost convention. Where an asset has been depreciated and is being carried at less than cost it may be revalued. However the revalued amount may not exceed historical cost.

Unrealised profits cannot be included in the financial statements but unrealised losses must be provided for. Liabilities or provisions cannot be set off against receivables or other assets, unless both items are currently due and relate to the same person.

Expenses incurred in relation to the formation of a company or the expansion of the business may be included as an asset in the balance sheet, but must be written off within four years, and an amount equal to the remaining value of such an asset must be treated as an undistributable reserve. Intangible assets can only be capitalised if purchased.

Group Financial Statements

Holding companies are required to produce and publish group financial statements incorporating the results of majority owned subsidiaries and associates worldwide. Holding companies which are themselves wholly owned subsidiaries (sub-holding companies) of an EC company are exempt from this requirement, provided that the group accounts prepared by the parent are published in German.

German sub-holding companies may also be exempt from preparing their own group financial statements even if the parent company is located outside the EC but does produce and publish in Germany group financial statements which contain the same information as required by the EC Eighth Directive.

Exemption will also be given if, during two consecutive financial years, the financial statements for the parent and subsidiary companies do not exceed two of the following three limits:

	Sum of Individual Financial Statements	Consolidated Financial Statements
Total Assets	DM 46.8m	DM 39m
Turnover	DM 96m	DM 89m
Average number of employees	500	500

A subsidiary must be excluded from the group financial statements if the business carried out by the subsidiary is so different from that of the rest of the group that its inclusion would be misleading. A subsidiary may be excluded if:

● there are considerable long-term limitations on the extent to which the parent company can exercise control over the subsidiary; or

● the investment in the subsidiary has been acquired solely with the intention of resale; or

● the necessary information concerning the subsidiary cannot be obtained without undue delay or expense for the group; or

● the subsidiary is immaterial to the truth and fairness of the group financial statements.

It is not compulsory for the financial reporting date of the group financial statements to coincide with that of the parent company, although this will normally be the case. The accounts for the companies included in the group financial statements should be made up to the group balance sheet date; this will involve production of additional financial statements if the year-end date of any of the companies occurs more than three months before the group accounting date. The form and content of the consolidated financial statements are prescribed by law and are substantially the same as for single companies.

The basis of consolidation is comparable to Anglo-Saxon methods, with the investment in the subsidiaries being replaced by the net value of the assets of those subsidiaries, generating goodwill or capital reserves on consolidation. If the parent company owns between 20 and 50 percent of the shares of another company, that company has to be consolidated on an equity basis.

All intragroup balances, transactions, profits and losses must be eliminated on consolidation.

A merger method of group accounting is also permissible under German law, but may only be applied in particular circumstances.

Depreciation

Depreciation is provided on all fixed assets. The total cost of and additions to fixed assets, the related accumulated depreciation and the book value at the end of the year are shown separately in the balance sheet and the annual depreciation charged in the profit and loss account is disclosed.

The depreciation provision may be calculated on a straight line or reducing balance basis, as the situation requires. Generally the rates are set by the tax authorities.

Where "special" depreciation is provided for tax purposes only (for example the allowances set up to provide incentives for investment in West Berlin or in East Germany), this may be credited to a special reserve (Sonderposten mit Rücklageanteil) and released over the same period as the related assets are depreciated on a commercial basis. Such reserves may only be created where the tax authorities require the tax allowances to be included in the financial statements.

Leasing

IAS17 describes the accounting and professional practice that has been in force in Germany for many years. Finance leases (those where substantially all the risks and rewards of ownership are transferred to the lessee) should be reflected in the balance sheet of the lessee by recording the asset and corresponding liability at the inception of the lease.

Research and Development

German law, in general, does not allow these costs to be carried forward in the balance sheet except where:

● the research resulting from such costs incurred by a third person has been acquired by the company in which case depreciation on a systematic basis is compulsory; or

● costs have been expended by the company to bring the product into production. These should be absorbed into production costs and not carried forward to the next year.

Inventories

These are split into three categories:

- Raw material, ancillary materials and supplies
- Work in progress
- Finished products and merchandise

Inventories must be valued at the lower of purchase price, or production cost, of each individual item as compared with its net realisable value. Groups of similar items may be treated together. The purchase price includes any additional expenses incidental to the purchase. Discounts must be deducted. Production cost includes, as a minimum, all items directly applicable to the goods produced and may include a reasonable proportion of production cost overheads but cannot include the cost of unused or unnecessary capacity. Certain elements of administration cost may be included in overheads, although this is not usual and distribution costs cannot be included. FIFO, LIFO and HIFO (highest in first out) valuations are all approved by law and are, except for LIFO, allowed for tax purposes. Average cost is usually used as it approximates to actual cost.

In the case of long-term production (construction business, shipbuilding industry, etc.), if the results are material, profits may be recognised not when the whole contract is fulfilled but on a pro rata basis. The necessary conditions for this are that:

- the final settlement of the work done is not possible until a reasonable time has passed and the project has been thoroughly researched; and

- no additional costs including financing costs will occur beyond those that have been included in the calculation.

In many cases, recognition of profits will not be possible but provisions for future losses must be made.

Capital and Reserves

Share Capital – Called but unpaid capital must be shown on the assets side of the balance sheet, but other unpaid capital may be deducted from the share capital figure on the liabilities side. However, companies must also create a reserve against the asset to protect creditors in the event of non-payment by the shareholders.

Capital Reserves – These reserves are set up to distinguish funds arising from "capital" sources from those generated by the company's business activities. Included here are share premium, loan capital and other amounts paid into the company by the investors.

Germany

Legal Reserves – All AGs are required to maintain a legal reserve by transferring 5% of the net profit each year until the total balance on this account together with the capital reserve reaches 10% of the share capital. This may only be used to absorb losses. Amounts in excess of 10% may be used to increase the share capital.

Revenue Reserves – The management of AGs may transfer a maximum of 50% of its net profit to revenue reserves, effectively as retained earnings. The balance on the profit and loss accounts can be used to pay dividends after approval by the shareholders. Dividends paid are not shown in the profit and loss account but deducted, without disclosure, from the retained earnings brought forward in the following year's financial statements.

Hidden Reserves – The law specifically disallows unjustifiable deductions from costs or valuations, and fictitious provisions, in an attempt to prevent the gross undervaluation of assets that was previously common practice. However, hidden reserves can arise where:

● assets, such as buildings, are depreciated, but effectively rise in value;

● additional tax allowances are only available if they are included in the accounting records (but see also the point concerning special depreciation); or

● over-cautious valuations are applied to assets such as inventories.

In these cases, the reserve is of course hidden in the relevant asset or liability valuation.

Provisions – Provisions must be made for uncertainties, accrued liabilities, warranties and indemnities, taxes (including deferred tax if necessary) and impending losses from incomplete business.

Provisions may be made for the cost of maintenance or repair not spent during the fiscal year, which will be incurred in the following fiscal year and warranties given without legal obligation.

Future pension payments must be shown under a separate heading.

Losses – In the event of a serious decrease in shareholders' funds when accumulated losses reduce the net assets to less than 50% of the issued share capital, a shareholders' meeting must be called to decide the company's future. If the losses diminish the share capital to nil, the executive board must apply to wind up the company.

Foreign Currency Translation

There are no legal or professional pronouncements on accounting for foreign currency items. The following details best practice:

● Short-term assets and liabilities denominated in a foreign currency should be translated at the exchange rate on the day of the transaction and adjusted at the end of the fiscal year to closing rates, where these are less favourable. This follows the basic valuation principle of recognising unrealised losses but not unrealised profits. If the possibility can be foreseen that the exchange position is likely to worsen further after the year end and before assets can be realised then consideration should be given to providing against this additional risk.

● Long-term investments including fixed assets and long-term loans must be translated using the market rate on the day of the transaction. If the exchange rate becomes worse, adjustments have to be made. If there is a permanent diminution in the value of these assets a provision must be made.

Where forward contracts for currency have been entered into in order to hedge against possible risks, it is permissible to use the contracted rate for translation of the related currency asset or liability.

The methods to be employed for the translation of the financial statements of foreign subsidiary companies into DM for the purpose of producing consolidated accounts are not laid down by law and discussions are still taking place in the profession as to the best method to be adopted. A guideline is currently being prepared and is under discussion.

Taxation

The tax calculation starts with the total annual profit of the company, and adjustments are made for taxes which are not deductible (corporation income tax and wealth tax) and other expenses which are not deductible for tax purposes. It is worth noting that undistributed profits are taxed at a higher rate than those distributed as dividends.

Under certain circumstances, part of the accounting income is not taxed in the current period. The untaxed reserves should be shown separately so that the reader of the financial statements is aware which part of the reserves has not yet suffered tax. Expenses not deductible for tax diminish the untaxed reserves. A provision is often made, even if not required on a commercial basis, for bad debts.

Treatment of Grants

Investment grants are credited to provisions and written off during the lifetime of the respective assets. These grants are not taxable.

Unusual and Prior Period Items

The notes to the financial statements include all changes in accounting policies and material unusual and prior year items. Adjustments to prior year figures are not usual as changes to financial statements are reserved for the shareholders at their annual meeting. Extraordinary income and charges are, if material, reported separately. Reserve accounting is generally not permitted.

Retirement Benefits

Prior to the implementation of the Bilanzrichtliniengesetz, companies had a choice as to whether to make provisions for retirement benefits or not. Under the current legal requirements, provision now has to be made, under the general clause that all uncertain liabilities must be provided for. There are, however, transitional concessions, under which the option not to provide is retained for pension liabilities that were entered into prior to 1 January 1987. The option to provide or not also remains open for liabilities indirectly related to pension obligations.

There is a view that these concessions are rather too generous and the IdW continues to stress the desirability of making full provision. The law does, however, require the amount not provided for to be disclosed in the notes to the accounts.

Price Level Changes

Present law does not allow the inclusion of price level adjustments in the financial statements. Nevertheless, the influence of inflationary changes and their effect on businesses is in some cases being reported to the shareholders. Guideline HFA2/1975 recommends a method for eliminating inflationary profits with disclosure in a supplementary statement.

Greece

Kolokotronis-Papakyriacou & Co

Greece became a member of the European Community in 1981. The country has recently been taking steps to deregulate most sectors of the economy including industry, commerce, banking tourism, shipping, agriculture, the stock exchange, capital movements and other areas of economic life including company financial reporting.

Several EC Directives have been incorporated into Greek company law. A General Accounting Plan has also been drawn up which became mandatory for large companies on January 1 1993. Companies are required to present financial statements in the standard form introduced by the General Accounting Plan and for practical reasons they have adapted their accounting records accordingly.

In Greece there are two professional accounting bodies:

- The Soma Orkoton Logiston (SOL) or Institute of Certified Public Accountants in Greece.
- The Association of Certified Accountants of Greece (SELE).

The accounting profession will be reorganised during 1993 since the Soma Orkoton Logiston (SOL) monopoly for statutory audits ends effectively with the completion of audits for the year ended December 31 1992. Thereafter statutory audits will be carried out by members of SOE, the new body of Auditors who will act either individually or as firms.

Foreign qualified accountants, who are holders of practising certificates, are recognised and individuals will be able to obtain the Greek qualification by passing certain examinations and completing fifteen years practical experience in total. Greek and EC Nationals with foreign qualifications and ten years practical experience, at least three years in Greece, will obtain the Greek qualification by passing special examinations, oral and written, in tax, audit and accounting.

Greece

There are two major types of companies:

- The Limited Liability Company (EPE) is required to have a minimum capital of 3,000,000 drachmae, with its capital divided into shares of not less than 10,000 drachmae each. The partners' liability is limited to their capital contribution. Taxable income is assessed 50% on the company and 50% on the individual partners.

- The Societe Anohyme (SA) is usually larger than an EPE. Its minimum paid-up capital is set at 10,000,000 drachmae with certain exceptions such as banks. An SA's shares may be either registered or bearer and the company may be private or public. The shareholders' liability is limited to their capital contribution.

This chapter deals mainly with SAs, which are by far the more important type of entity, as most business enterprises above a reasonable size are incorporated as an SA.

Form and Content of Financial Statements

The form and content of a company's books and records are prescribed by the Code of Books and Records.

The form and content of a company's financial statements are prescribed in detail in the recently amended company law which now incorporates the EC Directives. An SA's published financial statements should contain:

- Balance sheet
- Income statement
- Appropriation of profit statement
- Notes to the financial statements

The financial statements, which are filed with the Ministry of Commerce, must be accompanied by a directors' report and an auditors' report. Comparative figures must be shown. A statement of changes in financial position is not required and its compilation is not common practice.

Public Filing Requirements

All SAs must file audited financial statements (including directors' and auditors' reports) with the Ministry of Commerce at least 20 days before the annual general meeting of the shareholders. These are available for inspection by the public.

Companies must also publish the statutory auditors' report and the accompanying financial statements, with the exception of the notes, in one daily newspaper and one financial newspaper.

Following the annual general meeting, the minutes approving the financial statements must be filed with the Ministry of Commerce.

The directors of a company are responsible for the preparation, filing and publication of the financial statements. The financial statements are signed by the Managing Director, the General Manager, and the Chief Financial Officer.

Audit Requirements

Company law requires that the financial statements of every SA must be audited.

Up to the year ended December 31 1992 companies listed on the Athens Stock Exchange, banks, insurance companies, oil refineries and any other company meeting any two of the following three criteria must be audited by the SOL, the quasi-governmental body of auditors. The three criteria are:

- Total assets exceeding 200,000,000 drachmae
- Net turnover exceeding 400,000,000 drachmae
- Average labour force exceeding 50 employees

For the years ended on or after December 31 1993 all such financial statements will be audited by member of SOE.

The financial statements of all other companies must be audited by at least two auditors, who must be university graduates in economic studies of at least five-years standing and who must be at least 30 years old. SOL's audit report states whether:

- all information required has been received;
- the regulations have been complied with;
- the financial statements agree with the books and records of the company;
- the notes to the financial statements include the necessary legal disclosures;
- the content of the directors' report is in accordance with the financial statements; and
- the financial statements and the accompanying notes present the financial position of the company.

The old practice whereby in addition to the statutory auditors, many companies, particularly subsidiaries of multinationals, appoint a firm of accountants as independent auditors reporting to the ultimate shareholders or the parent company's auditors is expected to stop.

Valuation Principles

Greek companies are invariably required to adopt the historical cost convention to value their assets and liabilities. Land and buildings, plant and machinery are stated at cost subject to certain statutory revaluations. The revaluation laws stipulate how the surpluses arising from such revaluations can be used, such as to increase the share capital of the company or to write off any existing losses. The surpluses relating to land and buildings are usually taxed and the tax is charged to the shareholders. Such revaluations are imposed every two to three years.

Group Financial Statements

Since 1991 companies have been required to prepare consolidated financial statements in accordance with the relevant EC directive.

Depreciation

By law, the cost or valuation of any fixed asset, except land, should be depreciated and amortised over the predetermined useful life of the asset using the straight line method.

The depreciation rates allowed are:

● Buildings	5-8%
● Buildings on land owned by others	12%
● Machinery	12-15%
● Other equipment	20%
● Passenger vehicles	12%
● Transportation equipment	12-20%
● Telecommunication equipment	8-10%
● Furniture, fixtures, fittings, and office equipment	15-20%
● Computer equipment	20%

For each class of fixed assets, disclosure must be made of:

● the cumulative amount provided for depreciation at the beginning and the end of the financial year;
● depreciation charged during the year;
● the amount of any adjustment arising from disposals; and
● the amount of any other adjustments.

Leasing

There are no legal requirements regarding the accounting treatment of leases. Leasing costs are expensed in the period they are incurred.

Research and Development

Company law provides that these costs can either be written off in the year they are incurred or capitalised and amortised, applying the straight line method, over a period of five years.

Inventories

Inventories are divided into the following categories:

● Merchandise
● Finished goods, semi-finished goods, and by-products

- Work in progress
- Raw materials, consumables, spare parts, and packing materials
- Payments on account

Inventories are included at the purchase price or production cost of each individual item, unless the net realisable value is lower, in which case the lower value should be adopted. The loss due to an estimated lower realisable value is not tax allowable until it is realised.

The purchase price is the invoiced amount less any discounts plus any expenses incidental to acquisition. Production cost is the total of the purchase price of raw materials and consumables used, plus direct and indirect production costs, but excluding distribution costs.

In determining the purchase price or production cost, legislation allows FIFO, LIFO, weighted average, standard cost, replacement cost, base stocks and certain other methods. The method, once selected, must be used consistently.

Capital and reserves

If the net assets of a company fall below 50% of its paid-up capital, the directors of the company must call an extraordinary general meeting of the company to decide either to wind up the company or to increase the company's share capital.

If the net assets of a company fall below 10% of its paid-up capital, the company's operating license granted by the Ministry of Commerce will be revoked unless its share capital is increased.

A statutory reserve equal to one third of the share capital of the company must be built up through an appropriation of at least 5% of the annual net profits.

Where a company owns its own shares, a reserve must be set up equal to the acquisition cost of those shares. The shareholders may also vote to set up special reserves.

Profits are appropriated/distributed in the following order:

- Elimination of accumulated losses brought forward
- Statutory reserve
- First dividend
- Set up of reserve for own shares
- Supplementary dividend
- Board of directors' fees
- Issue of shares to employees
- Special reserves
- Retained earnings

In order to pay a dividend, the following conditions must be met:

● The unamortised part of capitalised installation costs, formation costs and research and development costs must be less than the voluntary reserves and retained earnings.

● The financial statements must be approved at the annual general meeting.

The first dividend and the additional dividend must amount to at least 6% of paid-up capital. Where 35% of the company's annual profits, after deducting the amount to be transferred to the statutory reserve, is greater than 6% of the company's paid-up capital, the dividend must be at least this amount, unless shareholders representing 95% of paid-up capital vote against such distribution at the annual general meeting. If no dividend is to be distributed unanimous approval of all shareholders is required.

Foreign Currency Translation

All realised gains or losses, with the exception of those relating to long-term loans used to finance the purchase of fixed assets, are credited/charged to operations.

Unrealised gains or losses, with the exception of those relating to long-term loans used to finance the purchase of fixed assets, are treated as follows:

● Exchange losses are charged to operations.
● Exchange gains are deferred and are transferred to operations in the following years as they become realised.

Realised and unrealised exchange gains or losses relating to long-term loans used to finance the purchase of fixed assets are treated as follows:

● Net exchange losses, per loan, are deferred and amortised over the remaining life of the loan. Losses during the construction period are capitalised and depreciated over a period after the completion of the construction.

● Net exchange gains, per loan, are credited to a liability "provisions" account and only the realised part is transferred to operating results.

Taxation

Companies pay income tax based on their profit for the accounting period after making certain adjustments to arrive at taxable profits. Some of these adjustments are for:

● tax-free income/reserves;
● various expenses not recognised by the tax laws;
● disallowed provisions including general bad debts reserves;
● depreciation in cases where the rates used for the accounts are different from the tax allowed rates; and
● tax losses which may, within five years, be set off against future profits.

Where accounting income differs from taxable income due to timing differences, no provision for deferred taxes is made.

Unusual and Prior Period Items

By law, the income statement should show unusual and prior period items arising in the year. Where unusual and prior period items are material, details must be provided in the notes to the financial statements and the effect on company taxation must be disclosed.

Retirement Benefits

The law requires a provision to be made in the financial statements for accrued retirement benefits.

Related Party Transactions

The law requires disclosure of the following amounts:

- directors' fees;
- liabilities to retired directors; and
- advances and loans given to directors.

Commitments and Contingencies

The law requires disclosure of the following:

- company guarantees;
- charges over assets;
- contractual commitments;
- contractual or other legal contingent liabilities; and
- commitments to related companies.

Price Level Changes

There is no legal requirement to provide for the effects of inflation in financial statements.

Guernsey

Michael Forrest International

Although the Bailiwick of Guernsey which is made up of the Islands of Guernsey, Alderney, Sark and Herm forms part of the British Isles, it is not part of the United Kingdom. Constitutionally, it owes allegiance directly to the Crown and has its own legislature and its own separate tax system.

Guernsey is not an associate member of the EC but, under special arrangements negotiated by the United Kingdom, it has many of the benefits of membership without many of the disadvantages. In particular, its fiscal autonomy is preserved and it does not have to comply with EC harmonisation policies.

The Bailiwick of Guernsey has its own laws, issued and updated by the States of Guernsey in the form of Acts. Company law, the most recent being Company (Guernsey) Law 1990, deals with the registration of companies whose liability is limited by shares.

Guernsey's Trust Law is incorporated in the Trusts (Guernsey) Law of 1989 as amended. As long as there are no beneficiaries resident in the Island, Guernsey taxation will not be levied on a trust formed in Guernsey.

Virtually all companies are private companies, only a very limited number of companies have publicly traded shares in Guernsey. Because neither private nor public companies (except banks, licensed deposit takers and insurance companies) are required to file financial statements with any authority in the Island, there is no distinction for practical purposes between the two types.

Guernsey has its own professional accountancy body, the Guernsey Society of Chartered and Certified Accountants (GSCCA) whose members are members of one of the professional bodies of accountants recognised in the United Kingdom and abroad.

Guernsey

Form and Content of Financial Statements

Guernsey company law does not dictate the form and content of financial statements for companies other than deposit-taking institutions and companies undertaking insurance business, which are controlled by the Protection of Depositors (Bailiwick of Guernsey) Ordinance 1971 to 1985 and the Insurance Business (Guernsey) Law, 1986. The accounting profession therefore seeks to comply with the concept of what is regarded as best practice by the professional bodies in the United Kingdom, as laid down in the Statements of Standard Accounting Practice (SSAP) and Financial Reporting Standards (FRS). These statements are not mandatory in law, though non compliance with them will generally result in reference to this fact being made in the audit report. The overriding concern is that the financial statements should show a true and fair view of the company's financial affairs and performance.

The directors are responsible for the preparation of a company's financial statements which give a true and fair view of the company's financial state of affairs. These are audited and presented to the shareholders.

Financial statements contain:-

● Directors' report
● Income statement
● Balance Sheet
● Statement of changes in financial position
● Notes to the financial statements including the accounting policies adopted by the company
● Auditor's report

Comparative figures must be shown.

There is no legal requirement for holding companies to produce group financial statements except, again, in the case of registered banks or deposit-taking institutions. In practice however holding companies do produce consolidated financial statements.

Public Filing Requirements

With the exception of registered banks, licensed deposit-taking companies and registered insurance companies, which have to file financial statements with the States Advisory and Finance Committee, there is no requirement for companies to file audited financial statements. Those which are filed with the States Advisory and Finance Committee are not available for public inspection. Nevertheless all companies are required to file with Her Majesty's Greffier (Registrar) an annual return that is available for public inspection.

The annual return contains details of:-

● The authorised share capital and issued share capital
● The directors

- The shareholders and their shareholdings
- The registered office

Audit Requirements

Every company requires an audit report on its financial statements unless it is exempt under the Companies (Exemption from Audit) Ordinance 1991. This ordinance applies to dormant companies and asset holding companies.

A company is an "asset holding company" during any period in which:

- its principal purpose is to own specified assets or assets of specified descriptions; and
- it does not engage in trade; and
- its activities (if any) are all directly connected with its ownership of those assets; and
- it receives no significant income other than income derived directly from its ownership of those assets; and
- it incurs no significant expenditure other than expenditure incidental to its ownership of those assets.

A company ceases to be an asset holding company when it not longer has all the above attributes. This ordinance does not apply to a company:

- which has more than 10 members; or
- which carries on banking, insurance or controlled investment business.

The auditor is appointed each year by the shareholders and must be appropriately qualified. The auditors' report states whether in his opinion the financial statements show a true and correct view of the state of affairs of the company and of the profit or loss for the financial year.

By law the auditor must also refer to any instances where:-

- proper accounting records have not been kept; and
- all the information and explanations required has not been received.

The auditor is required by the accountancy bodies to:-

- refer to any significant departures from SSAPs/FRSs unless they agree with the departure; and
- state whether the audit has been conducted in accordance with approved auditing standards.

Valuation Principles

Guernsey companies adopt the historical cost convention (that is, the assets and liabilities of the company are generally stated at original cost subject to depreciation or provisions). Certain fixed assets, in particular real property, may be revalued to market value. Any surplus or deficit arising on revaluation is transferred to a separate non-distributable reserve. There is no requirement to provide for the effects of inflation in financial statements.

Taxation

Guernsey resident trading companies pay income tax based on trading profits reported in their financial statements for the accounting period. Various adjustments may be made to the profit before tax shown in the financial statements in arriving at taxable profits.

The major adjustments are:

● Depreciation charged by the company is not deductible and fixed rate capital allowances are substituted instead.
● General or contingent provisions are not deductible.
● Dividends paid are not deductible.

Exempt companies pay tax at a flat rate, at present £500 annually, irrespective of the amount of profits, plus income tax on investment income from sources within Guernsey. These are companies which are incorporated in but not resident or controlled in Guernsey and which do not trade in Guernsey.

Exempt status may be granted to certain unit trusts and public investment companies. An annual fee of £1,000 is payable by exempted investment companies registered outside Guernsey and by exempted unit trusts. The annual fee for exempted investment companies registered in Guernsey is £1,300. No income tax is payable by exempted companies or trusts on income arising outside Guernsey or on deposit interest received in Guernsey.

Retirement Benefits

There is no legislation on the treatment of these items in the financial statements and little information is normally given.

Accounting Principles

In many cases, the law is silent on the accounting treatment to be adopted and on disclosure of information. In such cases, UK SSAPs/FRSs are normally followed and reference should therefore be made to the chapter on the United Kingdom.

The Guernsey Society of Chartered and Certified Accountants has issued a Statement of Guernsey Accounting and Auditing Practice which recommends that "Financial Statements of Guernsey incorporated companies and enterprises should be drawn up in such a manner so as to comply with Statements of Standard Accounting practice issued by the accountancy bodies in the United Kingdom. The information to be disclosed in the financial statements of Guernsey enterprises is derived from the disclosure of International Accounting Standard No.5".

Hong Kong

Charles Mar Fan & Co

It is natural that Hong Kong with its long history as a British Crown Colony should in the main follow UK accounting practices. The presentation of financial statements and disclosure requirements generally follow the requirements of the UK Companies Act of 1948, although in some cases, later UK requirements (e.g. the prohibition of loans to directors) have been taken up in Hong Kong legislation. However, the considerable foreign interest in Hong Kong does mean that where there are no local statutory accounting requirements, references are made to the practices in the countries of overseas parent companies (e.g. United States, Australia) as well as International Accounting Standards.

The accounting profession in Hong Kong, The Hong Kong Society of Accountants (HKSA), is responsible for developing generally accepted accounting principles that aim to show a true and fair view of a company's financial affairs and operating result.

Hong Kong has an active stock exchange with approximately 500 companies listed. It is a major international financial centre, as well as having an important manufacturing and export industry.

Form and Content of Financial Statements

The form and content of a company's financial statements are prescribed by law as set out in the Companies Ordinance as well as by Statements of Standard Accounting Practice (SSAP) and Accounting Guidelines promulgated by the HKSA. SSAPs are not mandatory in law, although non-compliance will generally result in reference to that fact being made in the report of the auditors. However, as required by the Companies Ordinance, the overriding concern is that the financial statements should show a true and fair view of the company's operating result and state of affairs.

It is the responsibility of the directors to prepare the company's financial statements for presentation to the shareholders at least once in each calendar year. Public companies are required to prepare financial statements made up to a date not more than six months prior to the company's annual general meeting whereas private companies, which are not also subsidiaries of groups containing public companies, must prepare financial statements made up to a date not more than nine months prior to their annual general meeting. Financial statements of a limited company incorporated under the Companies Ordinance must be audited.

The financial statements should contain:

- Directors' report
- Profit and loss account
- Balance sheet
- Notes to the financial statements
- Auditors' report

Notes to the financial statements will include the accounting policies adopted by the company as required by SSAP1. Comparative figures must be shown. Listed companies also publish a chairman's statement. SSAP4 requires companies with an annual turnover of more than HK$1,000,000 to include a statement of changes in financial position; non profit-making entities, financial institutions, insurance and shipping companies are exempt from this requirement.

Public Filing Requirements

The directors of a company are responsible for the preparation and filing of an annual return with the Registrar of Companies each year. The annual return contains, inter alia, details of:

- the registered office;
- the authorised share capital and the issued share capital;
- details of mortgages and charges on the company's assets;
- shareholders and their shareholdings; and
- directors.

A distinction is made in law between:

- a private company, which restricts the right to transfer its shares, prohibits any invitation to the public to subscribe for any of its shares or debentures, and limits the number of its shareholders, excluding employees, to 50; and

- a public company, which is a company that is not a private company.

A public company must file audited financial statements with its annual return. Private companies must file an annual return but need not file their audited financial statements. However, a private company must also file with its annual return a certificate confirming that the company has not invited the public to subscribe for its shares or debentures. All these documents are available for public inspection.

Listed companies are required by the stock exchange to file an interim unaudited report with the stock exchange in addition to their annual audited financial statements.

Audit Requirements

By law, an audit report signed by a member of the HKSA who holds a practising certificate has to be attached to a company's annual financial statements. This applies to all companies, both public and private.

The ethics and requirements of the HKSA and the fact that the auditor may not, by law, be an officer of the company ensures that the auditor is independent and sufficiently skilled to carry out an audit. In practice, a firm of accountants is appointed as auditor rather than an individual.

The auditor is appointed each year by the shareholders and, as a consequence, reports to them whether in his opinion the financial statements show a true and fair view of the operating result and state of affairs of the company and whether they have been properly prepared in accordance with the Companies Ordinance. The audit report will also state whether the statement of changes in financial position included in the financial statements presents a true and fair view.

By law, the auditor must refer in his report to any cases where:

● proper accounting records have not been kept; or

● the financial statements are not in agreement with the accounting records; or

● all the information and explanations considered necessary have not been received.

If no reference is made in the audit report, it may be assumed that none of the above cases applies.

Valuation Principles

Hong Kong companies generally adopt the historical cost convention, under which the assets of the company are stated at original cost less depreciation or provisions for diminution in value. Fixed assets, in particular property, may be revalued to market value. Any surplus arising on revaluation is credited to a reserve in the balance sheet.

SSAP1 requires that the accounting policies used should be disclosed in respect of items which have a material effect on the financial statements. The standard assumes that the fundamental accounting principles of going concern, accrual accounting, consistency and prudence have been followed.

Group Financial Statements

Group financial statements, normally in the form of consolidated financial statements, must be prepared when a company has subsidiaries unless it is also a wholly owned subsidiary of another body corporate.

Hong Kong

The group financial statements need not include those subsidiaries where, in the directors' opinion:

● the result would be misleading or harmful;

● the businesses are so different that they cannot reasonably be treated as a single undertaking; or

● it would be impracticable or of no real value to members in view of the insignificant amounts involved or would cause undue delay.

In cases where group financial statements do not include subsidiaries on the grounds that the result would be harmful or the businesses are different, the approval of the Financial Secretary of Hong Kong is required.

The form and content of group financial statements are prescribed by law and are substantially the same as for individual companies except that there is no requirement to present a profit and loss account for the holding company alone.

The financial year end of all subsidiaries should coincide with that of the holding company. If this is not the case, an explanation is usually required. SSAP7 requires uniform accounting policies to be applied in preparing consolidated financial statements. It also lays down certain guidelines in relation to the acquisition and disposal of subsidiaries.

The interest of the minority shareholders should be shown as a separate item wherever it appears in the financial statements.

Accounting Guideline 2.204 recommends the following treatments when accounting for goodwill.

● Positive goodwill arising in any single acquisition may be:
  – eliminated from the accounts, immediately on acquisition, against reserves; or
  – eliminated through the profit and loss account on a systematic basis over its useful economic life.
● Negative goodwill should be credited directly to reserves.

Under the Companies Ordinance, the merger or "pooling" method of accounting for a business combination may not be used.

SSAP10 deals with associated companies. An associated company is one in which the investing group or company has the ability to exercise significant influence over its commercial and financial policy decisions. Such influence is presumed to exist if the holding represents at least 20% of the equity.

An investing group's interest in associated companies should be accounted for by the equity method, whereby the group's financial statements include the group's post-acquisition share of the associated companies' profits or losses and reserves.

The audit report on the group financial statements will express an opinion as to whether the group financial statements have been properly prepared in accordance with the provisions of the Companies Ordinance and whether the group financial statements give a true and fair view of the state of affairs of the company and the group and of the profit or loss and changes in financial position of the group.

Depreciation

SSAP6 requires the cost of a depreciable asset, less its estimated residual value, to be depreciated or amortised systematically over its useful life.

Where depreciable assets are revalued in the financial statements, the provision for depreciation shall be based on the revalued amount and the current estimate of its remaining useful life.

For each major class of fixed assets disclosure should be made of:

● the depreciation methods used;

● the useful lives or the depreciation rates used;

● the total depreciation provided in the period; and

● the cumulative amount provided for depreciation at the beginning and end of the financial period.

There is no freehold land in Hong Kong. Land held under lease with an unexpired term of less than 50 years (including the renewal period) should be amortised over the remaining period of the lease. Buildings have limited useful lives and therefore are depreciable assets.

SSAP6 requires specific treatment for land and buildings in the course of development or redevelopment as follows:

● If held for resale, they may be regarded as trading stocks of a company and should be stated at the lower of cost and net realisable value in accordance with SSAP3 on accounting for stocks and work in progress.

● If held for other purposes, they may be stated at cost or at open market value. Depreciation of the buildings (and land where applicable) should be provided from the date the buildings can be brought into effective use by the company.

SSAP6 requires the following additional disclosures in respect of land and buildings:

● the amount at which land and buildings is carried in the balance sheet;
● the balances on any revaluation reserve together with movements during the accounting period; and
● any deficit on revaluation that has been taken to the profit and loss account during the accounting period.

Hong Kong

Separate disclosure is required by the Companies Ordinance of amounts ascribable to:

- land in Hong Kong held on long-term, medium-term, or short-term leases, respectively; and

- land outside Hong Kong held on freehold, long-term, medium-term, or short-term leases, respectively.

Investment Properties

SSAP13 deals with investment properties which are those held for rental income and potential appreciation in value.

Investment properties should not be subject to periodic charges for depreciation on the basis of SSAP6 except where the unexpired term of the lease is less than 20 years in which case depreciation must be provided on the carrying value over the remaining term of the lease.

Unlisted companies with investment properties, with a carrying value of less than HK$50 million or which comprise less than 15 per cent of the total group assets, may state investment properties at their carrying value.

Investment properties, other than those subject to depreciation or shown at the carrying value as referred to above, should be included in the financial statements at their open market value. Changes in the value of investment properties should not be taken to the profit and loss account but be treated as movements on an investment property revaluation reserve.

Leasing

SSAP14 accords very closely with the contents of IAS17 "Accounting for leases".

Finance leases (those leases which transfer substantially all the risks and rewards of ownership of an asset to the lessee) should be recorded in the financial statements of a lessee as an asset and as an obligation to pay future rentals. The amount due from the lessee under finance leases should be recorded in the financial statements of a lessor as a debtor.

Operating leases are accounted for as a normal hire of assets. The rental thereon should be charged on a straight line basis over the lease term unless another systematic and rational basis is more appropriate.

SSAP14 contains comprehensive accounting treatments and disclosure requirements covering all aspects of leasing activities.

Research and Development

There are no requirements regarding the method of accounting for research and development costs. However, generally accepted practice is that research and development costs, except those incurred on fixed assets, should be written off in the period in which they arise, unless they are reasonably certain of generating future income, when they may be capitalised and amortised on a systematic basis.

Inventories

SSAP3 requires inventories, other than long-term contract work in progress, to be valued at the lower of cost and net realisable value. Cost is defined as that expenditure which has been incurred in bringing each item or group of items to its present location and condition. In the case of work in progress and finished products, cost should include, in addition to the cost of purchase, the cost of conversion including direct labour, direct expenses and an appropriate proportion of indirect production overheads.

SSAP3 does not lay down the method used to arrive at cost except to state that the method used should provide the fairest practicable approximation to actual cost. The LIFO and base stock methods are unacceptable as they do not usually achieve this result.

SSAP3 also deals with long-term contract work in progress where the work extends for more than one year. Such contracts should be shown at cost to date, plus a proportion of attributable profit, less any foreseeable losses and progress payments received and receivable. Any excess of estimated losses over costs to date, less progress payments received and receivable, should be shown separately as a provision.

Capital and Reserves

There are no requirements to set aside amounts out of profits each year to special reserves.

A company may only make a distribution out of its accumulated realised profits (so far as not previously distributed or capitalised) less its accumulated realised losses (so far as not previously written off in a reduction or reorganisation of its share capital). Realised losses may not be offset against unrealised profits.

A company may only distribute its unrealised profit when the distribution is in kind (i.e. anything other than cash) and the unrealised profit arises from writing up the asset being distributed.

A further restriction is placed on distributions by listed companies whereby such a company may only make a distribution if, after giving effect to that distribution, the amount of its net assets is not less than the aggregate of its called up share capital and undistributable reserves.

Following IAS 1, AASB 1001 (AAS 6) requires that all material accounting policies applied to items in the financial statements be disclosed, together with details of any material changes in accounting policies.

Group Financial Statements

The directors of a company which has entities under its control (i.e. subsidiaries) are required by law to prepare consolidated accounts for each financial year, unless the economic entity, represented by the parent company and its controlled entities, is not a reporting entity. Control is defined in AASB 1024 (AAS 24) as being the capacity of an entity to dominate decision-making in relation to the financial and operating policies of another entity to enable that entity to pursue the objectives of the parent company. Indicators of control include the capacity to dominate the composition of the board of directors or the capacity to cast more than half the votes at a meeting of directors or shareholders. For financial periods ending on or after 31 December 1991, the "controlled entities" required to be included in consolidated accounts have been expanded beyond companies to include controlled non-corporate entities such as trusts and partnerships.

The consolidated accounts must be in the form of a single set of financial statements covering the parent company and its controlled entities. A controlled entity is required to change its year end to that of the parent company within 12 months of the parent gaining control of the subsidiary.

IAS 3 requires equity accounting for investments in associated companies in consolidated financial statements. In Australia, however, there is a legal impediment to this method. AASB 1016 (AAS 14) therefore requires information in relation to investments in associated companies calculated under the equity method to be disclosed in the notes to the financial statements.

Under AASB 1015 (AAS 21), all acquisitions of assets (including the acquisition of an entity) should be recorded at the cost of acquisition i.e. the purchase consideration plus costs incidental to the acquisition. On the acquisition of an entity, its identifiable net assets at the date of acquisition are required to be measured at their fair value and, to the extent that the cost of acquisition exceeds the fair value of the identifiable net assets acquired, the difference is treated as goodwill and is required to be systematically amortised to the profit and loss account over a period not exceeding 20 years.

The excess of the fair value of identifiable net assets acquired over the cost of acquisition is called discount on acquisition. AASB 1013 (AAS 18) requires the discount to be accounted for by reducing proportionately the fair values of the non-monetary assets acquired until the discount is eliminated. Any remaining discount is recognised as a gain in the profit and loss account.

The merger or pooling-of-interests method is not permitted in Australia.

Undistributable reserves comprise:

- share premium account;
- capital redemption reserve;
- the excess of accumulated unrealised profits over the accumulated unrealised losses; and
- any other reserve which the company is prohibited from distributing either by an enactment or by its memorandum or articles of association.

Foreign Currency Translation

SSAP11 deals with foreign currency translation and accords very closely with IAS21. It envisages two main types of transactions denominated in a foreign currency; those carried out individually by a company and those carried out by a foreign subsidiary or branch.

In the first case, the transaction is recorded at the exchange rate ruling on the date of the transaction. Any resulting exchange gain or loss is dealt with through the profit and loss account. At the balance sheet date, monetary assets or liabilities (for example, bank balances) denominated in a foreign currency are normally translated using the closing exchange rate and any exchange gain or loss is reported as part of the ordinary profit or loss for the year. Non-monetary assets (for example, fixed assets) are not normally retranslated except in certain specified circumstances.

In the second case, the closing rate/net investment method should normally be used whereby the balance sheet of the foreign enterprise is translated at the exchange rate ruling at the balance sheet date. The profit and loss account may be translated at either the closing or average rate provided that the method used is consistently applied. Exchange differences resulting from the retranslation of the opening net assets of a foreign enterprise, or in circumstances where foreign investments are financed by foreign currency borrowings, should be dealt with through reserves. Where the affairs of a foreign subsidiary or branch are closely interlinked with those of the investing company, the temporal method rather than the closing rate/net investment method is applied. Its rules are the same as those for individual companies.

Taxation

Companies pay profits tax based on the trading profits reported in their financial statements for the accounting period. Various adjustments are made to the reported profits before arriving at taxable profit. The major adjustments are as follows:-

- Interest or profits, less related expenses, not arising in or derived from Hong Kong are not taxable.
- Depreciation charged by the company is not deductible. Instead, fixed rate capital allowances are substituted. For example, at present, approximately 70% of the cost of new plant and machinery may be deducted from profits in the year of acquisition. There are also allowances on commercial and industrial buildings,

- Capital gains are not taxable.
- General or contingent provisions are not deductible.
- Dividends received are not taxable and dividends paid are not deductible.

Where accounting income differs from taxable income, SSAP12 requires provision to be made for deferred tax to the extent that it is probable that a liability or asset will crystallise on:

- short-term timing differences that arise on certain items mainly from the use of the cash basis for tax purposes and the accruals basis for financial statements purposes; and

- other timing differences likely to reverse in the foreseeable future, for example, depreciation allowances/depreciation charges.

Unusual and Prior Period Items

SSAP2 requires the financial statements to give particulars of any extraordinary income or charges. An extraordinary item is defined as one that is derived from events or transactions outside the company's ordinary activities and which is both material and expected not to recur frequently or regularly.

By law, where a material charge or credit arising in consequence of the occurrence of an event during a preceding financial period is included in the profit and loss account, the amount must be stated. Under SSAP2 where material adjustments applicable to prior years arise, either from changes in accounting policies or the correction of fundamental errors, they are accounted for by restating the financial statements for the prior period and may not be dealt with in the current period's profit and loss account.

Retirement Benefits

Employees are entitled to long service payments after a period of continuous employment with a company which varies between 5 and 10 years depending upon the conditions of employment. Provision should be made for long service payments if the payments will crystallise on termination of employment and the amount can be calculated with accuracy. In cases where it is possible that such a liability will crystallise, full disclosure of the contingency and a prudent estimate of the financial effects should be made.

There is no statutory requirement at present to disclose pension commitments or information on the funding thereof.

Related Party Transactions

The Companies Ordinance prohibits a company from making any loans to directors other than in specified circumstances. Where a company's shares are listed on the stock exchange or it is a member of a group which includes a listed company, the prohibition is extended to include persons connected with a director.

Hong Kong

There are exceptions to the above prohibition enabling public companies and private companies which are members of public groups to make such loans subject to an overriding limit of 5% of the company's net assets.

Private companies which are not members of public groups are permitted to make loans to directors provided the company approves the transactions in general meeting.

Details of any contracts in which a director has an interest must be disclosed in the annual directors' report and details of any management contracts, other than service contracts, in which any director has an interest must be available for inspection by members of the company.

Disclosure details in respect of relevant loans are governed by the Companies Ordinance.

Segmental Reporting

Listed companies are required by the stock exchange to disclose the turnover, profit contribution and growth trend of the different activities and different geographical areas in which they operate.

Under Accounting Guideline 2.206 and the Securities Rules, where any activity of a listed company contributes more than 10% of its aggregate turnover or results, it should give a description of that activity, its turnover and its contribution to the overall trading results.

Any changes in accounting policies which have a material effect on the segmented information should also be disclosed, explaining the reasons and the effect of the change.

Treatment of Grants

There is no statutory or other requirement in determining the nature of grants or assistance from government or other agencies.

Any grant, subsidy or similar financial assistance received is deemed to be a taxable income for tax purposes except when the grant is used for capital expenditure purposes.

Commitments and Contingencies

The Companies Ordinance requires disclosure of:

● the estimated amount and general nature of contingent liabilities not provided for;

● provision of security by the company for the liabilities of the company (the exact nature of the assets on which the liability is secured need not be disclosed);

- charges over assets given as security for liabilities of other persons;

- future capital expenditure contracted for or authorised; and

- other commitments not provided for but relevant in assessing the company's state of affairs (e.g. leasing).

Under SSAP8, contingent gains should not be disclosed unless it is probable that a gain will be realised. A material contingent loss should be accrued where it is probable that a future event will confirm a loss which can be estimated with reasonable accuracy. A material contingent loss not accrued should be disclosed except where the possibility of a loss is remote.

SSAP9 deals with treatment of events subsequent to the balance sheet date and requires disclosure of significant events for which no accounting adjustment has been made.

Balances not Reflected in the Balance Sheet

There is no statutory requirement to disclose any balance not reflected on the balance sheet except for potential deferred tax liabilities, commitments and contingencies which are covered in previous paragraphs.

Price Level Changes

There is no statutory or other requirement to provide for the effects of inflation in financial statements.

Future Developments

In view of the political situation in Hong Kong whereby after 1997 the sovereignty of Hong Kong will be reverted to China, it has become more common to use companies incorporated in other jurisdictions (e.g. Bermuda) as the holding company. As a result there has been a suggestion that the development of the future accounting principles of Hong Kong should follow International Accounting Standards rather than follow the UK Standards.

Hungary

CBI Konyvvizsgalo KFT

Hungary had played an active part in the world economy before World War II and the accountancy profession had developed accordingly. Accounting originally served the purposes of economic management, but later it became driven by tax considerations which had a significant impact upon the presentation of the balance sheet.

The recent changes in Hungary's socioeconomic structure required a profound transformation of accountancy. This was achieved by Act XVIII of 1991 which built upon European and international standards and is designed to help the process of integrating Hungary with the rest of Europe. The Act sets out various accounting provisions through which a realistic and fair view of the income generating capabilities, net assets, financial positions and future strategies of a company can be formed. This information is presented in such a manner that it is understandable by the shareholders.

The Act employed essentially European and international standards which were in issue at the time of its preparation. There are some areas, for example consolidation, where detailed provisions still have to be developed. The Act stipulates that entrepreneurs, government financed organisations, other organisations (associations, foundations etc) and the National Bank of Hungary shall follow the bases which it prescribes. The Act authorised the government to regulate by separate decrees how government financed organisations, insurance institutions, financial institutions and the National Bank of Hungary should prepare reports on their particular operations. These decrees have already been issued.

The Act does not take the needs of the tax authorities into account. The tax authorities use the balance sheet profit figure as the basis for their calculations but make various adjustments. Considerable adjustments are needed because taxation requirements are aimed at high profits whereas the Act requires the applications of the principle of prudence.

Form and Content of Financial Statements

The form and the content of the reporting statements are defined in detail by the Act which sets out provisions for:

● Annual reports
● Simplified annual reports
● Consolidated annual reports
● Simplified balance sheets

All entrepreneurs keeping double-entry books must prepare annual reports if their business exceeds two of the following three criteria:

● the total assets in the balance sheet exceed 150 million Hungarian Forints (HUF);
● the annual sales revenue exceeds HUF 300 million; or
● the average number of employees exceeds 100.

If their business falls below these limits simplified annual reports are prepared.

Consolidated annual reports must be prepared by entrepreneurs that either have a majority holding in another economic organisation or exercise decisive control over one or more other entrepreneurs. Simplified balance sheets are prepared by small enterprises whose net sales revenue does not exceed HUF 50 million.

The full annual report consists of:

● Balance sheet
● Profit and loss account
● Supplementary notes (the supplement)
● Business report

In simplified annual reports the balance sheet and the profit and loss account contain summarised data, and the business report is left out. The balance sheet and the profit and loss account conform to European and international standards.

All enterprises are required by law to have an accounting reference date of 31 December and this cannot be changed.

Public Filing Requirements

Entrepreneurs listed in the trade register who keep double-entry books must file with the court of registration their annual reports, or simplified annual reports, as well as their proposals or resolutions concerning the appropriation of its profit no later than 31 May following the enterprise's year end.

The business report need not be filed but must be available at the registered office of the business for inspection by all interested parties who may make copies of it. The annual report is available to the public and any person may obtain it at the court of registration and make copies of it.

For the time being company's limited by shares (Rt), limited liability companies (Kft) having an original capital in excess of HUF 50 million, a single member liability company and the issuer of bonds must publish their annual reports but not their business report. Publication of the whole or part of the supplement is not necessary if, according to the auditor's report, the information shown in the balance sheet and in the profit and loss account is sufficient for a true assessment of the entrepreneur's financial position.

Publication of the balance sheet is required for companies limited by shares. The balance sheet and proposals for the distribution of profit as well as the report of the company's supervising committee shall be made available at least thirty days before the general meeting. The balance sheet shall be published in two national newspapers and in the case of firms listed on the stock exchange in the official gazette of the stock exchange.

The annual report may be accepted as true and valid if it has been audited and reported upon by a chartered accountant. As from 1 January 1998 all entrepreneurs keeping double-entry books will be obliged to publish their annual report.

In the event of non compliance with the provisions of the Act on accountancy the general rules of the Civil Code will be applied and penalties may be imposed.

Audit Requirements

Hungarian socioeconomic circumstances means that it is not possible to require every enterprise to be audited. The Act on accountancy as well as other Acts prescribe that companies limited by shares, limited liability companies having a capital exceeding HUF 50 million, single member limited liability companies and the issuers of bonds, must have their annual reports audited. The same applies to other entrepreneurs who voluntarily publish their annual reports. As every entrepreneur keeping double-entry books will be obliged to publish their annual report from 1 January 1998 this means that they also will be obliged to appoint an auditor at that time.

An auditor must possess a certificate, which is issued by the Minister of Finance to a person who:

● is a qualified accountant; and
● before or after qualification spent four or six years, respectively, in the sphere of accountancy, finance or management; and
● has a clean record.

Chartered accountants entering the profession take an oath respecting legal rules and the norms of ethics and of official secrecy.

Hungary

The list of chartered accountants is issued in the official gazette of the Ministry of Finance. The Hungarian Chamber of Chartered Accountants keeps a record of the list on behalf of the minister.

An individual may qualify as chartered accountant who:

● has a qualification from a university or college and is a chartered associate accountant;

● has four years experience in accountancy, finance and supervising, before taking the first specialist chartered accountancy examinations; or

● has three years experience as an auditor with a chartered accountant before taking the first chartered accountancy examinations; and

● passes the examinations set by the examination board created by the Minister of Finance.

An organisation is entitled to practise as chartered accountants if the majority of its members, employees and senior officers are chartered accountants.

The specialist examinations cover auditing, accountancy, bookkeeping and preparation of annual reports, financial matters and legal knowledge.

The certificate issued on behalf of the Ministry of Finance is valid for five years and the Hungarian Chamber of Chartered Accountants keeps a register of the organisations possessing such a certificate. The audit report is signed by individuals who are chartered accountants even where they belong to an organisation which itself possesses certification as a chartered accountant.

Qualified accountants registered to practise in a country other than Hungary, may receive permission to act as an accountant in Hungary if proof is given, by examination, of their knowledge of Hungarian legislation. Permission may also be granted if reciprocal arrangements exist with the country in question.

The following activities fall into the framework of accountancy:

● the audit of the balance sheet, profit and loss account and supplement, verification of compliance with the Acts on accountancy and forming an opinion on the annual report;

● analysis of a company's financial condition and profitability;

● study and control of the consolidated annual report;

● checking the value of contributions in kind made on the formation of business organisations and a review of the balance sheet including valuations in the event of reorganisation of enterprises; and

● the review of calculations of business and goodwill valuations, examination and verification of balance sheets prepared in the case of liquidations and reporting thereon.

Principles of Valuation

A wide range of principles for the recording of transactions, assets and liabilities are set out in Hungarian legislation. The most important principles, during this period of transition in Hungary, are going concern and prudence. The application of each of the principles is, however, indispensable for the determination of revenues and costs.

The legislation sets out the following format for the profit and loss account:

● Trading profit
● Financial profit
● Pre-tax profit before extraordinary gains or losses
● Extraordinary gains or losses
● Pre-tax net profit
● Taxes
● After tax profit
● Dividend and profit sharing
● Balance sheet profit figure

The profit (or loss) may be determined using either the total cost method or the sales cost method.

Under the total cost method the profit (or loss) is the difference between the combined total of net sales revenues and the value of own work capitalised and the combined total of purchases of materials, payments to personnel, depreciation charges and other costs and expenditures charged during the calendar year.

Under the sales cost method the profit (or loss) is the difference between the total net sales revenues, and the aggregate of total sales costs, (direct and indirect) and other expenditure.

Investments and current assets must be valued at their purchase price or production cost. The Act on accountancy does not permit asset values to be higher than their purchase price or production costs although they may be modified for depreciation and decreases in asset values, respectively.

Group Financial Statements

The preparation of consolidated annual reports is obligatory only from 1 January 1995 although voluntary preparation may be implemented at an earlier date.

An enterprise which has a majority holding in, or which has control over the decision making of, a company (parent company) shall prepare summary accounts and a consolidated annual report which includes the income, expenditure, assets and liabilities of the parent, its subsidiaries and related companies as if they were one enterprise.

The consolidated annual report shall consist of the consolidated balance sheet, the consolidated profit and loss account and the consolidated supplement.

A parent company which is itself a subsidiary or is a business organisation whose founder is obliged to prepare consolidated annual reports and has a share of more than 90% in the parent need not prepare a consolidated annual report.

A majority holding is held by a parent company where it has control over either the decision making process of subsidiaries (and companies in which it has an investment), or more than 50% of the subscribed capital of the subsidiary company.

A significant holding is held by a parent company which has significant influence over the control of another company and the value of its investment exceeds 25%, but does not exceed 50%, of the subscribed capital of the other company.

Assets and liabilities appearing in the consolidated balance sheet must be valued on a consistent basis and appropriate adjustments made where necessary in the course of consolidation. The profit and loss account shall also be consolidated. Intra-group transactions and balances must be eliminated.

Depreciation

The purchase and production costs of tangible assets shall be depreciated over their useful lives from the date the relevant assets are brought into operation. Depreciation can be linear, regressive or related to performance.

Intangible assets must also be depreciated. The purchase price of rights, representing assets, shall be written off in six or more years, the goodwill of a business in at least five but not more than fifteen years and the capitalised value of research and development in five or less years.

Additional depreciation to reduce the value of tangible assets or investments to their market value shall be made if their value is permanently reduced due to the asset or investment becoming redundant owing to changes in the business or if it has become useless owing to damage or destruction.

Investments in company shares must be written down if, for a period of at least a year preceding the day when the balance sheet was prepared, the value of those shares fell below their book value.

The act specifies in detail the calculation of purchase and production costs of assets, which in general, are all the expenses incurred in the acquisition, establishment and installation of an asset, until it is operational or delivered into the warehouse and which can be individually attributed to the relevant asset.

Production costs include expenditure which:

- were directly incurred in the course of manufacturing, putting into service, expansion, remodelling and restoration of an asset to its original condition;
- were closely attributable to the manufacturing process; and
- can be charged to the asset (product).

Foreign Currency Translation

Foreign exchange cash and bank balances shall be shown at their original book value. If their forint value calculated at the official buying rate on the last day of the year is less than their book value, then the book value shall be reduced accordingly.

Cash payments made in foreign currency by a foreign member of a business organisation as a contribution to the subscribed capital shall be valued at the average rate valid on the day when the payment was made until it is used or converted into another currency.

Accounts receivable which are payable in foreign currencies shall be shown at the forint value calculated at the buying rate or at the valid free market rate, provided that the exchange rate of the relevant currency has not decreased and payment has not been made. If the exchange rate has decreased then the forint value shall be calculated using the buying rate valid on the last day of the year.

If payment of the account has been made by the day when the balance sheet is prepared, the accounts receivable figure shown in the balance sheet shall be calculated at the official buying rate valid on the day when payment was made.

Taxation

The Hungarian taxation system recognises several types of taxes:

- Personal income tax which is paid by Hungarian resident individuals based on their worldwide income and on foreigner's income arising in Hungary. No tax is payable on income up to HUF 100,000 and increases progressively with a maximum rate of 40% on income in excess of HUF 500,000.

- Value added tax is payable on the sales of products and services in Hungary and on the imports of services and products. Every entrepreneur is subject to VAT. The general tax rate is 25% although with effect from 1 January 1993 there are activities for which the rate of taxation is either 6% or 0%.

- Corporation tax is paid by enterprises which carry on activities aiming at or resulting in profit generation. Taxation is based on pre-tax net profit, as defined by the Act on accountancy, modified in accordance with the provisions of the Corporation Act. The rate of tax is currently 40%.

- Hungarian tax legislation furthermore recognises motor vehicle tax, land tax, excise tax and local tax whose importance is much less significant.

Hungary

Future Developments

The Hungarian accounting systems are now largely up to date and the process of developing an effective accounting profession has started. One of the major constraints on developments is the lack of appropriately trained accountants to serve the rapidly increasing number of companies.

A priority for the future is detailed regulations for and training in the field of consolidation.

India

Sharp & Tannan

Modern Indian Company Law and accounting date back to the latter half of the 19th Century when legislation was enacted to meet the growing needs of British businesses in India. Since independence in 1947 there have been continuing close political and economic relationships between India and the United Kingdom and English has been retained as an official language, particularly in legislation. Indian accounting and auditing practices continue to be modelled on those of UK. The Companies Act, 1956 is largely based on the UK Companies Act, 1948 although both disclosure requirements and the auditor's reporting responsibilities have been considerably extended.

The layout and contents of the balance sheet (but not the profit and loss account) are prescribed in detail in the Act and changes can only be made with Government permission. However, there are certain disclosure requirements relating to the profit and loss account. Despite the extensive information requirements, the financial statements generally follow the traditional UK pattern of disclosing profits or losses on a normal commercial basis and accounting treatment is not dictated by taxation requirements or regulations. Nevertheless, the degree of flexibility surrounding the preparation of financial statements is limited as it is only within the parameters of the Companies Act 1956, and certain other Acts and Rules, that the company and the auditor can exercise or develop their own judgement in determining policies.

There has not hitherto been any great user demand for changes, a majority of the core sector industries in India being Government companies (which includes deemed government companies and joint sector undertakings). Through their activities they control the country's natural resources such as oil, petroleum, steel and coal. They are also engaged in heavy engineering, specialised machine tool manufacture and similar activities. As a result, they exercise considerable economic influence on the private sector. These companies may be subjected to a special separate government audit. However, the Government has introduced new economic reforms which include liberalisation, privatisation and increased ownership/participation by foreign companies operating in India.

India

The Indian accounting profession became independent of the UK in 1949 when the Institute of Chartered Accountants in India (ICAI) was established.

The ICAI has formulated Auditing and Accounting Standards taking into account the recommendations included in international standards. Additionally, guidance notes are also published from time to time on various topics.

The Indian profession continues to strive for improvement in the education and professional qualifications of its members. India is a vast country and the principal firms of accountants are mainly established in the major cities and urban areas.

Form and Content of Financial Statements

The form and content of a company's financial statements are prescribed by the Companies Act 1956. Certain accounting standards (including disclosure of accounting policies, revenue recognition, etc.) issued by the ICAI are mandatory while others are only recommendations.

The directors are responsible for the preparation of a company's financial statements, which are audited and presented to the shareholders, to give a true and fair view of the company's financial state of affairs.

By law, the financial statements should contain:

- Balance sheet
- Profit and loss account
- Notes to the financial statements
- Directors' report
- Auditor's report

Comparative figures for the previous year are also required.

However, companies whose shares are listed on recognised stock exchanges are permitted to issue abridged financial statements in the prescribed form in lieu of the full balance sheet, etc.
Accounting policies adopted by the Company are disclosed as required by the ICAI. Many companies also publish a Chairman's statement.

The profit and loss account, in addition to certain prescribed disclosure requirements, should also contain by way of note detailed information of amounts paid to auditors, whether as fees, expenses or otherwise for services rendered. In many cases it also states in respect of each class of goods manufactured, the licensed and installed capacity and actual production. Companies are also required to disclose the value of imports in respect of:

- Raw materials
- Components and spare parts
- Capital goods

Any expenditure in foreign currency on account of royalty payments, know-how, consultation fees, interest and other matters must also to be disclosed. It is also necessary to disclose the consumption of all imported and indigenous raw materials, spare parts and components.

All remittances in foreign currencies, on account of dividends, to non-resident shareholders, the number of shares held by them and the year to which the dividends pertain has also to be disclosed. Similarly, earnings in foreign currency must be separately disclosed under the headings of exports, royalty, know-how, interest and dividends and other income indicating the nature thereof.

Public Filing Requirements

Public filing requirements are effected by a company's status. Indian law recognises the following types of companies:

- Public limited company: a company which is either not a private company or is a private limited company which is a subsidiary of a public limited company.

- Private limited company: a company where the public cannot be invited to subscribe for its shares, the shares are not freely transferable and which limits its members to 50.

- Deemed public company: a company which retains in its Articles of Association the criteria for a private company but loses the other privileges of a private company by virtue of

  - its turnover, or

  - shareholdings held by bodies corporate beyond the statutory limits, or

  - investment of funds in the share capital of a public company beyond statutory limits, or

  - invitation and acceptance of deposits from the public through an advertisement (other than from its members, directors or their relatives).

- Government company: a company where at least 51% of the paid up share capital is held by the Government.

All limited companies, both private and public, must file audited financial statements and an annual return each year with the Registrar of Companies. However, the profit and loss account is not available for public inspection in the case of:

- a private company;
- a private company whose entire paid-up capital is held by one or more bodies incorporated outside India; or
- a deemed public company where the central government prohibits inspection.

153

India

The Annual Return contains the following particulars of the company:

- Registered office
- Situation of foreign registers of members/debenture holders
- Shares and debentures, issued, subscribed and paid-up
- Particulars of indebtedness
- List of past and present members and debenture holders
- Directors, managing directors, manager and secretary, both past and present

Listed companies are also required to file audited financial statements with the Stock Exchange as well as having to comply with listing regulations, which include publication of unaudited half-yearly results.

Audit Requirements

Every company's financial statements require an audit report which must be signed by a member of the ICAI. In the case of a government company, appointment of an auditor is made by the Comptroller and Auditor General of India.

The law has been designed to ensure that the auditor is sufficiently independent to execute his functions properly. He cannot be an employee or officer of the company.

An auditor is appointed at an annual general meeting by the shareholders. He reports to them whether in his opinion, to the best of his knowledge and according to the explanations given to him, the financial statements reflect a true and fair view of the state of affairs of the company and of the profit or loss for the year. He also states whether proper books of account, as required by law, have been maintained.

If the auditor has not received sufficient information or has identified departures from the requirements of the Companies Act 1956, he must qualify the report.

Additionally, the auditor must also comment on certain matters which are specified in the Manufacturing and Other Companies (Auditor's Report) Order 1988, under the Companies Act 1956 including:

- loans taken from/given to other companies, firms or parties in which the directors are interested as shareholders or directors and companies under the same management;

- repayment of advances and loans where a repayment schedule is stipulated, including interest where applicable;

- physical verification and valuation of inventories;

- internal control procedures for the purchase of raw materials and assets, for the sale of goods and for the sale, or disposal, of realisable by-products and scrap;

- deposit of provident fund and employees state insurance dues within the stipulated period with the appropriate authorities; and

- non-payment of undisputed Government dues outstanding for more than six months as at the end of the financial year.

Valuation Principles

Indian companies adopt the historical cost convention (that is, the assets and liabilities of the company are generally stated at original cost, less depreciation). When fixed assets are revalued, any surplus or deficit arising is transferred to and maintained separately in a capital reserve. The auditor must state the basis of revaluation in his report.

Group Financial Statements

Group financial statements in the form of consolidated financial statements are not required and consequently consolidation principles as followed, for example, in the UK have no application. The Companies Act 1956, merely requires the financial statements of subsidiaries to be attached to those of the holding company.

A holding company is one which controls the composition of the Board of Directors of the subsidiary or holds more than 50% of the subsidiary's issued equity share capital.

If the financial years of the holding company and subsidiary do not coincide, the financial statements of the subsidiary for the year last ended before that of holding company should be attached together with a further statement setting out any material changes during this interval. The year end of the subsidiary should not however be more than six months prior to that of its holding company.

Depreciation

Either of the following two methods is generally used to calculate depreciation on buildings (but not land), machinery, plant and furniture in order to write off the assets over their economic lives:

- Written down value method: Depreciation is calculated with reference to the written down value of the asset at the rates specified under the Companies Act, 1956.

- Straight line method: 95% of the original cost of the asset is written off by way of depreciation over the useful life of the asset, at the rates specified under the Companies Act, 1956.

The value of leasehold land is generally amortised over the lease period.

India

By and large, depreciation rates are commercially realistic but if they are different from those prescribed under the Companies Act 1956 this is required to be disclosed in the accounts. Where depreciation is not provided in any year, this fact and the amount not provided is to be disclosed, as a note to the profit and loss account.

For each class of fixed assets the cumulative amount provided for depreciation at the beginning and the end of the financial year and the amount of any adjustments arising from additions and disposals must be disclosed.

Leasing

There are no statutory requirements regarding the method of accounting for leases. However, the ICAI has issued recommendations in a Guidance Note on Accounting for Leases. Lease premiums are allowed as revenue expenditure for income-tax purposes.

The leased asset is considered as a property of the lessor who enjoys depreciation and other deductions under the Income Tax Act. Normally there is an option for the lessee to buy the leased asset at the termination of the lease at approximately written down value.

Research and Development

The ICAI has issued an accounting standard on accounting for research and development which is mandatory. Research and Development costs of a project may be treated as deferred revenue expenditure whilst other expenses must be charged as expense in the year in which they are incurred.

Deferred research and development expenditure should be separately disclosed in the balance sheet under the heading 'Miscellaneous Expenditure'.

Capital and revenue expenditure on scientific research incurred prior to commencement of business is allowed as a deduction in the income tax assessment for the year in which the business commences, and thereafter in the year in which it is incurred.

Inventories

Inventories comprises:

- Raw materials and consumables
- Work-in-progress
- Finished goods

Inventories are uniformly valued at purchase price or production cost or at net realisable value, whichever is lower. Purchase price is the actual price paid plus expenses directly attributable to acquisition. Production cost comprises all direct costs, including material and labour costs plus a reasonable proportion of indirect costs but excludes distribution costs. The common methods followed are either FIFO, LIFO or weighted average, depending on the nature of the industry and other related factors.

The ICAI has issued an accounting standard, 'Accounting for Construction Contracts', which is mandatory. In the case of long term contracts, either the percentage of completion method or the completed contract method may be used. Under the percentage of completion method, the work-in-progress is valued at estimated realisable sale value after adjustment for progress payments and required provisions, when the contract has progressed to a reasonable extent, ie when at least 20% to 25% of the work is completed. Under the completed contract method, work-in-progress is valued at cost less progress payments.

Any loss foreseen for the entire contract, is to be provided irrespective of the amount of work done or the method of accounting followed.

An auditor has to report on the reasonableness of physical verification procedures and the frequency thereof, any discrepancies between book figures and physical count, whether the valuation is in accordance with normally accepted accounting principles and the effect of any change in the basis of valuation.

Capital and Reserves

The treatment of the capital redemption reserve, share premium account and the revaluation reserve follows UK practice. In addition the Indian Companies Act specifies that a general reserve and debenture redemption reserve should be maintained.

General Reserve

Instead of retaining earnings in the profit and loss account, companies try to build up their general reserve, since dividends may be paid out of the general reserve, up to a maximum of 10% of share capital, even if the company makes a loss in the year.

The directors can transfer as much as they like to the general reserve each year provided that the profit for the year has first been used to pay a dividend at a rate at least equal to that paid on average during the past three years. This requirement is waived if the profits for the current year are less than 80% of the average profit for the past two years. If profits are insufficient to cover this then the transfer to general reserve is restricted according to a sliding scale depending on the percentage dividend actually declared.

Debenture Redemption Reserve

Government guidelines require all companies issuing non-convertible debentures to create a debenture redemption reserve, equivalent to 50% of the value of the debentures, before redemption commences.

Dividend

A company can declare dividends only after providing for adequate depreciation, adjusting its accumulated losses, if any, and transferring profits to a General reserve (see above), as specified in the Companies (Transfer of Profits to Reserve) Rules 1975.

Managerial Remuneration

The Companies Act lays down the maximum remuneration, including commission, which may be paid to directors of a public company without the Government's approval. Appointment of a managing director, executive director or a manager can be made without the approval of central government only if he is a citizen of and is resident in India and satisfies certain other conditions set out in Schedule XIII of the Companies Act, 1956. All other appointments require central government approval.

The profit and loss account gives detailed information of payments made, or provided, during the financial year to the directors. In the case of low profits, the Companies Act 1956, provides for a cut of 10% in the salary payable to a director of a public company.

Foreign Currency Translation

The ICAI has issued an Accounting Standard giving recommendations on accounting for foreign currency translation. Disclosure is recommended with regard to:

- the methods used to convert assets and liabilities remaining unsettled at the end of the accounting period and translating financial statements of foreign branches; and

- the accounting treatment of exchange differences showing separately the amount of loss recognised in the profit and loss statement, the amount of loss or gain included in the carrying amount of fixed assets and the amount deferred in respect of losses related to long term liabilities.

In the case of current assets and current liabilities (other than those relating to fixed assets) if the result of conversion is an overall net gain, the ICAI recommends that it should not be taken into account.

Taxation

Companies are assessed to tax under the Income Tax Act 1961, at rates prescribed annually by the Finance Act, for the financial year from 1st April to 31st March. A substantial portion of the tax payable for the financial year is paid by way of "Advance Tax" on the estimated profits and/or by way of tax withheld at source. The "Return of Income" has to be filed on or before 31st December.

In addition to the above requirement, the Act has also made a tax audit of accounts compulsory if total sales, turnover or gross receipts exceed certain limits. The "Tax

Audit Report" has to be attached to the "Return of Income".

The trading profit, as reported in the financial statements, is adjusted for various allowances and disallowable items before arriving at the taxable profit. Some of the major adjustments are:

- Depreciation on the actual cost or the written down value basis only is fully allowable, without taking revaluations into consideration.

- Entertainment, travelling and advertising expenses are allowable subject to limits specified in the Income Tax Act.

- Contingent liabilities, though not provided as an expense, can be claimed as accrued expenditure for tax purposes on the basis of certain decisions of the Supreme Court of India.

- Statutory liabilities are allowable only on cash basis.

- Capital expenditure on scientific research, excluding land is fully allowable.

- Certain exemptions/deductions are also available in case of "eligible business" and for earnings in foreign exchange.

Since 1st April 1993, companies have been required to pay:

- wealth-tax at a flat rate of 1% where the net value of certain assets as on 31st March exceeds the prescribed limit; and

- capital gains tax at a flat rate of 40% on the income arising from transfer of long-term capital assets.

Unusual and Prior Period Items

The law requires the profit and loss account to disclose every material feature of non-recurring exceptional transactions. The ICAI has issued an accounting standard on prior period and unusual items which is mandatory.

Unusual items must be disclosed separately, together with their nature and amount, in such a way that their relative significance and their effect on the current operating results of the period can be clearly identified.

Prior period items must also be disclosed separately, together with their nature and amount, in such a way that their impact on the current years profit or loss can be identified.

Retirement Benefits

Retirement benefits are accounted for on the accruals basis, with corresponding payments being made to the recognised provident fund and superannuation trusts. Gratuity liability is generally based on an actuarial valuation as at the year end.

The Act requires disclosures of such contributions to be made separately in the profit and loss account. Unprovided liabilities are shown by way of a note to the financial statements.

Price Level Changes

The law does not require either disclosure of or provision for inflation accounting. Very few companies append inflation adjusted accounting information to the financial statements. Such disclosure is purely for information purposes and is not subject to audit.

Indonesia

Drs S Reksoatmodjo & Co

Financial reporting in Indonesia started to develop in the early 1970s as the economy became more industrialised. The Indonesian Commercial Code requires anyone carrying on a business to keep sufficient records to enable the determination, at any time, of that person's rights and obligations. The Code does not describe the form in which financial statements are to be presented.

The Indonesian Accounting Association (Ikatan Akuntansi Indonesia, IAI) has approximately 4,500 members of which 40% are in some form of government service. The IAI is a member of the International Accounting Standards Committee. There is a shortage of accountants in the private commercial and professional fields.

The IAI updated the old Indonesian Accounting Principles (IAP) at the end of 1984. These principles cover basic concepts, limitations and principles of financial statements and principles relating to income and expenses, assets, liabilities, and capital. In February 1988 the IAI issued its statements on foreign currency translation and capitalisation of interest incurred during construction contracts.

The reporting practices in the IAP are similar to those required in the USA and the stock exchange supervisory board (BAPEPAM) closely follows FASB rules in its requirements. The stock exchange is exerting efforts to stimulate the capital market which will put more emphasis on reliable financial reporting.

Form and Content of Financial Statements

There are no legal requirements concerning the form and content of financial statements. The IAP provides that financial statements must include :

- Balance sheet
- Statement of income and retained earnings
- Statement of changes in financial position/cash flows
- Notes to the financial statements

161

Indonesia

The management of the company is responsible for the preparation of the financial statements.

The Director General of Taxes requires the submission of supplementary information and schedules supporting the balance sheet and income statement together with a short-form report.

Public Filing Requirements

There are no public filing requirements. The financial statements of companies are not available for inspection by the public.

Audit Requirements

There is no statutory audit requirement in Indonesia except for public companies, banks, insurance companies and non-bank financial institutions. However, it is becoming increasingly common for the tax authorities and other government departments to request audited financial statements. As a result, it is generally necessary for foreign investors in Indonesia to have their financial records audited.

Valuation Principles

Indonesian companies adopt the historical cost convention (that is, the assets and liabilities of the company are generally stated at original cost subject to depreciation or provisions). Income and expenses should be recorded under the accruals method.

IAP do not permit the revaluation of fixed assets, except pursuant to government regulations, and require that significant accounting policies adopted by a company should be disclosed in the notes to the financial statements.

Group Financial Statements

There are no legal requirements relating to group financial statements. IAP state that, where one company owns more than 50% of the voting shares in another, this is an indication that a consolidated report should be prepared. However in the following cases a consolidated report is not required :

● where control is temporary in nature; or

● if the condition of the subsidiary is such that a majority of votes does not necessarily give control (eg, when a subsidiary is being legally reorganized or is bankrupt); or

● if the subsidiary operates in a different field of activity, not related to that of the holding company.

Subsidiaries should prepare financial statements for a period ending on a date the same as, or close to, the accounting period of the holding company. A difference of up to three months is acceptable so long as appropriate disclosures are made.

Both the purchase method and the pooling of interest methods of accounting for business combinations are acceptable.

Depreciation

Depreciation of fixed assets should be based on an adequate estimation of their useful lives. Fixed assets are to be stated at cost less accumulated depreciation. Accumulated depreciation can be disclosed in total as a deduction from fixed assets or as deductions from each category of fixed assets.

The method of depreciation used should be disclosed in the notes to the financial statements. Depreciation can be calculated using a variety of methods but the most commonly used are the straight-line method and the reducing balance method.

Leasing

The principle adopted is similar to that followed in the USA.

Research and Development

There are no requirements regarding the method of accounting for research and development expenditure. Generally pre-operating expenditure and research and development expenditure are capitalised and then amortised from the start of commercial production.

Inventories

Inventories cover :

- Trading/finished goods
- Work in progress
- Raw and auxiliary materials

Inventories are stated at the lower of cost or net realisable value. Cost includes all direct and indirect costs incurred in bringing the inventories to their current location and condition. Cost of inventory can be determined by using LIFO, FIFO or average cost method.

For long-term construction contracts, the construction work in progress at the end of an accounting period can be stated at cost plus an element of recognised profit, estimated using the percentage-of-completion method.

Capital and Reserves

A company's capital generally consists of preference shares, ordinary shares, capital in excess of par (paid-in surplus) and retained earnings. The authorised capital is stated in the articles of association of the company.

Indonesia

Issued capital is recorded at its par value. If the sum received on the issue of the shares is more than the par value of the shares issued, the excess is recorded as paid-in surplus.

Revaluation reserves only arise as a result of mandatory fixed asset revaluations pursuant to legislation and are presented in the balance sheet between paid-up capital and retained earnings.

Retained earnings represent the undistributed accumulated profits of the company. The balance is regarded as free from any distribution limitation, other than voluntary restrictions.

Under Article 47 of the Indonesian Commercial Code, when accumulated losses are equal to 50% or more of authorised capital, the directors are required to announce the fact in a court register and the official gazette. If the losses are equal to 75% or more of authorised capital, the company is dissolved by operation of law. However, in practice this does not often happen and many companies continue to trade with accumulated losses in excess of 75% of capital. Directors should be aware, nonetheless, that they become jointly and severally liable for the company's obligations when this point is reached.

Foreign Currency Translation

Foreign currency transactions are converted at the exchange rates ruling at the time the transactions occurred. Foreign currency assets and liabilities are converted into Indonesian rupiah at the exchange rates prevailing at the balance sheet date.

Conversion differences arising from the above and exchange rate gains (losses) arising from foreign currency transactions are to be credited (debited) in the current income statement.

Exchange gains or losses arising from devaluations or revaluations of the Indonesian rupiah may either be charged or credited in the year they occur or amortised. The treatment followed must be clearly stated in the notes to the financial statements.

Taxation

Corporate tax can be calculated based on the accounting profit or taxable profits multiplied by the rates determined by the tax authorities.

If the corporate tax calculation is based on the accounting profit, timing differences are recorded in a deferred tax account and allocated to the corporate tax charge in future years.

Unusual and Prior Period Items

Extraordinary items are those which are abnormal in nature and rare in occurrence. They are separately presented in the income statement and the nature of the transaction is disclosed.

Prior period adjustments are generally only made to correct material errors in prior period statements. Prior period adjustments are made by restating prior year figures and the opening balance on retained earnings.

The cumulative effect of a change from one acceptable accounting principle to another acceptable accounting principle is reported in the income statement for the period to which the change relates.

Retirement Benefits

There are no special accounting requirements regarding retirement benefits.

Commitments and Contingencies

A provision for contingent losses may be created if there is a strong indication at the balance sheet date that a liability will arise and there is a reasonable basis to determine its value.

If these two conditions are not met the item should be disclosed in the notes to the financial statements.

Related Party Transactions

The stock exchange supervisory board requires related party transactions to be disclosed in the notes to the financial statements.

Price Level Changes

There is no requirement to provide for the effects of inflation in financial statements.

Ireland

Oliver Freaney & Company

The Irish accountancy profession has developed in line with changes in the economy, in particular, the development of industry in a country whose economy was almost totally dependent on agriculture. The mainstay of the economy is still agriculture and its related industries. There has, however, been a large investment by overseas companies particularly in the electronics industry. The ethics and professional requirements of the accountancy bodies in Ireland ensure that auditing standards are of the highest quality.

The content and other requirements in relation to financial statements are contained in law and professional pronouncements. In the past such laws and pronouncements closely followed those of the United Kingdom. Nowadays, however, most legislation is as a result of EC directives.

The function of financial statements is to present to the shareholders an historical record of the performance and state of affairs of the company and the use it makes of available resources. Financial statements are prepared on a normal commercial basis and accountancy treatment of items is therefore not dictated by taxation requirements or regulations, as is the case in some countries.

Form and Content of Financial Statements

The form and content of a company's financial statements are prescribed by law embodied in the Companies Acts 1963 to 1990 and The European Communities (Companies:Group Accounts) Regulations 1992. In addition generally accepted accounting principles are established by the accountancy profession and are laid down in "Statements of Standard Accounting Practice" (SSAP) and other guidance notes. SSAP's are now gradually being replaced by "Financial Reporting Standards" (FRS). Neither the SSAP's or FRS's are mandatory in law, although many of the principles and practices in these statements are now embodied into the Companies Acts. The overriding requirement is that the financial statements show a true and fair view of the financial position of a company and this may in exceptional circumstances require a departure from legal and professional requirements.

Ireland

The directors of a company are responsible for the preparation of the financial statements which should contain:

- Directors report
- Income statement
- Balance sheet
- Cash flow statement
- Notes to the accounts
- Statement of accounting policies
- Auditors' report

The inclusion of a cash flow statement is a professional not a legal requirement.

The consolidated financial statements of a group contain all of the above, on a group basis, as well as the balance sheet and the related notes of the parent company. An income statement for the parent company is not required if certain requirements are complied with.

Some private companies may avail themselves of the exemptions, set out in the Companies (Amendment) Act 1986, relating to disclosures in the financial statements which are to be filed publicly.

The annual reports of most public companies contain additional information such as a chairman's statement, segmental information, historical summaries and value added statements.

The form and content of the financial statements of other bodies is usually governed by an Act or other document which governs that body.

Public Filing Requirements

Both public and private companies are required to annex financial statements to their annual return which is filed with the Registrar of Companies and is then available for public inspection.

Private companies may file abridged financial statements with the Registrar. The exemptions available are determined by the size of the company:

	Turnover Less than	Balance Sheet Total Less than	Number of Employees Less than
Small	IR£2.5m	IR£1.25m	50
Medium	IR£10m	IR£5m	250

To take advantage of the exemptions for small or medium sized companies a company must satisfy two of the above three criteria.

The annual return must be filed with the Registrar within 60 days of the annual general meeting which must be held within 9 months of the accounting year end. It is the directors' responsibility to ensure that the annual return and accounts are filed. Failure to do so can lead to fines and imprisonment.

Recent legislation requires that certain parent companies file group accounts with their annual return. These accounts should incorporate the results of all subsidiary undertakings which may include unincorporated bodies and other companies which are managed on a unified basis.

The accounts being filed must be prepared in either English or Irish. There are no legal requirements as regards currency.

Accounting periods may be of varying lengths although twelve months is normal. The legal requirement is that the directors present audited financial statements to the members of the company at an annual general meeting at least once in every calendar year with the proviso that no longer than 15 months may elapse between annual general meetings.

Audit Requirements

All companies incorporated under the Companies Acts are required to have their financial statements audited. Other bodies may be required to be audited under their constitution or other such document or legislation governing their operations.

The auditor must be an auditor recognised by the Minister for Industry and Commerce or registered with a recognised body of accountants, which are:

- The Institute of Chartered Accountants in Ireland
- The Institute of Chartered Accountants in England and Wales
- The Institute of Chartered Accountants in Scotland
- Chartered Association of Certified Accountants

The auditor may not be:

- an officer or servant of the company;
- a parent, spouse, brother, sister or child of an officer of the company;
- a partner of or in the employment of an officer of the company;
- a person disqualified for appointment as public auditor; or
- a body corporate

The auditors' report must state whether:

- they have obtained all the information and explanations which are necessary for the purposes of their audit;

- in their opinion, proper books of account have been kept by the company;

- in their opinion, proper returns adequate for their audit have been received from branches of the company not visited by them;

- the company's balance sheet and profit and loss account are in agreement with the books of account;

- in their opinion, the financial statements have been properly prepared in accordance with the Companies Acts;

- in their opinion, the financial statements give a true and fair view of the state of affairs of the company at the balance sheet date and of the profit and loss account for the year then ended;

- in their opinion, a financial situation exists that could require the convening of an extraordinary general meeting of the company, where the net assets have fallen to less than half the called up share capital; and

- the information in the directors' report is consistent with the financial statements.

The accountancy bodies require the auditor to:

- refer to any significant departures from SSAPs or FRSs unless he agrees with the departure;
- to give an opinion on the truth and fairness of the cash flow statement; and
- to state that the audit has been conducted in accordance with approved auditing standards.

Valuation Principles

Irish companies adopt the historical cost convention in that assets and liabilities are stated at original cost subject to depreciation or provisions. In some cases fixed assets, in particular land and buildings may be revalued on an existing use basis to current market value. By law, any surplus arising must be transferred to an undistributable reserve and any deficits, to the extent that they exceed previous surpluses, should be written off to the profit and loss account.

Accounting standards require companies which hold properties for investment purposes to revalue those properties to market value each year.

Group Financial Statements

The EC 7th Directive on group accounts has been incorporated into Irish legislation and is applicable to accounting periods beginning on or after 1st September 1992.

Parent companies which are limited by shares or guarantee are required to prepare and file with the Registrar of Companies group accounts which should incorporate the accounts of all subsidiary undertakings.

A subsidiary undertaking is a body corporate, partnership or unincorporated body of persons in which the parent company holds a majority of the voting shares or has the right to exercise dominant influence or has a participating interest or the subsidiary is managed on a unified basis.

A private parent company is exempt if the consolidated accounts meet two of the following criteria:

● Balance sheet total less than IR£6m
● Turnover less than IR£12m
● Average number of employees less than 250

There are very few circumstances in which a subsidiary may be excluded and FRS2 has further restricted the scope for exclusion.

The format of the group financial statements is basically the same as that of an individual company with notes being required for the group balance sheet as well as the parent company balance sheet.

The majority of group financial statements will be prepared under the acquisition method of consolidation. Merger accounting is now permitted where at least 90% of the nominal value of shares in the new subsidiary are acquired by the issue of shares in the parent or its existing subsidiaries, and the fair value of other consideration given did not exceed 10% of the nominal value of shares issued.

In the financial statements of the parent the investment in subsidiaries is usually stated at cost less a provision for any permanent diminution in the value of the investment.

The auditors' report will refer to all the matters noted above on a group basis with the exception of the financial situation which only refers to the parent company. The opinion will also refer to the truth and fairness of the state of affairs of the parent company as presented in its balance sheet.

Depreciation

Depreciation must be charged on all fixed assets, with the exception of investment properties. Depreciation is calculated to write off the assets over their useful lives.

Disclosure is required in the accounts of the amount charged to the profit and loss account, the accumulated depreciation, the method of depreciation and the useful lives or rates used.

Leasing

There are no legal requirements regarding accounting for leases with the exception of the disclosure of the financial commitment. SSAP21 sets out the rules for accounting for leases and distinguishes between operating and finance leases.

Ireland

Finance leases are those which transfer substantially all the risks and rewards of ownership to the lessee and should be accounted for as the acquisition of an asset and the assumption of the related liability.

Lessors should account for the amount receivable as a debtor and the repayments received should be split between the interest element and capital repayments.

Operating leases are accounted for as a normal hire of assets, rentals being charged to the profit and loss account on a systematic basis over the period of hire.

Detailed disclosures required by SSAP 21 include the net book value of assets acquired under finance leases and separate disclosure of lease liabilities.

Research and Development

Expenditure incurred on research must be written off to the profit and loss account as it is incurred. Development expenditure may be capitalised if there is a clearly defined project which is technically and commercially viable. The costs must be separately identifiable and the project must be expected to generate sufficient revenue to cover the costs.

Disclosure is required of amounts expended on research and development and any amounts committed in respect of subsequent years except where the directors feel it would be prejudicial to the interests of the company, in which case the fact that the information is not given must be stated.

Inventories

Inventories are described as stocks and work in progress. Stocks comprise raw materials, finished goods, and goods for resale and are valued at the lower of cost and net realisable value with full provision being made for obsolete and damaged items. Cost comprises the invoice value of the goods plus any costs incurred in bringing them to their present location and condition. Net realisable value is the expected sales price less any further costs to be incurred. Stock is usually valued on a first in first out basis.

Work in progress, including long term contract work in progress, is valued at its cost of production which includes materials and overhead expenses. Contract work in progress should be valued on a contract by contract basis. Revenue is recognised when invoiced as is the proportion of profit applicable to the particular stage of completion. Losses on contracts should be fully provided for as soon as they become apparent.

Disclosure is required of the various categories of stock i.e. raw materials, finished goods and goods for resale. If the replacement cost of stock differs significantly from the amount shown in the accounts it should be disclosed.

For long term contracts the amount by which recorded revenues exceed payments received should be shown within debtors as "amounts recoverable on contracts". Any costs incurred after deducting amounts transferred to the profit and loss account and after deducting foreseeable losses is disclosed under inventories as long term contract balances.

Intangible Assets

Only intangible assets acquired for valuable consideration may be capitalised. Intangible assets include development costs (dealt with above) goodwill, patents, trademarks and licences. Intangible assets cannot be revalued.

SSAP 22 prefers the immediate write off of goodwill, although it and company law does permit goodwill to be written off over its economic life. The financial statements must disclose the period chosen for writing off goodwill, the reasons for choosing that period and the amount of goodwill acquired, disclosing the amount for each acquisition separately.

Patents, licences and trademarks etc may also be capitalised if they were created by the company itself. While there is no requirement to depreciate these assets it is general practice to write them off over their economic life.

Capital and Reserves

The total of capital and reserves is referred to as shareholders funds and commonly comprises share capital, share premium, accumulated profit and loss and other capital reserves.

Disclosure is required of the authorised and issued amounts and numbers for each class of share capital. Details are also required of the number of shares held by the directors and secretary.

A share premium arises where the amount paid for a share is in excess of its nominal value. This is credited to a share premium account which may only be used to make a bonus issue of shares, for a capital redemption reserve fund or for the payment of a premium on redemption. The costs incurred on a share issue may be debited to this account.

Other capital reserves would be revaluation reserves or capital redemption reserve funds.

The share capital or debentures of a company may be repaid but a capital redemption reserve fund must be set up equal to the nominal value of the shares redeemed. This reserve may only be used to issue paid up bonus shares.

A company may only make a distribution from its revenue reserves if there are sufficient reserves to do so. A company's profits available for distribution are its accumulated realised profits, so far as not previously utilised by distribution or capitalisation less its accumulated realised losses, so far as not previously written off in a reduction or reorganisation of capital.

Foreign Currency Translation

Transactions of a company denominated in foreign currency are translated into Irish punts at the rate of exchange ruling on the date of the transaction. Exchange gains or losses arising due to differing exchange rates on the transaction date and payment date are dealt with through the profit and loss account.

Where a company has a foreign subsidiary or branch the closing rate method is normally used for the purposes of consolidation. The balance sheet of a foreign subsidiary is translated at the rate of exchange ruling at the balance sheet date, whilst the profit and loss account is translated at either the closing rate or an average rate for the year. Exchange differences arising on the retranslation of opening net assets are dealt with through reserves.

Taxation

Corporation tax is paid by companies. The charge for corporation tax is calculated based on the profit per the accounts with certain expenses being added back as they are not allowable under the Tax Acts. Disclosure is required of the amount and rate of corporation tax charged with any foreign taxes being shown separately.

SSAP 15 requires a provision for deferred tax to be made. Such a provision results from timing differences mainly due to the cost of fixed assets being claimed for tax purposes whilst charging depreciation, which is disallowed for tax purposes in the financial statements.

Unusual and Prior Period Items

Unusual items may be classed as exceptional or extraordinary.

Exceptional items are those arising in the normal course of business but are exceptional because of their size. These are included in the profit on ordinary activities and are described in the notes to the accounts.

Extraordinary items are those material items possessing a high degree of abnormality arising outside of the normal course of business and which are not expected to recur. They are shown separately on the face of the profit and loss account net of any related taxation before deducting any appropriations such as dividends. Following the implementation of FRS 3 it is expected that it will be very rare to find extraordinary items in a set of financial statements.

Retirement Benefits

Disclosure is required of:

- pension commitments provided for and not provided for in the financial statements;

- the nature of every pension scheme; whether it is a defined benefit or defined contribution scheme;

- whether it is internally financed or externally funded;

- whether pension costs are assessed in accordance with the advice of a professionally qualified actuary; and

- the date of the most recent actuarial valuation.

Related Party Transactions

For the purposes of consolidation all transactions with other undertakings within the group should be eliminated.

The Companies Act 1990 prohibits loans and certain transactions to directors of the company or to persons connected with a director, which includes a body corporate controlled by that director where such transactions exceed 10% of the net assets of the company. Where, however, such loans are made, disclosure is required of the name of the director, the balance at the year end and the maximum amount of the balance during the year. Some transactions are permitted if they are approved by the members of the company. The Act does not prohibit transactions between group companies or transactions made on the same terms as those offered to other customers in the normal course of business.

Segmental Reporting

An analysis of turnover on a geographical and activity basis is required for large companies but need not be given if the directors believe it would be prejudicial to the interests of the company.

Additional disclosures are required by SSAP 25, both geographically and by class of business, of profits, taxation, minority interests, extraordinary items, external and intra-segment turnover and net assets. These additional disclosures are only required for public companies and very large private companies. Again, where the directors are of the opinion that the disclosures would be prejudicial to the interests of the company, they need not be made.

Ireland

Treatment of Grants

Revenue grants are credited to the profit and loss account in the period in which the related expenditure is charged.

Capital grants are deferred and are amortised at the same rate as the related assets are depreciated.

Commitments and Contingencies

Disclosure is required of material contingent losses not accrued except where the likelihood of them crystallising is remote. Contingent gains should not be disclosed unless realisation of the gain is probable. Disclosures should give the nature of the contingency, the uncertainties expected to affect the outcome, a prudent estimate of the pre-tax financial effect, the tax implications, the legal nature of a contingent loss and whether any security has been given.

Material commitments must also be disclosed distinguishing between those contracted for and those not yet contracted for.

Balances not Reflected in the Balance Sheet

At present there are no legal or professional requirements in respect of balances not reflected on the balance sheet, a draft FRS is, however, in issue.

Price Level Changes

There are no longer any requirements in respect of accounting for price level changes.

Future Developments

The professional bodies are constantly reviewing professional standards and issuing proposed standards in draft form for discussion. The main development in progress at present is a revision of all SSAP's.

Italy

Consulaudit Sas – Arietti & Co

Since 1975 there have been considerable changes in the regime which governs the preparation of and reporting on financial statements in Italy. The Presidential Decree of March 1975, enacted in 1980 laid down audit and reporting requirements for listed companies and the law of April 1991 (the 1991 Law) introduced the requirements of the 4th and 7th European Community Company Law Directives into Italian law. This law becomes effective for accounting periods ending on 31 December 1993 for 4th Directive requirements and 31 December 1994 for 7th Directive requirements.

Until these laws become effective however, many companies will still follow the Civil Code. This outlines a highly formalised system of accounting based on the Napoleonic Code, which has been adapted to conform with the tax laws. The Civil Code makes little reference to consistency in the preparation of financial statements. However, according to the principles of the Dottori Commercialisti, all significant changes in accounting policies must be mentioned in the audit report and the net effect disclosed.

The implementation of the 4th Directive will have a significant impact on the format of the income statement and balance sheet and will enhance the level of disclosures made.

Form and Content of Financial Statements

The basic source for principles governing the contents and manner of preparation of financial statements has been the Civil Code. However, fiscal legislation requires that tax returns must be based on the accounting records and, consequently, financial statements have been somewhat affected by this consideration.

By law the directors of all limited companies must submit to their members at the annual general meeting the statutory financial statements containing:

- Balance sheet (Stato Patrimoniale)

- Income statement (Conto dei profitti e delle perdite)

Italy

- Directors' report (Relazione del Consiglio di Amministrazione) giving a clear and precise view of the financial position of the company.

Financial statements should also include details of the company's accounting policies. Where there are any changes this must be disclosed together with justification for the change and its effect on the current year's results.

The current approach to the preparation of the balance sheet is very mechanistic adopting a two sided balance sheet with assets on the left hand side. Provisions such as depreciation, amortisation, stock obsolescence, and bad debts, are shown as liabilities, as the setting-off against assets is not permitted. Furthermore, at the foot of the balance sheet, there must be a note of off-balance sheet items such as swaps, contingencies, and discounted bills.

The income statement should show items such as interest, dividends, profits or losses on sales of fixed assets and discounts, separately. The setting-off of income and expense items is not permitted and opening inventories are shown on the face of the income statement along with purchases of raw materials and finished goods, while closing inventories are included in the profit side of the statement as they reduce the charge to income.

The implementation of the 4th EC Directive at the end of 1993 will have a significant effect, and in particular:

- depreciation and other provisions will be deducted from the related assets;

- although a two sided balance sheet presentation will be retained, its structure will be quite different to current practices; and

- the traditional detailed two sided income statement will be replaced by a less detailed vertical format.

The directors' report should give any additional information considered necessary for a correct interpretation of the financial statements. Comparative figures are generally given for listed companies' financial statements.

The principles of Dottori Commercialisti require a statement of changes in financial position (Prospetto dei fabbisogni e delle coperture finanzianie) and a statement of retained earnings (Prospetto delle variazione del capitale netto) and so these are generally given for listed companies.

Public Filing Requirements

Under Italian law limited liability companies may be formed either as:

- Societa per Azioni (SpA) with a minimum capital of Lit 200 million; or
- a reponsibilita limitata (Srl) with a minimum capital of Lit 20 million.

Limited partnerships with shares, Societa in Accomandita per Azioni (SAPA), also exist, although these are less common.

For all such companies, the deed of incorporation, articles of association, copies of annual financial statements, and a list of directors are available for public inspection in the company files at the Register of Business Enterprises held by the local court.

Listed companies must also file their financial statements and the auditors' report with CONSOB.

In future small companies will be eligible to file financial statements whose balance sheet and notes have been abbreviated. To qualify as small, a company must not exceed two or more of the following criteria:

Turnover	4 Billion Lira
Balance sheet total	1.2 Billion Lira
Employees	50

Unlike certain other European countries there will be no exemptions for medium-sized companies.

Audit Requirements

Financial statements must be accompanied by a report of the directors and a report of the statutory auditors (sindaci). Furthermore, for all listed companies, state-controlled companies, and certain other companies the financial statements must be supported by a report of a registered auditing firm. Thus, a two tier system operates.

Any limited company with a share capital exceeding Lit 100 million is required to have a board of statutory auditors (collegio sindacale) who must report deviations from established accounting principles as well as monitor management to make sure that no illegal acts are carried out by them. The statutory auditors are appointed by the company's shareholders. A person may not act as a statutory auditor if he is a relative of a company director or bound to the company by a permanent relationship. He may, however, hold shares in the company.

Listed companies are required by CONSOB to publish unaudited half yearly reports.

No standard form of report has been developed for the sindaci. They do not perform an audit as the term is understood internationally. Only individuals may act as statutory auditors and in practice they are generally, though not exclusively, selected from members of the professional bodies which are:

● Dottori Commercialisti (doctor of commerce) having a university degree;

● Ragionieri (practising accountants) having a college degree; and

● Avvocati e Procuratori (lawyers).

Italy

The office of statutory auditor is a somewhat outdated institution and the office should not be confused with the role of a conventional auditor who examines financial statements and the underlying records in detail. This position will probably remain unchanged even after the 1991 Law becomes effective.

All companies quoted on the stock exchange are required to have their financial statements conventionally audited by firms approved by CONSOB. A list of such auditing firms is published regularly. This requirement also applies to a growing number of special categories of companies such as banks, insurance companies, shipyards, state-owned companies, newspapers, and others.

The report of the auditing firm must explain the procedures and tests carried out and "certify" that the balance sheet and the income statement agree with books and records prepared in accordance with the relevant legislation and reflect fairly the results of operations in conformity with correct accounting principles. Where the certification cannot be given or there are any reservations in any area, the reasons should be detailed in the audit report and the CONSOB committee informed.

The accounting principles referred to in the CONSOB audit report are those of the Consiglio Nazionale dei Dottori Commercialisti (CNDC). Where these might be lacking in detail, those of the International Accounting Standards Committee (IASC) are adapted to the extent that they do not conflict with current Italian legislation. The audit must be carried out in compliance with the auditing standard of the CNDC which includes standard auditing procedures similar to those generally accepted internationally.

Valuation Principles

The historical cost convention is required to be followed. However, a system of monetary revaluation to counter the effects of inflation was introduced under laws passed in 1975 and 1982, whereby certain categories of fixed assets or investments in subsidiaries could be revalued, at those dates, using specified indices. The resulting values can only be attributed to the asset if its current economic value is shown to exceed the revalued amount. The reserve arising from the revaluation should be shown separately in the balance sheet and can be used to increase the share capital or to cover losses.

Group Financial Statements

The Civil Code defines a controlled company as a company in which another company either directly or indirectly:

● holds a majority of the voting rights; or

● exerts a dominant influence, either because of the stock held or due to contractual ties.

An associated company is any company of which more than 20% (10% of investments in listed companies) of the capital stock is held. However, the Civil Code does not provide for the preparation of consolidated financial statements or for the adoption of the equity method of valuing shareholdings in controlled and associated companies.

In contrast, CONSOB may require listed companies to file consolidated financial statements whenever this is deemed relevant for public information purposes; however, this is not universal and such consolidated financial statements are not common.

For periods ending on or after 31 December 1994 the 1991 Law will be effective. It's main provisions are:

● all parents must prepare consolidated financial statements;

● the consolidation must include all subsidiaries, not just companies, irrespective of their legal form;

● the formats of the financial statements will be broadly the same as those currently being introduced for individual companies; and

● investments in associates will be valued, in group financial statements, on the equity basis.

Parent companies will be exempt from preparing group financial statements if:

● they are themselves a 95% subsidiary of an EC registered parent which prepares group financial statements in conformity with the 7th EC Directive; or

● the group does not exceed two of the following criteria:

Turnover	20 Billion Lira (Gross)
Balance sheet total	10 Billion Lira (Gross)
Employees	250

Any goodwill arising on consolidation will be capitalised and written off over a maximum of 5 years, unless there are special reasons for using a longer period. Negative goodwill should, depending upon the circumstances, be shown as a liability or a reserve.

Investments in associates and subsidiaries in the parent company's own balance sheet may, in future, be valued at either cost or on the equity basis. The tax effects of using the equity basis mean that the use of cost is likely to predominate.

Italy

Depreciation

The Civil Code provides that depreciation should be charged on all categories of assets on the basis of their estimated remaining useful lives. It should be noted that in practice most companies adopt the tax allowances as their depreciation policy.

Where accelerated depreciation charges are made which are in excess of those which are commercially necessary this should be disclosed in the directors' report. From the end of 1993 these charges will also be disclosed on the face of the profit and loss account.

Leasing

Italian law does not acknowledge the capitalisation of lease agreements and thus for statutory purposes all leases are treated as operating leases. It is a requirement, though, to disclose the total future lease obligations in excess of those already provided for in the balance sheet.

This position is unlikely to change in the near future.

Research and Development

The Civil Code does not deal specifically with research and development costs, but states that patents and trade marks must be stated at cost and amortised over their remaining life where definable or within a five-year period. Accounting practice tends to be derived from tax laws, which allow expenses of this nature to be either charged against income in the first year or deferred and amortised over a period of five years. Business start-up costs are often capitalised in this way, following the same principle of deferring costs which have a future benefit for the company.

Inventories

The Civil Code establishes the general rule that raw materials and finished goods should be stated at the lower of production cost, purchase price or net realisable value.

The fiscal legislation, however, is more detailed and may be summarised as follows:

● Work in progress existing at the year end is valued on the basis of average costs incurred in the tax period.

● Raw materials, consumables, and finished goods are valued at the lower of historical cost and the normal cost of the last quarter of the relevant tax period. Cost includes production overheads. The FIFO, LIFO and weighted average methods are allowed, although for tax reasons LIFO predominates.

Profit arising on long term contracts may be recognised as the contract progresses. Both the completed contract and the percentage of completion methods of valuing long term contracts are acceptable.

Intangible Assets

It is acceptable to capitalise intangible assets, such as formation expenses, which must normally be written off over a period not exceeding five years.

Brands may be capitalised if they have been purchased.

Capital and Reserves

In addition to the normal capital reserves, revenue reserves, revaluation reserves (including monetary revaluation reserves), there is a legal reserve to which an amount equivalent to at least 5% of the annual net profit is to be appropriated until the reserve is equivalent to 20% of share capital. This reserve is non-distributable but may be used to absorb losses.

In the event of a company accumulating losses of more than one-third of its capital, the directors must call a shareholders' meeting to consider its financial position and if the situation is not resolved by the end of the accounting period, the share capital should be reduced by the amount of the losses incurred, though not below the minimum levels prescribed by law (see Public Filing Requirements above).

Foreign Currency Translation

This subject is not specifically dealt with by the Civil Code. Monetary assets and liabilities are generally converted at the rate of exchange ruling at the transaction date or, if it gives a less favourable position, the rate ruling at the balance sheet date. Fiscal legislation requires that transactions in foreign currencies be translated into lira at the rates ruling at the transaction date. However, provision for any unrealised losses in the financial statements are allowed for tax purposes.

The financial statements of foreign subsidiaries are translated, generally using:

- the year end rate for balance sheet items; and
- the average rate for income statement items.

Translation differences arising are taken to reserves.

Taxation

A limited company is subject to:

- IRPEG – income tax on "legal persons"; and

- ILOR – local income tax that is deductible in calculating taxable income for IRPEG purposes.

As a rule, the taxable income of a company is based on the profit from operations as shown in the annual financial statements. However, various disallowed items must be added back to arrive at taxable profits. The major features are as follows:

- **Depreciation**: the Ministry of Finance has established maximum depreciation rates for various categories of fixed assets used in different business sectors. These rates generally correspond to the estimated useful lives and are applied to cost on a straight line basis. Depreciation charged using these official rules are allowable for tax purposes, but in the first three years of use of an asset, a company may choose to use accelerated depreciation for tax purposes which is calculated at a rate 50% higher than the official rate.

- **Repairs and maintenance**: expenses are deductible to a maximum of 5% of the aggregate book value of all tangible depreciable assets. Any excess must be capitalised and amortised over the next five years. Amortisation of patents, trademarks, and similar intangible assets is deductible in equal instalments over their useful lives.

- **Bad debts**: the provision for possible losses on doubtful accounts may be deducted annually up to a maximum of 0.5% of the total accounts receivable, until the provision is equivalent to 5% of the accounts receivable.

The Italian fiscal authorities may reassess tax liabilities for a particular year at any time up to 31 December of the fifth year subsequent to the year in which the declaration is filed.

The Civil Code requires limited companies to disclose income and other taxes separately in the profit and loss account, distinguishing prior years' taxes.

When an item of expense in the financial statements is disallowed by the fiscal authorities, due to the fact that it should be capitalised or deferred and subsequently amortised over a number of years, it is generally reinstated in the financial statements as a fixed asset or deferred charge, by crediting the Tax Reserve. This adjustment is made in the year when agreement is reached with the fiscal authorities and is amortised in subsequent years.

It is not usual to include provisions for deferred tax in the financial statements of individual companies although provisions are usually found in consolidated financial statements.

Unusual and Prior Period Items

Prior period adjustments are reflected in the current year results and it is best practice to disclose them separately.

There are currently no requirements relating to extraordinary items. With effect from 31 December 1993 extraordinary items, which are defined loosely in accordance with the EC 4th Directive, will be disclosed separately.

Retirement Benefits

There is a national social security fund to which all employers and employees contribute. There is therefore no need for any provisions or special disclosures to be made in the financial statements.

However, all companies are required to set up a "severance of employment" fund (fondo trattemento fine raporto) for employees. This involves making an annual provision, for each employee, of approximately one month's salary, plus an extra provision based on indexation of the fund's opening balance. On retiring or leaving work, employees are entitled to a lump sum payment out of the reserve. In certain circumstances, they can draw on their entitlements before the end of their employment.

Segmental Reporting

There are currently no segmental reporting requirements although, again, after December 1993 disclosure of segmental results by sector and market will be required.

Treatment of Grants

Grants received are normally taken to reserves and not taken to the profit and loss account.

Commitments and Contingencies

It is present practice to show contingent losses not provided for as a note, on the face of the balance sheet. It is not usual to disclose contingent gains.

Related Party Transactions

There are no particular requirements to make separate disclosures.

Price Level Changes

Although the purchasing power of the lira in recent years has declined, there is no requirement for businesses to recognise these effects in their financial statements. As described previously under valuation principles, legislation has in the past provided a means of periodically revaluing assets.

Future Developments

As explained previously the implementation of the 1991 Law, in stages, at the end of 1993 and 1994 will have a dramatic effect on the format of and disclosures given in company and group financial statements. Some of the key changes have been highlighted in earlier parts of this chapter. Their net result will be to bring reporting practices more into line with those now to be found widely throughout the European Community.

Japan

Actus Audit Corporation

The "Kabushiki Kaisha" or joint stock corporation is the most common type of corporation in Japan. For historical and regulatory reasons, there are two relevant laws relating to accounting and disclosure requirements: the Commercial Code (CC), promulgated in 1899 by the Ministry of Justice, and the Securities and Exchange Law (SEL), promulgated in 1948 by the Ministry of Finance.

The emphasis of accounting and disclosure under the CC has been towards the needs of creditors as much as shareholders and, as a consequence, great importance is placed on rules for valuing assets in a conservative manner, rather than measurement of earnings. The SEL applies to public corporations, which offer their own shares or bonds to the public in Japan either through a public offering or through a listing on a stock exchange. Disclosure requirements under the SEL are more detailed than those required under the CC in order to protect investors. A corporation regulated by the SEL, therefore, has to prepare two different sets of financial statements although the net income and shareholders' equity will be identical under both sets of regulations.

Since 1949, the Business Accounting Deliberation Council (BADC), an advisory body of the Minister of Finance, has issued Financial Accounting Standards for Business Enterprises and other pronouncements which are regarded as generally accepted accounting principles in Japan. In addition, the Japanese Institute of Certified Public Accountants (JICPA) has published many statements which provide guidelines for the interpretation and application of various accounting principles and the requirements of the CC and SEL.

Japanese tax laws and regulations have a strong impact on accounting practices, because certain accounting practices have to be followed in order to obtain tax benefits. The tax laws now allow more flexible treatments, or have been amended to comply more appropriately with commercial accounting principles and practices. However, they still have a significant influence on accounting practices in general.

The JICPA is a member of the International Accounting Standards Committee (IASC) and the International Federation of Accountants (IFAC) and has contributed to establish international accounting and auditing standards. The current accounting principles and practices generally accepted among Japanese companies are, with certain exceptions, similar to those prescribed in International Accounting Standards. Some larger corporations, whose shares are traded on foreign stock exchanges, disclose financial information in accordance with accounting principles generally accepted in the USA.

Form and Content of Financial Statements

Under the CC, all joint stock corporations must prepare statutory financial statements consisting of a business report, balance sheet, income statement, proposal for appropriation of retained earnings (or disposition of losses) and supplementary schedules. However, smaller corporations are permitted to omit certain information. Accounting periods may not be in excess of 12 months and the statutory financial statements must be submitted to the annual general meeting of shareholders within three months of the end of its financial year. Many Japanese companies have financial years ending on 31 March, which is also the end of the government fiscal year.

The form and content of financial statements required under the CC are dictated by the "Regulations Concerning the Balance Sheet, Income Statement, Business Report and Supplementary Schedules of Joint Stock Corporations". These regulations describe the form of presentation, classification of accounts, accounting policies and footnote requirements as well as the matters to be covered in the business report. Comparative figures are not generally shown in the statements and consolidated statements are not required.

Corporations under the SEL are required to prepare an annual financial report (Yuka-Shoken Hokokusho) which must be submitted to the Minister of Finance within three months of the end of the fiscal year. The annual report includes the audited financial statements consisting of:

- Balance sheet

- Income statement

- Statement of retained earnings and supplementary schedules

- Notes about accounting policies and other related matters

These are prepared in accordance with the "Regulations Concerning the Terminology, Forms and Preparation Methods of Financial Statements". The statements prepared under SEL rules disclose much more financial information, including comparative figures, than those prepared under the CC rules.

In addition, a half yearly report (Hanki Hokokusho) which includes the balance sheet and income statement, together with appropriate footnotes, is required to be submitted to the Minister of Finance within three months of the end of the half year. Separate regulations set out the content of these reports which are less detailed than the annual reports.

If a corporation, reporting under SEL, has significant subsidiaries and affiliated companies, in Japan or overseas, consolidated financial statements may be required. Consolidation accounting practices prevailing in Japan are similar to international practices in general but reporting regulations are also set by the Minister of Finance. Annual consolidated statements include comparative figures and are published within three months of the end of the year.

Public Filing Requirements

Under the CC, and the related regulations, a joint stock corporation falls into one of three categories dependening on its size. Auditing and reporting requirements are dependent on these classifications:

- Large corporation – Capital stock of not less than 500 million yen or total liabilities of not less than 20,000 million yen.

- Medium sized corporation – Capital stock of more than 100 million yen but less than 500 million yen and total liabilities of less than 20,000 million yen.

- Small corporation – Capital stock of 100 million yen or less and total liabilities of less than 20,000 million yen.

The audited statements are approved by the Board of Directors and are simply reported to the shareholders, although the appropriation of retained earnings has to be approved by the shareholders.

The financial statements together with auditor's report must be maintained at the corporation's principal office for five years and copies made available for inspection by shareholders and creditors at major branch offices for three years. A condensed balance sheet and income statement for large corporations and balance sheet only for medium sized and small corporations, must be published in newspapers or official gazettes immediately after their approval by the shareholders.

The annual financial report, including the audited financial statements, is required to be filed with the Minister of Finance within three months of the fiscal year end. At the same time, copies of the reports of listed corporations are also submitted to the stock exchange, or, to the governing securities association if a corporation's shares are traded on the over-the-counter market. These reports are then available for public inspection. The half yearly reports are filed with the same bodies as the annual reports.

Japan

Audit Requirements

There are varying audit requirements which are dependent upon a corporation's size and status.

- **General Rules** - Under the CC, all limited companies must have at least one statutory auditor (also referred to as the statutory examiner) who shall not be an employee or director of the company. There is no requirement that the statutory auditor should be professionally qualified as an accountant. The statutory auditor's responsibility is to review the business conduct of directors (except for small corporations) and to examine its books of account and statutory statements to ensure that they have been prepared according to the CC and the articles of the company. His function does not include the expression of an opinion on the truth and fairness of the financial statements.

- **Large Corporations** For large corporations, a CPA or Audit Corporation is elected as the independent auditor by the shareholders. The independent auditor shall examine the statutory statements and express his opinion on whether they give a true and fair view of company's financial condition and the results of its operations. The statutory auditor may rely, generally, on the audit procedures and opinion of the independent auditor, although it is possible to express a different opinion. The statements are finally approved by the shareholders.

- **Listed Corporations** Under the SEL, the financial statements of public corporations are required to be audited by a CPA or Audit Corporation. Their audit report is included in the annual financial report and it describes their opinion as to whether the financial statements fairly present on a consistent basis, the company's financial conditions and the results of its operations in accordance with generally accepted accounting standards and SEL reporting regulations. Audited consolidated financial statements are treated as supplementary information to the annual report. The half yearly report is also required to be filed.

- **Foreign Corporations** Foreign corporations listed on the Tokyo Stock Exchange are also required to submit their annual financial report, in Japanese, to the Minister of Finance and the Stock Exchange within six months after the end of the fiscal year. Reporting formats are fully regulated by the SEL and the financial statements together with an audit report issued by a Japanese CPA or Audit Corporation shall be included with the report.

Valuation Principles

- **Income and Expenses** – The accrual principle is applied to the recognition of income and expenses. Conservative methods are accepted for accounting for income from instalment sales or long term construction business. Small corporations are accustomed to apply cash accounting in practice.

- **Assets** – The historical cost convention is followed in Japan. Revaluation of assets is strictly prohibited, except for mergers and reorganisations, under the CC in order to protect creditors. If the market value of an asset is significantly less than its cost, the CC requires that the asset shall be reduced to market value. Inventories and marketable securities are normally valued at the lower of cost or market value.

- **Liabilities** – All liabilities outstanding at the balance sheet date shall be provided for in the accounts. Accruals for employee bonuses, after sales expenses, employee retirement benefits and other similar future expenses are provided for in accordance with Japanese income tax law and regulations. Some larger corporations, mainly listed companies, apply their own established methods to calculate such items, which may be more theoretically accurate and conservative. The excess of these provisions over the tax based amounts are disallowed for income tax purposes.

Banks, insurance companies and other public interest corporations are regulated by specific laws and accordingly, different accounting principles are applied.

Group Financial Statements

There is no requirement in the CC for corporations to prepare consolidated financial statements. However, the SEL requires public corporations to report consolidated statements as supplementary information to their annual report. Consolidation Accounting Principles were set by the BADC in 1975 and the disclosure of consolidated financial statements under the SEL commenced in 1978.

All subsidiaries in which the parent company owns more than 50% of the voting shares should be included in the consolidation, although they may be omitted where they account for less than 10% of total assets, total sales and total profit. A subsidiary must be excluded from the consolidation if:

- control is intended to be temporary; or

- the subsidiary is not considered to be a going concern; or

- its activities are so dissimilar that its inclusion would make the consolidation misleading; or

- severe restrictions over the operations of the subsidiary prevent effective control.

The equity method of accounting is used for investments in affiliated companies, in which the parent company owns between 20% and 50% of the voting shares and for non-consolidated subsidiaries. Any goodwill arising on consolidation is to be amortised within five years or written off immediately. Elimination of inter-company profits and account balances is normally made in accordance with the international consolidation practice. It is recommended that within a group there should be uniformity of accounting principles and accounting periods.

Japan

The SEL regulations set out the reporting formats to be used and additional information required, which includes details of significant consolidation accounting principles followed. Audits by a CPA or Audit Corporation are also required for consolidated financial statements. Multinational companies may have the audit of their overseas subsidiaries and affiliated companies carried out by other accountants. The auditors of the parent company would rely on the results of the work of these other auditors and, in such circumstances, appropriate references will be made in their report.

Depreciation

All fixed assets other than land must be depreciated and shown in the balance sheet at cost less accumulated depreciation.

The tax regulations specify a residual value of 10% of acquisition cost and lay down statutory useful lives for each class of asset. The reducing balance method is the most popular way of calculating the depreciation charge, although the straight line, sum of digits, and unit of production methods are all acceptable. Special or additional depreciation may be available under the tax laws which is shown as a charge against retained earnings. Few companies record depreciation in excess of the amounts deductible for tax purposes.

Disclosure must be made in a supplementary schedule to the financial statements of the aggregate depreciation for each category of fixed asset, including the charge and any other movements in the year. The major categories of fixed assets recognised are land, buildings, plant and machinery, furniture and fittings, vehicles and ships.

Leasing

There are no legal regulations on accounting for leases although there is a non-mandatory guideline produced by the JICPA setting out an acceptable practice, namely the capitalisation of finance leases and disclosure of future commitments.

Research and Development

Research and development expenditure on new products, new processes, and new knowledge may be carried forward to future accounting periods only if there is expected to be sufficient future revenue to cover these costs. Research and development expenditure incurred on existing products and operations should be written off in the year in which it is incurred.

The amount of research and development expenditure written off in the accounting period and the amount deferred should be disclosed in the financial statements.

Inventories

Inventories are normally stated either at cost or at the lower of cost and market value on a consistent basis. Companies may not use the cost basis where there has been a substantial and permanent reduction in the market value of the inventory.

Although cost should be the actual cost of purchase, approximations to actual cost derived from using either FIFO, LIFO, or a weighted average method may be used. Actual cost of production may include variable overheads and fixed overheads based on a normal level of capacity.

Inventories should be separated in the financial statements into the following categories:

- Supplies
- Raw materials
- Work in progress
- Semi-finished goods
- Finished goods

In the notes to the accounts, the company should specify which method has been used for valuation purposes for each of the above categories.

Intangible Assets

Patents, trade marks, know-how, goodwill, mining rights and other intangible assets are amortised under the straight line method. Useful lives, varying from five to twenty years, are set out in the tax law. Company formation costs, research and development costs, capital stock issue expenses and other deferred charges are also amortised under the straight line method. Useful lives are three to five years in general, but immediate write-off is also accepted. Details of additions, amortisation charges and balances on these accounts are shown in supplementary schedules.

Capital and Reserves

Capital accounts consist of the stated capital and additional paid in capital. When new stocks are issued, then as a minimum, their aggregate par values shall be recorded in the stated capital. When new stocks are issued at above par, up to half the subscription amount can be classified as additional paid in capital. The additional paid in capital is transferred to the stated capital in the event of stock splits or free share distributions (bonus issues).

A legal reserve must be set up as an appropriation of retained earnings. An amount equal to 10% of cash dividends must be transferred to the legal reserve until the reserve balance reaches 25% of the stated capital. Both the legal reserve and the additional paid in capital may be used in order to eliminate accumulated losses if an appropriate resolution is passed by the shareholders.

Japan

Director's bonuses are accounted for as an appropriation of retained earnings rather than as an operating expense, as they are not allowed for income tax purposes. Various tax reserves, such as reserves for special depreciation of assets, deferred capital gains and overseas investment losses, are provided as an appropriation of earnings in accordance with the tax law. Appropriations of retained earnings are subject to approval at the annual shareholders' meeting, although an interim dividend and the related transfer to the legal reserve is determined by the Board of Directors.

Foreign Currency Translation

Foreign currency transactions are recorded using the exchange rate ruling at the time of the transaction. At the year end, short-term monetary items are translated at rates ruling at the balance sheet date, although long-term assets and liabilities may remain at historical exchange rates. Differences arising from these transactions are recognised as exchange gains or losses in the current period.

When consolidating the financial statements of foreign subsidiaries the temporal method is recommended using historical rates for non-current monetary items and closing rates for current items and net income. Companies may choose to use historical rates for current monetary items. Exchange differences arising are recorded in the Foreign Currency Translation Adjustment Account which is shown in the balance sheet of the consolidated accounts and not in the profit and loss account.

Taxation

Japanese corporations pay national corporation tax, local inhabitant tax which is levied as percentage of the national corporation tax, and local enterprise tax. All these taxes are based on the corporation's profits. Taxable income is derived from the book income with some additions and deductions. Typical permanent differences are:

●   national corporation and inhabitant taxes;

●   entertainment expenses (an allowance of 3 or 4 million yen is available to smaller corporations);

●   donations, except for approved charity contributions;

●   director's bonus and excessive director's salary; and

●   80% of dividend income from affiliated companies is not taxable

Timing differences which may reverse over time are:

- inventory write-downs which are only allowable when the inventory is sold;

- provisions for bad debts in excess of tax limits;

- accelerated depreciation and amortisation in excess of tax limits;

- accrued expenses in excess of tax limits;

- accrued enterprise tax, which is only deductible when paid;

- finance costs for newly acquired land during its undeveloped period (up to 4 years); and

- tax reserves provided against retained earnings.

The national corporation and inhabitant taxes are shown as deductions from pre-tax income, although the enterprise tax is charged as an operating expense together with property tax, stamp duties and other sundry taxes. Consumption tax, equivalent to European VAT, is excluded from transactions and balances.

Because inter-period tax allocation accounting is not generally accepted in Japan, deferred tax on timing differences is not provided for in the accounts.

Unusual and Prior Period Items

A special gains and losses section is presented under the operating income section. Items to be reported in the section are not necessarily similar to extraordinary items reported under US, and other, accounting standards. Examples are:

- loss on the closure of specific businesses or factories;

- depreciation charged due to a shortened useful life of assets;

- reversal of accruals in excess of actual costs; and

- adjustments in respect of prior years.

Retirement Benefits

Most corporations have severance or retirement benefits schemes in addition to the national pension plan. Under these schemes, employees are entitled to lump sum payments on termination of their employment or pension annuities based on the length of their service, current salary and the reason for the termination.

Tax laws allow accruals to be made in the accounts up to a maximum of 40% of the aggregate benefits payable if all employees voluntarily terminated their employment at the balance sheet date. The tax practice is widely applied among smaller corporations, although some establish their own accounting methods based on actuarial assumptions.

Larger corporations fund their plans with the approval of the tax authorities and contributions to an approved plan are charged to income when paid. Accounting policies and related information about retirement and pension plans are disclosed in notes accompanying the financial statements.

Related Party Transactions

Under the CC the following information should be disclosed in the financial statements:

- amounts receivable from and payable to the parent or its subsidiaries;
- amounts receivable from and payable to directors and statutory auditors;
- investments in subsidiaries;
- sales to and purchases from the parent or subsidiary companies; and
- operating transactions with the parent or subsidiaries.

Further detailed information is required, under the CC, in supplementary schedules, relating to disclosure of transactions with other companies in which the company's directors are also directors. Annual salaries to directors and payments to statutory auditors are disclosed.

Under the SEL regulations related parties include the parent, subsidiaries and affiliated companies. Amounts receivable from and payable to related parties are classified separately in the balance sheet unless they amount to less than 1% of total assets in which case separate disclosure is not required.

Transactions with related parties, sales, purchases and non-operating income/expenses are also required to be shown separately in the income statement. There are exemptions from separate disclosure, where related transactions are less than 20% (10% for non-operating items) of the total. Detailed information is required to be given in supplementary schedules. In addition to the above, transactions with indirect related parties must be disclosed in the annual report.

Segmental Reporting

Following US disclosure practices introduced in 1985 the SEL implemented segmental reporting to be given in the supplementary notes to consolidated financial statements. Analyses by line of business and geographical analysis are required in respect of:

- sales to third parties and inter-group companies;
- cost of sales and operating expenses; and
- operating income.

A segmental analysis of assets will be required in the near future.

Treatment of Grants

Although accounting principles suggest that government grants should be credited to income, the CC requires such grants to be deducted from the acquisition cost of related assets. The amount of grants deducted is normally disclosed in the notes to the financial statements.

Commitments and Contingencies

Contingencies and commitments are required to be disclosed in the accompanying notes. They include guarantees of indebtedness, letters of credit, notes discounted at banks, purchase commitments and lease instalment payments.

Balances not Reflected in the Balance Sheet

As a result of recent developments in financial transactions, various off-balance sheet transactions are disclosed in the financial statements of listed companies. These include forward foreign exchange transactions, financial futures transactions and options and forward commodity transactions.

Price Level Changes

All financial statements must be prepared under the historical convention and there are no inflation accounting requirements.

Future Developments

There are no immediate significant changes expected in Japanese accounting and reporting systems, although some guidance notes are likely to be issued by the JICPA. However, Japan is under pressure to follow IASC pronouncements and the JICPA and the Ministry of Finance are considering how and when to implement these pronouncements. The following are major areas under consideration:

- Capitalisation of leased assets

- Capitalisation of research and development costs

- Capitalisation of interest costs during development

- Retrospective adjustments following changes in accounting policies

- Accounting for pension plans

- Extraordinary items

Jersey

Michael Forrest International

Although Jersey owes allegiance to the British Crown, it is self-governed. Jersey is part of the EC but has negotiated to retain its own internal government and tax structure. It is therefore excluded from EC requirements on harmonization policies but has free trade access. There are no exchange regulations regarding the transfer of funds.

The Island has its own laws, issued and updated by the States of Jersey in the form of Acts. Company law, the most recent being Company (Jersey) Law 1992, deals with the registration and conduct of companies whose liability is limited by shares. It is not possible to form unlimited liability companies in Jersey. There are very few companies with shares publicly traded in Jersey. Except for certain types of companies, there is no statutory requirement to have the company's accounts audited nor are accounts required to be filed with the public registry.

Jersey's Trust Law is incorporated in the Trusts (Jersey) Law of 1984. As long as there are no beneficiaries resident in the Island, Jersey taxation will not be levied on a trust formed in Jersey. No documents need to be registered or filed for public inspection although it may be necessary to submit the trust deed to the Comptroller of Income Tax in order to obtain Jersey tax clearance.

Jersey has its own professional accountancy body, the Jersey Society of Chartered and Certified Accountants (JSCCA) whose members are members of one of the professional bodies of accountants recognised in the United Kingdom and abroad.

Form and Content of Financial Statements

Jersey company law is limited in its requirements concerning the content of accounts and in general financial statements follow U.K. practice. Profits are shown on a normal commercial basis. There is no rigid form of accounts set down by company law nor is there a requirement in company law for a holding company to produce group accounts.

Jersey

In 1985, the JSCCA adopted a statement of accounting practice (SJAP) which drew on the disclosure requirements of International Accounting Standard No.5. The Islands of Jersey and Guernsey have issued a joint Statement of Channel Islands Accounting Practice, the objective of which is to ensure that the quality of financial reporting in the Islands is of the highest order.

Accounting practice generally accepted in the Island follows:

● SJAP for disclosure requirements.

● Statements of Standard Accounting Practice (SSAP) and Financial Reporting Standards (FRS) approved by the UK Accounting Bodies in respect of accounting principles.

Significant departures from the above standards must be disclosed in the accounts and the effects quantified.

The island's finance industry administers companies incorporated in many territories around the world. The overriding requirement for these companies is that, as well as complying with SJAP as far as possible, the financial statements should be prepared in accordance with Company law or other laws of those territories.

Public Filing Requirements

With certain exceptions, there is no statutory requirement for companies to file financial statements. The exceptions include public companies, companies listed under the Depositors and Investors (Prevention of Fraud) (General Provisions) (Jersey) Order 1986 and certain Unit Trusts. These accounts are filed with the Islands's Registrar of Companies.

New companies are required to file certain details with the Registrar of Companies and all companies are required to file with the Judicial Greffier (Registrar) in January of each year an annual return, available for public inspection, which contains details of:

● authorised share capital and issued share capital;
● shareholders and their shareholdings; and
● the registered office.

Audit Requirements

The standard table of articles of association of companies registered in the island of Jersey states that an audit report on the financial statements is required. This requirement may be waived by the members of a private company in general meeting, but is mandatory for a public company.

Companies holding a license under the Depositors and Investors (Prevention of Fraud) (General Provisions) (Jersey) Order 1986 (i.e., licensed banks) and "Classed

Funds" as defined by the Collective Investments Funds (Jersey) Law of 1988 are required by those laws to have their annual accounts audited.

For those companies requiring an audit report, the auditor must be independent and sufficiently qualified to carry out an audit. The auditor is appointed each year by the shareholders and reports to them whether in his opinion the financial statements show a true and fair view of the state of affairs of the company and the profit or loss for the period. By law, the auditors must also refer to any instances where:-

● proper accounting records have not been kept; or

● all the information and explanations required have not been received.

The auditor is required by the accountancy bodies to:

● refer to any significant departures from SSAPs and FRSs, unless they concur with the departure; and

● state whether the audit has been conducted in accordance with auditing standards.

Valuation Principles

Jersey companies adopt the historical cost convention. The assets and liabilities being generally stated at original cost subject to depreciation or provisions. Certain fixed assets, in particular real property and investments, may be revalued to market value. Any surplus or deficit arising is transferred to a separate non-distributable reserve.

Taxation

Jersey resident trading companies pay income tax based on trading profits reported in their financial statements for the accounting period ended in the calendar year prior to the year of assessment. The provision for tax based on the year's profits is shown in the balance sheet as future tax being payable more than 12 months from the year end. In the opening years, however, the tax charge is based on the accounts profit for the year of assessment and the change in basis to prior year may result in a double charge for tax being shown in the accounts of the first two years. In normal years, various adjustments are made to the profit before tax, shown in the financial statements, before arriving at taxable profit.

The adjustments are:

● depreciation charged by the company is not deductible. Instead, fixed rate capital allowances are substituted;

● general provisions and contingent liabilities are not deductible; and

● dividends paid are not deductible.

Jersey

Up to 31st December 1988, companies incorporated in, but not trading in, Jersey and in which no resident of Jersey had a beneficial interest could, by ensuring all meetings of directors were held outside Jersey, be deemed non-resident and pay corporation tax at a fixed rate of £500. From 1st January 1989 such companies could apply to be considered exempt companies which, although incorporated in Jersey, and considered resident for taxation in Jersey, paid no tax but paid a £500 exemption fee at the start of each calendar year.

Accounting Principles

As noted above, generally accepted accounting practice is determined for disclosure by IAS5 and for general principles by UK SSAPs/FRSs. For information on these practices the reader should refer to the UK chapter and the IAS chapter in this book.

Malaysia

Robert Teo, Kuan & Co

The Malaysian Companies Act (the Act) was first enacted in 1965. The Act adopted many features of the company laws then existing in the United Kingdom, Australia, New Zealand and India. Since then the Act has been extensively amended, particularly in 1985, 1986 and 1992.

The Malaysian Institute of Accountants (MIA) is the national accountancy body in Malaysia and was established in 1967 under an Act of Parliament, the Accountants Act, 1967. The functions of MIA are to:

- regulate the practice of the accountancy profession in Malaysia including the issue of accounting and auditing standards, guidelines and code of ethics;

- promote in any manner it thinks fit, the interests of the accountancy profession in Malaysia;

- provide for the training, education and examination by MIA, or any other body, of persons practising or intending to practice the accountancy profession; and

- to determine the qualification of persons for admission as members.

Under the Accountants Act 1967, any person who holds himself or herself out as an accountant must be a registered member of MIA. Admission to MIA is restricted to members of professional institutions and graduates of approved academic institutions who possess the prescribed years of approved work experience.

The other main accountancy body is the Malaysian Association of Certified Public Accountants (MACPA) which was formed in 1959. MACPA provides for qualification by examination combined with approved practical experience.

MIA and MACPA jointly approve and issue accounting standards derived from International Accounting Standards (IAS). On areas of accounting which are peculiar to Malaysia or not dealt with in IAS, Malaysian Accounting Standards (MAS) have been developed. There is no legal requirement to comply with accounting standards. However, MIA and MACPA may take disciplinary action against members for not observing the standards.

MIA has adopted to date IAS 1 to 28, except for IAS 16, 20, 22 and 24. MASs adopted to date by MIA are :

- MAS 1   Earnings Per Share
- MAS 2   Accounting for Acquisitions and Mergers
- MAS 3   Accounting for General Insurance Business
- MAS 4   Accounting for Life Insurance Business
- MAS 5   Accounting for Aquaculture

Form and Content of Financial Statements

The Act sets out various disclosure requirements relating to the form and content of accounts but does not promulgate any accounting standards. While compliance with IAS is not mandatory by law, non-compliance will generally result in a reference being made to this fact in the financial statements together with the justifications for the non-compliance. Where there is no disclosure of non-compliance with IAS this will usually result in a reference being made in the audit report.

The directors of a company are responsible for the preparation of financial statements, which are audited and presented to the shareholders, which give a true and fair view of the company's financial state of affairs and of its results and changes in financial position. Directors are required to maintain adequate accounting records of the company's transactions and in such a manner as to facilitate an audit. Under the Act, transactions must be recorded within 60 days of completion and the company must retain its records for at least seven years.

By law, the annual reports of a limited liability company must comprise:

- Directors' report
- Profit and loss account
- Balance sheet
- Statement of changes in financial position
- Notes to the financial statements including the accounting policies adopted by the company
- Statement by two directors that the financial statements show a true and fair view
- Statutory declaration by the director or the officer primarily responsible for the financial management of the company that the financial statements are correct
- Auditors' report

Holding companies must publish group accounts in the form of a consolidated balance sheet and profit and loss account dealing with the group as a whole. However, the Act provides for certain circumstances whereby a subsidiary company may be excluded from consolidation. Companies within a group are required by law to have co-terminous financial year ends.

Public companies listed on the Kuala Lumpur Stock Exchange are required to disclose, in addition to the requirements of the Act, the following information:

●   Segmental reports
●   Price earnings ratios
●   Analysis of equity structure
●   Particulars of major properties owned by the company

Financial statements of banks and finance companies and insurance companies are subject to modification by the Central Bank of Malaysia while the presentation of financial statements of co-operative societies are governed by the Co-operative Act 1948.

Public Filing Requirements

All limited companies, both public and private, must file an annual return with the Registrar of Companies within one month, or in the case of companies keeping a branch register at any place outside Malaysia, within two months, after the annual general meeting. Except for exempt private companies, all limited companies must also file with the annual return, audited financial statements together with directors' and auditors' reports. These are available for public inspection.

The annual return contains details of:

●   The registered office
●   The principal place of business
●   The principal nature of the business
●   The authorised, issued and paid up share capital
●   Mortgages and charges on the company's assets
●   Shareholders and their shareholdings
●   Directors, managers, secretaries and auditors

A distinction is made in law between:

●   a public limited company that has the word Berhad or Bhd as the last part of its name;

●   a private limited company (Sendirian Berhad or Sdn Bhd) whose constitution restricts the right to transfer its shares, limits the number of shareholders to 50 and prohibits any offer to the public to subscribe for its shares or debentures or to deposit money with the company; and

●   an exempt private company that is a private limited company with less than 20 shareholders, none of whom is a body corporate.

An exempt private company need not file audited financial statements together with its annual return. However, it must file, in place of the audited financial statements, a certificate relating to an exempt private company accompanied by an auditors' statement which states whether:

- the company has, in his opinion, kept proper accounting records and other books during the period covered by the financial statements;

- the financial statements have been audited in accordance with the Act;

- the auditors' report on the financial statements was made subject to any qualification or comment, and if so, particulars of the qualification or comment; and

- as of the date to which the income statement has been made up, the company appeared to have been able to meet its liabilities as and when they fall due.

Penalties are imposed for late submission of the annual returns and audited financial statements.

The accounts may be prepared in Bahasa Malaysia (the Malay language) or in English. However, the currency of presentation must be in the Malaysian currency, Ringgit Malaysia (RM).

Companies are required to present audited financial statements to shareholders annually. There is no specific date to which the financial statements must be drawn, but many companies choose 31 December to coincide with the tax year.

Usually the first accounting period may be more or less than twelve months and can end on any date during the year. However, the first accounts must be audited and ready for adoption at the first annual general meeting which must be held within eighteen months of the date of incorporation. In subsequent years, the financial statements must be presented to the annual general meeting of the company within six months of the date to which they are made up. The financial year end may be changed by resolution of the board of directors.

Audit Requirements

Under the Act, every company must appoint an approved auditor or a firm of approved auditors to report to the shareholders on the accounts of the company. An approved auditor must be a member of MIA and is additionally licensed by the Minister of Finance to perform a statutory audit under section 8 of the Act.

The directors may appoint the first auditors of the company, but the shareholders make subsequent appointments at the annual general meeting. An auditor holds office until the conclusion of the next annual general meeting.

The various ethical and other standards and rules of the accountancy bodies, the stringent audit licensing requirements as well as the fact that the auditor cannot be a director or an officer of the Company ensure that the auditor is independent and is sufficiently skilled to carry out an audit.

Auditing standards issued by MIA and MACPA prescribe the basic principles that their members are expected to follow when conducting an audit. These standards are modelled primarily on the International Auditing Guidelines issued by the International Federation of Accountants. Auditors are required by MIA and MACPA to:

- state in their report whether the audit has been conducted in accordance with approved auditing standards; and

- refer to any significant non-compliance with IAS and MAS if the fact on non-compliance is not disclosed in the financial statements.

The auditor must express an opinion on the following:

- whether the statutory accounts have been prepared in accordance with the provisions of the Act and whether they give a true and fair view of the state of affairs of the company, its results and its changes in financial position; and

- whether the company has kept proper books of accounts and other records and registers required under the Act.

In addition, the auditor is required to report to the Registrar of Companies all breaches or non-compliance with the provisions of the Act if the circumstances are such that in his opinion the matter has not been or will not be adequately dealt with by comment in his report or by bringing the matter to the notice of the directors.

Valuation Principles

The Act does not specify any applicable accounting convention. However, Malaysian companies commonly adopt the historical cost convention, that is, the assets and liabilities of a company are generally stated at original cost subject to depreciation or provisions.

The basis of valuation of the following assets have to be disclosed:

- **Real property and plant and machinery** – Freehold land and buildings are usually stated at cost less accumulated depreciation on the buildings. Leasehold land and buildings are usually stated at cost less amortisation in respect of the expired portion of the lease. Where real properties have appreciated in value, they may be revalued in the books to reflect the appreciation, and the surplus arising is reflected in non-distributable reserves. Plant and machinery is stated at cost less accumulated depreciation. The depreciation methods most commonly used are the straight line and reducing balance methods.

  The Capital Issues Committee prohibits public companies from incorporating revaluation of plant and machinery into their accounts.

Malaysia

- **Depletion of natural resources** – Amortisation of the cost of investments in natural resources is usually accounted for on a unit-of-production basis.

- **Quoted investments (marketable securities)** – Quoted investments held for the short term are included in current assets and stated at the lower of cost and net realisable value. Other quoted investments must be separately disclosed at cost and the market value shown. Provision is made for any permanent diminution in value.

- **Inventories** – Inventories are valued at the lower of historical cost and net realisable value. Cost includes an appropriate allocation of the overheads that relate to putting the inventories in their present location and condition. Cost is usually determined on the FIFO or the average cost method. The LIFO method is not acceptable by the tax authorities.

In accounting for results of the business of a company, the accrual method of accounting, prepared on a historical cost basis and in accordance with generally accepted accounting principles, is used. IAS No.18 deals with the bases for recognition of revenue arising from the ordinary activities of an enterprise.

Group Financial Statements

A Malaysian company with one or more subsidiary companies must prepare group or consolidated financial statements, unless the company is itself a wholly owned subsidiary company of another Malaysian company. For consolidation purposes, the subsidiary companies must draw up financial statements for the same period as those of the holding company, unless the Registrar of Companies has granted approval for the subsidiary company to have a different financial period.

A subsidiary may be excluded from consolidation if the directors are of the opinion that the following circumstances are applicable :

- consolidation would be impracticable or of no real value to the shareholders of the company because of the insignificant amount involved or because the accompanying expense or delay would greatly outweigh the value to shareholders of the company;

- the results would be misleading or would be harmful to the business of the company or any of its subsidiary companies; or

- the business of the parent and subsidiary companies cannot reasonably be treated as a single enterprise if their businesses are so diverse in nature.

Investments in subsidiary companies not consolidated are generally accounted for by using the equity method if the results are material. Otherwise, the investments are accounted for at cost. New subsidiaries are generally accounted for by the acquisition method.

Depreciation

Fixed assets with limited useful lives must be systematically depreciated to their estimated residual values over their expected useful lives. The depreciation method must reasonably allocate the cost to the periods in which the asset is expected to be used. No particular method is mandatory, but the straight line and reducing balance methods are the most common. If an asset has been revalued, depreciation should be based on the revalued amount rather than the cost. If the book value of an asset is not recoverable in full from future revenues it must be written down immediately to its recoverable amount.

The method of depreciation and the principal annual rates of depreciation have to be disclosed.

Leasing

Leases are classified as operating leases or financial leases. For an operating lease, the rental expense of the lessee is charged to income. A lease is presumed to be a financial lease if the present value of the minimum lease payments equals 90% or more of the fair market value of the leased assets at the beginning of the lease. A lessee must capitalise a financial lease and simultaneously recognise the obligation to make future payments.

Research and Development

Research and development costs may be deferred to future periods if they relate to a clearly defined and viable project and if recovery of these costs against future revenues from the project is reasonably assured. Any cost deferred in this manner is systematically amortised against the related future revenues or written off when the costs are recognised as non-recoverable.

Inventories

Trading inventory stock is valued at the lower of cost or net realisable value. In general, cost is determined using the FIFO method or the average cost method, unless specific identification is practical.

Intangible Assets

Presently, these is no approved guideline for the treatment of intangible assets, such as goodwill. IAS22, in respect of the treatment of goodwill, has not yet been adopted by MIA. Both MIA and MACPA are currently developing an MAS for goodwill and other intangible assets. However, it is common practice that only purchased goodwill is capitalised.

Malaysia

The more commonly used methods of accounting for goodwill are:

● Goodwill is treated as a non-current asset and amortised by systematic charges to profit over the estimated period of time during which the benefits are expected to arise.

● Goodwill is treated as a permanent item in the balance sheet. An annual review of the carrying value of goodwill is conducted and, where appropriate, its value is written down to the extent that it is no longer supported by probable future benefits.

Capital and Reserves

Capital

A company's issued share capital is stated in the balance sheet at the nominal value of the shares issued.

Share premium account

Any amount subscribed for shares, in excess of the par value, must be credited to reserves and separately disclosed as a share premium account.

The share premium account may be applied in:

● paying up unissued shares to be issued as fully paid up bonus shares;

● paying up in whole or in part the balance unpaid on shares previously issued;

● the payment of dividends if such dividends are satisfied by the issue of shares;

● the case of an insurance company, in appropriating or transferring monies to any statutory fund established and maintained pursuant to Malaysian insurance law;

● writing off the formation expenses of the company, or the expenses of, or the commission or brokerage paid or discount allowed on any duty, fee, or tax payable on or in connection with any issue of shares; and

● providing the premium payable on the redemption of redeemable preference shares.

Capital redemption reserve

Where a company redeems preference shares out of profits, it must transfer to the capital redemption reserve a sum equal to the nominal value of the shares redeemed. This reserve may only be applied in paying up unissued shares of the company to be issued as fully paid up bonus shares.

Revaluation reserve

Where any fixed asset is revalued by reference to current market value, any surplus must be transferred to a revaluation reserve. The revaluation reserve may be reduced to the extent that it is considered to be no longer necessary, but transfers out of this reserve may only be made in respect of distributable reserves if the amounts in question were originally charged to the income statement or represent realised profits.

Distribution of reserves

Apart from the requirement that dividends shall only be paid out of realised profits, there is no other restriction on the payment of dividends. However, income tax at the rate of 34% is deemed to be deducted from dividends at source.

In this connection, it would not be prudent to declare dividends in excess of the amount that can be franked by the available income tax credit under Section 108 of the Income Tax Act, 1967. To do so would result in the company having to pay additional income tax at 34% on dividends that are not franked.

Foreign Currency Translation

Transactions denominated in a foreign currency are recorded in RM, the reporting currency based on the applicable exchange rate on the dates of the transactions. If the rate does not fluctuate significantly, an average rate for a period may be used. Monetary assets and liabilities are reported using the closing rate on the balance sheet date.

In preparing group accounts, the financial statements of foreign subsidiaries are translated using the closing rate on the balance date. Exchange differences resulting from the translation of the opening reserves should be recorded as an increase or decrease in reserves.

Taxation

Income tax is payable at the rate of 34% on the taxable income of a company. The taxable income is determined after certain adjustments are made to the operating profit of the company. These adjustments are necessary mainly because the company, in reporting to the shareholders, is interested in showing a true and fair view of the results on a normal commercial basis whereas the government has other objectives.

The common adjustments are:

- Depreciation charges by the company are not deductible. Instead, capital allowances are claimable on the qualifying assets. Industrial buildings, but not commercial buildings, normally qualify for capital allowances.

- Entertainment expenses are not deductible.

Malaysia

- General (as opposed to specific) provisions are not deductible.

- Interest or royalty payments on which withholding tax has not been withheld and paid to the Inland Revenue are not deductible.

- Any other expenses incurred but not wholly and exclusively in the production of income, are not deductible.

- Capital expenditure charged to revenue are not deductible, but capital allowances are claimable on the qualifying assets.

- Tax incentives in the form of double deduction of certain expenses (eg export promotion expenses).

- Tax incentives in the form of certain allowances (eg export allowances and reinvestment allowances).

- Unabsorbed tax losses of previous years can be carried forward indefinitely or can be offset against the current year's business income.

Real Property Gains Tax covers gains on disposal of real property as well as shares in a Real Property Company. A Real Property Company is a company which owns real properties the market value of which is not less than 75% of the value of its total tangible assets.

It should be noted that the concepts of "Advance Corporation Tax", " Group Tax Relief" and "Carryback of Tax Losses" are not applicable in Malaysia.

Deferred Taxation

Where accounting income differs from taxable income, it is a standard accounting policy (IAS 12) to make a provision for deferred taxation on all significant timing differences except where it is thought reasonably probable that the tax effects of such deferrals will continue in the foreseeable future. Where provision is made the liability rather than the deferral method is preferred where the tax rate is constant. Deferred taxation benefits are only recognised where there is a reasonable expectation of realisation in the foreseeable future.

Unusual and Prior Period Items

Unusual items are gains or losses that derive from events or transactions that are distinct from the ordinary activities of the company and therefore are not expected to recur frequently or regularly.

Income from the ordinary activities of the company during a period should be disclosed in the income statement as part of the net income. Unusual items should be included in net income. However, the nature and amount of each such item should be separately disclosed.

Prior period items are charges or credits that arise in the current period as a result of errors or omissions in the preparation of the financial statements of one or more prior periods.

Prior period items and the amount of the adjustments, if any, resulting from changes in accounting policies should be either:

● reported by adjusting opening retained earnings in the financial statements for the current period and amending the comparative information in respect of prior years which is included in the financial statements; or

● separately disclosed in the current income statement as part of net income.

In either case the disclosure relating to these items should be adequate to facilitate comparisons of the figures for the periods presented.

Retirement Benefits

A retirement benefit plan often provides for separate funds to be set up into which contributions are made by the employer and sometimes by employees.

The objective of accounting for the cost of a retirement benefit plan is to ensure that the cost of benefits is allocated to the accounting period on a systematic basis relating to the receipt of the employees' services.

In a defined benefit plan the cost of retirement benefits is determined either using an accrued benefit valuation method or a projected benefit valuation method. The pay-as-you-go and terminal funding methods are not acceptable for accounting for the cost of retirement benefits. Current service costs are charged to income systematically over the expected remaining working lives of the employees covered by the retirement benefit plan. Past service costs, experience adjustments and the effects of changes in actuarial assumptions on retirement benefit costs are charged or credited to income as they arise or allocated systematically over a period not exceeding the expected remaining working lives of the participating employees.

In a defined contribution plan, the employer's contribution applicable to a particular accounting period is charged against income in that period.

If the defined contribution plan includes an element of past service cost or when a retirement benefit plan is amended with the result that additional benefits are provided for retired employees, such element of past service or the cost of additional benefits are accounted for in the same manner as for past service costs under a defined benefit plan.

Related Party Disclosures

IAS 24 which sets out the required disclosure concerning related parties has not been adopted in Malaysia. However, disclosure of the following information concerning related companies is required by statute:

- balances with other group companies at the end of the year;
- identity of the ultimate holding company; and
- transactions with related companies.

Segmental Reporting

Segmental reporting is only required for companies which are publicly traded. Industry and geographical segments are the usual bases for presenting information on operations. When consolidated financial statement are presented, segmental information needs to be prepared only in respect of the consolidated financial statements.

Industry segment information is usually presented by groups of related products and services, or by types of customer. Geographical segment information is sometimes presented on the basis of the location of operations of an enterprise, sometimes on the basis of markets and sometimes on both.

The company should provide reconciliations between the sum of the information on individual segments and the aggregate information in the financial statements.

Commitments and Contingencies

The amount of a contingent loss is accrued by a charge to the income statement if:

- it is probable that future events will confirm that, after taking into account any related probable recovery, an asset has been impaired or a liability incurred at the balance sheet date; and

- a reasonable estimate of the amount of the resulting loss can be made.

If a contingent loss is not accrued, its nature and an estimate of its financial effect are generally disclosed by way of note unless the possibility of a loss is remote. However, if a reliable estimate of the financial effect cannot be made, this fact is disclosed. Contingencies which are accrued may warrant separate disclosure.

Contingent gains are not accrued in financial statements. The existence of contingent gains is disclosed if it is probable that the gains will be realised. It is important that the disclosure avoids giving misleading implications as to the likelihood of realisation.

All material commitments are disclosed giving details of amounts committed for future capital expenditure including future operating lease payments or rental payments committed under contracts.

Price Level Changes

Price level changes or current cost accounting is not usually practised in Malaysia. IAS 6 on Accounting Responses to Changing Prices which was previously approved for adoption was subsequently withdrawn.

Future Developments

On accounting issues where there are no definitive standards in Malaysia and where there are wide divergences in practice, MIA and MACPA will initiate the development of a MAS for the improvement and harmonisation of accounting treatments adopted and the presentation of financial statements.

A discussion paper will be issued to obtain views on various issues and the approaches that could be adopted before proceeding to prepare an exposure draft for the accounting standard. The exposure draft will be addressed to accounting bodies, governmental authorities, securities markets, regulatory bodies and other interested parties. Adequate time is allowed for consideration and comment on each exposure draft before it is adopted.

Presently the issues under discussion are:

- Accounting for goodwill

- Accounting for property development activities

- Accounting for pre-cropping expenses in plantation companies.

Malta

Mizzi, Scerri, Said & Co

In view of its long connection with Great Britain and as a member of the Commonwealth the accountancy profession in Malta has been greatly influenced by the systems adopted in the United Kingdom. In the early 1960's Malta introduced a law, the Commercial Partnerships Ordinance, to regulate Commercial Partnerships, which was based on the United Kingdom Companies Act of 1948. Until 1967 most if not all of the qualified accountants in Malta were trained in the United Kingdom and had British qualifications. In 1967 Maltese candidates started sitting the local examinations of the Malta Institute of Accountants, which had been established in the 1940's, to obtain a Maltese qualification.

In order to practise as an accountant an individual must obtain a Minister's warrant to act as a Certified Public Accountant (CPA). This warrant may be obtained by an individual, having a degree from the University of Malta who also has the necessary practical experience. It may also be obtained by individuals who have passed the examinations of the Malta Institute.

Similarly if an individual wants to act as an auditor he must obtain the warrant of a Certified Public Accountant and Auditor (CPAA) before he can act as such. In order to obtain the CPAA warrant the individual, subsequent to his obtaining the CPA warrant, must have also been trained for a minimum of three years under a CPAA warrant holder.

The Malta Institute of Accountants is only now about to issue the first two accounting standards dealing with matters specifically relating to Maltese law and practice. Up to now most Maltese accounts have followed UK standards and International Accounting Standards (IAS) and the Malta Institute is in the process of enforcing requirements for the implementation of IAS's so far as these are not incompatible with local legislation.

Maltese subsidiaries of U.K. registered companies and also Maltese enterprises of some size have been adopting IAS's. They are not however enforced through local regulations though the Institute is endeavouring to have these standards included in the statute book. EC directives, have not so far been implemented, as Malta is not a member of the EC, although all new laws are being drafted with the requirements of those directives in view.

Form and Content of Financial Statements

The form and content of a company's financial statements are prescribed by law and form part of the schedules to the Commercial Partnerships Ordinance. All limited liability companies are required by this ordinance to present audited accounts to their shareholders. Furthermore the Malta Income Tax Act requires all limited liability companies to submit audited accounts with their tax returns although the taxation authorities do not insist on them being a specific format. In accepting the accounts presented with tax returns a serious view is taken of those that are not prepared in a professional manner.

The directors are responsible for presenting the company's financial statements, which are audited and presented to the shareholders, so as to give a true and fair view of the company's financial state of affairs as at the end of its financial year and of its results as at that date.

By law the financial statements of each limited liability company should include the following:

● Directors' report including a review of the business
● Profit and loss account, which may be abridged
● Balance sheet
● Notes to the financial statements
● Auditors' report

Comparative figures must also be disclosed.

It is not necessary in Malta for a holding company to publish group financial statements. Normally, however, the few public companies that exist in Malta, do publish consolidated accounts. The form of consolidated financial statements is not dealt with in the laws of Malta.

In Malta there is a small Stock Exchange which started operating in 1992 dealing with Malta Government Stocks and one public company's shares. It is anticipated that other companies may also be quoted and ultimately it is intended that the Exchange will also deal in foreign equities. The Stock Exchange may require quoted companies to make additional disclosures to those required by the Commercial Partnerships Ordinance.

Public Filing Requirements

Not all companies are required to file financial statements. Private exempt companies are not required to file financial statements while private non-exempt companies and public enterprises have to file their financial statements with the Registrar of

Partnerships. A public company is one that has 50 or more shareholders. Private non-exempt companies which are also required to file their financial statements include:

- those companies whose aggregate number of shareholders including corporate shareholders total more than 50;

- companies that have as their shareholders non-Maltese companies, in other words all subsidiaries of foreign companies; and

- companies who have as a director any other company even though that other company would be a private exempt company in its own right.

All companies must file an annual return with the Registrar of Partnerships. This form is prescribed by law and includes details of share capital (authorised and issued), details of shareholders and their holdings and directors. The form has to be made up to a date which is 14 days after the holding of the annual general meeting. Annual general meetings must be held within nine months of the end of a financial period or not later than fifteen months after the last annual general meeting. Financial statements where required are to be filed with this return.

As explained above the content of financial statements should comply with the Commercial Partnerships Ordinance and the filing of group accounts is not required. There are various penalties for non-compliance with the requirements for filing of the annual return and accounts. These penalties are normally very low for a first offender but subsequent defaults are penalised more heavily.

Financial statements filed with the Registrar of Partnerships must be in Maltese or English and are open for inspection to the public after payment of a nominal fee. Financial statements that do not comply with the requirements of the Commercial Partnerships Ordinance are not accepted by the Registrar. Accounting periods should be for 12 months or 52/53 weeks. Any change in the year-end must be agreed to by the Commissioner of Inland Revenue which is the taxation authority in Malta.

Audit Requirements

Every company is required to appoint an approved auditor i.e. either an individual or a firm of auditors. It is ensured that the auditor is independent and sufficiently skilled to carry out his duties both by the legislation contained in the Commercial Partnerships Ordinance and by the taxation authorities and also by the ethics and the internal regulations of the Malta Institute of Accountants.

The auditor is appointed each year by the shareholders and reports to them whether in his opinion the financial statements show a true and fair view of the state of affairs of the company and of the profit or loss and the source and application of funds and that they comply with the Commercial Partnerships Ordinance. The auditor should report any inconsistencies between the financial statements and the directors' report.

Malta

By law the auditor must also refer to any instances where:

- proper accounting records have not been kept; or
- all the information and explanations required for the purposes of the audit has not been received.

Although there is no legal requirement to do so an auditor also normally refers to non-compliance with International Accounting Standards.

Valuation Principles

All Malta registered companies adopt the historical cost convention. (i.e. the assets and liabilities of the company are stated at original cost subject to depreciation or provisions.) There is no law that regulates valuation principles and their disclosure in financial statements. However when a permanent diminution in value below depreciated original cost occurs the deficit is normally taken to the profit and loss account as a realised loss. The majority of accountants follow IAS's in this respect.

Group Financial Statements

There is no law in Malta that requires the preparation of group financial statements, however certain public companies and banks do publish group accounts. These group financial statements normally follow the presentation used by groups in the United Kingdom.

Depreciation

The cost or valuation (less estimated residual value) of any fixed asset that has a limited use for economic life should be depreciated or amortised systematically over that life. For each class of fixed asset disclosure must be made of the:

- cumulative amount provided for depreciation at the beginning and end of the financial period;
- amount provided in the period;
- amount of any adjustment arising from disposals; and
- amount of any other adjustments.

The requirements of IAS's as they relate to the treatment of depreciation, are widely adopted in Malta. The depreciation methods used should be those which directors consider most appropriate having regard to the types of asset and their use in the business. Generally either the straight line or reducing balance method is used.

Leasing

Other than the legal requirement to disclose financial commitments there are no statutory requirements regarding the disclosure of leases or the methods of accounting for them. The requirements of IAS 17 are normally followed.

Research and Development

There is no legal requirement relating to accounting for research and development and the requirements of the IAS on the subject are normally followed.

Inventories

Inventories are referred to as stocks in the Commercial Partnerships Ordinance and are divided into the following main categories:

- Raw materials and consumables
- Work in progress
- Finished goods and goods for sale
- Payments on account of contracts in progress
- Goods in transit paid for in advance

Inventories are included at purchase price, or production cost, of each individual item or group of similar items unless the net realisable value is lower in which case lower value should be substituted. Purchase price is the actual price paid plus any expenses incidental to acquisition. Production cost is the total of the purchase price of raw materials and consumables used, direct production cost and a reasonable proportion of indirect production costs but excluding distribution cost.

In determining purchase price or production cost FIFO, LIFO, weighted average, or any other similar method may be used but the method chosen must be the one which appears to the directors to be appropriate to the company's circumstances. IAS requirements are normally followed in the valuation of inventories.

Long term contracts should be assessed on a contract by contract basis and revenue and related expenditure should be recorded in the profit and loss account as contract activity progresses. Revenue should be recognised in a manner appropriate to the stage of completion of the contracts, the contractor's industry, the particular business and the customers involved. However no profit should be attributed to the part of the contract performed at the accounting date until the outcome of the contract can be assessed with reasonable certainty.

In the balance sheet the amount by which recorded revenue exceeds payments on account received from the customers is included in receivables (debtors) and separately disclosed as "amounts recoverable on contracts". Any balance of cost incurred on long term contracts after deducting amounts transferred to the profit and loss account, foreseeable losses and payments received on account, is disclosed as "long term contract balances". Compliance with IAS 2 and IAS 11 is normally adopted.

Capital and Reserves

In certain circumstances amounts must be transferred to special reserves that are defined in the Commercial Partnerships Ordinance and whose uses are restricted.

Malta

Where a company redeems shares out of profits, it must transfer to a Capital Redemption Reserve Fund a sum equal to the nominal value of the shares redeemed. This reserve may only be applied to issue bonus shares to the members. Where shares are redeemed out of a new issue the transfer to reserves is not necessary.

Where shares are issued at a premium over their nominal value the excess of the consideration over the nominal value must be transferred to a share premium account. The share premium account may not be distributed and can only be used for the issue of fully paid bonus shares.

Foreign Currency Translation

There are no legal requirements relating to foreign currency translation and IAS 21 is normally adopted.

Taxation

A company pays income tax which is at a rate of 35% based on its trading profit for the accounting period after making certain tax adjustments to arrive at taxable profits. These adjustments are necessary mainly because the company, in reporting to the shareholders, is interested in showing a true and fair view of the profit on a normal commercial basis whereas the government has other objectives.

The major adjustment is the disallowance of depreciation charged by the company and its replacement with capital allowances. There are no allowances on commercial buildings, such as retail shops, offices, houses or hotels but industrial buildings such as factories and mills usually qualify for some allowance. General or contingent provisions are not deductible.

Accounting income differs from taxable income due to either permanent differences or timing differences. Although there is no legally binding method of accounting for deferred taxation certain companies and banks do deal with this important matter. The assessment of whether deferred tax liabilities or assets will or will not crystallise should be based upon reasonable assumptions and a prudent view should be taken.

The most common causes of timing differences are the use of the cash basis for tax purposes and accruals basis for financial statements and the replacement of depreciation by the system of capital allowances for tax purposes.

Unusual and Prior Period Items

There is no law that covers this subject but IAS is normally followed by medium sized and large companies. A company's financial statements normally show extraordinary items separately in the profit and loss account and include notes which give an analysis and particulars of them.

Retirement Benefits

In view of social security laws in Malta no provisions for retirement benefits are normally necessary as all pensions are paid for by the state.

Related Party Transactions

There is no legal requirement in the Commercial Partnerships Ordinance for the disclosure of related party transactions. There is only one reference in the law which relates to loans made to directors. Details of and movements in these loans during the year are to be disclosed in the financial statements.

Commitments and Contingencies

Unless contingencies and commitments have crystallised and have been accounted for as accruals, items falling under this heading are normally included in the notes to the accounts. Balances not reflected on the balance sheet are included in the notes to the accounts.

Price Level Changes

There are no legal requirements for financial statements to disclose the effects of inflation. When SSAP 16 was issued in the U.K. certain large companies tried to adopt that standard. However since its withdrawal and the fact that inflation in Malta is not so high, companies have stopped using this system.

Mauritius

Hajee Abdoula & Ramtoola

Mauritius, being an ex-British Colony, has been greatly influenced by British accounting principles and practices. Most of the accountants in Mauritius are members of the six principal accountancy institutes in the United Kingdom and Ireland.

Until recently, there were no local accounting standards and the accounting profession has looked to the Statements of Standard Accounting Practice issued in UK for guidance in determining generally accepted accounting principles which aim to show a true and fair view of a company's financial affairs and performance. Tax laws have little influence in determining these generally accepted accounting principles. However, most companies use 30 June as their financial year end as this coincides with the tax year end.

In 1989, the Mauritius Accounting and Auditing Standards Committee was set up to prescribe accounting standards and auditing guidelines. This has resulted in a set of standards commonly known as the Mauritius Accounting Standards (MAS).

Form and Content of Financial Statements

The form and content of a company's financial statements, together with the accompanying notes as prescribed by the sixth schedule of the Companies Act 1984, are the responsibility of a company's management.

If there is any departure from the MAS, this fact, together with the reasons for the departure, should be disclosed by the directors in a note to the accounts. Failure to do so may lead to penalties.

A company's financial statements are prepared by the directors to give a true and fair view of the enterprise's financial state of affairs and to present a historical record to the shareholders annually of the use of the company's resources and its performance in the period being reported on.

Mauritius

The financial statements of public and non exempt companies must contain:

- Directors' report
- Income statement
- Balance sheet
- Notes to the financial statements, including the accounting policies adopted
- Statement of sources and application of funds
- Auditors' report

Comparative figures are required to be shown.

Holding companies are required to publish group financial statements in the form of consolidated accounts dealing with the group as a whole.

Companies listed on the Mauritian Stock Exchange also publish a chairman's statement giving brief details of changes in the financial position and the future development of the company. They must also adhere to the listing rules of the Mauritian Stock Exchange Limited.

Public Filing Requirements

The directors of the company are responsible for the preparation and filing of the financial statements and the annual return. Furthermore, quoted companies are required to file interim unaudited accounts with the stock exchange every six months.

A public company is empowered to offer its shares to the public and must state in its memorandum that it is a public company. In addition, the name of the company should include the word "Limited" or its abbreviation "Ltd" as the last part of the name.

A private company is not allowed to offer its shares to the public and must not have more than 25 shareholders.

A private company is an "exempt private company" if, for its last preceding financial year, it satisfies both of the following criteria:

- its issued share capital and reserves are less than two million rupees; and
- its turnover is less than four million rupees.

A private company which does not satisfy the above mentioned criteria is a "non-exempt private company".

All public and non exempt private companies must file financial statements with an annual return, each year, with the Registrar of Companies. These documents are available for public inspection at the Registrar of Companies' office.

The annual return contains details of:

- The registered office of the company
- The authorised and issued share capital
- The amount of mortgages and charges on the company's assets
- Shareholders and their shareholding
- Directors, secretaries and auditors (if applicable)

An exempt private company is not required to file a copy of its balance sheet and profit and loss account with its annual return. The return needs only to be accompanied by a certificate which includes summarised profit and loss and balance sheet information, signed by a director and the secretary of the company.

Audit Requirements

All public and non exempt private companies must have their financial statements audited. The shareholders appoint the auditor whose report has to give an opinion as to whether the financial statements:

- show a true and fair view of the state of affairs of the company and the operating results for the year;
- have been prepared in accordance with the requirements of the Companies Act; and
- have been prepared in accordance with Mauritius Accounting Standards.

The law requires that a person appointed to act as auditor of a company, other than an exempt private company, must:

- not be an officer or employee of the company;

- not be a partner, employer or employee of an officer or employee of the company;

- be a member of the:
  - Institute of Chartered Accountants in England and Wales
  - Institute of Chartered Accountants in Scotland
  - Institute of Chartered Accountants in Ireland
  - Chartered Association of Certified Accountants or
  - Chartered Institute of Management Accountants;

- in rare cases, hold a prescribed degree.

In practice, a firm of accountants is usually appointed as auditor of a company.

The auditor is required by the Mauritius Accounting and Auditing Committee Act to report on any departure from the MAS where the directors have not disclosed the departure.

Mauritius

An exempt private company is required to appoint at each annual general meeting an auditor, or auditors, who:

- need not be a qualified auditor;
- shall not be an officer of the company or a related corporation; and
- shall be ordinarily resident in Mauritius.

Their duty is however similar to that of an auditor of a public or non-exempt private company.

Valuation Principles

The historical cost convention is used to prepare financial statements in Mauritius. Certain fixed assets such as land and buildings may be revalued to market value. Any unrealised surplus or deficit arising should be transferred to a separate reserve shown in the balance sheet and should not be reflected in the profit and loss account.

Following IAS 1, MAS 1 requires all significant accounting policies used to be disclosed clearly and concisely by way of a note to the financial statements. Furthermore, MAS 1 requires disclosure of any changes in accounting policies that have a material effect in the current period or may have a material effect in a subsequent period.

Depreciation

MAS 7 requires that all fixed assets with a finite useful life should be depreciated. However, freehold land does not require a provision for depreciation unless it is subject to depletion.

Provision for depreciation should be made by allocating the cost (or revalued amount) less estimated residual value of the assets as fairly as possible to the periods expected to benefit from their use. The straight line method and the reducing balance method are both commonly used to calculate depreciation.

The financial statements are required to disclose the following information for each major class of depreciable asset:

- the depreciation method used;
- the depreciation rates used;
- total depreciation charged for the period; and
- the gross amount of depreciable assets and the related accumulated depreciation.

Leasing

Leases can be classified into two main categories, finance or operating.

According to MAS 15, if a lease is a finance lease, the recommended accounting method in the books of the lessee is to treat the lease as an asset and recognise a liability at an amount equal to the fair value of the leased asset, net of grants and tax credits receivable by the lessor or, if lower, at the present value of the minimum lease payments, using the interest rate implicit in the lease as the discount rate.

The leased asset is then amortised in a manner consistent with the lessee's normal depreciation policy for owned assets. If there is no reasonable certainty that the lessee will obtain ownership by the end of the lease term, the asset should be fully depreciated over the shorter of the lease term or its useful life. Payments made by the lessee should be apportioned between the finance charge and the reduction of the outstanding liability.

For operating leases, the lessee records the rental expense for the accounting period on a systematic basis that is representative of the time pattern of the user's benefit.

Inventories

MAS 5 classifies stocks as follows:

- Raw materials and consumables
- Work in progress
- Finished goods

MAS 5 allows stocks to be valued using the FIFO, weighted average, LIFO, base stock, standard cost, retail price less gross profit margin and latest purchase price methods.

For long term contracts, where the work extends for more than one year, the percentage of completion method should be used provided the contract is at a stage such that the outcome can be estimated reasonably. All foreseeable losses should be provided for in the financial statements.

Capital and Reserves

There are no legal requirements to set aside amounts out of the profits each year to special reserves. The only restriction on the payment of dividends is that they may not be paid out of share capital and capital reserves.

Group Financial Statements

The Companies Act requires the directors of a holding company to prepare group financial statements for each financial year unless the company is itself a wholly-owned subsidiary of another corporation incorporated in Mauritius. A company is a subsidiary of another company where the latter controls more than half of its voting power, controls the composition of its board of directors, or holds more than half of its issued share capital.

The group financial statements, whether listed or not, must be in the form of consolidated financial statements except in special circumstances where financial

Mauritius

statements for each company in the group would be preferable. A company incorporated in Mauritius is required to change its year end to that of its holding company within 2 years of becoming a subsidiary.

A holding company is required by MAS 11 to consolidate the financial statements of its associated companies using the equity method of accounting. Where there is a uniting of interests the pooling of interests method should be used to account for the business combination. Under this method the assets and liabilities for the combining enterprises and their revenues and expenses for the period in which the combination occurs, as well as any comparative periods disclosed, should be included in the financial statements of the combined enterprises as if they had been combined from the start of those periods.

Foreign Currency Translation

MAS 14 and IAS 21 are similar with regard to the accounting treatment and disclosure requirements of foreign currency translation.

Briefly, MAS 14 stipulates the following:

- Foreign currency transactions should be recorded in the reporting currency of an entity at the spot rate.

- At each balance sheet date foreign currency monetary items should be translated at the closing rate.

- Where there is a forward exchange contract the forward rate may be used for reporting the transactions.

- Exchange differences arising on settlement of monetary items or on translated short and long term foreign currency monetary items at the year end should be recognised in the profit and loss account.

- Exchange differences arising on foreign transactions on monetary items within a group should be taken to shareholders' interests in the consolidated financial statements.

- The closing rate is used to translate the balance sheet items of a foreign entity, whereas the spot rate is used to translate the profit and loss account items.

- The gain or loss on the transaction of foreign currency financial statements is not recognised in current net income, but as a separate component of shareholders' equity.

- For a foreign entity which is integral to the operations of the parent, the gain or loss on the translation of its financial statements is recognised in the current net income.

The financial statements must disclose the methods of translation used and the net exchange differences taken to the shareholders' interests or to income.

Taxation

A uniform rate of tax of 35% is applied to all profits chargeable to corporate income tax. However, as an incentive for companies to enter the stock exchange, publicly quoted companies are allowed a deduction of 30% off their tax liability.

Taxable income, which includes both income and capital profits, is arrived at after making the following adjustments to net profit:

● Depreciation is added back to trading profit and capital allowances given for investment in certain assets such as plant and machinery, furniture and fittings, electrical goods and motor vehicles.

● Increases in general provisions debited to profit and loss account are generally not allowable for tax purposes. Specific provisions can be claimed as deductions.

● Taxable losses of previous periods may be carried forward to be set off against future profits. However, where there is a change of more than 50% in ownership during one tax year previous tax losses cannot be carried forward.

● In principle, all interest payments on loan stock and other debts of a company are allowable, except for certain interest payments on debentures.

Dividends paid are not deductible in arriving at taxable income and are not subject to withholding tax.

MAS 13 requires deferred tax accounting for all timing differences that will crystallise in the very near future (within three years) using the liability method. Where it is expected that certain timing differences will not reverse for some considerable period ahead, the amount of timing differences, both current and cumulative, not accounted for should be disclosed by way of notes. Deferred tax balances should be disclosed separately from shareholders' funds in the balance sheet.

Unusual and Prior Period Items

According to MAS 8, exceptional items should be disclosed on the face of the profit and loss account or by way of a note, and described as such. Extraordinary items should be shown separately on the profit and loss account for the year together with the related tax charges or credits.

The preferred treatment for prior year adjustments is to adjust opening retained earnings in the current financial statements and amend the comparative information in respect of prior years. Such an amendment is required only where there is a change in accounting policies or a correction of a fundamental error.

Mauritius

Commitments and Contingencies

MAS 9 requires a probable contingent loss to be provided for in the profit and loss account whereas disclosure is required for a possible contingent loss. Contingent gains are not recognised until they are actually realised.

Future Developments

At the time of writing there are three accounting issues which are still at the exposure draft stage. These concern the accounting treatment of related party transactions, research and development and pension costs.

Mexico

Gossler, S.C.

The profession of Public Accountancy in Mexico dates from 1907, the year in which the first public accountant was licensed. The foregoing does not, of course, signify that there had been no accountants in companies previously to maintain the books and keep a record of operations; but it is considered that 1907 marked the commencement of the profession in an independent form, as we know it today.

In order to achieve the present state of the profession in this country, it was necessary for accountants to meet in associations until the Mexican Institute of Public Accountants (MIPA) was formed. MIPA is a federation, which groups institutes and colleges established in different cities throughout the country, and there are currently 54 institutes and colleges making up MIPA.

An important advantage of MIPA is that the profession is self-regulating as regards the acceptance of accounting principles, auditing standards and procedures, and rules of professional ethics.

There are legal codes regulating the professions in general, such as the Federal Law on Professions. The profession of Public Accountant is governed by laws such as the Fiscal Code of the Federation. However, these and other laws have very little influence on the doctrinal and technical aspects of the accountancy profession; they rather establish responsibilities, govern the presentation of supplementary information, or establish accounting policies to be followed by companies engaged in specific fields of activity, such as banks, insurance companies, broking companies and companies with state participation.

MIPA is an active member of the International Federation of Accountants (IFAC) and of the Interamerican Accounting Association (IAA). In addition, it is recognised for its leadership among Spanish-speaking countries in the technical field, particularly in the publication and dissemination of material covering generally accepted accounting principles and auditing standards and practices.

All the foregoing ensure that financial statements are prepared in basic compliance with international accounting standards and that audits are performed in accordance with generally accepted auditing standards similar to those established by the International Auditing Practices Committee of IFAC.

Form and Content of Financial Statements

The General Law of Mercantile Corporations regulates the formalities to be complied with by Sociedades Anonimas (which form the majority of business entities). This law provides that management should submit annually to a shareholders' meeting a report which includes at least:

● A report by management on the company's performance during the fiscal year, together with the policies followed by management and, if applicable, a report on the main projects in existence
● Balance sheet
● Income statement
● Statement of changes in shareholders' equity
● Statement of changes in financial position
● Notes to the financial statements which complete or clarify the information contained in the foregoing statements

Under this law, there is no specific obligation for the financial statements to be examined by a public accountant; however, it is good commercial practice for financial statements to be audited and audited statements are required, for example, for fiscal purposes (see comments under Audit Requirements). The requirements of the National Securities Commission for public offerings and annual reports also dictate that financial statements should be audited.

Public Filing Requirements

In order for a stock company to be able to issue shares to the general investing public, authorisation must be obtained from the National Securities Commission and the shares must be registered on the Mexican Stock Exchange.

The National Securities Commission is the organisation in charge of regulating the securities market and ensuring that the Securities Market Law and its regulating pronouncements are duly complied with.

Companies are required to supply periodic information (some of it quarterly) to the National Securities Commission, to the investing public and, if applicable, to the stock exchange. The financial statements of a company must be examined by a public accountant.

Financial statements of the companies registered on the Mexican Stock Exchange must be published in official newspapers, together with a summary of their Annual Report, containing a report by the Board of Directors, operating data and the financial statements audited by a Certified Public Accountant, to provide information to interested parties.

Legally the annual financial period for all companies, whether registered on the Stock Exchange or not, always ends on 31 December, except in cases of a merger, demerger or liquidation which may result in other dates being used.

Audit Requirements

All companies incorporated under Mexican law are required to appoint one or more statutory auditors (comisarios) who need not be public accountants. However, when public accountants are appointed as "comisarios", they have to carry out an examination of the financial statements in accordance with generally accepted auditing standards, as prescribed by the Mexican Institute of Public Accountants.

Each company listed on the Mexican Stock Exchange requires an audit report on its financial statements.

Since 1990 it has been obligatory for companies whose revenue, assets or number of workers, exceed certain limits to have their financial statements audited for federal tax purposes. For 1992, the limits above which companies are obliged to undergo a federal tax audit examination are as follows:

● Revenues of over N$5.85 million or with assets of over N$11.7 million or that have at least 300 workers.

● In a group situation if the group as a whole exceeds these thresholds all companies in the group are obliged to have this fiscal audit.

Companies which are merged into or demerged from a group requiring an audit, during a financial period, are required to have an audit in the current and the three subsequent periods.

Furthermore, any company may apply for an independent report for review by the Federal Tax Audit and Review Department of the Ministry of Finance. Most companies provide such audited financial statements to avoid lengthy direct audits by the tax authorities on the taxpayer's premises.

With regard to the report on consolidated financial statements, whenever there is more than one auditor within a group of companies, it is normal for the principal auditor to mention in his report the work performed by the other auditor(s), emphasising clearly the division of responsibilities between the auditors. This reference is not a qualification of opinion.

As part of this process, the principal auditor will, in preparing the audit report, evaluate the effect of their colleagues' work, together with their reputation and the adequacy of the auditing standards and procedures used by them.

Valuation Principles

Mexican financial statements follow a version of the historical cost convention, substantially modified to accommodate the effect of the high inflation rates which have been experienced in recent years.

The B-10 bulletin, issued by MIPA and obligatory since 1984, permits updating or restatement of figures in financial statements to be effected either by a method of indexation for changes in the general levels of prices or by using specific cost or replacement values. (see "Price Level Changes" below).

Group Financial Statements

When there is a group structure, consolidated financial statements must be presented. This will be the case where one company owns, either directly or indirectly, more than half of the voting power of another company.

However, since 1992, other criteria for assessing control of a company have been introduced, which do not require this degree of participation. If control is established the controlling company will have to recognise the other as a subsidiary and include it in their consolidated financial statements.

Also, new accounting principles have introduced the concept of an associated company where the investing company exerts significant influence and has at least a 10% investment. In some specific cases, an investment of less than 10% will be sufficient for a company to be an associate.

A subsidiary may be excluded from the consolidation if:

● it is an overseas subsidiary, in a country where exchange controls, restrictions on the remittance of profits, or uncertainty on monetary stability exist; or

● it is bankrupt and is being dissolved.

The individual financial statements utilised to prepare the consolidated financial statements should be prepared as at the same date or with a date which is not more than three months different from the date of the consolidated financial statements.

Where there are minority shareholders their interests should be shown under a separate heading in the financial statements as the last item of Stockholders' Equity.

In the consolidation process, any difference between the purchase value and the accounting value of the investment is dealt with either by adjusting the value of the underlying assets of the subsidiary company at the date of acquisition or recorded as "Surplus of cost over the net book value of shares in subsidiary companies", depending on the circumstances.

Positive "goodwill", should it exist, is written off against the consolidated results over a reasonable period. If there is negative goodwill, this should be recorded as a deferred credit, which must be transfered annually to future results over a period not exceeding 5 years.

Holding companies should, in addition to preparing consolidated financial statements, present their individual financial statements which comply with legal requirements. For this purpose, investments in the shares of subsidiary and associated companies should be valued by the equity method, which consists of valuing investments at cost plus, or minus, the holding company's share of post-acquisition profits or losses.

Depreciation

The cost of a tangible capitalised asset, sometimes less residual value, is systematically charged against income over the asset's estimated useful life except land which is not subject to depreciation. The process of depreciation is one of allocation, not valuation. The allocation may be made in accordance with two general criteria; one is based on time (which is most widely used) and the other on units produced.

The following should be disclosed:

● depreciation expense for the period;

● the balances of each major class of depreciable asset by nature or function, at the balance sheet date;

● accumulated depreciation, either by major class of depreciable asset or in total, at the balance sheet date; and

● a general description of the method, or methods, used in computing depreciation with respect to each major class of depreciable asset.

The estimated useful lives of assets used for the financial statements may be the same as those used for tax purposes, provided the latter fall within a reasonable range for the company's business.

Leasing

Accounting for leases largely follows internationally accepted standards:

● For a finance lease, the lessee records both an asset and an obligation equal, at the inception of the lease, to the lower of the market value of the leased property and the present value of the minimum lease payments during the lease term. Each payment is allocated between the interest charge and a reduction of the liability. The asset is depreciated over its useful life.

Mexico

● For an operating lease, the lessee records rental expenses in a manner which reflects the benefits obtained from the leased property over the lease term. This basis is usually the actual payment schedule provided in the lease.

Disclosure is required of all significant aspects of a company's leasing activities.

Research and Development

Accounting principles require that all research and development costs must be expensed when incurred. These charges must be disclosed for each period for which an income statement is presented.

Inventories

Inventories generally consist of:

● Raw material and supplies
● Work in progress
● Finished goods

Accounting principles require that inventories of trading and manufacturing companies be stated at the lower of cost and market value. For this purpose, the term "market value" means current replacement cost. Cost is the sum of all charges and disbursements, direct and indirect, incurred in bringing inventories to their respective condition and location. Direct cost, that is, raw material, labour and overhead, is also permitted, but seldom adopted.

Various methods are acceptable in determining inventory cost, including FIFO, LIFO, average and specific cost.

The basis for stating inventories must be consistently applied and disclosed in the financial statements. If the basis is changed, this must be disclosed, together with the effect on income.

Intangible Assets

Two kinds of intangible assets are recognised:

● Where items represent the utilisation of services or consumption of goods, which will directly produce specific income in the future, their charge to expenses is deferred and written off in the operating periods when the income arises.

Examples of this kind of intangible are the discount on the issue of debentures, expenses for placement of securities, and organisation expenses.

- Intangible properties, which imply some right or privilege or in some cases result in the reduction of costs of manufacture, improvement in the quality of a product or promotion of its acceptance in the market. These include patents, licences and brands.

Capitalisation of intangibles is permitted only when they have been bought, internally developed or acquired in any way. That is to say, they cannot be incorporated in the balance sheet of a company as a result of subjective assessment of their productive qualities.

Capital and Reserves

Capital stock is usually shown at par value. Any excess is shown separately as a premium on capital stock (see also "Price Level Changes" below). Additional contributions by shareholders are usually shown separately. Treasury shares are not permitted under Mexican law. No value is attributed to authorised shares which have not been issued.

In Mexico it is common for companies to be constituted as corporations with variable capital stock, which facilitates the increase and decrease of capital stock, with minimum requirements. In these cases, companies divide their capital stock into fixed capital (without the right of withdrawal) and variable capital, which can be altered easily.

From the fiscal point of view, income tax (35%) could be imposed in certain circumstances when capital is reduced, for example if the decrease exceeds the amount of capital stock remaining.

There is a requirement that each year 5% of the net income must be transferred to a legal reserve, until that reserve is equal to 20% of the capital stock.

Foreign Currency Translation

Foreign currency transactions are recorded at the exchange rate prevailing on the date of the transaction. Any resulting exchange gain or loss is dealt with through the income statement. At the balance sheet date, monetary assets and liabilities denominated in a foreign currency are normally translated using the closing exchange rate and any exchange gain or loss reported as part of the ordinary profit or loss for the year.

Taxation

Income tax is payable on a corporation's taxable income which is arrived at by adjusting net income shown in the financial statements and also recognising in some way the effects of inflation.

The most common adjustments to net income shown in the financial statements which are made in arriving at taxable income are:

- incentives offered by the federal government;

- employees' profit sharing, income tax itself, tax on assets and some other items of expenditure which are disallowed for tax purposes;

- interest and exchange fluctuations are included in, or deducted from, taxable income in real terms, that is, after taking into account the inflation for the related period;

- the "inflation" profit or loss resulting from holding monetary assets and liabilities is included in taxable income;

- inventory purchased is deductible, instead of the cost of sales shown in the income statement; and

- tax losses carried forward may be indexed using the inflation factor at the end of the month prior to the beginning of the fiscal year in which the loss is realised.

Tax is charged at 35% on taxable income.

Dividends paid, whether to resident or non-resident companies or individuals, are subject to tax (35%) only if the corporation has not paid the 35% tax mentioned above, on its annual profits. The tax is to be paid by the company not by the shareholders themselves.

Where accounting income differs from taxable income, it is standard accounting practice to make a provision for deferred tax on short term timing differences which arise on certain non-recurrent items.

Since 1989 there has been a so-called tax on assets payable by companies which have operated for more than three fiscal years. It is calculated at a rate of 2% on the company's assets minus certain debts for which deduction is authorised. The amount of this tax is compared with the income tax assessed in the same period and the highest of the two is paid.

The tax on assets paid in one fiscal year may be refunded by the fiscal authorities if in the next five years the income tax payable is greater than the tax on assets. The refund would be equivalent to the difference between the two taxes adjusted for the effects of inflation.

The employees' profit share, which is determined on a basis which does not take into consideration the effects of inflation, is 10% and must be paid regularly starting at the end of the second year of a company's activities.

Unusual and Prior Period Items

Accounting principles define extraordinary items as events and transactions which are unusual in nature and of infrequent occurrence. Extraordinary items, if material, must be separately disclosed net of any related income tax effect.

An event or transaction which is either unusual in nature or occurs infrequently, but not both, should be classified and reported as a separate component within net income.

Prior period adjustments are limited to the correction of errors in prior periods. In addition, adjustments (restatements) of previously issued financial statements are required if there is a change in certain accounting principles or an adjustment related to interim statements of the current fiscal period. All other revenues, expenses, gains and losses recognised during a period must be included in the net income of that period.

Retirement Benefits

Accounting principles for recording retirement benefits not actually payable at a balance sheet date are as follows:

- Provision should be made in full and charged to income in respect of amounts which can be determined or reasonably estimated in advance, such as pensions under a formal pension plan or past service premiums.

- No provisions are required for amounts that cannot be reasonably estimated in advance, such as indemnities which are payable upon dismissal of an employee.

Provisions for pensions and past service premiums are deductible expenses for tax purposes only if funded in accordance with plans that fulfil requirements established by income tax regulations.

Related Party Transactions

The following, among others, are considered to be a company's related parties:

- holding companies, subsidiaries, associates and affiliates;

- other companies and persons who possess, directly or indirectly, a significant influence on the voting rights of the reporting company; and

- members of the board, directors and high level executives together with the companies in which they hold the power to make decisions or exercise significant influence on operational and financial decisions.

Disclosure requirements in financial statements include:

- nature of the relationship;
- description of the transaction;
- amount of the transaction;
- the effect of changes on the conditions of recurrent transactions;
- balances due to or from a related party and their characteristics; and
- other information considered necessary in order to understand the transaction.

Mexico

Segmental Reporting

There are no requirements to disclose segmental information, such as industrial or geographic segments or export sales, in the financial statements of enterprises.

Treatment of Grants

There are no specific requirements for the treatment of grants or subsidies from the government although there are recommendations from MIPA, for example in the case of fiscal incentives. Generally grants etc are considered to be part of the income of the fiscal year and do not directly affect the stockholders' equity. Included in the notes to financial statements, there must be an explanation of the policy adopted and the nature and characteristics of the subsidies or incentives received.

Commitments and Contingencies

Accounting principles require financial statements to disclose commitments and contingencies.

Notes to the financial statements must disclose various matters, including unused letters of credit, long-term leases, assets pledged as security for loans, pension plans, and commitments such as those for plant acquisition, or obligations to reduce debts, maintain working capital, or restrict dividends.

In addition, an estimated contingent loss should be charged to income if it is probable that an asset was impaired or a liability was incurred at the date of the financial statements and the amount of the loss can reasonably be estimated. In the case of contingencies not meeting both of these conditions disclosure is required if some loss can be reasonably expected. Contingent gains should not be credited to income because to do so would recognise income prior to realisation.

Balances not Reflected in the Balance Sheet

As a professional rule, all material information should be disclosed which is necessary to make the financial statements clear and understandable.

Items disclosed in the balance sheet or elsewhere in the financial statements should be supplemented, if necessary, by additional information in the notes to make their meaning clear.

This being the basic principle, any significant item should be included in the financial statements.

Price Level Changes

The B-10 bulletin "Recognition of the Effects of Inflation on Financial Information" establishes the rules for adjusting financial statements to reflect the effects of inflation. The bulletin was issued by the Accounting Principles Commission of MIPA, and as such is compulsory for all companies. Two completely different methods are accepted in the bulletin:

- adjustment by reference to changes in the general price level. This consists of correcting the "measuring" unit utilised for traditional accounting, using constant pesos instead of nominal pesos; and

- restating to specific cost, also called replacement values. This is based on current values, instead of values assessed at the time the transactions were originally carried out.

The information obtained under these two methods cannot be compared, since each method is based on fundamentally different criteria.

Companies quoted on the Mexican Stock Exchange must, under the rules of the National Securities Commision, utilise the specific cost method.

The elements of the financial statements which should be restated are:

- all non-monetary items in the balance sheet including those making up the shareholders' equity; and

- the cost or expenses shown in the income statement associated with non-monetary assets and, if applicable, the income associated with non-monetary liabilities.

The method of restating by specific cost (replacement values) is, in the cases where this method is chosen, applicable only to inventory and tangible fixed assets, as well as to costs and expenses for the period associated with those assets. Other non-monetary items should be restated by reference to changes in the general price level.

The overall cost of finance, shown as a separate item in the income statement, should be calculated under both methods and will include, in addition to interest, the effect of both the company's monetary position and currency exchange fluctuations.

Bulletin B-10 has been updated since it was first introduced to ensure that financial statements reflect more appropriately the effects of inflation. The figures in the financial statements now have to be restated to reflect the purchasing power of the peso at the balance sheet date rather than the date on which the transaction took place.

When comparative financial statements are prepared, the financial statements of the previous period should be updated to reflect the purchasing power of the peso as at the last balance sheet date.

Mexico

Future Developments

As a member of IFAC and IAA, Mexican accounting and auditing standards will continue to advance along with the development of these worldwide standards.

Nevertheless, some situations particular to this country will continue to require specific solutions, for example the effects of inflation on financial information.

From 1 January 1993, a new Mexican monetary unit came into effect, with the name of "New Peso" ("N$") and equivalent to 1,000 original pesos. This means that all financial statements must be expressed in "new pesos" from this date.

Netherlands

Horlings, Brouwer & Horlings

Dutch accounting and reporting practices are well developed and have a good international reputation. High professional standards rather than statute have been responsible for this because there was little legislation regarding the format of financial statements prior to the EC Fourth Directive. In many ways, Dutch practices are similar to those found in the United Kingdom and the United States; the most widely acknowledged difference is in the area of current cost accounting. Here the Dutch have for many years held that the true profitability of a company can only be measured when the current cost of resources consumed is matched against the income produced.

The objective of Dutch financial statements is to provide enough information to allow a user to judge the financial position and profit or loss of a company.

The financial statements should be drawn up fairly and systematically. Tax legislation does not have a direct influence on the figures produced, nor is uniformity considered an objective in itself.

Both the Fourth and the Seventh EC Directives have been implemented in Dutch legislation which is found mainly in Book 2, Title 9 of the Civil Code. This applies to companies, co-operative societies and mutual insurance companies. When implementing these Directives the Netherlands did not follow the French practice of establishing a General Accounting Plan detailing all items to be disclosed. However the legal provisions set out rules for valuation and provide standard layouts for financial statements.

Where areas are not covered by legislation, the concept of generally acceptable Dutch accounting practice, as set out in the Guidelines (Richtlijnen), retains a central position in the preparation of annual financial statements.

The Guidelines have been developed as a result of consultation between the Dutch Institute of Registered Accountants (Nederlands Instituut Van Register Accountants, NIVRA) and the representative bodies of employers and employees, all of whom

Introduction

IAS are not mandatory, but the members of IASC – the principal accounting bodies in more than 60 countries – make every reasonable effort to comply with the standards. Some countries, such as Malaysia, adopted IAS almost in their entirety as national standards while others use IAS as the base for preparing their own standards. As well as issuing its own standards, IASC acts as a forum for the discussion by countries of differences in accounting principles and the ways in which these differences might be eliminated. One of its most important current projects is to restrict the number of choices of accounting treatment that are allowed in some already issued IAS, aiming at further increasing comparability.

IFAC is seeking to achieve international harmonisation of auditing, ethical, and education standards; and its International Auditing Practices Committee (IAPC) is producing a series of International Standards on Auditing to develop and harmonise auditing practices throughout the world.

Within the European Community (EC), harmonisation has been addressed through the promulgation of accounting directives that must be incorporated into the national laws of the countries within the EC. The most important of these directives so far issued are the Fourth, which deals with the form and content of financial statements (and prescribes precise formats for the balance sheet and income statement), the Seventh, which governs the preparation of consolidated financial statements, and the Eighth which introduces rules for the regulation of auditors.

Disclosure/Measurement

Many countries require the basic financial statements to be expanded by explanatory notes in varying amounts of detail. These often include what is known as an "accounting policy" note, in which the company describes the particular methods it has adopted in preparing its financial statements. Many fundamental concepts (and some not-so-basic ones) are not disclosed. Variations across nations in the level and quality of disclosure is rarely a problem to those familiar with financial statements prepared in their own country but can leave a great deal of room for misinterpretation by foreigners. It is this area of uncertainty, in particular, that this book hopes to help remedy.

IAS1, "Disclosure of Accounting Policies", describes certain fundamental accounting assumptions that underlie the preparation of financial statements. These are:

- The enterprise is a going concern.

- Accounting policies have been applied consistently.

- Revenues and costs are recognised as they are earned or incurred.

participate in the Council for Annual Reporting. Judgements of the Enterprise Chamber and the Supreme Court are incorporated in the Guidelines, in so far as they are considered to be generally applicable. The international standards of the International Accounting Standards Committee (IASC) are also included, in so far as they are considered acceptable in the Dutch situation.

Form and Content of Financial Statements

The form of financial statements and the required notes, together with the contents of the directors' report, are prescribed by law. Depending upon its size a business may be able to take advantage of various exemptions available relating to the form and content of its financial statements. For public filing purposes further exemptions might also be applicable.

Financial statements comprise the balance sheet (balans), the profit and loss account (winsten verliesrekening) and explanatory notes.

The management of the company is responsible for the preparation of the annual report, which should include:

- the directors' report (Verslag van de raad van be stuur, directieverslag);
- the financial statements as described above;
- other information, including at least the following:

  – the audit report or a statement as to the reason for its absence,

  – a summary of the provisions in the Articles of Association in respect of the appropriation of the result,

  – a statement of the appropriation of the profit or the treatment of the loss or, if not finalised, the proposed appropriation or treatment,

  – a summary of the provisions in the Articles of Association in respect of the contribution to a deficit of a co-operative or mutual insurance company, in so far as these differ from the statutory provisions,

  – a list of names of people having special rights of control over the enterprise with a description of the nature of such rights,

  – a statement of the number of profit sharing certificates and similar rights, mentioning the rights conferred thereby,

  – a statement and a financial quantification of any post balance sheet events which have material financial consequences for the enterprise and the companies included in its consolidated annual financial statements.

Comparative figures should be shown.

In general, an enterprise which, solely or jointly with another group company, heads a group shall, in the notes to its annual financial statements, include consolidated annual financial statements, showing its own financial information together with that of its subsidiaries and other group companies.

There is no requirement for a statement of source and application of funds to be included in the annual report.

Public Filing Requirements

In principle, every enterprise is required by law to file its financial statements with the Trade Register of the Chamber of Commerce. The public has access to these records. Companies are, however, categorised as either small, medium or large and the category into which they fall affects the information required by law to be filed.

Companies are categorized as small or medium-sized if during two consecutive financial years the size of the business is not greater than at least two of the following three limits:

	Small	Medium
Balance sheet totals	Dfl. 5m	Dfl. 20m
Net turnover	Dfl. 10m	Dfl. 40m
Average number of employees	50	250

When these criteria are not met the company is considered as large.

In order to determine the size of a parent company the value of its assets, net turnover and the number of employees of all group companies shall be aggregated as they would have been in the consolidation if the parent had prepared consolidated annual financial statements. This does not apply if the parent is itself an intermediate holding company and the financial information which should be consolidated has been included in the consolidated annual financial statements of a larger entity, prepared in accordance with the provisions of the Seventh EC Directive or, if these provisions need not be observed, in an equivalent manner.

All large enterprises must file full financial statements together with the directors' report and the additional information specified above. The enterprise may state, however, that the annual report of the directors is held at its offices and that it will be made available upon request. Medium-sized enterprises have only to file limited financial statements, the so called "other" information and the directors' report. Small enterprises need to file a shortened balance sheet and limited explanatory notes thereto. If a small enterprise is set up with the objective of being a non-profit making organisation there is no filing obligation provided that it:

● immediately and at no charge sends to creditors and shareholders, upon their request, the shortened balance sheet and notes thereto or makes them available for inspection at their registered office; and

●   has filed at the Trade Register a certificate from a public accountant certifying that the enterprise did not perform any activities during the financial year outside its objectives and that this exemption is applicable.

Companies have to file their annual financial statements within eight days after adoption by their members. If the annual financial statements require approval, such period will commence on the date of approval.

The financial statements filed should be in Dutch or, if such a text has not been prepared, in French, German or English. If the activities of the enterprise or the international structure of its group justifies this, the annual financial statements, or the consolidated annual financial statements, may be prepared in a foreign currency.

Any interested party may issue proceedings demanding that the enterprise shall fulfil its filing obligations.

In the case of the involuntary liquidation of a company there is an implication, in principle, that each executive director can be jointly and severally liable for the company's liabilities to the extent that these cannot be met out of the liquidation of its assets.

Unless there are specific provisions in its articles an enterprise's financial year ends on 31 December. Its year end can only be changed by amending the articles of association.

Audit Requirements

The financial statements of all enterprises other than those classified as small are required to be audited. Only members of the NIVRA or duly authorized foreign accountants may carry out audits.

In his report the auditor states that he has performed an audit of the financial statements. His conclusion is directed towards the truth and fairness of the financial position and result, as presented in the financial statements. The auditor also verifies that the financial statements are in compliance with legal requirements which deal directly with the financial statements. The auditor does not express an opinion on compliance with other specific legal regulations, such as tax, labour and environmental laws. He must be alert, however, in connection with his audit, to the possibility that regulations which potentially have a significant impact on the financial statements have not been complied with properly and to the possible financial implications of this.

The following types of opinions are possible:

●   unqualified opinion: the financial statements are proper;

●   adverse opinion: the financial statements are incorrect as a result of mis-statements that impair their truth and fairness;

- qualified opinion ("except for" or "subject to"): the financial statements contain material mis-statements and/or a material uncertainty regarding specific aspects of the audit; and

- disclaimer: uncertainties regarding the audit exist which cannot be resolved and which could impair the truth and fairness of the financial statements.

Valuation Principles

In choosing a principle for the valuation of an asset or a liability and for the determination of the results, an enterprise shall follow the general provisions that the annual financial statements shall fairly, clearly and systematically reflect the amount and composition of the assets and liabilities at the end of the financial year and the result for that period and the items of income and expenditure upon which it is based.

Principles which may be considered are acquisition price or manufacturing cost and, in respect of tangible and fixed financial assets and stocks, their current value.

Generally, if the current value basis would more succesfully fulfil the central requirement of providing a true and fair view, the enterprise must use this basis in preparing the financial statements. The Decree on the Valuation of Assets indicates in more detail how the concepts of replacement value, business value and realizable value can be used. In general, replacement value can be used only if replacement in the economic sense is possible.

Such principles must be applied in a prudent manner. Profits shall be recognised only to the extent that they have been realised at the balance sheet date. Losses and risks originating before the end of the financial year shall be taken into account if identified before the preparation of the annual financial statements.

The valuation of assets and liabilities shall be based on the assumption that the entire activities of the enterprise will be continued (the going concern basis), unless such an assumption is incorrect or open to serious doubt.

The principles of valuation of the assets and liabilities and determination of the results shall be disclosed in respect of each material item in the financial statements.

Group Financial Statements

It is important to make a distiction between group companies, subsidiary companies and participating interests.

A group company is a company or partnership bound to a group, that is part of an economic entity, under common management and decisive influence.

Netherlands

A subsidiary is:

- a legal entity in which the company, or one or more of its subsidiaries, pursuant to an agreement with other persons can exercise, solely or jointly, more than one-half of the voting rights at a general meeting; or

- a legal entity in which a company, or one or more of its subsidiaries, is a member or shareholder and, pursuant to an agreement with other persons, can appoint or dismiss, solely or jointly, more than one-half of the directors or supervisory directors; or

- a partnership in which the participating entity is fully liable.

A participating interest is:

- a legal entity in which, directly or together with subsidiaries, capital is beneficially owned to further group operations on an intended long-term basis; or

- an interest in a partnership of which the legal entity, or a subsidiary thereof, is a partner, with joint and several liability, or a partner with the objective of being connected on a long-term basis to further group operations.

The law presumes a participating interest exists where at least 20% of the issued capital is held either directly by an entity alone or together with its subsidiaries.

For every participating interest that an entity has, the following information must be made publicly available:

- name and registered office;
- percentage share of the issued capital held (where applicable); and
- equity and results for the last period for which the information is available.

This information is not required where the participating interest is not material to the group. Information on equity and results may also be omitted if the participating interest is:

- included in the consolidation or;
- accounted for on the basis of net asset value or;
- is a minority interest (less than 50%) and there is no filing requirement in the country of incorporation.

Unless there is no legal obligation for a parent company to disclose its interest in a company, this latter company has to give the following information:

- name and registered office of the ultimate parent company;
- name and registered office of all intermediate parent companies which prepare consolidated financial statements.

The information required does not need to be included in the notes to the financial statements provided that it is filed separately at the Chamber of Commerce and notice of the filing is given in the notes to the financial statements.

A legal entity which, solely or jointly with another group company, heads a group shall, in the notes to its annual financial statements, include consolidated annual financial statements which include its own financial information with that of its subsidiaries and other group companies.

A subsidiary or group company may be excluded from the consolidation if:

- a group company has totally different activities;
- group companies, in total, are immaterial to the group;
- group companies are only held for disposal; or
- the required information can only be obtained, or estimated, at disproportionate expense or with great delay.

A part of a group may be excluded from the consolidation, provided the financial information which the legal entity should consolidate has been included in the consolidated annual financial statements of a larger entity and these financial statements have been prepared in accordance with the provisions of the Seventh EC Directive or, if these provisions need not be observed, in an equivalent manner.

Small groups are exempt from preparing consolidated financial statements.

The provisions on the form and content of financial statements for individual companies apply equally to the consolidated annual financial statements.

Consolidation is generally carried out by the full consolidation method, so that the net asset value of the parent company itself is nearly always equal to the consolidated net asset value.

No reserves or goodwill arise on consolidation since a parent company must value its investment in a subsidiary on the basis of net asset value.

The financial information relating to joint-ventures may, if certain provisions are satisfied, be included in the consolidated annual financial statements on a proportional basis, pro rata to the percentage interest held therein.

Depreciation

Tangible fixed assets which are subject to physical or economic wear and tear should be depreciated. Depreciation should be applied consistently from the time the asset is ready for use and in such a way that, by the end of its expected useful life, an asset or group of similar assets will have been written off to their estimated (average) residual value. The depreciation charges should, as far as possible, reflect the decline in value of the asset's performance potential.

Netherlands

The straight line basis of depreciation is the preferred and most widely used method. Other acceptable methods are:

- progressive methods;
- regressive methods; and
- unit of production method.

A change in method of depreciation is to be regarded as a change in the principles of valuation and determination of results, and is only allowed under certain conditions.

Leasing

The law has no specific requirements on accounting for leases. The Guidelines state that in the case of financial leases, both the assets and the related debts should be valued initially by lessees at the price that would have to be paid if the assets were acquired for cash. The assets should then be depreciated in the normal manner and the debt should be valued anually at the present value of the instalments to be paid. The interest rate applicable is calculated on the basis of the lease agreement.

Research and Development

Research and development costs may be capitalised if prudent, but should be written off over a maximum of five years. However, when such costs are capitalised, a legal reserve equal to the costs capitalised shall be included in the balance sheet.

Inventories

Inventories form part of current assets and should be split as follows:

- Raw materials and consumables
- Work in progress
- Finished goods and trading goods

Inventories are shown at the lower of purchase or production cost and net realisable value and valued on a consistent basis. If the policy is changed, this should be stated in the notes to the annual financial statements together with the reasons for doing so.

The purchase cost is the price paid plus any acquisition expenses. The production cost is the total of direct materials and production expenses and may be increased by a mark-up for indirect expenses and, if necessary, interest. In valuing inventories of a similar nature a system of weighted average prices, FIFO, LIFO, or similar bases may be used.

Inventories of raw materials and consumables which are regularly replaced and whose total value is of relatively minor importance may be shown at a fixed quantity and value if the quantity, make-up and value are subject only to minor changes.

The valuation of work in progress at the balance sheet date is not specifically dealt with by law. For long-term work in progress, the Guidelines state that taking profit whilst the contract is still in progress is acceptable only if both the proceeds and the expenses of that part of the work already completed can be determined with sufficient reliability.

Here, too, the valuation must also be in accordance with generally acceptable accounting practice, so that a responsible opinion may be formed.

Intangible Assets

Under intangible fixed assets the following shall be shown seperately:

- capitalised share issue expenses;
- research and development costs;
- concessions and licences;
- intellectual property rights;
- goodwill; and
- advance payments on intangibles.

Concessions and licences, intellectual property rights and goodwill may only be included in the balance sheet where they have been acquired for valuable consideration.

In addition to the intangible fixed assets referred to in the law, there may be others such as preparatory and start-up costs, trade names and membership rights.

Intangible fixed assets are, however, only shown in the balance sheet if there is a well-founded expectation that the future yields from these assets allow sufficient scope for depreciation.

If the costs of formation and increases in share capital and research and development expenditure are capitalised, a legal reserve equal to the capitalised amount should be created under shareholders' equity. This reserve is realised as and when these assets are depreciated.

Capital and Reserves

Capital and reserves are divided into:

- issued shares;
- share premium;
- revaluation reserve;
- statutory reserves;
- legal reserves;
- other reserves; and
- undistributed profits.

In the notes to the financial statements, details of the type and number of outstanding shares are also given.

Netherlands

The law prescribes certain legal reserves, which are not available for distribution, including reserves covering capitalised share issue expenses and research and development costs.

Certain other reserves are required by law or by the Guidelines in special cases. The articles of an enterprise may also include requirements regarding transfers that must be made to reserves. There are extensive disclosure requirements, and in particular, the reserves available for distribution must be identified.

There are no restrictions on the distribution of distributable reserves as long as the proposed distribution does not reduce shareholders' funds below the amount of issued share capital plus legal and statutory reserves. If shareholders' funds become negative, the company can continue to trade. Neither the directors nor the shareholders are required to take action to improve such a situation.

Foreign Currency Translation

The law contains no specific rules for the treatment of foreign currencies in the financial statements.

In the Guidelines for accounting for exchange differences a distinction is made between:

● transactions in foreign currencies; and
● foreign-based operations.

Transactions in foreign currencies relate to transactions which lead to the creation or extinction of receivables or liabilities expressed in foreign currencies or which lead to the acquisition or disposal of liquid assets or financial instruments expressed in a foreign currency.

Foreign based operations are those carried on in a country other than that of the reporting company through participating interests, group companies or branch establishments which draw up their financial statements in a foreign currency.

There are two types of foreign based operations:

● activities in foreign entities, that is the foreign activities take place independently; and

● direct foreign operations where the reporting (parent) company regards the foreign participation's assets and liabilities as its own.

As far as transactions in foreign currencies are concerned, in general, the following policies should be applied:

● transactions which have been settled during the reporting period should be reported at the settlement rates; and

254

- where transactions have not been settled at balance sheet date, the receivables or liabilities arising from those transactions should be carried in the balance sheet at the closing rates, except where forward contracts have been concluded as a hedge against the exchange difference.

The exchange differences which arise as a result of the application of these policies should be shown in the income statement in the period in which they have arisen.

As far as activities in foreign entities are concerned, their assets and liabilities should be translated at the closing rate. The translation difference arising on the shareholders' equity as at the beginning of the reporting period should be credited or charged directly to the shareholders' equity of the reporting parent company.

As far as direct foreign operations are concerned, the assets, liabilities, income and expenditure should be translated as if they directly formed part of the financial statements of the reporting parent company. The corresponding translation differences should be shown in the profit and loss account as part of the results from ordinary operations.

Taxation

The balance sheet and the profit and loss account which are included in the financial statements also form an appendix to the corporate income tax return which has to be filed after the end of each financial year. The return itself is based on a comparison of the net fiscal assets at the beginning and end of the financial period. The financial period normally runs for a period of twelve months.

The net assets for corporate income tax purposes do not have to be equal to the net assets shown in the annual financial statements. Differences can arise as a result of the following:

- depreciation of assets shown in the financial statements is not always on the same basis as the tax authorities consider acceptable;

- the methods of valuing stock which are normally acceptable for fiscal purposes are limited to the lower of historical cost price or net realisable value. The only other systems allowed are the base stock system and LIFO but only under restricted conditions;

- the equalisation reserve for certain grants, related to assets, given by the government up to and including 1989;

- unrealised gains on revalued assets are not taxable until realised;

- dividends paid are not deductible for corporate tax purposes; and

- dividends received (generally even from abroad) are not subject to corporate income tax.

The above differences may result in a deferred tax liability usually accounted for in the financial statements on the basis of the actual (that is, not discounted) tax rate.

Unusual and Prior Period Items

The law states that extraordinary income and expenditure includes that which does not result from the normal business operations of the enterprise. Unless this income and expenditure is immaterial in comparison with the result for the year, its nature and size should be explained in the notes.

This also applies to income and expenditure that should be allocated to another accounting period, to the extent that it is not included in extraordinary income and expenditure.

There are no legal provisions relating to items of income and expenditure which are considerably greater than normal. The Guidelines, however, state that if these arise out of normal business activities, they should not be shown as extraordinary income or expenditure. However, the size of such items may well imply that they should be shown seperately in the income statement or in the notes to the financial statements.

Retirement Benefits

The Guidelines state that if an enterprise has granted unconditional rights to a pension, this should be shown in the financial statements. The same rule applies in respect of a definite intention to make legally binding pension arrangements. Unconditional pension obligations should be shown in the balance sheet to the extent that they are not already financed.

Under the Pensions and Savings Act where these funds provide legally enforceable pensions they should be held by a life insurance company or a company pension fund or a special pension fund for companies in a particular industry.

If a funding deficit arises it should be accounted for in the financial statements. The notes to the financial statements should disclose the policies relating to pension charges and provisions for pension liabilities, adopted in determining the company's financial position and results.

Charges arising from pension entitlements are part of the operating result, with the exception of back service charges arising from new schemes or improvements in the way entitlements are regulated. These back service charges should be considered as extraordinary charges.

Provision should also be made in the annual financial statements for liabilities arising from early retirement schemes. The provision should be made in respect of all employees who have opted to avail themselves of the scheme for the entire period for which those employees have been promised payments under such a scheme. It should be explained in the notes to the financial statements how the provision has been calculated.

Although there are similarities between the early retirement provisions and the provision for pension liabilities the essential difference lies in the limited duration of early retirement schemes.

Related Party Transactions

The following is required by law to be disclosed in the financial statements:

● receivables arising from loans and advances to members or holders of registered shares and balances with group companies;

● the aggregate amount of remuneration, including pension charges, and of any other distributions to directors and former directors and, separately, to supervisory directors and former supervisory directors. In a group situation the amounts disclosed should include payments made by the parent, its subsidiaries and other group companies; and

● receivables and guarantees to or for directors and supervisory directors given by the enterprise, its subsidiaries and the companies included in the consolidation. Any amounts outstanding, the rate of interest, the other principal provisions and the repayments made during the financial year should also be disclosed.

Segmental Reporting

If an enterprise, classified as large, carries on business in different sectors, net turnover must be analysed between those sectors. Similarly net turnover must be divided into the various geographical areas in which the enterprise supplies goods and services. This information should also be disclosed on a consolidated level where relevant.

The Minister of Economic Affairs may grant dispensation from these obligations if satisfied that this disclosure may be prejudicial to the interests of the enterprise.

Treatment of Grants

The Guidelines contain provisions relating to the following subsidies and facilities provided by the government or equivalent bodies:

● operating subsidies;
● investment subsidies;
● finance facilities; and
● development credits.

A subsidy may not be credited directly to shareholders' equity.

Operating subsidies should be credited to the period in which the subsidised expenditure is charged or in which the revenues have been lost.

Netherlands

Investment subsidies should either be accounted for separately through an equalisation account or be deducted from the cost of the investment. Each year a part of the equalisation account should be released to the profit and loss account.

The amount of a finance facility should be included as a liability in the balance sheet. If at a later date it is decided that the credit need not be repaid, the amount which becomes available should be regarded as either a cost subsidy or as an investment subsidy.

Development credits should be deducted from the related development costs themselves. If, subsequently, the financial results of the project are such that repayment of the credits is required, the repayment and any interest due are treated as costs of future turnover.

Commitments and Contingencies

Where a provision for a liability is not included in the balance sheet because it is not possible to make a reasonable estimate of the amount of such an obligation, the notes should disclose the nature of the contingencies and commitments, the uncertain factors affecting the future outcome and the fact that a reasonable estimate cannot be made.

Contingent income should not be accounted for in the annual financial statements unless it is almost certain that the income will be received.

Balances not Reflected in the Balance Sheet

The law requires that any major financial commitments entered into by an enterprise for a number of years in the future and which are not shown in the balance sheet, such as those arising out of long term contracts, shall be disclosed, identifying separately commitments relating to group companies.

Price Level Changes

The law does not require the effect of inflation to be shown in the financial statements. However, if the financial statements have been drawn up on the basis of historical cost the Guidelines state that, in order to comply with the general requirements of a true and fair view, consideration must be given to including financial information on the basis of current value in the notes.

Future Developments

Since the implementation of the Fourth and Seventh EC Directives no major developments in accounting have occurred or are to be expected.

The implementation of the Eighth EC Directive, however, will have a significant impact on the requirements of persons who are qualified to carry out an audit. At the moment only members of the NIVRA or duly authorised foreign accountants may carry out audits. The expectation is that, under the requirements of the Eighth EC-Directive, Accountants Administration Consultants, members of the NOVAA, may also be qualified to carry out audits. This will result in a new qualification: the Certified Accountant.

New Zealand

Spicer & Oppenheim

As a member of the Commonwealth with a strong English and Scottish element in its population, it is natural that New Zealand should closely follow accounting principles established in the United Kingdom. The Companies Act of 1955 embodies to a considerable extent the requirements of UK Companies Acts prior to the implementation by the United Kingdom of the EC Fourth Directive. Financial statements are prepared on the basis of a true and fair view and follow the traditional concept of presenting to shareholders a historical record of the performance and state of affairs of the company and the use it makes of available resources. As in the United Kingdom, the inclusion of items in the financial statements is based on a normal commercial view and is not dictated by tax requirements or regulations.

There is only one professional body of accountants in New Zealand, the New Zealand Society of Accountants (NZSA), which is responsible for the control and regulation of its accountancy profession. Members of the Society are designated Chartered Accountants and no person who is not a member is permitted to carry out company audits. Only public companies are required to have an audit; private companies can dispense with an audit if the shareholders unanimously so resolve.

Although the Companies Act sets the minimum disclosure requirements, the NZSA prescribes its own Statements of Standard Accounting Practice (SSAP's) or Financial Reporting Standards (FRS's) as some are now called. These effectively govern the standard and content of the financial statements of reporting entities and members are expected to observe these standards.

Farming and farm-based products are an important sector of the New Zealand economy. Diversification is taking place and other commodities, for example, forestry-based products, and manufacturing industries, are growing in importance. Deregulation of foreign exchange and banking has allowed entrepreneurial ventures more freedom, particularly in expanding their offshore activities.

As in similar overseas economies, small to medium-sized businesses predominate and, in New Zealand, constitute nearly 90% in number of all businesses. New Zealand has three active stock exchanges in Auckland, Wellington and Christchurch.

New Zealand

Form and Content of Financial Statements

The form and content of a company's financial statements are prescribed by law (Companies Act of 1955). In addition, generally accepted accounting principles are established by the NZSA and laid down in SSAP's, FRS's and other guidance statements. These are not mandatory in law, even for quoted companies, though reference to non-compliance will be made in the audit report. The directors are responsible for the preparation of a company's financial statements which should contain:

- Directors' report
- Income Statement
- Balance Sheet
- Notes to the financial statements including the accounting policies
- Statement of cashflows
- Audit report

Comparative figures must be shown. Holding companies must publish group financial statements, normally in the form of consolidated financial statements, dealing with the group as a whole. Many companies also publish a chairman's statement.

Companies listed on the stock exchange are subject to additional regulations, including:

- prerequisites for admission to the official list;

- prerequisites for quotation of issues;

- continuing listing requirements;

- the production of:

  - a half yearly report to be lodged with the Exchange within four months of the end of the half year,
  - a year end announcement to be made within three months of the end of the financial year, and

- the production of an annual report to be published and issued to the shareholders within four months of the end of the financial year which includes details of:

  - the largest 20 shareholders.
  - the directors' holdings.
  - a detailed spread of shareholders within one month of publishing the report.

A company, to be considered for a standard listing, must have a minimum issue of securities of NZ$10m, and either:

- at least 200 shareholders holding at least 25% of the issued capital; or

● at least 500 shareholders, with marketable parcels of shares, holding 15% of the share capital.

Public Filing Requirements

A distinction is made in law between a private company and a public company:

● A public company issues a prospectus inviting the public to subscribe for shares. The company cannot allot any such shares unless the minimum subscription has been subscribed and the sum payable on application has been received by the company.

● A private company is expressly prohibited from issuing a prospectus inviting subscriptions from the public for shares. It must have a minimum of 2 but not more than 25 members and all of its share capital must be subscribed for in the memorandum, which must state that the company is a private company.

All public companies and overseas companies must file audited financial statements (including the directors' and auditors' report) and an annual return each year with the Registrar of Companies. Private companies need only file the annual return. These are all available for public inspection.

The annual return contains details of:

● the registered office;
● the authorised share capital and issued share capital;
● the total amount of mortgages and charges on the company's assets;
● shareholders and their shareholdings; and
● directors and secretaries.

A public company has four months after the year end to file audited financial statements with the Stock Exchange and their accounts are required to be laid before the members within nine months of their year end. The penalty for non-compliance with this provision is a fine of $NZ400.

All financial statements presented in New Zealand are required to be either in English or able to be readily convertible into the English language.

The standard accounting period of accounts in New Zealand is twelve months.

Valuation Principles

New Zealand companies follow the historical cost convention, the assets and liabilities of the company generally being stated at original cost subject to depreciation or provision for diminution of value. Exceptions to the historical cost convention have been introduced through SSAP17 and SSAP28.

New Zealand

Under SSAP17, properties meeting the definition of investment properties must be revalued on a yearly basis by an independent valuer. SSAP28 allows for the revaluation of Fixed Assets.

The surplus or deficit arising on revaluation must be transferred to a revaluation reserve which is reflected under Capital on the Balance Sheet.

SSAP1 requires that the accounting policies applied to items which are material or critical to the financial statements should be disclosed. It also assumes that the fundamental principles listed in the introduction to the Standard have been followed unless stated to the contrary.

Group Financial Statements

Group financial statements, normally in the form of consolidated financial statements, must be prepared when one company controls directly, indirectly, or beneficially, the majority of another company's equity share capital, its voting rights, the voting rights of the board of directors, or the right to more than 50% of earnings or dividends.

SSAP8 provides guidelines for determining the appropriate method of consolidation.

● The purchase method: when one of the parties to a business combination can be identified as the acquirer.

● The pooling of interests method: when none of the parties to a business combination can be identified as the acquirer.

● The equity method: to be used for accounting for associates and subsidiaries or "in-substance" subsidiaries which have not been consolidated.

A company is deemed to be an "in-substance" subsidiary of another if that other company obtains by any plan, arrangement or device, in substance, the benefits or risks of majority ownership or control.

Group financial statements need not include those subsidiaries where, in the directors' opinion:

● it would be impracticable or would be of no real value;
● the result would be misleading or harmful; or
● the businesses are so different that they cannot reasonably be treated as a single undertaking.

The form and content of the group financial statements are prescribed by law and are substantially the same as for single companies.

The audit report for consolidated financial accounts gives an opinion as to the company and its subsidiaries as a whole.

Depreciation

SSAP3 states that the cost of any fixed asset which has a limited economic useful life, less its estimated residual value, should be depreciated or amortised systematically over that life. For each class of fixed asset, disclosure must be made of:

- the cumulative depreciation at both the beginning and the end of the financial year;
- the economic lives or the depreciation rates used;
- the amount provided in the year and methods used; and
- the amount of any other adjustments (including those arising from disposals).

SSAP3 requires depreciation to be charged on fixed assets, including buildings but not freehold land.

Leasing

SSAP18 requires a finance lease to be reflected in the balance sheet of a lessee by recording an asset and a liability at amounts equal, at the inception of the lease, to the fair value of the leased property. Lease payments should be apportioned between the finance charge and the reduction of the outstanding liability.

The basis used to allocate income, which should be disclosed in the financial statements, should be designed to produce a constant periodic rate of return. The disclosures given should indicate whether the return relates to the net investment outstanding or the net cash investment outstanding in the lease.

The gross investment in finance leases should also be disclosed in the financial statements together with the related unearned finance income and unguaranteed residual values of leased assets.

Research and Development

SSAP13 prohibits the inclusion of research costs (other than market research activities) as an asset in the balance sheet but allows development costs to be deferred in specific circumstances. If development costs of a project are deferred, they should be amortised on a systematic basis by reference either to the sales or use of the product or process or to the time period over which the product or process is expected to be sold or used. Costs written off cannot later be reinstated.

There is no requirement to disclose the total charged to the profit and loss account, although movements in and the balance of unamortised deferred development costs should be disclosed, together with the basis of amortisation.

The accounting policy adopted for the costs of research and development activities should be included in the statement of accounting policies. If development costs are deferred, the basis of amortisation should be disclosed.

Inventories

Inventories are usually divided into three categories:

- Raw materials and consumables
- Work in Progress
- Finished Goods

Inventories are included at the purchase price or production cost of each individual item, or groups of similar items, or at net realisable value if lower. Purchase price is the actual price paid plus any expenses incidental to acquisition. Production cost is the total of the purchase price of raw material and consumables used and direct production overheads which relate to putting the inventories into their present location and condition.

In determining purchase price or production cost, the tax legislation allows FIFO, weighted average or any other similar method to be used, although SSAP4 considers that in most cases FIFO or weighted average should be used.

SSAP14 deals with long-term contracts where the work extends for more than a year. Such contracts should be shown at cost to date plus an appropriate portion of attributable profit less foreseeable losses and progress payments.

There should be a separate disclosure in the financial statements of:

- the gross amount of contract work in progress; and
- the total of cash received and receivable as progress payments, advances and retention on account of contract work in progress.

Intangible Assets

The most common form of intangible asset is goodwill. This is becoming less common in recent years. The usual treatment of goodwill is to amortise it over a 25 year period. Goodwill is required to be disclosed separately in the financial statements.

Capital and Reserves

The treatment of capital redemption reserves, share premium accounts and revaluation reserves follows UK practice. New Zealand law, however, has not followed the UK Companies Act 1981 that incorporated the requirements of the EC Fourth Directive relating to distributions. It would therefore seem that UK practice prior to 1981 would be followed, which means that accumulated prior period losses need not necessarily be made good before distributing current year's profit.

Proposed dividends are provided in the financial statements for the year to which they relate.

Any movement in capital or reserves should be disclosed in the balance sheet by way of a note.

Foreign Currency Translation

SSAP21 deals with accounting for the effects of changes in foreign currency exchange rates. Exchange gains and losses should be recognised in the profit and loss account in the period in which the exchange differences occurred. At the balance sheet date all foreign assets and liabilities should be translated at the closing rate in the case of an independent foreign operation, and in the same way as the underlying transactions in the case of an integrated foreign operation.

Exchange differences should not be classified as an extraordinary item unless the difference relates to an item that is itself extraordinary.

The following disclosures are required:

● the methods used to translate foreign currency transactions and the financial statements of foreign operations;

● the net exchange difference included in the profit and loss account for the period;

● a reconciliation of the opening and closing balances of the foreign currency translation reserve showing separately the aggregate amount offset in the reserve as a result of hedging foreign currency liabilities against foreign currency non-monetary assets and/or investment in independent foreign operations; and

● the exchange difference remaining to be amortised as a result of hedging a foreign currency liability by a future income stream, or vice versa.

Taxation

Companies pay company tax based on their trading profit as reported in their financial statements for the accounting period after making the following adjustments:

● General or contingent provisions are not deductible.

● Dividends paid are not deductible. Under the imputation credit system however, a shareholder can receive credit for the company tax paid.

● Depreciation is usually charged in the financial statements at the rates published by the Inland Revenue Department. For this reason little or no adjustment is required for tax purposes.

Where accounting income differs from taxable income, it is standard accounting practice (SSAP12) to make provision for:

● permanent differences arising from special legislation, that is economic, political, or administrative reasons. The tax cost or saving is included in the normal charge for the year;

New Zealand

- timing differences in charges and credits to income. These require an allocation of taxes to be made between those years affected by setting up a deferred tax account; and

- differences arising from direct charging or crediting to retained earnings, or extraordinary gains/losses included in the computation of taxable net income. These require an allocation of taxes to be made among the items affected in the year.

Income tax benefits arising from income tax losses should be recognised only to the extent of accumulated net credits from timing differences in the deferred tax account unless there is virtual certainty that they will be realised.

Extraordinary and Prior Period Items

Two recent exposure drafts have been released in NZ dealing with these issues.

ED57A,which is expected to become a standard in 1993 tightens the definition of extraordinary items. To be extraordinary under the new definition, an item must meet all of the following criteria:

- infrequency of occurrence (not more than every three years);

- the event or transaction is outside the ordinary operations of the entity; and

- the event or transaction is outside the control or influence of managers or owners.

The effect of this tightening of definition means that events such as the sale of an investment not acquired with the intention of resale is no longer classed as extraordinary.

Related Party Transactions

Related party disclosures are dealt with in SSAP22. This states that where there has been a material transaction between the reporting entity and its related party or parties, there needs to be disclosed:

- the identity of each related party involved and the nature of their relationship;

- the type of transactions involved;

- total debts with related parties that have been written off or forgiven during the reporting period; and
- the recorded value of the transactions with related parties expressed either in dollar terms or as a percentage of the value of all transactions and the terms of settlement for these balances.

When the reporting entity is controlled by another entity, the name of that related party and also, if applicable, the name of the entity ultimately controlling that party should be disclosed.

If a transaction between related parties takes place at a nil or nominal value, a brief description of the transaction and the fact that no charge has been made must be given.

Segmental Reporting

A new SSAP was introduced in April 1990 dealing with segmental reporting. This states that for each industry and geographical segment, the following information should be disclosed:

- segment revenue, distinguishing between revenue derived from customers outside the reporting entity and revenue derived from other segments;

- segment result;

- the carrying amount of segment assets;

- the basis of inter-segment pricing; and

- abnormal items.

The SSAP also states that where the reporting entity presents consolidated financial statements, segmental information need only be presented in the consolidated financial statements and not in the parent entity's financial statements.

Treatment of Grants

SSAP16 requires that Government grants should be recognised in the income statement on a systematic basis. However, no recognition should occur until all conditions attached to the grant have been complied with. Grants in the income statement should be recognised as separate items.

Commitments and Contingencies

The treatment of contingencies is dealt with in SSAP15. This states that the amount of the contingent loss should be accrued if:

- it is expected that future events will confirm that, after taking into account any related probable recovery, an asset has been impaired or a liability incurred at the balance sheet date; and

- a reasonable estimate of the amount of the resulting loss can be made.

New Zealand

The disclosure of a contingent liability or capital commitment should be given by way of a note to the financial statements if either of the above two conditions is not met.

Contingent gains should not be accrued in financial statements. Their existence should be disclosed by way of a note if it is probable that the gain will be realised.

If disclosure is required, the following information should be given:

● the nature of the contingency;

● the uncertain factors that may affect the future outcome;

● an estimate of the financial effect net of any tax implications, or a statement that such an estimate cannot be made; and

● the existence of counter claims that could reduce the financial effect of exposure.

Price Level Changes

There are currently no guidelines for dealing with price level changes in NZ. The previous guidelines in place have been removed.

Future Developments

The structure of financial statements in NZ is expected to change significantly in the near future. A new framework is being introduced, which will result in a change to the financial statements produced. These changes will include statements of:

● financial performance;
● changes in financial wealth (unless exempt);
● financial position;
● cashflows (unless exempt); and
● service performance (unless exempt).

This new framework also introduced the concept of Differential Reporting. This concept presents the notion that some entities should be able to depart from particular requirements of accounting standards in their financial records.

The framework establishes the criteria which will enable entities to determine whether or not they are eligible. This criteria basically operates on a cost/benefit basis taking into consideration the size and ownership of the business.

Major changes are also being proposed for the Companies Act. These changes are presently before Parliament and the Bill is expected to be passed in July 1993.

The major proposals in the Bill are as follows:

- There will no longer be any distinction between private and public companies.

- Instead of companies having Articles and Memoranda of Association, the Companies Bill allows for them to have a Constitution. This will now have a statement of deviations from the Constitution which will be embodied in the Act.

- Par value and nominal capital will no longer be applicable.

- Companies will be able to purchase and finance their own shares.

- More protection will be available for minority shareholders.

- Directors will be more tightly controlled.

Nigeria

Sulaimon and Co

In recent years a number of changes have taken place in the development and preparation of Nigerian Financial Statements. There has been important new legislation which superseded previous laws and a major change in the economic policy of the country whereby substantial controlling shareholdings held by Government in parastatals and major banks have been relinquished. This privatisation exercise has not however affected the strict requirements involved in the preparation of financial statements.

As regards legislation, the Companies and Allied Matters Decree 1990 has been promulgated to supersede the Companies Act of 1968, as a result of which there have been changes to the presentation and contents of and disclosures in published financial statements.

The Nigerian Accounting Standards Board (NASB), established in 1982, is still the major body involved in setting Accounting and Reporting Standards. It has a broad membership drawn from all relevant sectors of the economy and it is charged with formulating and publishing Accounting Standards to be observed in the preparation of financial statements, promoting and sponsoring legislation and, from time to time, reviewing standards developed in the light of changes in the socio-economic and political environment.

The Taxation Authorities' criteria for determining acceptable accounting treatment are based on the requirements of the relevant sections of the Companies and Allied Matters Decree 1990.

Form and Content of Financial Statements

The form and contents of a company's financial statements are prescribed by the law embodied in the Companies and Allied Matters Decree 1990. The Directors are charged with the responsibility for preparing the financial statements of a company which are subsequently audited. The basic contents of a set of financial statements are:-

Nigeria

- Report of the Directors

- Report of the Auditors

- Balance Sheet

- Profit and Loss Account

- Statement of Source and Application of Funds

- Statement of Value Added

- Five Year Financial Summary

- Notes to the Financial Statements

- General Information such as the names of Directors, the Auditors, registered office and secretaries

Comparative figures must be given where applicable. Holding companies must publish group financial statements in the form of consolidated financial statements dealing with the group as a whole.

Filing Requirements

All companies, both private and public, are required to file their audited financial statements together with their annual returns with the Registrar of Companies, Corporate Affairs Commission at Abuja, the new capital of the country.

The audited financial statements only are expected to be filed at least 42 days after the Annual General Meeting for the year, whether or not that meeting is the first or only ordinary general meeting of the company in the year. By virtue of the financial statements being publicly filed, any interested party has access to the published financial statements.

If a company, which is required to comply with any of the provisions of the Companies Decree in respect of filing, defaults then the company and every director or officer of the company in default shall be liable to a fine.

The annual return contains details of:-

- the name and address of the registered office of the company;

- the situation of the registers of members and their shareholdings;

- particulars of mortgages and charges on the company's assets;

- particulars of Directors and Secretaries; and

- the issued, authorised and total paid-up capital.

Financial statements which are filed must be in English and denominated in Naira (N). Normally financial statements filed are for a 12 month period. This could however vary where a company commences or ceases business in which case it may be more or less than 12 calendar months.

Audit Requirements

All limited liability companies are by law required to have auditors. Only members of the Institute of Chartered Accountants of Nigeria (ICAN), currently the only recognised body of Accountants established in Nigeria, are qualified to act as company auditors.

They are expected to report on whether in their opinion:

● all information and explanations considered necessary have been received;

● proper books of account have been kept;

● the financial statements are in agreement with the books of accounts and returns and give a true and fair view of the state of financial affairs;

● the requirements of the Productivity, Prices and Income Board Guidelines have been complied with; and

● the requirements of the relevant legislation have been complied with.

Valuation Principles

Nigerian companies still adopt the historical cost convention in the valuation of their assets and liabilities although provision is made for the revaluation of fixed assets at their market value from time to time.

Group Financial Statements

Group financial statements are required to be prepared by the directors of a holding company where it has one or more subsidiary companies at the end of the period, except where:

● the company is the wholly owned subsidiary of another body corporate incorporated in Nigeria; or

● the directors are of the view that:-

    – it is impracticable in view of the insignificant amounts involved, or
    – it would involve expense or delay out of proportion to the value to members of the company, or
    – the result would be misleading or harmful to the business of the company or any of its subsidiaries, or
    – the business of the holding company and that of the subsidiary are so different that they cannot reasonably be treated as a single undertaking.

Nigeria

The group financial statements of a company consist of:

● a consolidated balance sheet of the company and its subsidiaries; and

● the profit and loss account of the company and its subsidiaries.

The equity method of accounting may be used for accounting for investments in subsidiaries.

Accounting Issues

The accounting treatment allowed and/or required and the disclosure requirements for each of the following areas are as set out in the relevant standards issued by the Nigerian Accounting Standards Board (SAS). Where no SAS has been issued the relevant International Accounting Standard (IAS) is followed.

● Depreciation – SAS 9 which complies with IAS 4 and the relevant parts of IAS 25

● Leasing – SAS 11 which complies with IAS 17

● Research and Development – Compliance with IAS 9 is required

● Inventories – Compliance with IAS 2 is required

● Intangible Assets – There is no Nigerian Standard in this regard

● Capital and Reserves – Compliance with the relevant parts of SAS 2 is required

● Foreign Currency Translation – SAS 7 which complies with IAS 21

● Taxation – Compliance with IAS 12 is required

● Unusual and Prior Period Items – Compliance with IAS 8 is required

● Retirement Benefits – SAS 8 which complies with IAS 19 and 26

● Related Party Transactions – Directors and others – Compliance with IAS 24 is required

● Segmental Reporting – Compliance with IAS 14 is required

● Treatment of Grants – Revenue and Capital – Compliance with IAS 20 is required

● Contingencies and Commitments/Balances not reflected on the Balance Sheet – Compliance with IAS 10 is required

● Price Level Changes – Compliance with IAS 15 is required

Future Developments

The professional requirements as to the form, content and audit of financial statements are expected to change in the near future to accommodate the country's ever changing social and economic environment.

The Nigerian Accounting Standards Board (NASB) is also expected to issue additional standards. It is doing its best to ensure the adoption and implementation of the standards with the active participation of its member organisations.

Pakistan

S M Masood & Co

Pakistan's accounting legislation was originally embodied in the Companies Act 1913, a legacy of the British Empire. In 1984, to cater for the changing environment of industry, commerce and communication, major legislation relating to Company Law was consolidated. Accounting legislation is now contained in the Companies Ordinance 1984, Banking Companies Ordinance 1962 and Insurance Act 1938, as subsequently amended. With the advent of the Institute of Chartered Accountants of Pakistan (ICAP) in 1961, the accounting profession has developed generally accepted accounting principles which attempt to ensure accounts show a true and fair view of a company's financial affairs. The accounting standards have legislative backing.

The pronouncements and guidelines issued by ICAP are influenced by International Accounting Standards (IAS). Generally IAS are adopted unchanged. Wherever necessary, however, modifications or supplementary guidelines are issued by ICAP to meet local requirements. The Ministry of Finance, through the Corporate Law Authority (CLA) (the regulatory body for the affairs of companies) and the State Bank of Pakistan, to a lesser extent but particularly in respect of banking companies and non-banking financial institutions, are also involved in the setting of accounting disclosure requirements.

Professional requirements are normally adhered to when preparing financial statements for organisations other than companies, such as co-operative societies.

Financial statements are prepared in accordance with the accounting standards, notwithstanding the specific legal provisions in tax laws.

Form and Content of Financial Statements

The form and content of a company's financial statements are prescribed by law embodied in the Companies Ordinance 1984 and other statutes such as the Banking Companies Ordinance 1962 and Insurance Act 1938 (as amended) supplemented by pronouncements from the CLA and, in respect of banking and non-banking financial institutions, by the State Bank of Pakistan.

Pakistan

The responsibility for the preparation and presentation of financial statements for shareholders, showing a true and fair view of the company's financial state of affairs, is that of the directors of the company. The financial statements must contain:

● Directors' Report

● Balance Sheet

● Profit and Loss Account or Income and Expenditure Account

● Notes to the Financial Statements, including the accounting policies adopted

● Auditors' Report

Where fundamental accounting assumptions of going concern, consistency and accruals are not followed, the background to and the reasons for this must be disclosed.

In addition to the above for companies listed on stock exchanges, the financial statements are required to:

● be prepared in accordance with International Accounting Standards and other standards as notified by the CLA;

● include a Statement of Sources and Application of Funds; and

● where applicable give notes about the capacity of the industrial unit, its actual production and the reasons for any shortfall and credit facilities available but not used.

The financial statements of a holding company must include financial statements for each of its subsidiaries together with a statement of the holding company's interest in the subsidiary companies. Where the financial year of the holding company and subsidiaries do not coincide, additional details are required to be included in the financial statements regarding any change in the holding company's interest and material changes in a subsidiary's fixed assets, investments, monies lent and long term borrowings by it, between the end of the financial year of the subsidiary and that of the holding company.

Under the Companies Ordinance 1984, the directors' report includes a commentary on the state of the company's affairs, the dividend recommended and amounts proposed to be transferred to reserves. For a public company or private company which is a subsidiary of a public company, the directors are also required to report on:

● material changes and commitments affecting the financial position of the company between the end of the company's financial year and the date of the report;

- any changes during the financial year concerning the nature of the company's business or that of its subsidiaries; and

- reservations and qualifications contained in the auditors' report.

and to include:

- information about the pattern of shareholdings; and

- the name and, if established outside Pakistan, the country of incorporation of its holding company.

Comparative figures are also required to be shown in the financial statements for all companies.

Companies listed on a stock exchange are required to prepare their financial statements in accordance with the Fourth Schedule to the Companies Ordinance 1984 and other companies in accordance with the Fifth Schedule. Insurance, banking and other companies or organisations regulated by separate statutes are required to prepare their financial statements in accordance with those statutes. Insurance companies are also required to include in the financial statements a classified summary of their assets, giving both their book value and their market value.

There is only one permitted format of financial statements both for presentation to shareholders and for public filing.

Public Filing Requirements

Presently the Companies Ordinance 1984 recognises the following type of companies:

- Private limited company, whereby the company cannot invite the public to subscribe for its shares, the shares are not freely transferable and its members are limited to fifty.

- Public limited company being a company which is not a private company.

- Listed company being a company or a body corporate or other body, whose securities are listed on a stock exchange.

Whereas all companies are required to file Annual Returns with the Registrar of Companies, only listed companies are required to file financial statements with the CLA the Registrar of Companies and the Stock Exchanges.

Every company is required to hold its first Annual General Meeting within eighteen months of its incorporation and thereafter at least once in every calendar year, within six months of its financial year end and not more than fifteen months after the holding of its last preceding Annual General Meeting. This timescale for holding annual meetings, except the first, may be extended by up to ninety days at the discretion of the CLA or the Registrar of Companies.

Pakistan

Financial statements are required to be filed simultaneously with the notice of the Annual General Meeting which must be issued at least twenty-one days before the meeting. The Annual Return is filed within forty-five days of the Annual General Meeting for listed companies and within thirty days for other companies.

The Annual Return contains the following particulars of the company:

- Registered Office, Principal or Head Office of the Company

- Share Capital and Debentures

- Indebtedness

- Holding Company and Subsidiaries of the Company

- Past and Present Members and Debenture Holders

- Past and Present Directors, Chief Executive, Managing Agents, Secretary, Auditors and Legal Advisors

The financial statements and the Annual Returns filed with the Registrar of Companies are open to public inspection.

No exemptions or alternatives are available for filing financial statements for listed companies and for filing of the Annual Return for all companies. Accordingly there are no remedies for filing financial statements which do not comply with legal/professional requirements.

Penalties for non-compliance with the provisions of the relevant laws include imprisonment for up to one year and a fine of up to Rs. 20,000 with additional fines for each day the default continues. Penalties of imprisonment and fines are also imposed on auditors but to a lesser degree as compared with directors and other officers of the company.

Financial statements and Annual Returns are normally prepared in English and the reporting currency is Pakistan Rupees.

The length of the accounting period is twelve months except where special permission has been granted by the Registrar of Companies. The directors of a holding company are required to ensure that the financial year of each of its subsidiaries coincides with the company's own financial year, unless in the opinion of the directors there are good reasons for not doing so. Taxation authorities have specified year ends for certain industries like textiles and sugar. With the exception of stipulated industries, any variation in the length of the accounting period and year end can only be made after the approval of the taxation authorities.

Audit Requirements

Every company under the Companies Ordinance 1984 is required to have auditors.

Only chartered accountants within the meaning of the Chartered Accountants Ordinance 1961 are qualified to act as auditors of a public company or a private company which is a subsidiary of a public company. There are no qualifications specified for auditors of private companies except that private companies with share capital of Rs. 3 million, or more, are required under the Income Tax Ordinance to have their financial statements audited by Chartered Accountants. A body corporate or a person who is a director, officer or employee of a company or who is indebted to the company cannot be appointed as its auditor.

The auditor is appointed each year by the shareholders in the Annual General Meeting (AGM) and reports to them whether in his opinion the financial statements show a true and fair view of the state of affairs of the company and of the profit or loss for the year and, in the case of listed companies, of the changes in the financial position or the sources and application of funds for the year. Additionally, the auditor must also comment and express an opinion on certain matters as specified by the Companies Ordinance, 1984 including whether:

- the auditor has obtained all the information and explanations necessary for the purposes of the audit;

- proper books of account have been maintained;

- the financial statements are in agreement with the books of account and whether they have been drawn up in compliance with the Companies Ordinance 1984;

- expenditure incurred was for the purpose of the company's business; and

- the business conducted, investments made and expenditure incurred were in accordance with the objects of the company.

The audit report also refers to:

- the consistency of accounting policies applied or any changes since the previous years; and

- departures from standard accounting practices and whether the auditor concurs with these departures.

Where in addition to the Companies Ordinance 1984 a company is also regulated by any other legislation such as the Banking Companies Ordinance 1962 or the Insurance Act 1938, the auditor also reports whether compliance has been made with the requirements of those statutes. The Insurance Act & Rules specifically require the auditor to report whether any assets of the life insurance funds have been applied in contravention of the provisions of the Act and to certify that he has verified the cash balances and securities relating to insurers' loans, reversions and life interests and investments. The auditor must also report on the extent to which he has verified investment transactions relating to any trusts undertaken by the insurers.

Valuation Principles

In preparation of the financial statements Pakistani companies adopt the historical cost convention. In recognising income and expenses and in determining the value of assets and liabilities, commercial reality prevails over legal form and the fundamental accounting assumptions of consistency, going concern, accruals and prudence are followed.

Fixed assets may be revalued and any surplus or deficit arising on such a revaluation is transferred to a separate non-distributable reserve. The Insurance Act 1938 allows the recognition of the Appreciation of Investments in the Profit and Loss Account.

Group Financial Statements

The legal framework for the corporate sector in Pakistan does not recognise the concept of Consolidated Financial Statements. Furthermore, taxation legislation does not have provisions that promote the need for preparation of Consolidated Financial Statements. However, the Accounting & Auditing Practices Committee (AAPC) of ICAP has issued a draft Statement of Standard Accounting Practice recommending a phased approach for the adoption of IAS 27 and 28.

Under the Companies Ordinance 1984 the balance sheet of the holding company is required to include certain particulars of its subsidiaries. The Ordinance defines that a company is a subsidiary of another company if the latter holds, or controls directly or indirectly, more than 50% of its voting securities or otherwise has power to elect and appoint 50% of its directors.

Exemptions are only available to the holding company for exclusion or variations in the treatment of a subsidiary on application to and approval of the CLA.

Group Financial Statements are prepared by attaching to the financial statements of the holding company, in respect of each subsidiary, the following:

● latest financial statements;

● directors' report;

● auditors' report on the financial statements; and

● a statement showing the extent of the holding company's interest in the subsidiary.

- a statement showing changes, if any, between the end of the financial year of the subsidiary and the end of the holding company's financial year in respect of the following:

  - the holding company's interest in the subsidiary,
  - the subsidiary's fixed assets,
  - the value of the investment,
  - money lent by the subsidiary, and
  - money borrowed by the subsidiary for purposes other than meeting current liabilities;

- a statement showing the net aggregate amount of profits, less losses, of the subsidiaries, so far as it concerns members of the holding company, which are not dealt with in the company's accounts; and

- a statement showing the net aggregate amounts of profits, less losses, of the subsidiaries, as far as those are not dealt with, or in case of losses not provided for, in the company's accounts.

As the financial statements of the subsidiary companies, which are prepared and audited by their directors and auditors, are attached to the accounts of the holding company, its auditor is only required to give his report on the financial statements of the holding company.

Depreciation

The application of IAS 4 on depreciation is mandatory for listed companies and is also generally adopted by other companies.

Recognised accounting principles require the cost of assets, less any salvage value, to be spread over their expected useful economic life in such a way as to allocate it, as equitably as possible, to the periods during which services are obtained from the use of the asset. Most physical assets including buildings, but not land, are deemed to have a limited useful life and are therefore depreciable.

The reducing balance method of depreciation is most commonly used. The depreciation method selected must be applied consistently from period to period unless altered circumstances justify a change. Where the method is changed, its effect must be quantified and disclosed together with the reason for the change. The financial statements are also required to show:

- the depreciation method and rates used;

- the amount charged or provided for depreciation during the year;

- the aggregate cost (or valuation) of each class of asset;
- the aggregate amount written off in respect of each class of asset since acquisition (or revaluation);

Pakistan

- the net book value of the asset after deducting the accumulated depreciation since the date of acquisition (or revaluation);

- where no depreciation is provided on any class of assets, the reasons must be disclosed and the effect quantified; and

- where any borrowing costs are capitalised, or any exchange variance included in the carrying value of the assets, their amounts and the depreciation policy relating to them must be disclosed.

Leasing

The law recognises IAS 17 on leasing. The method to be used for accounting for a lease depends upon whether the lease is classified as a finance lease or an operating lease.

A finance lease is reflected in the financial statements by recording an asset and liability at the lower of the fair value of the leased asset and the present value of the minimum lease payments for the lease term. Rentals are apportioned between the finance charge and a reduction of the liability. The finance charge is allocated over the lease term, so as to produce a consistent periodic rate of interest on the remaining balance of the liability for each accounting period. The leased asset is amortised in a manner consistent with the lessee's normal depreciation policy for owned assets. If there is uncertainty as to whether the lessee will obtain ownership by the end of the lease term, the asset is depreciated over the shorter of the lease term or its useful life.

The financial statements are required to identify separately each major class of asset subject to finance leases and to disclose:

- the aggregate amount of liabilities, differentiating between the current and long term portion;

- the interest rates used as the discount factor;

- the amount of minimum future lease payments and the periods in which they become due;

- purchase options; and

- financial restrictions imposed.

Where an operating lease exists, the charge to income is the rental expense for the accounting period recognised on a systematic basis which is representative of the benefits obtained from the use of the assets over the lease term.

For non-cancellable operating leases with a term of more than one year, disclosure must be given in summary form of minimum lease payments and the periods in which the payments will become due.

Research and Development

IAS 9 is followed and research and development costs are charged as an expense in the period that they are incurred. Where the costs are related to a product or process, which is clearly defined, technically feasible and commercially viable and adequate resources for completing and marketing the project are available, the development costs are deferred to future periods.

The deferred development costs are then allocated on a systematic basis to future accounting periods by reference either to the sale or use of the product or process or to the time period over which the product or process is expected to be sold or used.

Development costs once written off cannot later be reinstated.

The financial statements must disclose total research and development costs. Where any such costs are capitalised the financial statements must disclose the amounts capitalised, the amortisation for the year, any other movements in the year and the un-amortised balance at the year end. The reasons for carrying forward any such costs must also be disclosed.

Inventories

The principles set out in IAS 2 are applied and inventories are valued at the lower of historical cost and net realisable value.

Costs include production overheads and where applicable other overheads, to the extent that they clearly relate to putting the inventories into their present location and condition. Historical costs are generally accounted for using the FIFO or weighted average cost methods. Standard costing and the retail method of valuing stocks are only used where they give a fair and consistent approximation to actual costs.

The LIFO or base stock methods are rarely used. Where these methods are used, disclosure must be made of the difference between the carrying amount of stock and the amount arrived at using either the FIFO, weighted average or current cost methods.

Estimates of net realisable values are based on the most reliable evidence available at the time. The estimates are made as to what the inventories are expected to realise.

Under the Accounting Legislation, inventory should where practicable be analysed between stores, spares, loose tools, raw material and components, work in progress, finished goods and other stocks. SAP1 of the ICAP recommends that where a company holds stock to produce fixed assets for its own usage that stock should be shown as 'Capital Work in Progress' under Fixed Assets and described as Stores and Spares held for capital expenditure.

Other disclosure requirements include:

● reasons for not classifying inventories as specified above;

● the basis of valuation; and

● provisions for diminution in the value of inventory made as a deduction from the gross amount of stores, spares and tools, and stock in trade.

Intangible Assets

Presently accounting legislation does not specify the required treatment of Intangible Assets. However disclosure requirements are specified which are similar to those of tangible fixed assets.

These are:-

● the accounting policy used including amortisation/depreciation;

● the method of determining the carrying value (original cost or valuation) and movements in the period;

● amortisation/depreciation rates; and

● amounts written off.

Capital and Reserves

Capital and Reserves, commonly referred to as shareholders' equity, comprises issued share capital, reserves and retained earnings or unappropriated profits. Under the Companies Ordinance 1984 there is only one class of share capital that is ordinary shares, which must be fully paid and therefore the question of 'called up capital' or 'paid up capital' does not arise. The financial statements disclose Authorised, Issued and Subscribed Share Capital differentiating between shares issued for cash, other than cash and as bonus shares. In the case of a subsidiary company, the shares held by the holding company are identified.

Another form of capital, which is redeemable (participatory or otherwise), has been introduced in accordance with tenets of Islam. The most common types are 'participation term certificates' and 'term finance certificates'. The disclosures required include: the nominal value, material terms and conditions, nature of consideration, mode and basis of repayment or redemption, arrangements for sharing of profits and losses, provisions for participatory reserves, options for conversion into shares and the manner in which the redeemable capital has been secured.

Reserves are classified between capital and revenue reserves. Capital reserves include capital redemption reserve, share premium account and surplus on revaluation of fixed assets. Where a company issues shares at premium, whether in cash or otherwise, a sum equal to the aggregate amount or the value of the premiums on those shares is transferred to the share premium account.

The share premium account can only be utilised for:

● writing off preliminary expenses and any discount on the issue of shares;

● providing the premium payable on redemption of capital; and

● the issue of fully paid bonus shares.

Where a company revalues its fixed assets, an amount equivalent to the increase in the value is transferred to a surplus on revaluation of fixed assets account. This surplus cannot be applied to set off or reduce any deficit or loss, except to the extent that it is realised on the disposal of the assets, or diminution (deficit) arising from the revaluation of any other fixed assets of the company.

Revenue reserves include retained earnings (unappropriated profit and loss) and general reserves created out of retained earnings on the recommendation of the directors. Banks and financial institutions are required by their respective governing legislation and the pronouncements of the State Bank of Pakistan to maintain a specified level of capital and reserves.

Where accumulated losses exist these are deducted from capital and reserves.

Bonus shares can be issued out of distributable reserves to the extent that these reserves, after the bonus issue, are not less than 25% of the increased share capital.

Dividends, as recommended by the directors and approved by the shareholders, can only be paid out of the profits of the company, with the exception that no dividends can be paid out of profits arising out of the disposal of immovable property or assets of a capital nature, unless the business of the company is that of selling and purchasing such assets.

Dividends and bonus shares are charged to retained earnings when declared. In other situations, the amount transferred from retained earnings is governed by law. Movements in each reserve must be disclosed on the face of the balance sheet unless shown in the profit and loss account or notes to the accounts.

There are specific prohibitions in the Companies Ordinance. Companies are not allowed to buy their own shares or those of their holding companies, nor can they provide financial assistance to buy shares in their company unless the company is a private company which is not a subsidiary of a public limited company.

Foreign Currency Translation

The Companies Ordinance 1984 only deals with the treatment of exchange gains or losses relating to foreign currency borrowings used to buy assets. Such exchange

Pakistan

gains or losses can be added to or deducted from the value of the respective assets so long as the amounts involved, and the depreciation policy to be followed, are disclosed. For other purposes IAS 21 on Accounting for the Effects of Changes in Foreign Exchange is followed.

The financial statements disclose the methods used, net exchange difference taken to shareholders' interest or income or included in the carrying value of assets, the procedures selected for translating the income statement of foreign entities and, in respect of exchange differences deferred, the cumulative deferred amount still to be credited or charged to income.

Taxation

The accounting treatment of taxation is governed by the provision of the Companies Ordinance 1984 and the requirements by IAS 12 on Accounting for Taxes on Income.

Tax is payable at the rate of 44% by listed companies and 55% by other companies. Banking and insurance companies are subject to different rates and rules. Taxable income is arrived at after adjustments are made to the profits of the company.

The most common adjustments are:

● Depreciation. Accounting depreciation is substituted by depreciation calculated on the basis of rates specified by the taxation statutes.

● Lease Rentals. The Income Tax Ordinance recognises legal form and accordingly finance lease rentals are tax allowable deductions, whereas in the financial statements commercial form is recognised.

● Provisions. Increases in provisions are generally not deductible, nor are decreases in provision assessable. Only when amounts are actually incurred can they be claimed as deductions.

● Certain Expenses. Limits have been specified in the Income Tax Ordinance for allowing deduction of certain expenses such as donations etc.

● Tax Losses Brought Forward. Tax losses may be carried forward and off set against business income for a period of six years. Losses arising due to depreciation allowances can be carried forward indefinitely.

Where accounting income differs from taxable income provision for deferred taxation is made unless there is a reasonable probability that the timing differences will not reverse in the foreseeable future. Deferred tax debit balances should only be carried forward if there is a reasonable expectation of realisation.

The financial statements should disclose:

● the current tax charge, tax charges relating to prior periods, deferred taxation and tax on unusual or prior period items;

- an analysis of taxation between Pakistan Taxation, Overseas Taxation and taxation on income, capital gains and any other taxes;

- the relationship between the tax charge and accounting income, where it is not apparent from the application of effective tax rates, due to timing differences etc;

- details of both the effect of tax losses available and losses carried forward;

- the tax effects, if any, related to assets that have been revalued;

- the method used to account for deferred taxation;

- the extent to which, and the reasons for, provisions for deferred taxation have not been made; and

- the element of the deferred tax liability relating to the current financial year.

Unusual and Prior Period Items

IAS 8 on Unusual and Prior Period Items and Changes in Accounting Policies is followed.

Unusual items are included in net income, the nature and amount of each such item being separately disclosed.

Prior period items are reported either by adjusting opening retained earnings in the financial statements for the current period and making amendments to the comparative information in respect of prior years or including and separately disclosing them in the current income statement. Whichever method is applied, adequate disclosure must be made to facilitate comparison of figures.

A change in an accounting estimate is normally accounted for as part of income from the ordinary activities. Where the revision of an estimate relates to an item that was originally treated as an unusual item, it will also be treated as unusual.

The Companies Ordinance 1984 therefore only requires separate disclosure of losses or expenses and provision in respect of unusual and prior period items.

Retirement Benefits

In addition to obligatory statutory retirement schemes such as the Employees Old-Age Benefit Scheme, employers provide retirement benefits through participatory provident funds and superannuation schemes. Most of the retirement schemes and particularly the provident funds are established under a deed of trust, the operations of which are subject to detailed regulations. For other schemes provisions are made in financial statements in accordance with established legal commitments. Provisions are made for the accrued liability arising in accordance with the terms and conditions of the scheme.

Pakistan

The Companies Ordinance 1984 requires disclosure of deferred liabilities for pension, gratuity and other staff benefit schemes together with the accounting policy applied. Where the liability is secured on any assets of the company, this must be disclosed together with details of the classes of assets given as security. Where deferred liabilities are covered by investments, details must be given. Where full provision for pension liabilities has not been made, this fact, together with reasons for non-provisions, must be disclosed.

Related Party Transactions

Related parties include directors, the chief executive, managing agent and other executives, subsidiary and associated companies, or undertakings, and other organisations over which control exists.

Under the Companies Ordinance 1984 associated companies, or undertakings, are defined as those which are under common management, have common directors and where one company, or undertaking, or their directors, holds or controls shares, directly or indirectly, carrying not less than 20% of the voting power in another company or undertaking.

Extensive disclosures are required on the nature, extent and basis of a wide range of transactions with related parties, including purchase and sale of goods, interest payments and guarantees given.

If there are no transactions with related parties, disclosure is made of relationships which exist which give rise to control as required by IAS 24 on related party disclosures.

In addition to the above any balances, due to or from related parties, must be disclosed separately together with the maximum aggregate amount outstanding at the end of any month during the period.

Segmental Reporting

Under the Companies Ordinance 1984, where an undertaking has more than one line of business, the results of each one should be given separately provided that its turnover exceeds 20% of the total turnover of the company. Further disclosures are made in accordance with IAS 14 on Reporting Financial Information by Segment, as follows:

- a description of the activities of each reported industrial segment and the composition of each reported geographical segment;

- details of sales or other operating revenues distinguishing between revenue derived from customers outside the enterprise and revenue derived from other segments;

- segment results and assets employed;

- the basis of inter segment pricing;

- a reconciliation between the sum of the information on individual segments and the aggregated information in the financial statements as a whole; and

- material changes in identification of segments and in accounting practices used in reporting segment information.

Treatment of Grants

The government in Pakistan presently does not provide any grants. Concessions are usually available in the form of tax holidays and rebates on excise duty on exports. The accounting treatment for these concessions is to adjust the related provisions and charges to income.

Commitments and Contingencies

Disclosure and accounting treatment of contingencies and commitments are prescribed by the Companies Ordinance 1984 and IAS 10 on Contingencies and Events Occurring after the Balance Sheet Date.

Contingent losses are provided for if it is probable that future events will confirm that an asset has been impaired or a liability has been incurred at the balance sheet date and a reasonable estimate of the amount of the resulting loss can be made. Contingent gains are not accrued in the financial statements.

Disclosure is made of:

- the amount where practicable, together with a general description of any material guarantees given by the company, on behalf of related parties, employees and any other person required to be specified separately;

- contingent losses not accrued and contingent gains, together with the nature of the contingency, the uncertain factors that may affect the future outcome and an estimate of the financial effect, or a statement that such an estimate cannot be made;

- the amount or estimated amount, where practicable and if material, of commitments for capital expenditure to the extent they have not been provided for; and

- any other sum for which a contingent liability exists and the general nature of any other commitment, if material.

Balances not Reflected in the Balance Sheet

Balances not reflected in the balance sheet relate to contingencies and commitments already dealt with above and to events occurring after the balance sheet date.

Where events occurring after the balance sheet date do not affect the condition of assets or liabilities existing at the balance sheet date, no adjustments are made. Where such events are significant, however, disclosure is made of the nature of the event and an estimate of the financial effect or a statement that such an estimate cannot be made.

Price Level Changes

There is no statutory requirement or prevailing practice to account for price level changes.

Future Developments

Presently the CLA has invited recommendations from various interested bodies for proposed amendments to the Companies Ordinance 1984. The areas which are being examined include qualification of auditors of private limited companies, additional disclosures in the financial statements and adoption of accounting treatments recommended by International Accounting Standards.

Pakistan closely follows the International Accounting Standard Committee. Accounting issues which are emerging in Pakistan are more or less the same as that at international level. However, recent important developments, namely the change in the industrial climate, privatisation and the liberalisation of foreign investments, have brought to the forefront accounting issues such as consolidation, segmental reporting, business combinations and investments.

Saudi Arabia

Usamah Ali Tabbarah

The Kingdom of Saudi Arabia is amongst the foremost in the Middle East where the process of a modern renaissance has been successfully instituted and is continuing. All laws for governance of the Kingdom, designed to promote the harmony dictated by the canonical law of Islam – the Shari'ah, are promulgated by Royal Decree. The principal regulations and standards governing accounting and auditing activities and the governmental agencies which regulate them are:

- Regulations for Companies: The General Administration for Companies Division of the Ministry of Commerce.

- Regulations for Zakat and Income Tax: The Zakat and Income Tax Department of the Ministry of Finance and Planning.

- Foreign Capital Investment Code: The Foreign Capital Investment Committee under the aegis of the Ministry of Industry and Electricity.

- Saudi Arabia Auditing Standards: The Ministry of Commerce published the Saudi Arabian Auditing Standards.

- Saudi Arabian Accounting Concepts and Objectives were issued as an officially approved document by the Minister of Commerce, by Ministerial Resolution No.692 of 28/02/1406H, to provide guidance to professional accountants licensed to practise in the Kingdom.

Additional rules and regulations applicable to commercial banks have been issued by the Saudi Arabian Monetary Agency.

In the development of Accounting Standards attempts are being made to keep abreast of Standards issued and updated by the relevant international accounting bodies. However, it is the practice of major accounting firms to comply with International Accounting and Auditing Standards.

Saudi Arabia

The Zakat and Income Tax Regulations of the Kingdom have a predominant influence on the accounting treatment of transactions as well as the presentation of financial statements, in some situations overriding the general commercial viewpoint.

The Income Tax Regulations of 1951 incorporating the subsequent amendments by Royal Decrees, Ministerial Resolutions and ZITD Circulars form the principal body of tax legislation.

Form and Content of Financial Statements

The form and content of the financial statements of a corporation, which are specified in the Regulations for Companies, must as a minimum comprise a balance sheet; a financial report on its operations reflected in a profit and loss statement; and the financial position for the last financial year setting out the proposed method for allocating net profits.

The Companies' Regulations further stipulate that in preparing the accounts the classifications used in the previous year must be used and the bases for valuing assets and liabilities must also remain unchanged. The auditor may recommend altering classifications or evaluation bases, in which case alterations are allowed if they are approved by members in general meeting. No official determination has been made regarding the format of financial statements. Therefore each business entity and its auditor are free to select a format of their own.

It is a requirement of the Ministry of Commerce that all books of account, shown below, be maintained in Arabic and kept within the Kingdom:

- Journal
- General ledger
- A comprehensive trial balance of all assets and liabilities as well as constituent elements of the operating results.

The auditor is required to confirm that the relevant books of account and accounting records have been maintained in Arabic within the Kingdom. All submissions to the Government Authorities must be made in Arabic.

The financial statements presented comprise the following elements:

- Balance sheet
- Profit and Loss account
- Cash flow statement
- Notes to the financial statements
- Auditors' report

The Companies' Regulations gives the responsibility for the preparation of the financial statements and reports on the operations and financial position of a limited liability company to its managers.

Public Filing Requirements

Entities, including individuals, that are required to file tax declarations with the Zakat and Income Tax Department (ZITD) namely resident corporations, limited liability partnerships (companies), partnerships, contractors and practising professionals must prepare audited financial statements for the purpose of assessment by ZITD of taxes and the zakat levy.

The tax filing requirements as well as the submission deadlines apply, notwithstanding the fact that the foreign shareholders in a limited liability partnership (company) are entitled to a tax holiday.

The directors of a company are responsible for the submission of the annual tax declaration which should be supported by audited financial statements, irrespective of who actually prepares the documentation. The generally accepted basis for validating information in the tax declaration is by reference to the audited financial statements.

Limited liability partnerships (companies) with foreign participation as well as branches of foreign companies are required to file the final tax returns and pay the tax and or zakat dues within two and a half months of the end of the year. Filing extensions are permissible if requested from and approved by ZITD before the due date and on payment of tax due on an estimated basis. For companies wholly owned by Saudi nationals, the final Zakat returns must be filed within one month from the financial year-end. For sole practitioners and professional partnerships the filing deadline is 15 days from the year-end and no extensions are allowed by ZITD. Late filing is subject to penalties of up to 25 percent of the tax due.

In the case of a corporation, the board of directors must prepare, at least 60 days before the annual general meeting, the corporation's balance sheet, profit and loss statement and reports on the corporation's operations and its financial position. The board must also make proposals for the distribution of the corporations net profits. These documents together with the auditor's report on the financial statements must be filed with the General Administration for Companies division of the Ministry of Commerce at least 25 days prior to the general meeting.

In the case of a limited liability partnership the managers must, within 4 months after the end of each financial year, prepare a balance sheet of the partnership, a profit and loss statement and a report on its operations and financial position as well as on their proposals for the appropriation of net profits. These documents together with a copy of both the Directors' and auditors' reports must be filed with the General Administration for Companies division of the Ministry of Commerce within two months of their preparation.

In the case of companies with variable capital and cooperative companies the requirements for the preparation of financial statements are the same as those for either corporations or limited liability partnerships. A cooperative partnership with limited liability is permitted under the Companies' Regulations.

Saudi Arabia

Foreign companies operating in the Kingdom are subject to the provisions of the Companies' Regulations (other than those relating to incorporation). Therefore, they are subject to the same requirements for the preparation and filing of financial statements as apply to Saudi corporations.

The directors of a corporation must, within 30 days from the date of their approval by the members' general meeting, file copies of the balance sheet, the profit and loss statement, the board of directors' report and the auditors' report with the Commercial Register Office as well as the General Administration for Companies division of the Ministry of Commerce.

The managers, or those deemed to be the principal officers, of the above mentioned corporate entities, except for general partnerships, limited partnerships and joint ventures, are required to publish, in a newspaper distributed in the locality of the head office of the corporate entity, the balance sheet, the profit and loss statement, a comprehensive summary of the board of principal officers' (Chief Executive Officer's) report and the full text of the auditors' report. A copy of each of these documents must also be sent to the General Administration for Companies division of the Ministry of Commerce at least twenty five days prior to the date set for the members' general meeting.

Late filing of returns with the Ministry of Commerce, may, at the discretion of the Authorities, give rise to penalties.

Audit Requirements

The auditing standards used in practice are International Auditing Standards.

The constituent general meeting of shareholders appoints the first auditor of a corporation. The shareholders' general meeting shall appoint one or more auditors (from among those licensed to practise in the Kingdom) and determine their remuneration and term of office. A retiring auditor may be re-appointed.

The auditor is required:

● to submit a report to the annual general meeting indicating whether he has obtained all the information and explanations requested from the corporation and in his opinion, the extent to which the company's accounts are in conformity with reality. The auditor is also required to report on any violations of the Companies' Regulations or of the company's bye-laws.

● to prepare a special report, to accompany the chairman of the boards statement to the general meeting, relating to transactions and contracts in which any director has a personal interest. The chairman's statement must be made available to the auditor at least fifty five days prior to the date fixed for the general meeting.

● to report any violations of the requirement that a director, within 30 days of his appointment, must own shares in the Company's stock to a value of not less then SR 10,000.

Any auditor who knowingly includes false information in the balance sheet or the profit and loss statement or in reports prepared by him, for the partners or general meeting, or who conceals essential facts from his reports with the intention of concealing the financial position of the company from the partners or third parties, without prejudice to the requirements of the Islamic Shari'ah, shall be liable to imprisonment of not less than three months and not more than one year or to a fine of not less than SR 5,000 and not more than SR 25,000.

Valuation Principles

Financial statements are based on the historical cost convention. Assets are stated initially at the amounts paid to acquire them and liabilities are stated at the amounts received when the related obligation was incurred. These are subject to depreciation and amortisation provisions respectively.

The upward revaluation of property, plant and equipment is not permitted in order to prevent possible mis-statement of values. The historical cost of assets may not therefore be adjusted to reflect price level changes.

In accordance with rules relating to the disclosure of accounting policies, the basis for asset valuation, depreciation methods and inventory pricing are given. Generally, an accounting policy, once adopted, is not changed, except under exceptional circumstances in which case the reporting entity has to obtain the approval of its shareholders.

Group Financial Statements

The Tax Regulations require each entity in a group to file a separate tax return directly with the tax authorities which must be accompanied by its own individual audited accounts.

Consolidated financial statements are prepared, usually in accordance with International Accounting Standards IAS27 and IAS28, for the parent company shareholders, to reflect the financial position and results of operations of the group of enterprises as a whole. Further, the financial statements for business combinations are prepared and presented, generally in accordance with International Accounting Standard IAS22.

Depreciation

Because of its effects on the profits of taxpayers, the Zakat and Income Tax Department (ZITD) has issued rules on and specified the rates of depreciation allowed for fixed assets. The straight-line method has been adopted by ZITD and a rate table has been provided for use by taxpayers.

Saudi Arabia

Disclosure of the method of depreciation adopted is usually made in the notes to the financial statements which are required to show:

- the amount charged or provided for depreciation during the year;
- the aggregate cost or value of each class of asset;
- the aggregate amount written off in respect of each class of asset since acquisition; and
- the net book value after deducting the accumulated depreciation since the date of acquisition.

Leasing

International Accounting Standard 17 sets down the generally accepted accounting practices for lease accounting. Where a lease transfers substantially all benefits and risks of ownership to the lessee it should be accounted for as the acquisition of an asset and the recognition of an obligation by the lessee (a finance lease). Other leases should be accounted for as the rental of assets (an operating lease).

The basic accounting principles applied to lease transactions, for lessees, are:

- A finance lease should be reflected in the balance sheet of a lessee by recording an asset and a liability at amounts equal, at the inception of the lease, to the fair value of the leased property or if lower at the present value of the minimum lease payments. Rentals are apportioned between the finance charge and the reduction of the outstanding liability.

- The finance charge is allocated over the lease term so as to produce a constant periodic rate of interest on the remaining balance of the liability for each accounting period. Depreciation charged on the leased asset is computed on the same basis as other similar fixed assets.

- For operating leases the rental expense for the accounting period is charged as an expense for the period.

Capital and Reserves

Under the Regulations the share capital of a company must be fully subscribed and cannot be issued at less than par value. Partial allotments are not permitted. Shares may be issued at a premium, if allowed by the Company's bye laws, or if approved at a general meeting.

Ten percent of the annual net profit of a company must be transferred to a statutory reserve until it equals 50 percent of the share capital. A premium arising on the issue of shares can be added to this reserve, even if it has reached the maximum limit prescribed in the Regulations. Interim dividends can only be paid after the approval of the accounts at the shareholders' annual general meeting.

If the accumulated losses of a corporation reach three quarters of its capital, the members at an extraordinary general meeting have to consider whether the company shall continue to operate or be dissolved. Accordingly the members must provide additional funding depending upon their decision.

Foreign Currency Translation

Transactions in foreign currencies are translated into Saudi Riyals (functional currency) at the rates prevailing at the date of the transaction. Assets and liabilities expressed in foreign currencies at the balance sheet date are translated into Saudi Riyals at the rates prevailing at the balance sheet date. Any gains or losses arising out of these transactions are credited or charged to the results of the period in which they arise.

Taxation

The profits of foreign companies and the profit share of non-Saudi shareholders in Saudi companies attract company tax whilst zakat is applicable to Saudi individuals and Saudi companies as well as to Saudi Partners in mixed companies. Generally, there is no accounting for deferred taxation.

Dividends are paid to members after deduction of income tax for non-Saudis and non-GCC citizens and zakat for Saudis and GCC citizens. Income tax is assessed after aggregating taxable income for non-Saudis and non-GCC citizens and the zakat levy is assessed after aggregating the zakat leviable base for Saudi and GCC citizens.

Increases made in provisions for liabilities are not tax deductible and decreases are not assessable. The amounts claimable as deductions for tax are only those expenses actually disbursed during the accounting period.

A tax loss of an entity occurring in a year of tax assessment is not allowed to be carried forward and set off against the taxable income of a subsequent period.

Income tax is withheld from payments to non-residents or residents who do not have a valid tax clearance certificate for services by entities such as sub-contractors if such services were rendered within the Kingdom of Saudi Arabia.

Charges such as royalties and consultancy services attract withholding tax whether or not such services are carried out within the Kingdom of Saudi Arabia.

Unusual and Prior Period Items

Unusual items are those which are non-operating, unusual in nature and infrequent in occurrence. They are added to net income and shown separately, disclosing the description and the amount of each item.

Amounts relating to prior periods are separately disclosed in the current income statement as an element of net income. Prior year figures are not restated.

Saudi Arabia

Retirement Benefits

When an employment contract for a specified period comes to an end or when an employer cancels a contract in respect of an unspecified period the employee has the right to receive an award for the period of service. This is computed on the basis of half a month's pay for each of the first five years, and one month's pay for each of the subsequent years. This is the statutory minimum which most employers account for on a pay-as-you-go basis. Some employers reflect the accrued benefits in a provision for termination benefits.

Related Party Transactions

Transactions with related parties, which include parent and subsidiaries, other affiliates, principal owners and management, are separately disclosed.

A corporation may not give a cash loan to, or guarantee any loan taken out by a director. Banks and other financial institutions are exempt from this provision.

Treatment of Grants

When grants are made available to business enterprises there are generally certain terms and conditions attached. The accounting treatment of the grants is dependent upon evidence being available that these terms and conditions have been complied with.

The related transactions should be identified and documented separately from other transactions. This is to facilitate the financial reporting of the economic and the social benefits derived from the grant.

Contingencies and Commitments

Contingent liabilities that may arise from probable future commitments, such as unused letters of credit, are disclosed in the notes to the financial statements.

Price Level Changes

No accounting information is required to be disclosed in respect of price level changes.

Future Developments

Practices are expected to evolve in the future in order to achieve harmony, to the extent that it is possible, with International Accounting Standards.

Singapore

Teo Foong & Wong

Accounting standards and guidelines codified in the Statements of Accounting Standards (SAS) issued by the Institute of Certified Public Accountants of Singapore constitute the principal source of accounting principles and practices in Singapore. The Institute is established under the Accountants Act 1987 and it represents the official accounting body in Singapore.

The Institute expects its members who assume responsibilities in respect of financial statements to observe Statements of Accounting Standards, auditing and other pronouncements issued by the Institute. Disciplinary action may be taken against any of its members that have prepared or audited financial statements which are in violation of the pronouncements.

The standards and guidelines concern both accounting measurements and disclosure. Their application is not confined to corporations but apply to all entities, unless specifically exempt by a particular pronouncement, that prepare financial statements which are intended to give a true and fair view. The standards are not legally binding and departures are permitted if they conflict with disclosure exemptions granted by law, such as the Singapore Companies Act.

Accounting standards in Singapore follow closely the standards set by the International Accounting Standards Committee (IASC) of which the Institute of Certified Public Accountants of Singapore is a member.

Tax laws have little impact on accounting methods and principles because different conventions are used for tax and for accounting purposes.

Form and Content of Financial Statements

The form and content of a company's financial statements are prescribed by law as embodied in the Companies Act (Chapter 50). In addition, the requirements of the accounting profession and the Stock Exchange of Singapore need to be followed.

Singapore

The directors are responsible for the preparation of a company's financial statements which give a true and fair view of the state of its financial affairs. These are audited and presented to the shareholders.

Financial statements comprise the following items:

- Balance sheet
- Profit and loss account
- Statement of changes in financial position
- Notes to the financial statements including accounting policies

The balance sheet and profit and loss account must be accompanied by the directors' and the auditors' reports as well as a signed statement by the directors that the financial statements show a true and fair view and that there are reasonable grounds to believe that the company will be able to pay its debts as and when they fall due.

A statement of changes in financial position is required except where:

- the company is an exempt private company (as defined by the Companies Act); or
- the company is not public and has turnover and other operating revenues of S$1 million or less.

The financial statements must be stated in Singapore dollars and comparative figures must be shown as required by Ninth Schedule of the Companies Act. Holding companies must publish group financial statements, normally in the form of consolidated financial statements, dealing with the group as a whole. Many companies also publish a chairman's statement.

The Stock Exchange of Singapore requires listed companies to disclose certain additional financial data, for example earnings per share, segmental information, information on business activities and details concerning directors and officers.

Public Filing Requirements

All limited companies, except exempt private companies, must file audited financial statements together with the directors' and auditors' reports and an annual return each year with the Registrar of Companies. These are available for public inspection.

The first annual meeting of a company incorporated under the Companies Act has to be held within 18 months of the company's incorporation and subsequently, once in every calendar year at intervals not exceeding 15 months.

An annual return consisting of the date of meeting, details of the company's capital structure, amounts due on mortgages and other charges, information relating to shareholders and a list of directors and managers together with the audited financial statements need to be filed with the Registrar of Companies within one month after the annual general meeting. Failure to comply with the requirement is an offence and may render the company as well as its directors liable to a penalty or to prosecution by the Registrar of Companies.

Every company with securities listed on the Stock Exchange of Singapore must supply on a yearly basis certain information, which includes the company's financial statements, the auditors' report and the directors' report, to the Council of the Stock Exchange as well as to each member of the company and to every holder of securities issued by the company. The submission must be made not less than 14 days before the date of the company's annual general meeting and not more than six months after the end of that financial year.

Audit Requirements

The Companies Act requires every company incorporated under the said Act to appoint one or more auditors to report to members on the financial statements of the company. With the exception of the company's first auditor, who may be appointed by the directors, auditors are appointed by shareholders at the general meeting and hold office until the conclusion of the next annual general meeting.

Under the Companies Act, approved company auditors, who must be appointed within three months of incorporation, are certified public accountants qualified for appointment under the Accountants Act. It is not mandatory for a non incorporated business to be audited. However, Singapore branches of foreign corporations need to be audited by approved company auditors.

Standards applying to auditing principles and practices are set out in Statements of Auditing Guidelines issued by the Institute of Certified Public Accountants of Singapore. Supplementing the guidelines are Statements of Auditing Practice dealing with the detailed work that the auditor has to carry out in accordance with the guidelines.

An auditor must state in his report whether the financial statements are properly drawn up so as to give a true and fair view of the company's affairs and its profit or loss and whether the accounting and other records of the company have been properly kept in accordance with the provisions of the Companies Act.

If the auditor is not satisfied that the financial statements or records are in order, a qualified auditors' report will be issued.

Valuation Principles

The historical cost convention is normally applied, the assets and liabilities of the company being generally stated at original cost subject to depreciation or provisions. However, it is frequently modified by the incorporation of the revaluation of certain assets.

- Freehold land is stated at cost or appraisal value. Buildings on freehold land are stated at cost or appraisal value less depreciation at rates calculated to write off the value of the buildings over their useful lives. Real property held for investment need not be depreciated. Any appreciation in the value of real property arising from an appraisal is taken to revaluation reserves.

- Stocks are normally stated at the lower of cost (on an actual, average or FIFO basis) and net realisable value. The LIFO method is uncommon but may be used, provided the difference resulting from using this and not one of the preferred methods is disclosed in the notes to the financial statements.

- Marketable securities, held as long-term investments, are stated at either the lower of cost and market value on a portfolio basis or at cost less provision for a decline in value other than a temporary decline. Securities held as current assets are carried at either market value or the lower of cost and market value on a portfolio or individual investment basis.

Generally, the recognition of income and expenses is based on the 'accruals' concept; that is revenue and costs are recognised as they are earned or incurred, not as money is received or paid. This concept implies that revenue and profit dealt with in the profit and loss account will be matched with related costs and expenses where these are material and identifiable.

SAS 16 deals with the bases for recognition of revenue which sets out the following requirements:

- In a transaction involving the sale of goods, revenue is recognised when the seller has transferred to the buyer the significant risks and rewards of ownership and no significant uncertainty exists with regard to the sale consideration, the associated costs incurred, or to be incurred and the extent to which the goods may be returned.

- In a transaction involving the rendering of services, performance should be measured either under the completed contract method or under the percentage of completion method, whichever relates the revenue to the work accomplished. In any case, such performance should be regarded as being achieved when no significant uncertainty exists regarding the consideration that will be derived from rendering the service, and the associated costs incurred or to be incurred in rendering the service. This relates in particular to the recognition of income on construction contracts which is dealt with specifically under SAS11.

Revenues such as interest, royalties and dividends should only be recognised when no significant uncertainty as to measurability or collectability exists. These revenues are recognised on the following bases:

- Interest: on a time proportion basis taking account of the principal outstanding and the rate applicable;

- Royalties: on an accrual basis in accordance with the terms of the relevant agreement;

- Dividends from investments not accounted for under the equity method of accounting: when the shareholder's right to receive payment is established.

The recognition of revenue for specialised industries such as insurance and banking is governed by the rules, regulations and guidelines issued by the Monetary Authority of Singapore.

Group Financial Statements

Where a company has one or more subsidiaries, the directors must ensure group financial statements are presented. Normally, this means consolidated financial statements, unless the company is a wholly owned subsidiary of another company incorporated in Singapore. A company is deemed to be a subsidiary of another company if the other company controls the composition of its board of directors, controls more than half of its voting power or holds more than half of its issued share capital.

A subsidiary may be excluded from consolidation if the company's directors are of the opinion that:

- the business of the holding company and that of the subsidiary are so different that they cannot reasonably be treated as a single undertaking; or

- the result would mislead or be harmful to the business of the company or any of its subsidiaries; or

- consolidated financial statements would be impracticable, would be of no real value to members of the company in view of the insignificant amount involved, or would involve expense or delay to members of the company.

The financial statements for a group of companies may be in the form of one set of consolidated financial statements, or separate financial statements for each corporation in the group in which case the directors must certify that:

- it is impractical to prepare consolidated financial statements and in the interests of the shareholders not to do so, in which case the reasons must be given; and

- the financial statements are not significantly affected as a result of the non-elimination of intercompany transactions and balances, except to the extent disclosed in the notes.

The auditors must state whether they agree with the directors' reasons for not preparing a single set of consolidated financial statements. All intercompany transactions are to be eliminated from the consolidated profit and loss account and from the consolidated balance sheet.

Singapore

A note must still be shown in the financial statements of the holding company or any document attached to them stating for each subsidiary :

● its name;

● its place of its incorporation;

● the name of any foreign country in which it operates;

● the percentage of each class of shares held by the holding company;

● the amount of the holding company's investment in each class of its share capital; and

● its financial year-end, where it is not the same as that of the holding company.

The balance sheet date of a subsidiary must be altered to coincide with that of its holding company, if necessary, within two years of its acquisition.

The consolidated financial statements and the directors' report thereon can only be issued once the audited financial statements, directors' report and the auditors' report from a subsidiary have been received.

If directors of the holding company cannot obtain the financial statements, directors' report, auditors' report or other information of a subsidiary which require to be consolidated, the directors may still issue consolidated financial statements and directors' report by omitting the financial statements of this subsidiary. However, directors must provide an explanation for the omission so as to prevent the consolidated financial statements and reports from being misleading.

When the directors of a holding company finally receive the financial statements of the subsidiary, these financial statements and reports must be sent within one month of receipt to all shareholders of the holding company with explanations or qualifications.

For group financial statements, the financial statements of foreign subsidiaries are normally translated at an exchange rate approximating that on the last day of the accounting year. The resulting exchange difference should be recorded as a reserve account on the balance sheet.

A company that is not a subsidiary of an investing company is an associated company if the investing company holds a long-term investment of 20% or more of the equity shares and is in a position to exercise significant influence over the investee company's commercial and financial policies. Singapore accounting principles require the use of the equity method of accounting for such investments.

Depreciation

Fixed assets should be depreciated on a systematic basis over the useful life of the assets. The depreciation method selected should be consistently applied from period to period unless a change in method is justified and disclosure made of its effect on the financial statements. If an asset has been revalued, depreciation must be based on the valuation rather than the cost. When it becomes apparent that the book value of an asset will not be recoverable in full from future revenues, it must be written down immediately to its recoverable amount.

Leasing

SAS 15 deals with accounting for leases. Leases are classified as either operating leases or financial leases. In an operating lease, only the rental is taken into account by the lessee. A lease is presumed to be a financial lease if the present value of the minimum lease payments equals 90% or more of the fair market value of the leased assets at the inception of the lease. The lessee must capitalise a financial lease and recognise the obligation to make future payments.

Research and Development

Research costs are normally expensed as incurred. Development expenditure is also normally expensed, but may be deferred to future periods if it can be identified as relating to a specific and viable project and if recovery of such expenditure against future revenues from the project is reasonably assured. Any expenditure deferred in this way is amortised on a systematic basis against these future revenues or written off when recognised as non-recoverable.

Inventories

The basis of valuation of inventories is the lower of cost and net realisable value. Cost should be accounted for using the FIFO method or a weighted average cost formula. Where appropriate, the specific identification method may be used. Net realisable value is the estimated selling price less anticipated cost of disposal, with allowances made for damaged, obsolete and slow-moving items.

The standard also requires a systematic allocation of production overhead costs that relate to bringing the inventories to their present location and condition. Overheads other than production overheads should be included in inventory cost, only to the extent that they relate to bringing inventories to their present location and condition. Exceptional wastage and idle capacity should not form part of inventory cost.

Intangible Assets

If material, the major elements of intangible assets should be shown separately, eg goodwill, franchises, patent rights, copyrights and trade marks. The basis of valuation for each type of intangible asset also should be disclosed. Where an intangible asset has been acquired other than through payment of cash, or its equivalent, the basis of valuation should be fully described as, for example, 'at cost, being the values assigned to shares issued therefor'.

Intangible assets having a limited useful life should be amortised over that life and this fact should be disclosed. Purchased goodwill should be accounted for in accordance with SAS 22 which states that it should be amortised to income on a systematic basis over its useful life or if it is found not to be supported by future income it should be charged to income immediately.

Capital and Reserves

The treatment of capital redemption reserves, share premium account and revaluation reserves follows UK Companies Act 1981. However, with regard to dividends UK practice prior to 1981 would be followed, which means that accumulated prior period losses need not necessarily be made good before distributing current year's profits. Proposed dividends are provided in the financial statements for the year to which they relate.

Foreign Currency Translation

Normally each asset, liability, revenue or cost resulting from a transaction denominated in a foreign currency should be translated into the reporting currency at the exchange rate in effect on the date on which the transaction occurred. If the rates do not fluctuate significantly, an average rate for a period may be used. At each balance sheet date, recorded monetary balances that are denominated in a foreign currency are adjusted to reflect the rate at the balance sheet date. All these exchange adjustments are to be taken to the profit and loss account.

Financial statements of foreign subsidiaries and branches (which are not an integral part of the head office) are translated at the rate of exchange ruling at the balance sheet date. Foreign currency translation adjustments are taken directly to reserves.

Generally, companies pay income tax on profits derived from or accrued in Singapore. Various adjustments are made to the accounting profit for the period, as shown in the financial statements, to arrive at taxable profits. The major adjustments are:

● Depreciation is not deductible; instead allowances are made according to the Tax Act.

● Capital gains are not taxable.

● General reserves against inventories and bad debts are not deductible.

Tax effect (deferred tax) accounting is required under the SAS. Where provision is made, the liability rather than the deferral method tends to be used.

Related Party Transactions

SAS 21 governs the disclosure of related-party transactions. If control exists, related-party relationships should be disclosed regardless of whether the parties have engaged in any transactions with each other. If such transactions have occurred, the reporting enterprise should also disclose in the financial statements the types of transactions and other details necessary to gain a full understanding of them. Related-party transactions of a similar nature may be disclosed in aggregate, except when separate disclosure is required for an understanding of their effects on the financial statements.

Unusual and Prior Period Items

In accordance with SAS 8, income from the ordinary activities of the enterprise during the period should be disclosed in the income statement as part of net income. Unusual items should also be included in net income, but the nature and amount of each unusual item should be separately disclosed. However, SAS 8 is silent in terms of presentation. RAP 1 recommends that unusual items (less attributable income tax) be shown separately in the profit and loss statement after the results derived from ordinary activities. Abnormal items may require disclosure if a true and fair view is to be given. If disclosure is appropriate, they should be reflected before unusual items, giving separate disclosure of their nature and amount.

Prior period items, and the amount of the adjustments, if any, resulting from changes in accounting policies should be treated in one of the following two ways:

- by adjusting opening retained earnings in the financial statements for the current period and amending the comparative information given in respect of prior years; or

- by separate disclosure in the current income statement as part of net income.

In either case, the disclosure should be adequate to facilitate comparison of the figures for the two periods presented.

Retirement Benefits

At present it is unusual in Singapore to find many companies that operate pension and retirement plans because of the Central Provident Fund Scheme. However, some companies do have such plans for senior executives or arrangements under trade union agreements. In addition certain companies historically operated such plans under which certain liabilities still exist.

As a minimum the following should be disclosed:

- a statement that such plans exist, identifying or describing the employee groups covered;

Singapore

- the methods used (actuarial, accrual, discretionary, etc) to recognise pension or retirement costs; and

- all contractual obligations in connection with pensions, provident funds and retirement benefits; and in particular:

  - where the employer has given a guarantee (for example, to maintain the solvency of the scheme or to ensure a minimum rate of interest on, or rate of, accumulation of the funds), there should be an appropriate note in the financial statements of the employer,

  - where there is an obligation to provide retirement benefits which are not covered by contributions to a scheme; provision should be made if the amount is material. If no provision is made this should be stated by way of note.

Segmental Reporting

Industry segments and geographical segments are the usual bases for presenting information on operations by segment. An enterprise would provide information on both bases if both are applicable to its operations. Industry segment information is usually presented on the basis of general groupings of related products and services, or by types of customer.

Geographical segment information is sometimes presented on the basis of the location of operations of the enterprise, sometimes on the basis of markets and sometimes on both. An enterprise's domestic operations are generally considered to be a separate geographical segment. In Singapore the following information is generally considered necessary for each reported segment:

- a description of the activities of each reported industry segment and an indication of the composition of each reported geographical area;

- an analysis of sales or other operating revenues, distinguishing between revenue derived from customers outside the enterprise and revenue derived from other segments;

- segment result; and

- segment assets employed, expressed either in money terms or as percentages of the overall totals.

Treatment of Grants

The standard prescribes that government grants should not be recognised in the income statement until there is reasonable assurance that the enterprise will comply with the conditions attaching to them, and that the grants will be received. Crediting grants directly to shareholders' funds is not permitted. Grants should be recognised in the income statement on a systematic basis which matches the grants with the related costs (ie those costs which the grant is intended to contribute towards).

Grants for compensation of losses or expenses already incurred, or giving immediate financial support to an enterprise, are recognised in the income statement when they become receivable. Where a grant is related to an asset, the grant may be set up as deferred income, or deducted in arriving at the carrying amount of the asset. Disclosure is required in the financial statements of:

● the accounting policy adopted;

● the method of presentation of government grants;

● the nature and extent of grants recognised;

● an indication of other forms of government assistance from which the enterprise has directly benefitted; and

● contingencies related to the assistance.

Commitments and Contingencies

With regard to contingent gains/assets disclosure must avoid giving misleading implications as to the likelihood of their realisation. The amount of the contingent loss should be based on management's "best estimate", and if an estimate cannot be made, the existence and the nature of the contingency should be disclosed.

Where a contingent liability/loss is not accrued in the financial statements, the existence of the contingency should be disclosed in the notes to the financial statements, stating the nature of the contingency, the uncertain factors affecting its future outcome, and an estimate of the financial effect, or a statement that such an estimate cannot be made.

The Singapore Companies Act requires the disclosure of commitments relating to capital expenditure contracted but not provided for in the financial statements.

Balances not Reflected in the Balance Sheet

The accounting standard and guidelines on off balance sheet financing, E40 Financial Instruments, are still under review by the Institute's Accounting Standards Committee. However, the Stock Exchange of Singapore has issued directives to require all listed companies with financial instruments to disclose the information in the notes to the financial statements.

Price Level Changes

Accounting for price level changes is not normally practised in Singapore.

Future Developments

Financial reporting in Singapore has, not surprisingly, been influenced by the United Kingdom. All International Accounting Standards (IAS) issued by the IASC are

Singapore

considered by the Institute's Accounting Standards Committee before they are recommended to the Council for adoption as Statements of Accounting Standards. Where appropriate the IAS are amended to take into account local circumstances.

Presently the following IASC exposure drafts are under review:

- E40 Financial Instruments

- E41 Revenue Recognition

- E42 Construction Contract

- E43 Property, Plant and Equipment

- E44 The effects of changes in Foreign Exchange Rates

- E45 Extraordinary items, Fundamental Errors and Changes in Accounting Policies

- E46 Business Combinations

A move to make financial statements more comparable is underway and the trend is therefore to narrow the differences both in accounting practices followed locally, and also as between practices in Singapore and those in other countries around the world.

Spain

Audihispana SA

Application of the General Accounting Plan approved by Royal Decree 1643 of December 1990 which reforms the 1973 plan is obligatory for years commencing on or after 31 December 1990. Spanish generally accepted accounting principles are set out in the General Accounting Plan, the Commercial Code, which adapts the plan for different economic sectors and in accounting regulations laid down by The Audit and Accounting Institute. Controlling bodies, such as the Bank of Spain, and the Directorate General of Insurance, also issue accounting regulations which conform with EC Company Law Directives.

For any issues not covered by the aforementioned bodies, it is common practice to refer to International Accounting Standards. With the implementation of the new General Accounting Plan, accounting standards are free from tax influences to enable financial statements to give a true and fair view of a company's state of affairs.

Form and Content of Financial Statements

The financial statements prescribed by the General Accounting Plan, which must be prepared by company directors, include:

- Balance sheet

- Income statement

- Annual report including the company's accounting policies

Comparative figures are required.

The Annual report also includes a statement of changes in the financial position and a statement of movement in shareholders' equity. There is an abbreviated format for financial statements if during the two years prior to the presentation of the financial statements to be issued at least two out of the following three requirements are complied with :

Abbreviated Balance Sheet and Annual Report	Assets less than 230 million pesetas Sales less than 480 million pesetas Average number of employees per year less than 50
Abbreviated Income Statement	Assets less than 920 million pesetas Sales less than 1,920 million pesetas Average number of employees per year less than 250

Public Filing Requirements

The financial statements must be filed with the Mercantile Register within one month of their approval by the general shareholders' meeting. The Mercantile Register will keep the financial statements for six years during which time they are available to interested parties. Non-filing with the Mercantile Register results in fines being levied of between 200,000 and 2,000,000 pesetas for each year of delay. Companies required to prepare financial statements are:

- Limited companies
- Private limited companies
- Limited partnerships with shares

Audit Requirements

All companies' financial statements and management reports must be reviewed by independent auditors except that those companies preparing an abbreviated balance sheet and annual report are exempt from this obligation.

The general shareholders' meeting appoints the auditor. The appointment, which is for between three and nine years, must be made prior to finalisation of the year to be audited. Auditors may not be re-appointed at the end of the nine year period until three years has elapsed.

In Spain there are two audit institutes:

- The Institute of Certified Accounts Examiners (Instituto de Censores Jurados de Cuentas de Espana, ICJCE)

- The Economists Auditors Register (Registro de Economistas Auditores, REA)

Members of both groups are included in the Official Register of Accounts Auditors (Registro Oficial de Auditores de Cuentas, ROAC). Members of both audit institutes enjoy the same rights and privileges. The creation of audit companies is permitted.

Both institutes have strict ethical standards that ensure the independence and technical ability of the auditor. ROAC and both audit institutes have the right and responsibility to verify the technical quality of all work and to see that standards are being met by their members.

Independent auditors must give their opinion on both individual and, where appropriate, consolidated financial statements. They will also be involved in other company matters such as:

- capital increases charged to reserves;

- capital increases through offsetting loans;

- mergers;

- capital reductions; and

- changing the company's status eg to limited company.

Valuation Principles

Income and expenses are charged in terms of the actual flow of the assets and services which they represent, irrespective of when cash or financial flow occurs. However, foreseeable, or possible, risks and losses are recorded when first identified.

Financial statements are based on historical cost. This means that, generally, assets are stated initially at the amounts of cash or cash equivalents paid to acquire them and liabilities are stated at the amounts of cash or cash equivalents received when the related obligation was incurred. These are subject to depreciation and amortisation provisions, and, under certain circumstances, downward adjustments to market or current net realisable values.

Assets acquired free of charge are recorded on acquisition at their estimated sales value, at that date, bearing in mind the condition of the asset.

Group Financial Statements

It is compulsory for groups of companies, being a parent company and one or more subsidiary companies to prepare consolidated financial statements if they comply with at least two of the following three requirements:

- Consolidated assets are greater than 2,300 million pesetas

- Consolidated sales are greater than 4,800 million pesetas

- The average number of employees per year is greater than 500

A company is considered to be a parent when, apart from being a partner, it holds a majority interest in the voting rights of an enterprise, even if only with the agreement of other partners, or it has the right to appoint the majority of the Board of Directors.

However, a company is exempt from consolidation when the parent company is also the subsidiary of a Spanish, or EC domiciled company, or when the subsidiaries carry out such different activities to those of the parent company that it would be inappropriate to prepare consolidated financial statements.

Consolidation methods used are:

● Global integration: Applied to investments where the majority of votes are held by the parent.

● Proportional integration: Applied to investments where joint management exists.

● Equity method: Applied to investments which give ownership of either more than 3% of listed or 20% of unlisted companies.

In the individual financial statements of the parent company long term investments are valued at the lower of cost or market value.

Intercompany balances and transactions are eliminated in the consolidation process and adjustments made where the accounting policies of a subsidiary are not consistent with those of its parent.

The excess of the cost of an investment over its equity value is treated as goodwill and is reflected under assets in the balance sheet. Goodwill is depreciated over a period of not more than 10 years. If a minority interest exists it is shown under liabilities in the balance sheet.

Consolidated financial statements must be filed with the Mercantile Register within one month of their approval by the parent company's general shareholders' meeting.

Depreciation

The cost of tangible fixed assets assigned to productive operations is systematically amortised over their estimated useful lives. Depreciation is generally calculated on the straight line method, although other methods such as sum of the digits and reducing balance are acceptable.

Additional provisions are made for those fixed assets which are obsolete or whose market value is lower than the net book value.

The main disclosures given in the annual report are:

● the movements during the year on each relevant item in the balance sheet;

● accumulated depreciation and provisions;

- in the case of revalued assets, details of authorisation for the revaluation and its amount will be shown;

- a description of depreciation methods and useful lives by groups of assets;

- tax burdens; and

- firm purchase and/or sales commitments at the year end.

Leasing

Finance lease contracts entered into from 1 January 1991 must be accounted for as a credit purchase provided there is no reasonable doubt that a purchase option will be carried out. For contracts commencing prior to that date transitional arrangements exist which permit them to be accounted for either as explained above or as straight rental agreements on condition that only one of the two methods will be applied for all contracts in effect at 1 January 1991.

The annual report will contain information regarding leased assets indicating the original cost of the asset, the purchase option value, the contract term, the number of years elapsed, instalments made during previous years and the current year and outstanding instalments.

Research and Development

Research and development costs are normally written off in the year they are incurred. Those relating to specific projects which are expected to be technically successful and economically and commercially profitable, are capitalised and depreciated at the year end.

Costs capitalised must be depreciated, using the straight line method over a maximum term of five years from the finalisation of the research or development project.

Inventories

Inventories generally consist of:

- Raw materials and supplies
- Work in progress
- Finished goods

Inventories of mercantile and manufacturing companies are stated at the lower of cost or market value. Cost is the sum of all expenditure, both direct and indirect, necessarily incurred in bringing inventories to their respective condition and location. Various methods are acceptable in determining inventory costs including FIFO, LIFO, average and specific identification. In general, the term "market value" means current replacement cost, except that it should not exceed net realisable value nor should it be less than net realisable value reduced by a normal profit margin.

Spain

The annual report must provide information regarding the existence of firm purchase and/or sales commitments and any type of charges which restrict the availability of inventories.

Intangible Assets

In general, valuation rules applicable to tangible fixed assets are applicable to intangible fixed assets, but depreciation of goodwill must not exceed ten years.

Capital and Reserves

Share capital   This is represented by bearer or registered shares, and must be at least 25% paid up. Registered shares must be issued when the capital has not been fully paid up and transmission restrictions exist. Amounts outstanding are shown under assets in the balance sheet. Share capital for limited companies may not be less than 10 million pesetas. The company can buy back a maximum of 10% of the share capital provided that:

● the purchases have been approved by the general shareholders' meeting which fixed the price, term and number of shares to be bought; and

● the shares are fully paid.

If these conditions are not satisfied the purchase is null and void.

When a purchase of its own shares takes place a company must either sell the shares within one year or set up a reserve equivalent to the payment made and reduce the share capital. Cross holdings between companies is limited to 10% of the companies' share capital except for cross holdings between parent and subsidiary companies.

Non-voting shares can be issued, up to a maximum of 50% of the paid up share capital, with a minimum annual dividend of 5% of the paid up capital. If distributable profits are not available to meet these dividends shareholders will be paid over a five year term, during which time they will have voting rights. These shares have preferential rights in the case of a liquidation and are not affected by capital reductions as a result of losses.

Legal reserve   10% of profit for the year is allocated to this reserve until the balance reaches 20% of the share capital. To the extent that the legal reserve exceeds 10% of the issued share capital it may be used to increase share capital. Otherwise, this reserve may only be used to offset losses, provided that no other available reserves exist for such a purpose.

Freely distributable reserves   In essence retained earnings are distributable. However, they may include a non-distributable element to the extent that goodwill, start up expenses and research and development expenses have not been totally depreciated or that their net book value is equal to or higher than these reserves.

Accumulated losses If shareholders' equity is reduced to half the share capital or less, as a result of accumulated losses, the law requires that a company must take appropriate steps, eg reduce share capital, or it must be dissolved.

Foreign Currency Translation

Foreign currency items are translated using the market rate of exchange valid at the date of the transaction. Balances at the year end are valued at the exchange rate valid at that date.

Unrealised exchange rate differences at the year end, calculated in accordance with the General Accounting Plan, are included under liabilities in the balance sheet as deferred income if positive and charged to the income statement if negative.

Positive exchange rate differences deferred in previous years are released to the income statement in the year that the related credits and debits fall due or alternatively they are treated in the same way that negative exchange rate differences, relating to similar transactions, of an equal or higher amount are recognised.

Overseas subsidiaries' financial statements will be translated into pesetas by means of the following methods:

Monetary/non-monetary This is the recommended method when the subsidiary's transactions are closely linked with those of the Spanish parent company. This consists of converting non-current account balances into pesetas using the exchange rate valid at the subsidiary's year end . Income statement items will be converted into pesetas using a weighted average rate of exchange, except for results generated by non-current balance sheet items such as depreciation and amortisation. The differences arising from conversion are included within the results for the year.

Year end exchange rate method With this method all assets, rights and obligations will be converted into pesetas using the exchange rate at the subsidiary's year end and the income statement will be converted into pesetas applying a weighted average rate of exchange. The difference between the equity amount of the subsidiary converted at the historical excha nge rate and the net equity position resulting from conversion of assets, rights and obligations will be recorded under shareholders' equity as a reserves account.

When foreign subsidiaries are affected by high inflation rates their financial statements must, prior to conversion, be adjusted, following regulations established in the country where the subsidiaries are domiciled, so that the effect of inflation is recognised.

Taxation

The Corporation Tax charge is calculated on profit before taxation (as adjusted for tax purposes) at a rate of 35%. Tax incentives to which the Company has a right are then deducted.

Spain

Temporary timing differences create deferred tax or advance tax balances which are reflected under liabilities or assets, respectively. Where temporary differences are expected to reverse in more than one year the amount of the deferred or advance tax will be classified as long term.

The value of tax credits carried forward to be offset against future profits may only be recognised if the generation of those future profits is reasonably certain.

Unusual and Prior Period Items

Extraordinary income and expenses are shown separately on the income statement.

In exceptional cases, when the application of an accounting principle is changed and justified in the annual report, the effect of the change is recorded by adjusting opening reserves, and the effect on the current year will be recorded under extraordinary results in the income statement for the year.

Some valuation bases used are dependent upon estimates made by the company eg estimated useful lives of assets for depreciation purposes. Where a change is made to these estimates this does not amount to a change in accounting principles and therefore their effect will be reflected in the current years results.

Retirement Benefits

For accounting periods ending after 30 June 1990, companies are required to make provisions, based on actuarial calculations, for expenses accrued during the year which relate to internal pension plans.

Appropriate provisions must be made to correct funding deficits existing at 30 June 1990, as follows:

- For pensions accrued by personnel who had already retired at the beginning of the first fiscal year which ended on or after 30 June 1990, the deficit has to be corrected over seven years.

- For pensions accrued by personnel who had not retired at the beginning of that fiscal year, the deficit has to be corrected over fifteen years.

Related Party Transactions

Balances and transactions carried out with subsidiary companies must be disclosed in the financial statements. The financial statements are also required to disclose, globally, the remuneration of the Board of Directors as well as the amounts of loans to and obligations incurred, concerning pensions, for members of the Board.

Segmental Reporting

There are no specific Spanish rules and the provisions of IAS 14 apply.

Treatment of Grants

Non-repayable capital grants are treated as deferred income and released to the income statement over the life of the asset to which they relate. Where the assets are not depreciated the grants are released to income in the year in which they are sold or withdrawn from use.

Commitments and Contingencies

The notes to the financial statements must disclose a number of matters involving commitments and contingencies, including unused letters of credit, long-term leases, assets pledged as security for loans, pensions plans, the existence of cumulative preferred stock dividends in arrears, and commitments such as those for plant acquisitions or obligations to reduce debt, maintain working capital, or restrict dividends.

In addition, the estimated loss arising from a contingent liability is charged to income if:

● it is probable that an asset had been impaired or a liability had been incurred at the date of the financial statements; and
● the amount of the loss can be reasonably estimated.

Disclosure is required for contingent liabilities which do not meet both those conditions if the loss is reasonably possible. Contingent gains are not recognized until they are realised.

Balances not Reflected in the Balamce Sheet

As a general principle assets and liabilities should not be sct off and all balances accounted for separately.

Price Level Changes

In Spain, at present, there is no legal obligation to adjust financial statements for the effect of price level changes.

Future Developments

There are two main developments in progress:

● a draft General Accounting Plan for construction companies, which whilst still awaiting approval is already in use; and

● a draft General Accounting Plan for sports companies.

Switzerland

Experta Révision S A

Swiss financial statements have a reputation of being less useful than those prepared in other European countries. This partly stems from the fact that Switzerland has not joined the EC and therefore it is not bound to implement EC company law Directives.

The preparation of financial statements is regulated by the Swiss Code of Obligations. Special rules apply to banks, insurance companies, mutual investment funds and to pension funds. The Code of Obligations has recently been updated and new requirements have applied since 1 July 1992 which aim to increase the standard of accounting policies followed.

The new regulations have increased the level of disclosure and are more likely to meet international standards. The gap between the Swiss principle of "proper rendering of accounts in such a manner that it offers a most reliable picture of the financial and income situation" and the "true and fair view" is now not very wide. Nevertheless, the creation of hidden reserves decided by the board of directors is still authorised.

Professional accounting standards are not as developed as in the USA, the UK and in the EC. The Swiss professional body "the Fiduciary Chamber" (the Chamber) publishes an Audit manual which includes comments on the preparation of financial statements. The Chamber also publishes a professional magazine. Several audit recommendations and professional communications have been issued by the Chamber as at the end of 1992. A Foundation for accounting and reporting recommendations "FER" related to the Chamber has also issued eight recommendations.

Whoever is obliged by law to have their company name entered in the Commercial Register is also obliged to keep such books of account as are necessary for the company depending upon the nature and the extent of its business.

The most common legal entity used in Switzerland is the corporation (limited company). The commentary in this chapter is based on the practices which apply to corporations.

Switzerland

Form and Content of Financial Statements

The minimum content of financial statements is prescribed by the Swiss Code of Obligations.

The annual financial statements are prepared by the board of directors and are approved by the general meeting of shareholders and comprise:

- Profit and loss statement
- Balance Sheet
- Attachments

Inventories must also be prepared.

The board of directors prepares for each year a business report which is composed of the annual financial statements, the annual report and the consolidated statement, if it is required by law.

The annual financial statements shall be prepared in accordance with the principle of "proper rendering of accounts in such a manner that if offers a most reliable picture of the financial and income situation of the company". It also contains the previous year's figures. The proper rendering of accounts shall, in particular, follow the principles of:

- completeness of the annual financial statement;

- clarity and materiality of the statements;

- prudence;

- continuation of the Company's activity (going concern);

- consistency in presentation and valuation; and

- prohibition of setting off assets and liabilities, as well as of expenses and income.

The principles of proper rendering of accounts may be overruled in that hidden reserves may be created by the board of directors. Hidden reserves, which exceed the fairly assessed depreciation, value adjustments and provisions, are permitted, taking into account the interests of the shareholders to the extent that they can be justified having regard to the continuing prosperity of the company and the need to maintain a stable dividend policy. The creation of hidden reserves is not disclosed in the annual financial statements although the auditor must be informed of their existence. Nevertheless, any material reduction in the hidden reserves must be disclosed in the attachments to the financial statements.

The profit and loss statement shows operational and non-operational, as well as extraordinary, income and expenses. The balance sheet shows the current assets and the capital assets, the outside funds and the equity. Each of the sections is divided into individual figures which follow, but in less detail than and with some small differences to, the layout of the balance sheet and the profit and loss statement prescribed in the EC 4th Directive.

The attachment includes additional information such as guarantees, indemnity liabilities and pledges in favour of third parties; assets pledged or assigned for the security of the company's liabilities; liabilities from leasing contracts; the fire insurance value of the assets; liabilities to personnel welfare institutions; amounts, interest rate and maturities of bonds issued; the net total decrease of the hidden reserves if this causes the business result to be shown considerably more favorably than is in fact the case; revaluations; own shares acquired; share capital movements; deviations from the principle of proper rendering of accounts when authorised; important shareholders (more than 5%) for stock exchange listed companies; and consolidation principles.

The Code of Obligations does not make any distinction between small and large companies regarding the Form and Content of financial statements. Large stock exchange listed companies may disclose additional information, but they are not obliged to do so. A law on stock exchanges and securities trading is being developed in Switzerland (a preliminary draft was issued in March 1991) which may increase the level of information to be published by quoted companies.

Public Filing Requirements

Companies whose shares are traded on a stock exchange, or companies which have bond issues outstanding, must publish their annual financial statements and their consolidated statement as approved by the general meeting of shareholders in the Swiss Official Gazette of Commerce, or a copy shall be sent to every person requesting it.

Other corporations must make their annual financial statements, consolidated statement of account and the auditors' report available to creditors who can provide evidence that they need access in order to protect their own interests.

Banks, insurance companies, mutual investment funds and pension funds have to file their annual financial statements with the Swiss supervisory body. Public banks and insurance companies have to publish their financial statements (annually, half yearly or quarterly, depending on size) in the Swiss Official Gazette of Commerce.

There is no general requirement for annual financial statements to be filed at a commercial registry as exists in EC countries.

The annual financial statement must be approved by a general meeting of shareholders within six months (four months for banks) after the end of the financial year. At least twenty days notice of the meeting must be given. For this purpose, the

Switzerland

annual report, the annual financial statement, the consolidated statement and the auditors' report must be made available for inspection by the shareholders at the company's registered office. Any shareholder may also request that a copy of these documents be sent to him.

There are no specific penalties for non-compliance with legal requirements or failure to file annual financial statements. In the case of non-compliance, the supervisory body will investigate if the corporation is a bank or an insurance company and in all cases, the auditors will react, and, if necessary, call a general meeting of shareholders.

If the annual financial statement does not comply with the law, the auditors will qualify their report and the general meeting of shareholders may not approve the annual financial statement presented to them. If the corporation is monitored by a supervisory body then this authority may take appropriate action.

The annual financial statement shall be expressed in Swiss Francs and written in one of the four official Swiss languages: German, French, Italian or Romanch.

The first accounting period may be for a period of up to twenty-four months. Thereafter the annual financial statements shall be prepared every year. A company is free to choose its year end. Once it has been selected however a subsequent change requires a modification of the articles of incorporation approved by a general meeting of the shareholders.

Audit Requirements

Switzerland has a well-organised auditing profession. It is a long and difficult process to qualify as a registered accountant and accordingly all the standards in the profession are very high. Even if the financial statements are not very informative, it is unlikely that the figures themselves will portray the financial situation of the company as being better than it actually is. This is particularly true for larger companies which are usually audited by a recognised accountant.

Corporations must appoint one or more auditors who must be qualified to fulfil their duties with the company to be audited. The auditors are elected by the general meeting of shareholders for a maximum term of three years although re-election is possible. A limited liability company (Sarl) does not have to appoint an auditor.

The auditors report to the general meeting of shareholders and they must be independent from the board of directors and from any shareholder who has a majority vote. Anybody, provided he is qualified to fulfil his duties, may be appointed as auditor of a corporation.

If the company has its shares listed on the stock exchange or has outstanding bond issues the law requires the auditor to meet special professional qualifications. The special professional qualifications required are set out in a government ordinance and broadly represent the Swiss equivalent of CPA or Chartered Accountant.

The same special requirements apply if a company exceeds two of the following in two consecutive years:

● a balance sheet total of 20,000,000 Swiss Francs;

● revenues of 40,000,000 Swiss Francs; and

● an average annual number of employees of 200.

The auditors of banks and insurance companies must be approved by their supervisory body.

At least one auditor must have his domicile, registered office, or a registered branch office in Switzerland.

The auditors examine whether the books and records and the annual accounts, and the intended appropriation of profits comply with the law and the articles of incorporation. They then recommend to the shareholders acceptance or rejection of the financial statements. Without a report from the auditor no resolution concerning the financial statements may be passed in general meeting.

Where a company is required by law to have specially qualified auditors, the auditors prepare a report for the board of directors in which they comment on the conduct of and the result of their audit. If such a company is required to prepare consolidated financial statements, its auditor shall examine and report on whether the statements comply with the law relating to the rules of consolidation.

The auditors shall be notified in detail of the creation and dissolution of replacement reserves and hidden reserves.

Auditors are also required by law for duties other than auditing the annual financial statements, for example formation and dissolution of a company, increase and decrease of share capital, etc.

Valuation Principles

The policies of prudence and accruals underly the recording of income and expenses. Income is recognised only when realised. Losses/expenses must be recorded as soon as they are known by the company, even if they are not realised.

The historical cost principles underly the valuation of assets. The valuation of fixed assets may not exceed the acquisition, or manufacturing, costs less the necessary depreciation. The lower of cost or market value principle is applicable for current assets.

Quoted securities are an exception to the cost basis. They must be valued at, as a maximum, their average stock exchange price during the month preceding the date of the balance sheet. As stated above, hidden reserves may be created by the board of directors without disclosing their impact on the annual financial statements. Consequently the result for the period, disclosed in the financial statement, may not reflect the true position.

If, due to a loss shown in the balance sheet, half of the share capital and legal reserves has been eroded, real property whose value has risen above its acquisition or manufacturing cost may, for the purpose of eliminating the balance sheet deficit, be revalued to its current value. The revaluation surplus shall be shown separately as a revaluation reserve.

Alternative valuation principles such as replacement value or current value are not permitted in Switzerland for the annual financial statement of a corporation.

For banks and insurance companies, the valuation principles stated above are generally applicable with some minor differences.

Group Financial Statements

Swiss law does not describe in great detail what comprises a group of companies. The principle of "common management" is the most important criterion to follow when determining whether or not a company has to prepare consolidated financial statements.

A company which, by majority vote or by another method, controls one or more companies under common management (a group of companies), shall prepare group financial statements. The company is exempt from doing so if, during two consecutive financial years, together with other group companies, it does not exceed two of the following:

● a balance sheet total of 10,000,000 Swiss Francs;

● revenues of 20,000,000 Swiss Francs; and

● an average annual number of employees of 200.

However, consolidated financial statements must be prepared if:

● the company has outstanding bond issues;

● the company's shares are listed on a stock exchange; and

● shareholders holding at least 10% of the share capital request them.

Intermediate holding companies, included within consolidated financial statements examined according to the provisions of Swiss or equivalent foreign law, need not prepare separate consolidated statements of account if it communicates the parent's consolidated statements, in the same way as its own annual statements, to its shareholders.

They are, however, obliged to prepare their own separate consolidated financial statements if they are required to publish an annual report or if requested to do so by shareholders holding at least 10% of the share capital.

The group financial statements include a balance sheet, a profit and loss account and an attachment. A statement of cash flows may be added. The attachment states the consolidation and valuation principles. The minimum layout prescribed for annual financial statements is also applicable for group financial statements. Swiss practice is mostly influenced by international standards. The level of information given by larger groups depends on the importance of the group and its international connections.

Group financial statements may use replacement cost, book value or historical cost valuation bases, but the valuation principle used must be disclosed in the attachment. Historical cost or book value are the most commonly used methods, although the Audit manual recommends replacement cost.

The basis of consolidation is not prescribed by law but the trend is to meet international standards and principles. The group financial statement is required to show a "most reliable picture of the financial and income situation".

In the parent company's own annual financial statement, its investment in subsidiaries shall be shown at cost less depreciation. In certain cases the investment may be revalued.

If a company is required to prepare a consolidated statement, an auditor with appropriate qualifications shall examine whether it complies with the law and the rules of consolidation. The auditor of the consolidated statement may not necessarily audit the parent's own financial statements.

As the general meeting of shareholders of the parent company has to approve the consolidated statement of account, the group auditors' responsibilities, in case of fault, are similar to the responsibility of the company's auditor. Consolidated statements must be audited in the same way as the company accounts. The valuation principles should be carefully checked, especially if the consolidated valuation principles differ from those used in the company's accounts.

Switzerland

Depreciation

Fixed assets cannot be included in the balance sheet at more than purchase or production cost, less depreciation appropriate to the circumstances. Depreciation rates are determined as a rule by the life of the asset. The tax authorities have laid down the following standard rates which are widely used in Switzerland:

	Percentage of Cost
● Property	1 – 4
● Office furniture and equipment	7.5 – 15
● Purchased goodwill	12.5 – 33.3
● Plant and machinery, motor vehicles, computer installation and software	20

These rates are based on the straight line method. Depreciation is also permitted using the reducing balance method, in which case the rates stated above are doubled.

In the balance sheet, depreciation is either deducted directly from the fixed assets, which is the most widely used method, or shown separately as a provision.

Leasing

Lease contracts may either be capitalised in the balance sheet and the corresponding lease liability recognised or the instalments paid charged directly to the profit and loss statement as a rental. Whilst both methods are permitted the Audit manual recommends the capitalisation method in the case of finance leases.

If leasing contracts are not included in the balance sheet the total amount of future liabilities must be disclosed in the attachment.

Research and Development

Capitalisation of research and development costs is only permitted if those costs can be identified with a definite product which has been shown to be commercially viable based on a carefully prepared plan.

Capitalisation is not permitted for basic research, that is, expenditure on general research, on development activities to acquire new scientific knowledge, or on product development in the wider sense.

Inventories

Inventory is valued at the lower of cost or market value. Raw materials, work in progress, finished goods and merchandise may be stated separately or together in the balance sheet. Inventory may be valued by the reference to average cost, LIFO, FIFO or selling price less estimated profit margin.

Changes in the valuation method are allowed if they can be justified in which case the change should be disclosed in the attachment to the financial statements.

Additional provisions, which form part of the hidden reserves, are often made against the value of inventory.

Intangible Assets

This includes concessions, patents, goodwill, research and development, software, know-how and the company's formation expenses. The capitalisation of these items is restrictive and in particular internally generated goodwill may not be capitalised. The maximum value allowed is cost less depreciation. The principle of prudence prevails and the economic value of each item should be assessed and not exceeded.

Company formation expenses may be capitalised and depreciated over a legal maximum of five years.

Capital and Reserves

The share capital of the company (corporation) shall amount to a minimum of 100,000 Swiss Francs and the minimum paid in capital allowed is the greater of 20% of the issued capital and 50,000 Swiss Francs.

Shares may be issued either in the name of a holder or to a bearer. The par value of each share shall not be less than 10 Swiss Francs. The company may create ordinary, authorised and conditional capital as well as participation certificates and profit sharing certificates.

It is possible to reduce share capital but this is subject to special regulations designed to protect the company's creditors.

Accumulated profits may be distributed after certain allocations have been made to the legal reserves and the statutory reserves. The board of directors propose the profit allocation to the general meeting of shareholders who approve it (or not) based upon the auditors' recommendation.

At least 5% of the annual profit shall be allocated to the general reserve until it has reached 20% of the paid up share capital. In addition, further allocations must be made equal to 10% of any dividend which is in excess of 5% of the paid up capital until the total general reserve equals 50% of the share capital. Other allocations are also required by the law. The legal reserves may be used only in special circumstances.

Certain other reserves, such as a revaluation reserve, may only be utilised if the requirements of the law are fulfilled.

Switzerland

The general meeting of shareholders may approve the creation of reserves, which are neither provided for by law nor by the articles of incorporation or which exceed these requirements, to the extent that they are:

- necessary for replacement purposes; or
- justified with regard to the continuing prosperity of the Company or the maintenance of a stable dividend policy.

Allocations to welfare institutions may be decided upon by the general meeting of shareholders.

Swiss quoted companies usually try to maintain a regular dividend policy. They are helped in this by the control they have over their hidden reserves.

Foreign Currency Translation

The prudence principle prevails. Gains on foreign currency may be accounted for only when they are realised whilst unrealised losses must always be accounted for.

For fixed assets, the historical rate shall not be exceeded. Current assets and liabilities may be valued at current rates so long as the prudence principle is respected. In some cases, the prudence principle is not followed (for example banks). Stock exchange quoted securities may be valued at the current rate even if this results in the recognition of an unrealised profit.

There are various methods which are acceptable, such as "current/non-current", "monetary/non-monetary"; "modified monetary" and "current rate", although the prudence principle is the overriding consideration.

Taxation

Taxes on profit and on equity are levied on a State (Canton) and on a Federal level. The combined rate ranges from 8 to 45%. The international requirement for tax provisions has become more common in Switzerland, especially by large groups and by companies affiliated to a foreign group.

Dividends paid are submitted to a withholding tax of 35% recoverable by shareholders who are resident in Switzerland. Foreign resident shareholders may recover the withholding tax subject to appropriate double taxation treaties.

Unusual and Prior Period Items

Non-operational and extraordinary income and expenses, as well as the profits from the sale of capital assets, should be shown separately in the profit and loss account. The company may give additional disclosure in its accounts and in some cases the basic requirement for accounts to give "the most reliable picture of the financial and income situation" may oblige the company to provide additional information.

Operational Prior Period Items such as valuation adjustments may be reflected by adjusting the reserves brought forward and the comparative figures. Prior Period Items which correct errors made in previous periods will be treated in the same way as extraordinary items.

Retirement Benefits

Contributions to the social security system as well as to a pension fund (welfare institutions) are treated as expenses in the profit and loss account in the year they are paid or become payable.

In Switzerland, the pension fund must be a separate entity (usually a foundation with its own legal existence). Therefore, provisions for retirement benefits are not shown in the balance sheet of the company.

The law prescribes that a retirement indemnity shall be paid to employees over fifty who leave the company after twenty years of employment. Such retirement indemnity provisions are not usual since the welfare institutions have replaced this system.

Related Party Transactions

Transactions with related parties should be made at arm's length. Claims and liabilities against other companies in a group or against shareholders who hold a participation in the company shall be separately shown in the balance sheet.

Shareholders' contributions made in kind when a company is formed are acceptable but valued prudently.

Shareholders and members of the board of directors, as well as connected persons, who have unjustifiably and in bad faith received dividends, shares of profits, other profit shares, and interests etc to the extent that they are obviously disproportionate to the economic situation of the Company, are obliged to return them.

The obligation to return lapses, in law, five years after the receipt of the benefit.

United Kingdom

Neville Russell

The United Kingdom was one of the first countries to institute modern financial reporting. Company law and the accountancy profession both have their origins in the mid-nineteenth century with the formation of the limited liability company. The Industrial Revolution and the spread of international trading links from Britain at that time sowed the seeds of financial reporting in all corners of what is now the Commonwealth. Today, British accounting still plays a major role as the number of multinational companies continues to grow.

Legislation in the United Kingdom relating to financial statements and auditing is set out in the Companies Act 1985 (which reflects amendments introduced by the Companies Act 1989). This Act has implemented European Community legislation up to and including the Eighth Company Law Directive.

Traditionally, the function of the financial statements has been to present an historical record to the shareholders of the performance and state of affairs of the business and the uses which management, who are not necessarily the owners, have made of the available resources.

The Companies Act requires that financial statements should always show a true and fair view of the financial affairs and performance of a company and this requirement ultimately overrides other provisions of the Companies Act and the pronouncements of professional bodies.

In addition to company law there are also professional pronouncements which have to be taken into account when preparing financial statements. The main pronouncements are Financial Reporting Standards (FRSs) issued by the Accounting Standards Board (ASB) and Statements of Standard Accounting Practice (SSAPs) issued by the ASB's predecessors and which they have adopted. Unlike the provisions of the Companies Act which only have to be followed in law by limited companies, FRSs and SSAPs must be followed by the preparers of any financial statements which purport to show a true and fair view. FRSs and SSAPs are usually compatible with, if not more stringent than, International Accounting Standards.

United Kingdom

Although not strictly part of company law the legislation does give weight to FRS/SSAPs as companies are required to disclose whether or not they have complied with them in the preparation of their financial statements. If they have not, the reasons must also be disclosed. The requirements of the Companies Act, FRSs and SSAPs are generally totally independent of the requirements of taxation authorities (the Inland Revenue).

The profession also plays an important part in the interpretation and implementation of company and tax legislation. Representation to the relevant government departments is made through a series of committees and there is generally a high degree of liaison and co-operation between the profession and the government.

In addition to the Companies Act 1985 there is other legislation which requires certain enterprises, which are not necessarily companies, to produce annual financial statements, many of which require to be audited. These include: trades unions, pension funds, charities, housing associations and friendly societies.

Form and Content of Financial Statements

The directors are responsible for the preparation of financial statements which give a true and fair view of the company's financial state of affairs and of its results. The form and content of a company's financial statements are prescribed by the Companies Act, FRSs and SSAPs. Non-compliance with any of their requirements will usually be referred to in the auditors' report.

The financial statements of limited liability companies which are presented to shareholders should contain:

- Directors' report including a review of the business

- Profit and loss account

- Statement of total recognised gains and losses

- Balance sheet

- Cash flow statement (unless exempt)

- Notes to the financial statements including the accounting policies adopted by the company

- Auditors' report (except for dormant companies)

The company's activities should be divided into continuing operations, acquisitions (as a component of continuing operations) and discontinued operations. The results of each should be disclosed separately in the profit and loss account and notes.

The requirement to present a statement of total recognised gains and losses was introduced in FRS 3. This statement will include not only the realised profit or loss reported for the year but also any unrealised profits and losses, such as surpluses arising on the revaluation of properties and currency translation differences on foreign currency net investments.

Parent companies must publish group financial statements in the form of consolidated financial statements, dealing with the group as a whole. Many companies also publish a chairman's statement.

Listed and USM companies are obliged to comply with additional disclosure requirements that are imposed on them by the International Stock Exchange (ISE) or their securities may be suspended from listing. The general principle underlying these requirements is that any information necessary to enable holders of a company's listed securities and the public to appraise the position of the company and to avoid the establishment of a false market in its listed securities must be notified to the ISE.

Special requirements also exist for foreign companies whose securities are traded on the ISE or which have a branch in the United Kingdom.

Small companies are generally permitted to provide less detailed information than other companies in the financial statements they prepare for shareholders and are exempt from preparing a cash flow statement.

Companies are categorised as small or medium-sized if during two of the last three financial years they did not exceed at least two of the following three limits:

	Small	Medium
Balance sheet totals	£1.4m	£5.6m
Turnover	£2.8m	£11.2m
Average number of employees	50	250

These limits were set in November 1992 and are revised from time to time.

Shareholders in companies listed on the ISE can chose not to have the full financial statements, in which case the company is required to provide them with a Summary Financial Statement, the contents of which are prescribed by law.

Public Filing Requirements

A distinction is made in law between:

- a public limited company (plc) that must have a minimum allotted share capital of £50,000 (at least one quarter paid up), state that it is a public company in its memorandum of association and have the words "Public Limited Company" or "plc" as the last part of its name; and

- a private company (Limited or Ltd) which may not offer shares to the public.

United Kingdom

Limited companies, both public and private, must each year file with the Registrar of Companies, their financial statements together with the directors' and auditors' reports (where required) and an annual return. These are available for public inspection.

For public filing purposes only, small private companies are permitted to exclude the directors' report, the profit and loss account and many of the notes to the financial statements. Medium- sized companies may exclude certain elements of the profit and loss account disclosures. These are known as abbreviated financial statements.

Companies listed on the ISE or quoted on the USM are required to publish half-yearly reports on their activities and results during the first six months of each financial year. Such reports need not be audited. These reports comprise, essentially, profit and loss account information and supporting narrative.

Financial statements will normally cover a period of twelve months. A company is permitted to change its accounting reference date as long as the resulting accounting period is for not less than six months and not more than eighteen months. A company may normally only have an accounting period which is longer than twelve months once every five years. There is no similar restriction for companies shortening their accounting period.

Public companies are required to file their financial statements with the Registrar of Companies within seven months of their accounting reference date and private companies within ten months. They must be in English, except for companies whose registered office is in Wales, which may file financial statements in Welsh. There is no restriction on the currency in which the financial statements are denominated. The filing of financial statements denominated in European Currency Units (ECUs) in addition to those filed in Sterling, or other functional currency, is expressly permitted within the Companies Act.

Where financial statements are filed after the due date, or if they are defective in any way, the company and/or its directors are liable to a fine, the limit of which is prescribed by law. There are also provisions to force companies to rectify defective financial statements, the cost of which has to be borne personally by the directors.

The annual return must be filed once every calendar year, and in any event not later than one year after the previous return. It contains details of:

● The registered office

● The authorised share capital and allotted share capital

● Mortgages and charges on the company's assets

● Shareholders and their shareholdings

● Directors and the company secretary

Audit Requirements

Every company, unless it is dormant, is required to appoint a registered auditor. It is ensured that the auditor is independent and sufficiently skilled to carry out his duties both by the legislation contained in the Companies Act and by the ethics and internal regulations of the professional bodies. Members of these professional bodies are not automatically registered auditors but are eligible if they satisfy certain regulations introduced by those bodies. In practice, a firm of accountants is usually appointed rather than an individual auditor.

Registered auditors may be members of:

● The Institute of Chartered Accountants in England and Wales

● The Institute of Chartered Accountants of Scotland

● The Institute of Chartered Accountants in Ireland

● The Chartered Association of Certified Accountants

Holders of overseas auditing qualifications may also be eligible to become registered auditors.

The auditor is appointed by the shareholders and reports, to them, whether in his opinion the financial statements show a true and fair view of the state of affairs of the company, its profit or loss for the year and comply with the Companies Act. He should refer in his report to any inconsistencies between the financial statements and the directors' report. Where group financial statements are prepared the auditor must report on them in addition to reporting on those of the individual companies within the group.

By law, the auditor must also refer to any instances where proper accounting records have not been kept or where he has not received all the information and explanations required by him for the purpose of his audit.

An auditor is required to:

● refer to any significant departures from FRS/SSAPs or requirements of the Companies Act unless he concurs with the departure; and

● state whether the audit has been conducted in accordance with the auditing standards.

The audit report will also include a statement of the auditors' responsibilities and a brief summary of the audit process followed.

United Kingdom

Valuation Principles

UK companies generally adopt the historical cost convention. (That is, the assets and liabilities of the company are stated at original cost subject to depreciation or provisions). Certain fixed assets, in particular property, may be revalued to market value. By law, any surplus or deficit so arising must be transferred to a non-distributable revaluation reserve which is separately shown on the balance sheet. However, when a permanent diminution in value below depreciated original cost occurs, the deficit must be taken to the profit and loss account as a realised loss.

Investment properties (as defined by SSAP 19) are required to be stated at market value and the investments of pension funds are required to be stated at their valuation (as determined by an actuary).

Both the Companies Act and SSAP 2 require that the accounting policies applied to items that are material or critical to the financial statements should be disclosed. They also assume that in the preparation of the financial statements, four fundamental concepts (going concern, accruals, consistency, and prudence) have been followed unless stated to the contrary.

Group Financial Statements

Detailed rules for the preparation of group financial statements are set out in the Companies Act 1985, FRS 2 and SSAPs 22 and 23. They will be in the form of consolidated financial statements, and must be prepared by every company that has one or more subsidiary undertakings unless it qualifies for one of the following exemptions:

● it is itself a subsidiary of another company, incorporated in the European Community, which in turn prepares consolidated financial statements which comply with the 7th EC Company Law Directive; or

● the group as a whole qualifies as either a small or medium-sized group. The limits which have to be satisfied to qualify as a small or medium-sized group are broadly similar to those for small or medium-sized companies referred to above.

A subsidiary undertaking is an enterprise, normally but not necessarily a company, which is controlled by the parent. Control is normally demonstrated by controlling more than 50% of the votes attaching to the shares of the enterprise or 50% of the votes of the board of directors. Where control can be demonstrated by other means, an enterprise may be regarded as a subsidiary undertaking.

Ordinarily consolidated financial statements will incorporate those of the parent and all its subsidiary undertakings. However a parent is required to exclude a subsidiary undertaking from consolidation if any of the following conditions are satisfied:

● its inclusion would involve expense or delay disproportionate to the benefit gained and if more than one subsidiary is excluded they are in aggregate not material to the group;

- long term restrictions substantially hinder effective management by the parent;

- its shares are held exclusively for resale; or

- the business of the subsidiary undertaking is so different, that if consolidated in the group financial statements they would not show a true and fair view.

The form and content of group financial statements are prescribed by law and are substantially the same as for single companies except that there is no requirement to present a profit and loss account for the holding company alone. The interest of the minority shareholders should be shown as a separate item wherever it appears in the financial statements.

The accounting reference dates of the subsidiaries should coincide with that of the holding company and, if they do not, this should be explained in the financial statements. If the year end of a subsidiary undertaking is more than three months apart from that of the parent, it must prepare financial statements as at the date of the parents' year end for inclusion in the consolidated financial statements.

FRS 2 requires the effective date for accounting for both acquisition and disposal of subsidiaries to be the date on which control passes to or from the parent.

There are two possible methods of accounting for subsidiaries: acquisition (which is the most widespread) and merger accounting. Where acquisition accounting is used the purchase consideration should be allocated between the subsidiary's underlying net assets (other than goodwill) on the basis of their fair values to the acquiring company. Under the acquisition method the results of the subsidiary are consolidated from the date control passes.

Any excess of the consideration over the fair values of the subsidiaries net assets is called positive goodwill. Conversely, where the fair values of the net assets exceed the consideration, the difference is termed negative goodwill. SSAP 22 provides that any goodwill arising on acquisition should be written off immediately against reserves, although amortisation (over its useful economic life) through the profit and loss account is also permitted. Negative goodwill should be credited directly to reserves.

The merger method of accounting for a business combination may only be used if certain restrictive criteria, as set out in SSAP 23 and the Companies Act 1985 are satisfied. The effects of using the merger method are that the consolidated financial statements incorporate the combined companies' results as if they had always been combined and no goodwill arises on consolidation.

When a subsidiary is sold, the consolidated profit and loss account should include the results of that subsidiary up to the date of sale and the gain or loss arising on the disposal of the investment.

United Kingdom

By law, investments in related undertakings must be shown separately on the balance sheet. A related company is one in which the investing company holds shares on a long term basis for the purpose of securing a contribution to that company's own activities by exerting its influence over the related company. Such influence will be assumed if the holding of equity shares with unrestricted voting rights is more than 20%. A related company is normally accounted for in the group financial statements under the equity method whereby the group's share of the company's profits or losses and reserves from the date of acquisition are brought into account.

SSAP 1 also requires investments in non-corporate enterprises such as joint ventures and consortia to be accounted for under the equity method in the group financial statements.

The auditor of the parent company is required to form an opinion on the consolidated financial statements even though the audit of the subsidiaries may have been performed by someone else. There is no exemption from audit and filing of financial statements for subsidiary undertakings. Where a parent is exempt from preparing group financial statements the reason why must be given and if exemption is being claimed on the grounds that it is a small or medium-sized group, the auditor is required to report whether, in his opinion, the group qualifies for that exemption.

Depreciation

The cost or valuation (less estimated residual value) of any fixed asset that has a limited useful economic life, must be depreciated or amortised systematically over that life. For each class of fixed asset, disclosure must be made of:

- the cumulative amount provided for depreciation at the beginning and end of the financial year;

- the amount provided in the year;

- the amount of any adjustment arising; and

- the depreciation methods, useful economic lives and depreciation rates used.

Depreciation is not normally charged on freehold land unless it is subject to depletion (for example by extraction of minerals) or is adversely affected by other factors such as location.

The depreciation methods used should be those which the directors consider most appropriate having regard to the types of assets and their use in the business. Generally, either the straight line or reducing balance method is used to write off the cost less residual value of the assets over their useful economic lives.

Under SSAP 19, investment properties (those held for rental income and potential appreciation in value) should be revalued annually to their open market value and should not be depreciated unless held on a lease with an unexpired term of less than 20 years.

Leasing

Accounting for leases is governed by SSAP 21 which broadly follows IAS17 in distinguishing different treatments for finance and operating leases. Other than the general legal requirement to disclose financial commitments, there are no statutory requirements regarding the disclosure of leases or the methods of accounting for them.

Finance leases (those leases which transfer substantially all of the risks and rewards of ownership to the lessee) should be accounted for by lessees as the acquisition of an asset and the assumption of a liability. Lessors should account for finance leases as a receivable. Each rental payment should be allocated between an interest element and a reduction of capital outstanding on a basis which gives a constant rate of return: in the case of lessees, on the outstanding liability; in the case of lessors, on the net cash investment (ie, after tax allowances) in the lease.

Lessees account for operating leases (all other leases) as a normal hire of assets, with rentals being recorded on a systematic basis (usually based on actual payments) over the period of hire. The lessor continues to recognise the leased asset within its own tangible assets.

SSAP 21 contains comprehensive disclosure requirements covering all aspects of a company's activities as a lessor and the future financial commitments of lessees under the terms of leases entered into.

Research and Development

The law prohibits the inclusion of research costs as an asset in the balance sheet and allows development costs to be capitalised only in special circumstances.

Under SSAP 13, development costs may only be capitalised if they can be separately identified with a technically and commercially viable project, are expected to produce sufficient net revenue (after all other costs) to cover development costs and there are adequate resources to complete the project. Costs written off cannot subsequently be reinstated.

The amounts capitalised should be amortised on a systematic basis from the start of commercial production.

SSAP 13 imposes additional disclosure requirements for larger and public companies. Such companies will not only have to show the movements on deferred development expenditure and the amount carried forward at the beginning and end of the period, but they will also have to disclose any research and development expenditure written off and development costs amortised in a period. Deferred development expenditure should be shown as an intangible fixed asset in the balance sheet. The accounting policy on research and development expenditure should be explained.

United Kingdom

Inventories

Inventories are referred to as stocks in the Companies Act and are divided into four categories:

- Raw materials and consumables

- Work in progress

- Finished goods and goods for resale

- Payments on account

Inventories are included at purchase price or production cost of each individual item, or group of similar items, unless the net realisable value is lower, in which case the lower value should be substituted. Purchase price is the actual price paid plus any expenses incidental to acquisition. Production cost is the total of the purchase price of raw materials and consumables used, direct production costs and a reasonable proportion of indirect production costs, but excluding distribution costs.

Legislation allows the use of the FIFO, LIFO, weighted average, or any other similar method to be used but the method chosen must be the one which appears to the directors to be most appropriate. SSAP 9, however, requires the use of a method which provides a fair approximation to actual cost and does not consider that LIFO and the base stock method will normally meet this requirement.

SSAP 9 also deals with long-term contracts where the work normally extends for more than one year. Long-term contracts should be assessed on a contract-by-contract basis and the revenue and related expenditure should be recorded in the profit and loss account as contract activity progresses. Revenue should be recognised in a manner appropriate to the stage of completion of the contracts, the contractor's industry, the particular business and the customers involved. However, no profit should be attributed to the part of the contract performed at the accounting date until the profitable outcome of the contract can be assessed with reasonable certainty.

In the balance sheet, the amount by which recorded revenue on contracts exceed payments on account received from customers, is included within receivables (debtors) and separately disclosed as "amounts recoverable on contracts". Any balance of costs incurred on long-term contracts, after deducting amounts transferred to the profit and loss account and after deducting foreseeable losses and payments received on account, is disclosed under inventories as "long-term contract balances".

Where payments on account exceeds the aggregate of revenue recognised to date and the balance of costs not yet released to profit and loss account, the excess should be included within creditors, described as Payments Received on Account.

Intangible Assets

Intangible assets may be included at their cost (less provision for permanent diminution in value) or at current cost, and include:

- research and development;

- patents and trademarks;

- concessions and licences;

- purchased goodwill (which may not be revalued above cost); and

- brands.

By law, non-purchased goodwill cannot be included as an asset but a company may temporarily have purchased goodwill in its balance sheet. SSAP 22 dictates that this should normally be written-off against reserves immediately but the option exists to amortise goodwill through the profit and loss account over its estimated useful life.

Accounting for brands has become a major issue in financial reporting in the United Kingdom and research into the most appropriate methods is still continuing.

Capital and Reserves

In certain circumstances, amounts must be transferred to special reserves that are defined by law and whose uses are restricted.

Capital Redemption Reserve. Where a company redeems or purchases shares (ordinary or preference) out of profits, it must transfer to the capital redemption reserve a sum equal to the nominal value of the shares redeemed. This reserve may only be used to issue paid-up bonus shares to the members.

Share Premium Account. Where shares are issued at a premium, the excess of the consideration over the nominal value must, in most circumstances, be transferred to a share premium account. The share premium account may not be distributed and can only be used to:

- issue fully paid bonus shares;

- write off preliminary expenses;

- write off the expenses of share or debenture issues;

- write off any discount allowed on a debenture issue; and

- provide the premium payable on the redemption of debentures.

Revaluation Reserve.   Where an asset is revalued by reference to current cost or market valuation, any surplus or deficit must be transferred to a revaluation reserve. A permanent diminution below depreciated original cost must be taken to the profit and loss account as a realised loss.   The revaluation reserve must be reduced to the extent that it is considered to be no longer necessary.   An amount may be transferred from the revaluation reserve to profit and loss account if the amounts were previously charged to that account or represent realised profits.   The revaluation reserve may be capitalised for the issue of additional shares.

Distributions.   If the directors of a company wish to make a distribution to shareholders, for example by paying a dividend, the company must have profits available to do so.   In very broad terms, these "distributable" profits are accumulated realised profits less accumulated realised losses insofar as they have not already been distributed.   Realised profits are determined for this purpose in accordance with generally accepted accounting principles.

A public company must also comply with the further legal requirement that when it has made a distribution out of distributable profits, its remaining net assets must not be less than the total of its called-up share capital and undistributable reserves. Undistributable reserves include the capital redemption reserve, share premium account, and revaluation reserve.

Where the latest financial statements (which will normally be used to decide whether a distribution can be made) have been subject to a qualified audit report, the auditor must state in writing whether the qualification is considered material for determining the legality of a proposed distribution.

The profit and loss account of every company must show the aggregate amount of any dividends paid and proposed.   Certain related details must also be included in the directors' report.

Accumulated Losses.   Where the directors of a public company are alerted to a "serious loss of capital" (that is the net assets fall to 50% or less of the called-up share capital), they must by law call an extraordinary general meeting of the company to consider what, if any, measures should be taken to deal with the situation.   There are no similar legal requirements for private companies.

Foreign Currency Translation

SSAP 20 envisages two main types of transactions denominated in a foreign currency:

- those carried out individually by a company; and
- those carried out by a foreign subsidiary or branch.

In the first case, the transaction is recorded at the exchange rate ruling on the date of the transaction.   Any resulting exchange gain or loss is dealt with through the profit and loss account.   At the balance sheet date, monetary assets or liabilities (eg, bank balances) denominated in a foreign currency are normally translated at the year end rate except in certain specified circumstances. Once non-monetary assets (eg machinery and property) have been translated and recorded they will not normally be retranslated.

In the second case, the closing rate/net investment method should normally be used whereby the balance sheet of the foreign enterprise is translated at the exchange rate ruling at the balance sheet date. The profit and loss account may be translated at either the closing or average rate, provided that the method used is consistently applied.

Exchange differences resulting from the retranslation of the opening net assets of a foreign enterprise, or in circumstances where foreign investments are financed by foreign currency borrowings, should be dealt with through reserves. Where the affairs of a foreign subsidiary or branch are closely interlinked with those of the investing company, the temporal method rather than the closing rate/net investment method is applied. Its rules are the same as those for individual companies.

Taxation

A company pays corporation tax which is based on its trading profit for the accounting period after making certain adjustments to arrive at taxable profits. These adjustments are necessary mainly because the company, in reporting to the shareholders, is interested in showing a true and fair view of the profit on a normal commercial basis, whereas the Government has other objectives. Advance Corporation Tax (ACT) is payable when dividends are paid.

The major adjustments are:

- depreciation charged by the company is not deductible. Instead, fixed rate allowances are substituted. There are only very limited allowances for buildings;

- general or contingent provisions are not deductible; and

- dividends paid are not deductible.

Accounting income differs from taxable income due to either permanent differences or timing differences. SSAP 15 requires any tax which has been either deferred or accelerated by the effects of timing differences to be accounted for to the extent that it is probable that a liability or asset will crystallise. The most common causes of timing differences are:

- the use of the cash basis for tax purposes and the accruals basis for financial statements; and

- the replacement of depreciation by the system of capital allowances for tax purposes.

United Kingdom

Debit balances on deferred tax should not be carried forward as assets, unless they are expected to be recovered without replacement by equivalent debit balances.

Unusual and Prior Period Items

By law, a company's profit and loss account must separately identify any extraordinary items arising in the year. Extraordinary items should be disclosed on the face of the profit and loss account, after the tax charge. The financial statements must also give a further analysis of such items and particulars of any extraordinary income or charges in the notes. However, the provisions of FRS 3 are such that there is little likelihood of any items qualifying to be treated as extraordinary.

FRS 3 does recognise that certain elements of income or expense, whilst not extraordinary, may be sufficiently unusual to merit separate disclosure. These are referred to as exceptional items and their disclosure will normally be given as a note to the financial statements. FRS 3 requires certain items to be shown, if material, on the face of the profit and loss account, before the tax charge. These are:

● profits or losses on the sale or termination of an operation;

● costs of a fundamental reorganisation of the business; and

● profits or losses on the disposal of fixed assets.

By law, where a material amount relating to a preceding financial year is included in the profit and loss account, the effect must be stated. Under FRS 3, material adjustments applicable to prior years, which arise from changes in accounting policies or from the correction of fundamental errors, are accounted for (net of taxation effects) by restating prior years' figures and the opening balance of retained profits. Such adjustments may not be included in the current year's profit and loss account. Prior year adjustments do not include normal recurring corrections and adjustments of accounting estimates.

The cumulative effect of these adjustments should also be noted at the end of the statement of total recognised gains and losses.

Retirement Benefits

The law requires disclosure of:

● pension costs charged in the profit and loss account;

● any pension commitments for which provision has been made in the financial statements; and

● any commitment for which no provision has been made.

SSAP 24 requires disclosure of further information including:

- the nature of the pension plan;

- the accounting policy followed; and

- for certain types of plan only, an outline of the results of the most recent actuarial valuation including the main actuarial assumptions and the market value of the fund's assets at the date of the valuation.

SSAP 24 states that the cost of pensions should be charged against profits on a systematic basis over the service lives of the employees. For a defined contribution plan, the pension charge will be the sum of the contributions payable to the plan in the period. For a defined benefit plan, the annual charge should identify both the regular cost and any variations therefrom. The method of calculating the regular cost should ensure it is a substantially level percentage of the current and future payroll costs and any variations from regular cost should normally be recognised over the expected average remaining service lives of the employees. Exceptions to this general principle are described in the standard.

The same principle of accounting also applies to other post-retirement benefits given to employees eg, health care insurance.

Segmental Reporting

Listed companies and other large companies are required to provide segmental information based on both the business and the geographic sectors in which the company operates.

For each business and geographic sector an analysis of turnover, net profit and assets is required. Geographic sectors are defined either by the location of the company's operations or the markets served. Many companies provide this segmental information on both bases.

Treatment of Grants

Grants are generally divided into revenue and capital based grants.

Revenue based grants are credited to income in the period that they become due unless they relate to specific items of expenditure, in which case they are credited to income in the period that the expenditure is charged.

Capital based grants are either deducted from the cost of the related assets or credited to a deferred revenue account and released to income over the life of the related assets. The latter method is to be preferred as the former, although historically the one which has been most common, conflicts with the Companies Act requirement for fixed assets to be stated at cost, less depreciation.

Commitments and Contingencies

The Companies Act requires disclosure of:

- the estimated amount and legal nature of any contingent liabilities;

- charges given over the enterprise's assets as security for liabilities of other persons;

- future capital expenditure contracted for or authorised at the balance sheet date;

- pension commitments of the company; and

- other commitments not provided for but relevant when assessing the company's state of affairs eg future lease commitments.

Under SSAP 18 a contingent gain should not be disclosed unless it is probable that the gain will be realised. Uncertainties expected to affect the outcome of contingencies should be disclosed.

Under SSAP 17 events subsequent to the balance sheet date should be adjusted for in the financial statements only if they provide additional evidence of conditions existing at the balance sheet date eg resolution of litigation which was incomplete at the year end. Other material events occurring after the year end should be disclosed but no adjustments made to the financial statements.

Balances not Reflected in the Balance Sheet

Major financial commitments and contingent assets and liabilities must be disclosed in the notes to the financial statements.

Where a company enters into complex financial arrangements which result in assets/liabilities not being reflected in the financial statements full disclosure of the nature of the transactions and their consequences should be given.

Related Party Transactions

There is currently no UK standard which corresponds to IAS24 although an exposure draft has been in existence for some time. There are however, complex provisions concerning related party transactions in the Companies Act and these are almost exclusively restricted to transactions with directors or their connected parties. The main features of these provisions are that:

- there are very extensive restrictions on loans, and on provision of guarantees or security for loans, to directors;

- details of loans to, and guarantees or security given on behalf of, directors must be disclosed if they exist at any time during the reporting period; and

- transactions and arrangements between the company and any director or person connected with him (including close relatives, business partners and companies under his control), together with outstanding balances in respect of these, must usually be disclosed.

However, it is essential that all financial statements drawn up under the Companies Act show a true and fair view and this provision may be used to require disclosure of other related party transactions not otherwise mentioned in the legislation.

Price Level Changes

There is no legal requirement for financial statements to reflect the effects of inflation. A system of accounting for price level changes was developed by the professional bodies but the relevant standard has been withdrawn. However, companies may still present supplementary information in their financial statements which reflects changes in price levels and guidance is contained in "Accounting for the Effects of Changing Prices: A Handbook".

Future Developments

The Accounting Standards Board has commenced a major review of Accounting Standards in the United Kingdom and has already implemented several changes. More are likely to follow. Areas where new standards are expected include:

- capital instruments and off-balance sheet financing; and

- insurance companies.

The law relating to the appointment of auditors is under review and it is likely that the requirements for small companies will be relaxed.

United States of America

Chastang, Ferrell & Associates P A
Clifton Gunderson & Co
Eide Helmeke & Co
Hutchinson & Bloodgood
Lerman, Bauer, Altman & Co P C
Madsen, Sapp, Mena Rodriguez & Co P C
Schmaltz & Company P C
Weber Lipshie & Co
Withum, Smith & Brown
Wolf & Company of Massacheusetts P C

The United States has some of the most comprehensive and detailed accounting and reporting requirements in the world. These requirements, with few exceptions, are developed within the private sector, principally by the Financial Accounting Standards Board (FASB). Other groups establish accounting standards in specialised areas, including:

- Governmental Accounting Standards Board (GASB) - establishes accounting standards for governmental entities

- Accounting Standards Executive Committee (AcSEC) - provides supplementary guidance on financial reporting problems not addressed by the FASB or GASB

- Emerging Issues Task Force (EITF) - provides guidance on narrowly defined emerging issues and implementation problems

"Generally accepted accounting principles" (GAAP) consist of the rules, conventions, and procedures that determine how financial information is presented in financial statements. A major influence on GAAP for companies whose securities are publicly traded is the Securities and Exchange Commission (SEC). The SEC was created by federal legislation in 1934 and given the authority to prescribe accounting and auditing standards to be used by companies in financial reports required to be filed with the SEC. The SEC has historically looked to the FASB and its predecessors, the Accounting Principles Board (APB) and the Committee on Accounting Procedure (CAP) to set those standards, while retaining primarily an oversight role. In recent years, however, the SEC has increasingly expressed its attitudes on accounting and auditing issues in order to influence the standard-setting process.

Corporations are usually formed under state rather than federal law. Certified public accountants (CPAs) are licensed by each state and may not practice in other states unless they are licensed there also. While this would not seem to be conducive to a strong national accounting profession, most CPAs belong to the American Institute of Certified Public Accountants (AICPA) which promotes uniform technical and ethical standards.

Federal tax laws have little influence on generally accepted accounting principles or on the form and content of financial statements.

Form and Content of Financial Statements

Except for publicly held companies and certain regulated industries, there are no legal requirements regarding the form and content of companies' financial statements. They are based instead on GAAP that has been developed over the years. Statements of Financial Accounting Standards (SFAS) issued by the FASB are the primarily private-sector sources of GAAP in the United States. The SEC has established additional requirements for the form and content of financial statements of publicly held companies.

The content of a company's financial statements, which includes their accompanying footnotes, is the responsibility of the company's management, regardless of who actually prepares the statements or whether they are audited.

The statements are designed for general purposes and are primarily intended to address the needs of present and potential investors and creditors.

Under GAAP, the minimum elements of a company's basic financial statements are:

- Balance sheet (sometimes called a statement of financial condition)

- Income statement (sometimes called a statement of operations)

- Statement of changes in stockholders' equity

- Statement of cash flows (required by GAAP when both a balance sheet and income statement are presented)

- Notes to the financial statements

Publicly held companies must present comparative financial statements: two years of balance sheets and three years of income statements and statements of cash flows. Non public companies usually present comparative financial statements, for the most recent two years, although they are not required to do so.

Public Filing Requirements
Publicly Held Domestic Companies
The Securities and Exchange Commission (SEC) administers the statutes which govern the activities of companies whose securities are held and traded by the public. These statutes require the filing of reports with the SEC at various intervals if the company fits any of the following descriptions:

● companies with securities listed on a national securities exchange such as the New York Stock Exchange;

● companies whose securities are traded "over-the-counter", including companies listed on the National Association of Securities Dealer Automated Quotation (NASDAQ) system, if they have over $5 million in total assets, and a class of equity securities held by 500 or more holders;

● "over-the-counter" companies which do not meet the tests in the above paragraph, but which have voluntarily elected to comply with reporting requirements by registering under the relevant statue;

● companies with over 300 holders of a class of securities registered under the Securities Act; or

● companies with a class of securities registered under the Securities Act, for the fiscal year in which a registration becomes effective.

Both listed and "over-the-counter" companies registered under the Exchange Act must file certain reports, among which are the following:

Form 10K. This is an annual report which must be filed within 90 days after the end of a company's fiscal year. The annual report requires full description of business activities, including changes since the previous year; competitive conditions; backlog information; availability of raw material requirements; important patents and trademarks; research and development costs; new products information; environmental problems; segment information; and information on foreign operations. Required sections of the Form 10-K include:

● Selected financial data and a discussion and analysis by management of the company's financial condition, results of operations, and liquidity.

● Description of properties used in the business.

● Description of important legal actions, including civil rights and environmental cases and the disposition of previously reported proceedings.

● Names, ages and family relationships of executive officers.

● Financial statements audited by independent CPA's.

United States of America

- Holdings of the company's securities by management and principal security holders.

- List of directors and their background.

- Compensation of officers and directors including pension and deferred payment plans and unaccountable expense allowances.

- Options to buy company securities granted to its officers and directors.

- Transactions between the company and its officers, directors, major security holders and their families.

Form 10Q. This is a quarterly financial report which must be filed for each of the first three quarters of a company's fiscal year, no later than 45 days from the end of each quarter. Form 10-Q consists of two parts. Part I includes comparative balance sheets, statements of income and statements of cash flows, an analysis of significant changes in financial condition and results of operations and other data. Part II includes, among other things, information with respect to legal proceedings, changes in the rights of securities holders, defaults, and results of votes by holders of the company's securities.

Form 8K. This form must be filed within a specified time after the occurrence of certain events. In addition, this form is used for the voluntary reporting of other materially important events. Generally, the SEC considers a material event as one which is important enough to influence a reasonable person in making an investment decision. Events that must be reported include:

- change in control of a company (due within 15 calendar days);

- acquisition or disposition of a significant amount of assets (due within 15 calendar days);

- appointment of a receiver for a company or its parent under the Bankruptcy Act (due within 15 calendar days);

- changes in the company's independent accountant, including the reason(s) for the change, together with a description of any differences relating to accounting principles (due within 15 business days);

- resignation of directors (due within 5 business days);

- change in fiscal year (due within 15 calendar days); and

- form 8-K should also include any other events believed to be important for security holders to know.

All reports are required to be expressed in English and to be stated in US currency.

The duty to file reports is suspended for any year on the first day of which each class of the company's registered securities was held by less than 300 holders. The first time this event occurs Form 15 should be filed with the SEC 30 days after the beginning of the year. This serves as notification to the SEC that the company no longer has to file. However, the reporting duty resumes whenever a company exceeds 300 security holders as of the first day of a fiscal year.

All financial statements filed with the SEC must conform to GAAP and, in addition, they are subject to the more stringent reporting requirements promulgated by the SEC. In the event the SEC disagrees with a financial statement presentation or disclosure, the SEC customarily communicates its position in writing to the company and requests the filing of a revised document. After the SEC approves any revisions, it accepts the report as filed, which then becomes public information available to any interested party. Failure to comply with all of the requirements can result in penalties and sanctions. One of the most severe penalties is the ability of the SEC to prevent the company from effecting an offering of securities.

The foregoing represents a brief, and very condensed description of the responsibilities of a domestic public company to comply with the regulations of the SEC. It does not include a description of the process of registering a company's securities with the SEC. This process, whether it be an initial public offering (IPO) or a secondary offering, is extremely complex, and mandates the use of different forms not mentioned in this chapter. This requires the use of a skilled and experienced team of CPA's and special legal counsel. Whether a company is contemplating an IPO, or has attained public status, this team should be actively and continuously involved.

Publicly held Foreign Companies

Securities of a foreign private issuer may trade in the US either directly or in the form of American Depository Receipts (ADRs). An ADR is a certificate issued by a U.S. bank that represents the right to receive a specified number of foreign securities on deposit with a foreign depositary bank affiliated with the domestic ADR-issuing bank.

A foreign private issuer can register securities under the 1934 Act by filing a registration statement on Form 20-F with the SEC. Form 20-F is the keystone of the SEC's integrated disclosure system for foreign private issuers. It requires audited financial statements as well as extensive narrative non-financial disclosure. The required disclosure is less extensive than that required for US issuers. The same form will serve as the issuer's "annual report" in years subsequent to the 1934 Act registration.

The non-financial disclosures required in the Form 10-F include a description of the company's business and properties; information as to legal proceedings, including pending or contemplated governmental proceedings; exchange controls affecting security holders; identification of all control parties together with total shareholdings of all officers and directors as a group; information as to taxes in the issuer's home country as they affect US security holders; selected financial information, including a five year history of key income statement and balance sheet items; a management discussion and analysis of the results of operations, financial condition and liquidity, and descriptive information concerning the directors and officers of the company, including their compensation. Much of this information is similar to the requirements of a domestic company on Form 10-K.

The issuer will be required to file an annual report on Form 20-F within six months after the end of each fiscal year. Copies of the Form 20-F are not required to be furnished to security holders.

All of the primary financial statements included in these reports are generally stated in the currency of the country in which the issuer is incorporated or organised. In addition, in the event that GAAP of the foreign country differs significantly from US GAAP, a reconciliation of the financial statement effects of such differing practices is to be provided.

The issuer will be required to report on Form 6-K whatever material information, not previously furnished, it (i) is required to make public in the country of its domicile or in which it is incorporated or organised or (ii) filed with a foreign stock exchange on which its securities are traded and which was made public by that exchange, or (iii) distributed to its security holders promptly after the material contained therein has been made public.

Audit Requirements

Publicly held companies must have their annual financial statements audited. Many non-public companies also engage independent auditors to report on their financial statements, to comply with requirements of creditors or contractual agreements, or for other business reasons. Non-public companies sometimes engage CPAs to provide a level of service regarding their financial statements that is less than an audit. CPAs can issue a "review report" (expressing limitedassurance as to the fairness of presentation) or a "compilation report" (expressing no assurance as to the fairness of presentation) on companies' financial statements.

In the United States, accountants obtain and retain CPA designation by fulfilling certain educational requirements, passing a uniform CPA examination, fulfilling any experience requirements mandated by the state in which they practice, and complying with continuing professional education requirements. Non-public companies may select any CPA or firm of CPAs to audit their financial statements. Public companies must be audited by accounting firms which have voluntarily elected to comply with requirements for membership in the SEC Practice Section of the American Institute of Certified Public Accountants.

The standard form of the audit report was revised in 1989. The new standard form identifies the financial statements audited in an opening (introductory) paragraph, describes the nature of an audit in a scope paragraph, and expresses the auditors' opinion in a separate opinion paragraph.

The basic elements of the report are the following:

- a statement that the financial statements identified in the report were audited;

- a statement that the financial statements are the responsibility of the company's management and that the auditor's responsibility is to express an opinion on the financial statements based on the audit;

- a statement that the audit was conducted in accordance with generally accepted auditing standards (GAAS);

- a statement that GAAS requires that the auditor plan and perform the audit to obtain reasonable assurance about whether the financial statements are free of material misstatement;

- a statement that an audit includes:

  - examining, on a test basis, evidence supporting the amounts and disclosures in the financial statements,

  - assessing the accounting principles used and significant estimates made by management,

  - evaluating the overall financial statement presentation;

- a statement that the auditor believes that the audit provides a reasonable basis for the opinion expressed; and

- an opinion as to whether the financial statements present fairly, in all material respects, the financial position of the company as of the balance sheet date and the results of its operations and its cash flows for the period then ended in conformity with GAAP.

In addition to expressing an opinion on the financial statements, the auditor has a responsibility to evaluate the company's ability to continue in existence for a year from the date of the financial statements. If the auditor concludes there is substantial doubt about the company's ability to continue as a going concern, the auditor must describe the problem in the auditors' report.

Valuation Principles

To provide a structure for developing accounting standards, the FASB established in the early and mid 1980s a conceptual framework for financial reporting. This framework sets forth the objectives of financial reporting, qualitative characteristics of financial information, and definitional, recognition, and measurement criteria for elements of the financial statements.

United States of America

Revenues and gains are generally recognised when realised and earned, that is, when the goods or services are exchanged for cash or claims to cash and when the company has substantially completed the activities needed to be entitled to the benefits represented by those revenues. Revenues are measured at the exchange values of the assets (goods or services) or liabilities involved. Expenses and losses are recognised when a company's economic benefits are used up or when previously recognised assets are expected to provide reduced or no further benefits.

In general, assets and liabilities are initially recorded at historical cost. In other words, an asset is stated initially at the amount of cash or cash equivalents paid to acquire it and a liability is stated at the amount of cash or cash equivalents received when the related obligation was incurred. Assets recorded at historical cost are subject to depreciation and amortisation provisions, and under certain circumstances, downward adjustments to market or current net realisable values, as defined by GAAP for the particular circumstances.

GAAP requires a description of all significant accounting policies used. This description is usually the first footnote accompanying the financial statements and includes disclosures such as depreciation and inventory pricing methods used. A presumption exists in preparing financial statements that an accounting principle once adopted should not be changed in accounting for similar transactions and other events. That presumption may be overcome only if the company justifies use of another accounting principle on the basis that it is preferable. This practice promotes consistency between financial reporting periods. If another principle is deemed preferable, the nature of the change and effects of the change on net income must be disclosed.

Group Financial Statements
Consolidated Financial Statements
Consolidated financial statements must be presented for a parent company and all subsidiaries in which the parent company has direct or indirect ownership of a majority voting interest. A majority-owned subsidiary must be consolidated unless the parent's control is likely to be temporary, or the parent does not have the ability to control the subsidiary (for example, if the subsidiary is in bankruptcy or operating under foreign exchange restrictions or controls).

In consolidated financial statements, the financial position, results of operations, and cash flows of the parent and consolidated subsidiaries are presented as if they were a single entity. Intercompany transactions and balances are eliminated, but no adjustments need be made to bring the subsidiaries' accounting principles into line with those of the parent, if they differ.

A difference in financial periods of a parent and subsidiary does not of itself justify a subsidiary's exclusion from consolidation. If the difference is not more than three months, it is usually acceptable to consolidate the subsidiary's statements. However, if this is done, disclosure is made of the effects of any intervening events that materially affect the consolidated financial position or the results of operations.

Minority interests, if material, are generally shown as separate items in the consolidated statements.

When the parent and its eligible domestic subsidiaries file a single consolidated tax return, the subsidiaries generally record the tax expense on the basis on which the total consolidated tax liability is allocated among the companies in the group.

Combined Financial Statements
Combined financial statements are often used for companies under common control in other than a parent-subsidiary relationship (for example, when several companies with related operations are controlled by a single owner). Elimination of intercompany transactions and balances, and other areas such as minority interests, income taxes, and so on, are treated in the same manner as in consolidated statements.

Equity Method
The equity method is used to account for an investment where the investor company has the ability to exercise significant influence over the investee company's financial and operating policies. A holding of 20 to 50% of the investee company's voting stock is presumed to give the investor company that ability.

Under the equity method, an investor company initially records an investment at cost. It adjusts the carrying amount of the investment at the end of each year by the investor company's proportionate share of changes in the investee company's net assets and for the effects of intercompany profits.

Cost Method
If consolidation and the equity method are not appropriate, the cost method is used. Under the cost method, an investor company records dividends received as income and adjusts the carrying amount of its investment for reductions in market value which are other than temporary.

Business Combinations - Purchase and Pooling of Interests Methods
The two generally accepted methods of accounting for business combinations are the pooling of interests method and the purchase method. The two methods are not alternatives. The pooling of interests method may be used only when certain prescribed criteria are met. Otherwise, the purchase method must be used.

The purchase method, in effect, accounts for the combination as the acquisition of a controlling interest in a company by another company. The assets and liabilities of the acquired company are initially reported in consolidation at their fair values at the date of combination. A difference between the cost incurred by the acquiring company to acquire the controlling interest and the aggregate of those amounts is treated as goodwill, which is recorded as an asset. Goodwill is amortised over a period not to exceed 40 years, with annual amortisation reported as an expense in the income statement.

Under the purchase method, adjustments to fair values are usually made in worksheet entries (consolidation adjustments) when grouping the accounts of the separate companies for financial reporting. Assets and liabilities of a purchased subsidiary may be adjusted to fair value in the subsidiary's separate financial statements if a substantial change in ownership has occurred. This accounting treatment is termed "push down" accounting. "Substantial change in ownership" is not defined in the accounting literature and has been interpreted to mean anywhere from an 80 to 100% change.

The pooling of interests method accounts for a business combination as the uniting of the ownership interests of two or more companies resulting from the exchange by those companies of equity securities. Pre-existing bases of accounting are retained, and pre-existing recorded amounts of assets and liabilities are recorded by the combined entity at their previous amounts.

Auditors' Reports on Consolidated Financial Statements

In the auditors' report, the auditor expresses an opinion on the consolidated financial statements taken as a whole. The auditor does not take audit responsibility for the separate financial statements of each company included in the consolidated group.

Depreciation

Under GAAP, the cost of a tangible asset, less salvage value, is systematically charged to operations over the asset's estimated useful life. The cost includes all expenditure incurred to bring the asset to the condition and location necessary for its intended use. Typically, one of the following depreciation methods is used:

- Straight line

- Declining balance

- Sum of the years' digits

- Units of production

The straight line method is the most common for publicly held companies. The cost of land is not subject to depreciation. Because of the significant effect of depreciation on the financial position and the results of operations, the following disclosures are required:

- depreciation expense for the period;

- balances of major classes of depreciable assets, by nature or function, at the balance sheet date;

- accumulated depreciation, either by major classes of depreciable assets or in total, at the balance sheet date; and

- a general description of the method or methods used to compute depreciation of major classes of depreciable assets.

Depreciable lives for financial reporting purposes are based on the economic useful lives of the assets, which frequently differ from the depreciable lives permitted for income tax purposes.

Leasing

Lease accounting is one of the more detailed and complex areas in US accounting literature. The basic premise is that a lease which transfers substantially all benefits and risks of ownership should be accounted for by the lessee as the purchase of an asset (a "capital lease"). Other leases should be accounted for as the rental of assets (an "operating lease").

The basic accounting principles used by lessees for lease transactions are:

● Capital lease: the lessee records an asset and a liability both equal to (a) the market value of the leased property or (b) the present value of the minimum lease payments for the lease term, whichever is lower. Each payment is allocated between interest expense and reduction of the liability. The leased asset is amortised in a manner consistent with the lessee's normal depreciation policy for owned assets. The amortisation period cannot be longer than the lease term, unless the lease provides for the transfer of title to the lessee or gives the lessee a bargain purchase option.

● Operating lease: the lessee records periodic rental expense equal to the total lease payments spread ratably, normally straight line, over the lease term.

Required disclosures in the financial statements and footnotes are intended to provide a general description of leasing activity (i.e., types of leases), the flow of lease income and expense, and the future cash flows of the leasing activity. Additional disclosures are required to describe leases between related parties and sale-leaseback transactions.

Research and Development

In general, all research and development costs, including indirect costs, must be expensed when incurred. However, the cost of machinery and facilities with alternative future uses are capitalised and depreciated over their estimated useful lives. Total research and development costs charged to expense are disclosed in the notes to financial statements.

Inventories

Inventories generally consist of:

● Raw materials and supplies

● Work in progress

● Finished goods

United States of America

GAAP requires, in nearly all cases, that inventories of mercantile and manufacturing companies be stated at the lower of cost or market value. Cost is the sum of all expenditures, direct and indirect, incurred in bringing inventories to their respective condition and location. Various methods are acceptable in determining inventory costs including FIFO, LIFO, average, and specific identification. In general, the term "market value" means current replacement cost, except that it cannot exceed net realisable value nor can it be less than net realisable value reduced by a normal profit margin.

Depending on the nature of the inventory, the rule of "lower of cost or market" may be applied to individual items or to the total inventory.

Disclosure requirements include:

● the basis of valuation (for example, lower of cost or market value);

● the method of determining costs (for example, FIFO);

● the amounts of each major category of inventory; and

● a description and amounts of inventories pledged as collateral.

Additional disclosures are required when the LIFO method is used to determine cost.

Intangible Assets

Common types of intangible assets include goodwill, patents, trademarks, copyrights, licenses and franchises. Intangible assets are initially recorded at cost and amortised into income over their useful lives. The amortisation period may not exceed 40 years. The straight line method of amortisation is generally used. Disclosure requirements include:

● the basis of valuation;

● a description of the assets;

● amortisation expense for the period;

● the amortisation method; and

● the amount of accumulated amortisation.

Capital and Reserves

Capital of a corporation, commonly called stockholders' equity, generally consists of common stock, preferred stock, additional paid-in capital, and retained earnings.

A corporation may re-acquire its own shares unless restricted by its certificate of incorporation or the law of its state of incorporation. Most state laws allow a corporation to re-acquire its own shares out of retained earnings or capital, except when the corporation is insolvent or would be made insolvent by the transaction. The shares re-acquired may be held as "treasury stock" or may be retired. If a company re-acquires its own shares, the cost of those shares is generally shown as a deduction from equity. Gains and losses on reissuance or retirement of stock are accounted for as adjustments to equity rather than as part of income.

Cash and property dividends are charged to retained earnings when they are declared. Property dividends are recorded at the fair value of the assets transferred, and any difference between the book and fair value of the assets transferred is included in income.

Accounting for stock dividends and stock splits depends on the relative number of shares involved and legal requirements. When the number of shares issued in relation to the number of shares already outstanding is small, an amount equal to the fair value of the shares issued is usually transferred from retained earnings to capital stock and paid-in capital. For other situations, the amount transferred from retained earnings is only that required by law.

Restrictions on retained earnings are usually disclosed in the notes to the financial statements.

Foreign Currency Translation

US accounting standards require the "functional currency" approach to translation. The economic environment of a foreign company is viewed as the critical element in determining the functional currency. The functional currency, therefore, may or may not be the local currency.

A brief summary of foreign currency accounting follows:

- Foreign company financial statements must be expressed in the functional currency of the entity and conform to GAAP before they are translated. If the foreign company's local currency is not its functional currency, assets and liabilities are first remeasured using the functional currency before translation into US dollars.

- The current exchange rate at the balance sheet date is used to translate revenue, expenses, gains, and losses of a foreign company.

- The weighted-average exchange rate for the period is used to translate revenue, expenses, gains, and losses of a foreign company.

- The gain or loss on the translation of foreign currency financial statements is not recognised in current net income, but as a separate component of stockholders' equity.

United States of America

- In highly inflationary economies (those where cumulative inflation is approximately 100% or more over a three-year period), the functional currency is the reporting currency of the parent.

- A foreign currency transaction is one that requires settlement in a currency other than the functional currency of the reporting entity. Gains or losses resulting from a foreign currency transaction are generally recognised in net income for the period.

Financial statements disclosures include:

- the aggregate exchange gain or loss included in net income, including gain or loss on forward exchange contracts;

- an analysis of the changes in the separate components of equity for cumulative translation adjustments for the period; and

- material exchange rate changes after the balance sheet date, and their effect on unsettled balances.

Taxation

Corporations pay income tax on their computed taxable income at the federal level and, in many instances, at state and sometimes local levels. Federal, state, and local taxable income are rarely the same as financial statement income before taxes. They differ because income for federal and state tax purposes is computed in accordance with the prevailing tax laws, whereas financial accounting income is determined in accordance with GAAP. Some common differences between financial statement income before taxes and federal taxable income are:

- Depreciation: Methods permitted by the tax authorities may be different from GAAP.

- Dividend income: A corporation may deduct, subject to certain limits, a portion (currently 80%) of the dividends it receives from most domestic corporations.

- Bad debts: Estimates of uncollectible receivables are reported as an expense in the financial statements, but a bad debt cannot be reported on the tax return until the receivable is considered worthless.

GAAP requires the income tax effects of transactions to be reported in the financial statements when the transaction occurs, regardless of when the transaction is reported in the tax return. Deferred income taxes are recorded for differences between financial statement accounting and income tax accounting.

Accounting for income taxes has changed significantly in recent years. Before 1988, corporations computed deferred taxes based on differences between financial statement income and taxable income. In 1987, Statement of Financial Accounting

Standards No. 96 was issued. Under that Statement, deferred taxes were recognised on differences between the financial statement and income tax bases of assets and liabilities. Statement 96 was criticised for being extremely complex and for prohibiting, in many cases, recognition of deferred tax assets. Statement 96's effective date was postponed several times and then rescinded before it ever became effective. Some companies did, however, adopt and use Statement 96 accounting between 1988 and 1992.

Statement of Financial Accounting Standards No. 109, Accounting for Income Taxes, was issued in 1992. The provisions of this Statement are required for years beginning after 15 December 1992. They may be used for earlier periods. Under Statement 109, deferred taxes are calculated on differences between the financial statement and income tax bases of assets and liabilities that will result in taxable or deductible amounts in the future. Deferred tax assets are recorded if there is more than a 50% likelihood that the related tax benefits will ultimately be received.

Deferred taxes are not provided for on undistributed earnings of a subsidiary if the tax law provides a means by which those earning may ultimately be recovered tax-free and the parent company expects to use that means.

Disclosure requirements under Statement No. 109 include:

- components of the net deferred tax liability or asset;

- the net change in the "valuation allowance" (that is, deferred tax assets which are not recorded because there is less than a 50% likelihood that the related tax benefits will ever be received);

- the tax effect of each type of significant temporary difference or carry forward;

- significant components of income tax expense such as amounts currently payable, amounts deferred, and benefits of operating losses carried forward;

- reasons for differences between the "expected" and actual income tax expense shown in the financial statements; and

- amounts and expiration dates of operating losses and tax credits carried forward.

Unusual and Prior Period Items

Extraordinary items are transactions and other events that are both unusual in nature and infrequent in occurrence. Extraordinary items, if material, are separately disclosed in the income statement, net of any related income tax effect.

A transaction or other event that is either unusual in nature or infrequent in occurrence, but not both, is reported as a separate component of income from operations. Unusual or infrequent items are not reported net of their income tax effect.

United States of America

Previously issued financial statements may not be restated except to correct an error or to change to an accounting principle whose effects are required to be reported retroactively rather than in current income.

Retirement Benefits

For defined contribution retirement plans, the pension benefits received by retirees depend solely on amounts contributed by the employer and investment earnings on those contributions. The pension expense for these plans generally equals the employer's contribution for the year.

Defined benefit pension plans provide a promise to pay specified benefits to retirees based on such factors as age, years of service, and compensation. The basic premise of accounting for these plans is that the pension expense should be recorded by the employer in the period in which the employee provides the related services. A specific actuarial method, the unit credit method, must be used to allocate pension expenses to the years in which employee services are provided. Pension cost is based on the plan's benefit formula.

Statement of Financial Accounting Standards No. 106, Employers' Accounting for Post-retirement Benefits Other Than Pensions, is effective for years beginning after 15 December 1992. The effective date is postponed for two years for (1) plans outside the United States and (2) non-public companies with 500 or fewer plan participants. Statement No. 106 requires that costs of benefits provided to employees or their beneficiaries after retirement, such as health care and life insurance, be accounted for in a manner similar to defined benefit pension costs. Prior to Statement No. 106, employers generally used "pay-as-you-go" accounting, that is, benefits were recorded as expenses when paid. When a company initially adopts Statement No. 106, it may either record the entire effect immediately or amortise the initial effect over the average remaining service period of active participants in the plan.

Related Party Transactions

Information about transactions and relationships with related parties must be disclosed. Related parties include parent and subsidiary companies and other affiliates, principal owners, and management. The required disclosures include the nature of the relationship involved and a description and dollar amount of related party transactions. Accounting for related party transactions is the same as accounting for transactions with outside parties.

Segmental Reporting

Publicly held companies must present information within or accompanying their financial statements about business segments, foreign operations, export sales, and major customers. A business segment is determined based on factors such as the nature of the product, the nature of the production process, and markets or marketing methods. Data which must be disclosed for all business segments and foreign operations includes:

- sales to unaffiliated customers and sales or transfers to other industry segments;

- operating profit or loss; and

- the aggregate carrying amount of identifiable assets.

The accounting principles used in presenting segmental information are the same as those used in the underlying financial statements, except that most intersegment transactions are not eliminated.

Commitments and Contingencies

The footnotes to the financial statements must disclose a number of matters involving commitments and contingencies, including unused letters of credit, long-term leases, assets pledged as security for loans, pension plans, the existence of cumulative preferred stock dividends in arrears, and commitments such as those for plant acquisitions or obligations to reduce debt, maintain working capital, or restrict dividends.

In addition, an estimated loss from a contingent loss is charged to income if (1) it is probable that an asset had been impaired or a liability had been incurred at the date of the financial statements and (2) the amount of the loss can be reasonably estimated. Disclosure is required for contingencies not meeting both conditions if a loss is considered reasonably possible. Contingent gains are not recognised in income until they are actually realised.

Balances not Reflected in the Balance Sheet

A financial instrument is defined as cash, evidence of ownership in an entity (stock, for example) or a contract requiring an exchange of financial instruments between entities. Some financial instruments carry a risk of loss from failure of another party to fulfil the terms of a contract or from changes in market prices. If those losses could exceed amounts reported on the balance sheet, information about those risks must be disclosed. Examples of such items include guarantees of the debts of others, commitments to lend, and interest rate swaps. Disclosure requirements for financial instruments with off-balance-sheet risk of credit or market loss include:

- the face, or contract, amount;

- a discussion of the credit and market risks, the cash requirements of the instruments, and the accounting policies regarding the instruments;

- the accounting loss that would result if a party completely failed to perform under the contract and collateral, if any, proved worthless; and

- the company's policy for requiring collateral or other security.

United States of America

Price Level Changes

Other than for certain specialised industries that use fair value, the historical cost of assets and liabilities is not adjusted to reflect price level changes. As a result of high rates of inflation in the 1970s, the United States required supplementary disclosures for price-level changes on an experimental basis. Since 1986, price level disclosures have been voluntary, and few companies furnish them. However, publicly held companies are still required to discuss the effect of changing prices in management's discussion and analysis which accompanies the financial statements.

Future Developments

The FASB is working on a range of projects which will take many years to complete. Some of those projects may ultimately change some fundamental financial accounting and financial reporting principles. These projects include the following.

Consolidations and Related Matters

This project covers all aspects of accounting for affiliations between entities, including consolidation policies and procedures; accounting for corporate and noncorporate joint ventures; use of the equity method of accounting for investments; segmental reporting; and similar matters for not-for-profit entities.

Financial Instruments and Off-Balance-Sheet Financing Issues

Many innovative and complex financial instruments have been created in recent years. The goal of this project is to determine what, if any, broad accounting and disclosure changes are needed for financial instruments and transactions. Changes may result, for example, in accounting for mandatorily redeemable preferred stock and other obligations to repurchase equity instruments.

Accounting for Marketable Securities

Investments in debt securities are currently reported at cost, net of unamortised premiums or discounts. The FASB is considering whether to expand the use of fair value accounting for investments in debt securities. Because market values of debt securities are sensitive to interest rate fluctuations, such a change would have a large impact on financial institutions and other entities which carry large investment portfolios in debt instruments.

Impairment of Long-Lived Assets and Identifiable Intangibles

Divergent practices exist for writing down the value of long-lived and intangible assets and how to determine the amounts to write down. The major issues in this project include how to identify assets for evidence of impairment, how to quantify impairment, financial statement presentation and disclosure of impairment write-downs, and whether assets previously written down should ever be subsequently written up.

Present-Value-Based Measurements in Accounting

This project considers when amounts should be recognised in financial statements based on the present value of estimated future cash flows; when accounting allocations should be made over the life of an asset or liability using an interest method; and how the interest revenue or expense element associated with present value measurements should be reported in the income statement.

Table of International Comparisons

With many countries around the world adopting International Accounting Standards as the basis for their accounting practices and disclosures and with the strong influence of European Community Company Law directives on European accounting, practices worldwide have never been closer. However wide variations are often to be found.

The tables set out on the following pages identify some of the practices followed in nine different countries around the world. They provide an "at a glance" comparison between those countries and illustrate how close world accounting practices have become in some areas and how far apart they remain in others.

Table of International Comparisons

Australia	Brazil	Canada

Public Filing of Financial Statements

Australia

All companies, except proprietary companies, file financial statements and an annual return with the Australian Securities Commission.

Exempt companies file only the annual return. Public companies are also required to file an interim audited report with the Stock Exchange every 6 months (mining companies every 3 months).

Brazil

All corporations registered as an SA publish their financial statements in the official gazette prior to the annual shareholders' meeting. A company whose shares are publicly traded must also file information annually and to a lesser extent, quarterly with the Securities Commission (CVM). Limited companies (LTDA's) do not have to comply with these filing requirements.

Canada

Companies with total revenues of more than C$15m and total assets of more than C$10m file their annual financial statements and annual return. Companies listed on a stock exchange also file quarterly unaudited financial information with the relevant securities commission.

Audit of Financial Statements

Australia

A company's financial statements must be audited unless it is an exempt proprietary company and all the shareholders have agreed to dispense with the audit.

The auditor must be a member of one of two Australian accounting bodies or a similar overseas body.

A true and fair type audit report is given.

Brazil

Audited financial statements are mandatory only for publicly held companies, financial institutions, public institutes, government controlled companies and other organisations.

The auditor being an individual or a firm must be registered with the Consellio Federal de Contabiliade and in the case of publicly held corporations with the Security and Exchange Commission (CVM).

The auditor reports, inter alia, on whether the accounts conform with generally accepted principles and if the effects of inflation have been fully recognised.

Canada

Public companies and private companies with turnover in excess of C$10 million or gross assets in excess of C$5 million must be audited. Other companies need not have an audit if there is the unanimous agreement of the shareholders.

Regulation of auditors is a provincial responsibility and therefore varies throughout Canada. Some provinces require auditors to be licensed.

A true and fair type audit report is given.

France	Germany	Japan

Public Filing of Financial Statements

Both SA's and SARL's must file their financial statements, and certain supplementary information with the Registrar of Companies. Where auditors have been appointed the audit report must be filed. Listed companies must also publish, in a legal bulletin, certain information on a quarterly or half yearly basis. They must also publish their unaudited financial statements within 4 months of the year end.

AG's, large GMBH's and certain other enterprises publish their audited financial statements in the Federal Gazette and file them with the trade register.

Medium sized corporations file only their audited financial statements with the trade register whilst small corporations file unaudited financial statements. Listed companies file copies of their financial statements and the report of the executive board with the stock exchange.

The audited financial statements are filed with the Minister of Finance and, if the company is listed, with the stock exchange. Half yearly reports are filed with the stock exchange where relevant. Limited financial information (depending upon a company's size) is also published in a newspaper or official gazette.

Shareholders and creditors may inspect the financial statements at the principal office of the company for five years or at branch offices for three years.

Audit of Financial Statements

Société Anonyme and other companies exceeding certain size criteria are required to have an audit.

The auditor must be state registered and is appointed for a period of six years.

If consolidated accounts are prepared two auditors must be appointed.

A true and fair audit report is given.

All companies, except those satisfying the criteria to be classified as small must be audited.

For large companies only the auditor must be a qualified individual or audit corporation.

In addition to a true and fair type audit report the auditor prepares a long form report although this is strictly confidential and is not published.

All companies have a statutory auditor and in addition large corporations have an independent auditor.

There is no requirement for the statutory auditor to be qualified and they have a limited role in reviewing the conduct of the business and the preparation of the books and records.

The independent auditor must be a Public Accountant or an Audit Corporation and performs a true and fair type audit.

Table of International Comparisons

Singapore	United Kingdom	United States of America

Public Filing of Financial Statements

All limited companies (except exempt private companies) must file audited financial statements, a directors' report and an annual return with the Registrar of Companies. Companies listed on a stock exchange must file the above (except the annual return) with the Council of the Stock Exchange and supply them to every member and to every holder of securities issued by the company.	All companies must file audited financial statements with the Registrar of Companies (dormant companies file them unaudited). Financial statements filed by small and medium sized companies are abbreviated and include less information than in the financial statements issued to shareholders. Quoted companies file their annual financial statements, a half yearly unaudited report and a preliminary announcement of their results for the year with the stock exchange.	Public filing requirements are limited to companies whose securities are held and traded by the public. These companies have to file with the SEC annual reports (including the audited financial statements) and quarterly reports which include comprehensive financial information. The SEC must also be notified of a wide range of materially important events which affect a company.

Audit of Financial Statements

All companies and branches of foreign corporations must be audited by approved company auditors. Approved auditors are Certified Public Accountants qualified for appointment under the Accountants Act. The auditor gives a true and fair type opinion on the financial statements.	All companies, except those which are dormant are required to appoint an auditor. The auditor must be registered with a supervisory body before carrying out a company audit. The auditor gives a true and fair type opinion on the financial statements.	Only publicly held companies are required to have an audit although many others do. Many companies chose to have a limited scope review by a Certified Public Accountant (CPA). Public companies must be audited by CPA's who are members of the SEC practice section of the AICPA. The auditor gives a true and fair type report.

Australia	Brazil	Canada

Valuation Principles

Historical cost is normally followed with the revaluation of certain fixed assets being permitted.	Original cost adjusted using either monetary correction or constant currency methods to reflect the effects of inflation.	Historical cost basis. Assets are generally not revalued to market value,

Group Financial Statements

Parent companies are required to prepare consolidated financial statements. Equity accounting is not allowed for investments in associates – although this information is given in the notes. Goodwill is amortised through the profit and loss account over 20 years. The merger (pooling of interest) method is not permitted.	Publicly held parent companies are required to prepare consolidated financial statements – this is optional for all other parents. Investments in associates and subsidiaries excluded from consolidation are valued on the equity basis.	Parent companies are required to prepare consolidated financial statements. Associates are valued on the equity basis. Uniting of interests (merger) method is allowed in limited circumstances. Goodwill is written off over a maximum of 40 years. It is not permissible to recognise negative goodwill.

Foreign Currency Translation
Group Financial Statements

The financial statements of "integrated" overseas subsidiaries are translated using the temporal method and translation adjustments are included in the current income statement.	The financial statements of a subsidiary may be translated at either the closing or the average rate, but the method used must be consistent from year to year.	The financial statements of "integrated" overseas subsidiaries are translated using the temporal method and translation adjustments are included in the current income statement.

Table of International Comparisons

France	Germany	Japan

Valuation Principles

France	Germany	Japan
Historical cost with revaluation of certain fixed assets permitted.	Historical cost. Assets may not be revalued above it.	Historical cost. Revaluation of assets is strictly prohibited.

Group Financial Statements

France	Germany	Japan
All parents are required to prepared consolidated financial statements unless they are included within a larger group producing consolidated financial statements or the group falls below certain size limits. Equity accounting is used for associates or excluded subsidiaries. Proportional consolidation is recommended for investments in joint ventures. Goodwill is written off over its expected life (normally 5 to 20 years). In some instances it may be written off against retained earnings.	Parent companies are required to prepare consolidated financial statements unless they are included within a larger group which prepares consolidated financial statements in German and, for non-EC parents, publishes them in Germany. Groups falling below certain size criteria are also exempt. Associates are valued using the equity method. The merger (pooling of interests) method is permitted if certain conditions are satisfied.	Only public corporations produce consolidated financial statements which are included as supplementary information in the parent's annual report. Equity accounting is used for associates and for subsidiaries excluded from consolidation. Goodwill is either written off immediately or amortised over five years.

Foreign Currency Translation

Group Financial Statements

France	Germany	Japan
Foreign subsidiaries are most commonly translated using the closing rate for the balance sheet and the average rate for the profit and loss account. Translation differences are usually shown as a movement on shareholders equity.	There is no fixed rule for the translation of foreign subsidiaries and discussions are currently taking place within the profession as to the most suitable method.	The temporal method is recommended (using historical rates) for non-monetary items. Current rates are recommended for monetary items although companies may use historical rates.

Singapore	United Kingdom	United States of America

Valuation Principles

Historical cost modified, frequently, by revaluation of certain assets.	Historical cost with revaluation of certain fixed assets/inventory permitted.	Historical cost.

Group Financial Statements

Group accounts are prepared unless the parent is wholly owned by another Singapore company. They are normally in the form of consolidated statements although other formats may be acceptable.	A parent company must produce consolidated financial statements unless it is a subsidiary of an EC parent which produces group accounts or the group falls below certain size criteria.	A parent company must prepare consolidated financial statements. The equity method is used to value associates. Goodwill is written off through the profit and loss account over a maximum of 40 years. The pooling of interests (merger) method is used when certain criteria are met. Combined financial statements are often prepared for companies under common control which do not have a parent – subsidiary relationship. The principles applied are the same as for consolidation.
Equity accounting is used for valuing associates.	The equity method is used for associates and certain excluded subsidiaries.	
Goodwill is written off over its useful life.	Goodwill is either taken directly to reserves or amortised over its estimated useful life.	
	The merger method is permitted in certain circumstances.	

Foreign Currency Translation
Group Financial Statements

Financial statements of subsidiaries are translated at the rate ruling at the balance sheet date. Foreign currency translation differences are taken directly to reserves.	The temporal method of translation is used for translating "integrated" foreign subsidiaries and adjustments included in the profit and loss account.	Translation rules follow a "functional" currency approach which reflects the economic environment of the subsidiary.
		Where the functional currency is the US dollar a method similar to the temporal method is used.

Table of International Comparisons

Australia	Brazil	Canada

Foreign Currency Translation

Groups (Continued)

Australia	Brazil	Canada
Financial statements of other subsidiaries are translated at the year end rate and translation differences reported through shareholders equity.		Financial statements of other subsidiaries are translated at the year end rate and translation differences reported through shareholders equity.

Individual Entities

Australia	Brazil	Canada
Transactions settled during the period are translated at the rate ruling at the transaction date.	Transactions settled during the period are translated at the rate ruling at the transaction date.	Transactions settled during the period are translated at the rate ruling at the transaction date.
Monetary assets/ liabilities are translated at the year end rate and exchange differences included in the current year's income statement.	Monetary assets/ liabilities are translated at the year end rate and exchange differences included in the current year's income statement.	Monetary assets/ liabilities are translated at the year end rate and exchange differences included in the current year's income statement.
Non-monetary assets/ liabilities are translated at the rate ruling at the transaction date.	Non-monetary assets/ liabilities are translated at the rate ruling at the transaction date.	Non-monetary assets/ liabilities are translated at the rate ruling at the transaction date.
Differences arising on assets under construction may be included within the cost of the assets.		Gains or losses on a long term item are deferred and amortised over its life.

Taxation

Australia	Brazil	Canada
Taxable income comprises a company's income and capital profits. It is derived from adjusted operating profit.	Taxable income is derived from accounting net profit, subject to various adjustments.	Taxable income is based on reported earnings subject to various adjustments.

France	Germany	Japan

Foreign Currency Translation
Groups (Continued)

France	Germany	Japan
	Both the temporal method and the current rate method are acceptable with translation adjustments being reported as part of income or shareholders equity respectively.	Exchange differences are recorded in the Foreign Currency Translation Adjustment Account in the balance sheet and do not go through the profit and loss account.

Individual Entities

France	Germany	Japan
Transactions settled during the period are translated at the rate ruling at the transaction date.	Transactions settled during the period are translated at the rate ruling at the transaction date.	Transactions settled during the period are translated at the rate ruling at the transaction date.
Receivables/liabilities are translated at the year end rate. Exchange differences are shown on the balance sheet. Unrealised losses are deducted from the profit and loss account.	Monetary assets/liabilities are translated at the rate ruling at either the transaction date, or, if worse, the year end rate. The same basic rules apply to long term investments. If there is a permanent diminution in value of these assets a provision must be made.	Monetary assets/liabilities are translated at the balance sheet date, although long term assets/liabilities may remain at historical rates.

Taxation

France	Germany	Japan
Taxable income is based on reported trading profit subject to various adjustments.	Taxable income is based on reported trading profit subject to various adjustments.	Taxable income is based on reported trading profit subject to various adjustments.
There are rarely any material differences between accounting and		

Table of International Comparisons

Singapore	United Kingdom	United States of America

Foreign Currency Translation

Groups (Continued)

Singapore	United Kingdom	United States of America
	Other subsidiaries should be translated at the closing rate (average rate may be used for profit and loss account items) and translation differences treated as movements on reserves.	For other subsidiaries the year end rate is used for balance sheet items and a weighted average rate for income statement items. Translation adjustments are reported as a separate component of shareholders equity.

Individual Entities

Singapore	United Kingdom	United States of America
Transactions settled during the period are either translated at the rate ruling at the transaction date, or, if there have been no significant fluctuations at an average rate for the period.	Transactions settled during the period are either translated at the rate ruling at the transaction date or, if there have been no significant fluctuations, at an average rate for the period.	Transactions settled during the period are translated at the rate ruling at the balance sheet date. Assets and liabilities are translated at the year end rate and any translation differences included in the current year income.
Monetary assets/liabilities are translated at the year end rate whilst other assets/liabilities are recorded at their historical rates.	Monetary assets/liabilities are translated at the year end rate whilst other assets/liabilities are recorded at their historical rates.	
All exchange adjustments are taken to the profit and loss account.	All exchange adjustments are taken to the profit and loss account.	
Where a trading transaction is covered by a related, or matching forward contract the rate of exchange specified in the contract may be used.	Where a trading transaction is covered by a related, or matching forward contract the rate of exchange specified in the contract may be used.	

Taxation

Singapore	United Kingdom	United States of America
Taxable income is based on reported trading profits subject to various adjustments.	Taxable income is based on reported trading profits subject to various adjustments.	Tax is often payable at federal, state and local levels. Taxable income is calculated on adjusted trading profits.

Australia

Brazil

Canada

Taxation (Continued)

Deferred tax accounting is followed using the liability method. A deferred tax asset is only recognised where realisation is assured beyond any reasonable doubt.

Where the tax charge varies significantly from notional tax based on the reported profits a reconciliation between the two must be given.

There is no tax-effect (deferred tax) accounting in Brazil.

Deferred taxation is provided using the deferral method.

The future benefits of tax losses may only be recognised if there is virtual certainty that they will be utilised within the prescribed period.

Retirement Benefits

Employers are required to provide retirement/ pension benefits usually through a separately constituted pension fund.

Contributions are expensed in the period in which they are made.

Certain corporations, including those which are listed, are required to disclose details of the company's superannuation commitments.

Provision is made in the financial statements for long service leave costs.

Payments to the public and private pension plans are charged against income when due to be paid. Employer's contributions are made at a fixed rate.

Apart from disclosures relating to private plans no other provisions or disclosures are made.

Employers usually set up a separate pension fund.

Disclosures and accounting treatment in the employer's financial statements depend on whether the fund is benefit or cost based.

In a benefit based plan an actuary assesses, triennially, the level of contributions to be made which are charged to income as they accrue. Where an actuarial valuation highlights a deficit or where additional costs arise, due to enhancement of the scheme, to be met by the employer, these will usually be amortised over the expected remaining service lives of the employees.

There are comprehensive rules on actuarial methods and valuation bases and on the detailed disclosures which are required.

Table of International Comparisons

France	Germany	Japan

Taxation (Continued)

France	Germany	Japan
taxable income so deferred tax provisions are rarely found except in consolidated financial statements.	Deferred taxation is calculated on the liability method. Deferred tax assets are only recognised in very limited circumstances.	Deferred tax is not found in the accounts of individual companies although it may be in consolidated financial statements.
Where deferred tax is calculated either the deferral or the liability method may be used.		

Retirement Benefits

France	Germany	Japan
Employees and employers contribute to a government fund for pensions and other retirement benefits. Private funds are rare.	For pension commitments entered into prior to 1 January 1987 companies can choose whether or not to make full provision for them although they are encouraged to do so.	Where a company sets up a scheme to cover pensions, in addition to state pensions, tax laws allow 40% of accumulated pension liabilities to be accrued. Most smaller companies follow this in their financial statements.
Companies are required to disclose details of retirement benefits in the notes to the financial statements.	For commitments entered into after that date full provision should be made in the financial statements.	Larger corporations fund their plans, with the agreement of the tax authorities and charge contributions to income as they are paid.
	Where full provision has not been made the amount not provided should be disclosed.	The notes to the financial statements set out the accounting policy followed and other related information.

Table of International Comparisons

Singapore	United Kingdom	United States of America
Taxation (Continued)		
Deferred taxation is calculated either using the liability method, which is most common, or the deferral method.	Deferred tax is calculated using the liability method. Deferred tax assets may not be recognised except to the extent that they are recoverable without replacement by equivalent debit balances.	Deferred tax is calculated on the differences between the value of assets and liabilities for tax purposes and their value for the financial statements. Deferred tax assets are recorded if there is more than a 50% likelihood that the related tax benefits will ultimately be received.
Retirement Benefits		
Most pensions are paid through the Central Provident Fund Scheme and company plans are unusual. Where company plans do exist comprehensive disclosures are required and companies should provide in full for their commitments. If full provision is not made this should be disclosed.	Private pension funds set up by employers are very common. Disclosures and accounting treatment in the employers financial statements depend on whether the fund is a benefit based or cost based plan. In a benefit based plan an actuary assesses, triennially, the level of contributions to be made which are charged to income as they accrue. Where an actuarial valuation highlights a deficit or where additional costs arise, due to enhancement of the scheme these will usually be amortised over the expected remaining service lives of the employees. There are comprehensive rules on actuarial methods and valuation bases which are acceptable and on the detailed disclosures which are required.	Disclosures and accounting treatment in the employers financial statements depend on whether the fund is a benefit based or cost based plan. In a benefit based plan an actuary assesses, triennially, the level of contributions to be made which are charged to income as they accrue. Where an actuarial valuation highlights a deficit or where additional costs arise, due to enhancement of the scheme these will usually be amortised over the expected remaining service lives of the employees. There are comprehensive rules on actuarial methods and valuation bases which are acceptable and on the detailed disclosures which are required.

387

Table of International Comparisons

Australia   Brazil   Canada

Retirement Benefits (Continued)

For a cost based plan the charge is normally expensed as it accrues. Disclosure requirements are less onerous and actuarial valuations are not required.

Leasing

Finance

A liability equal to the present value of minimum lease payments is recognised at the inception of the lease. The liability is reduced by the capital element of any lease payments.

The interest element of payments is calculated by reference to the rate implicit in the lease agreement.

Assets held under finance leases are capitalised at an amount equal to the liability recognised and amortised over its useful life.

All leases are generally treated as operating leases. If at the end of a lease the company acquires the asset it will be treated as an acquisition at that time.

A liability equal to the present value of minimum lease payments is recognised at the inception of the lease. The liability is reduced by the capital element of any lease payments. The interest element of payments is calculated by reference to the rate implicit in the lease agreement.

Assets held under finance leases are capitalised at an amount equal to the liability recognised and amortised over its useful life.

Operating

Lease payments are expensed in the period in which they fall due.

Comprehensive disclosures are required relating to both finance and operating leases.

Periodic rentals are charged against income in the year they are due and disclosed in the notes to the financial statements.

Lease payments are expensed in the period in which they fall due.

Comprehensive disclosures are required relating to both finance and operating leases.

France	Germany	Japan

Retirement Benefits (Continued)

Leasing

Finance

France	Germany	Japan
In individual companies all leases are invariably treated as operating leases. In consolidated financial statements leased assets are often capitalised and an equal liability recognised. Treatment of the liability and asset is broadly similar to that followed in Australia.	An asset and a liability is recognised at the lower of fair market value or present value of lease payments. Each lease payment is allocated between a reduction in the outstanding liability and interest. The asset is amortised in a manner consistent with the lessees normal depreciation policy for other owned assets.	There is no requirement for capitalisation of finance leases and it is therefore rarely to be found in practice. Where capitalisation does take place IAS is generally followed.

Operating

France	Germany	Japan
The lease expense should be charged in a way that reflects the economic substance of the contract. In practice costs are usually expensed as incurred. Comprehensive disclosures are required relating to both finance and operating leases.	Lease payments are normally expensed as they accrue.	Lease payments are normally expensed as they are made.

Table of International Comparisons

Singapore	United Kingdom	United States of America
Retirement Benefits (Continued)		
	For a cost based plan the charge is normally expensed as it accrues. Disclosure requirements are less onerous and actuarial valuations are not required.	For a cost based plan the charge is normally expensed as it accrues. Disclosure requirements are less onerous and actuarial valuations are not required.

Leasing

Finance

| Leases qualifying as finance leases are capitalised and a corresponding liability recognised.

The treatment of the asset and the liability follows, broadly, other international practice. | A liability equal to the present value of minimum lease payments is recognised at the inception of the lease. The liability is reduced by the capital element of any lease payments.

The interest element of payments is calculated by reference to the rate implicit in the lease agreement.

Assets held under finance leases are capitalised at an amount equal to the liability recognised and amortised over its useful life or the lease term if shorter. | Under a finance (or capital) lease an asset and liability are recognised both being equal to either the market value of the leased asset or the present value of the lease payments whichever is lower.

Each lease payment is allocated between interest expense and reduction of the liability.

The asset is amortised over its useful life or, unless the lease provides for the transfer of title to the lessee, the lease term whichever is shorter. |

Operating

| Lease payments are expensed as they accrue. | Lease payments are normally written off on a straight line basis over the life of the lease irrespective of when the cash payments are made.

Comprehensive disclosures are given for both finance and operating leases. | Lease payments are normally written off on a straight line basis over the life of the lease irrespective of when the cash payments are made.

Comprehensive disclosures are given for both finance and operating leases. |

International Technical Contact Partners

Jacques Priorollo
Bergé, Giordano, y Asociados
Riva Davia
1367 Piso 11*A
1033 Buenos Aires
ARGENTINA

Telephone No: (1) 381 0416, 383 1687/ 0412
Fax No: (1) 381 0416, 383 1687, 383 0412

Andrew Gordon
Duesburys
140 Sussex Street
Sydney NSW 2000
AUSTRALIA

Telephone No: (02) 950 8000
Fax No: (02) 950 8111

Dr V Hamerle
Hamerle-Reinold EWB Revisions-
und K-Treuhandgesellschaft m b H
Am Modenapark 10
1030 Vienna
AUSTRIA

Telephone No: (0222) 715 1982 0
Fax No: (0222) 715 1982 80

Dominic Rousselle
André Hoste & Partners
Avenue Chateau de Walzin 10
B-1180 Brussels
BELGIUM

Telephone No: (02) 347 25 00
Fax No: (02) 347 06 49

Douglas Hillen
Neville Russell
The Williams Building
2nd Floor
20 Reid Street
Hamilton HM11
BERMUDA

Telephone No: 292 3862
Fax No: 295 1349

Ricardo Julio Rodil
Trevisan Auditores e Consultores
Rua Francisco Tramontano 100
05686-010 Sao Paulo - SP
Sao Paulo
BRAZIL

Telephone No: (011) 844 6833
Fax No: (011) 844 6932

Gerard Pilache
Societé Africaine d'Audit et
    d'Expertise Comptable
Douala
CAMEROON
*(Correspondence via Alain
Penanguer, Paris, France)*

J Max Wiebe
Hudson & Company
600-1015 4th Street S W
Calgary
Alberta
T2R 1J4
CANADA

Telephone No: (403) 265 0340
Fax No: (403) 265 3142

Michael Weston
Michael Forrest International
Langtry House
PO Box 124
La Motte Street
St Helier
Jersey
CHANNEL ISLANDS

Telephone No: (534) 73921
Telex No: 4192069 FIDES
Fax No: (534) 24668

Patricio Da Forno
Humphreys y Cla
Providencia 199
Piso 6
Santiago
CHILE

Telephone No: (2) 2047316 - 2047293
Fax No: (2) 22 34937

John P Poyiadjis
Pavlou, Poyiadjis & Co
Chanteclair House
2 Sophouli Street
8th Floor
PO Box 1814
Nicosia
CYPRUS

Telephone No: (02) 453406
Telex No: 4173 CHARTACO CY
Fax No: (02) 453276

Antonin Janda
Antonin Janda & Co
Prague
CZECH REPUBLIC
(Correspondence via Frédéric
Mazière, Paris, France)

Peter W Viereck
Revisionsfirmaet Preben Larsen
Overgaden neden Vandet 9C
PO Box 1930
1023 Copenhagen K
DENMARK

Telephone No: (32) 96 20 00
Fax No: (32) 96 20 40

A Hamdi Abou Saada
Abou Saada & Partners
122 El Tahrir Street
El Dokki
PO Box 183 Orman
Cairo
EGYPT

Telephone No: (02) 3614561, 3614562, 3614563
Telex No: 20388 HABS UN
Fax No: (02) 3614560

Thierry Karcher
Calan Ramolino & Associés
2 Rue Paul Cézanne
75008 Paris
FRANCE

Telephone No: (01) 40 76 60 60
Fax No: (01) 42 89 26 25

Gerard Pilache
Societé Africaine d'Audit et
d'Expertise Comptable
Libreville
GABON
(Correspondence via Alain Penanguer,
    Paris, France)

Gerhard Nolze
BTR Beratung und Treuhand Ring G m
    b H Wirtschaftsprufungsgesellschaft
Burchardstrasse 17
2000 Hamburg
GERMANY

Telephone No: (040) 33 97 110
Fax No: (040) 32 64 85

Loizos E Kolokotronis
Kolokotronis-Papaakyriacou & Co
Veritas House
27-31 Hatzikyriakou Avenue
185 38 Piraeus
GREECE

Telephone No: (1) 4539750, 4539754, 4523212
Telex No: 211457 EQUI GR
Fax No: (1) 45 39 755

Philipe Saingolet
Cabinet Saingolet
38 Le Lys Dugazon
Petit-a-Pérou
97139 Abymes
Pointe-à-Pitre
GUADELOUPE

Telephone No: (590) 902314, 890679, 827094, 838011

Selwyn Mar
Charles Mar Fan & Co
11th Floor Belgian House
77-79 Gloucester Road
GPO Box 982
HONG KONG

Telephone No: (852) 520 0333
Telex No: 83982 CMFCO HX
Cable No: MARFAN HONG KONG
Fax No: 529 4347

József Koblencz
CBI Konyvvizsgáló Kft
Vigado Ter 1
1051 Budapest
HUNGARY

Telephone No: (1) 176 4048, 176 0048
Fax No: (1) 176 7994

Farook M Kobla
Sharp & Tannan
Bank of Baroda Building
Bombay Samachar Marg
Bombay 400 023
INDIA

Telephone No: (22) 2047722/23, 2042961,
2044818, 2045963, 2046647, 2040422
Telex No: 118 6150 STCA IN
Telegrams: DOCQUET
Fax No: (022) 2045963

Drs Santoso Reksoatmodjo
Drs S Reksoatmodjo & Co
J1 K H Wahid Hasyim No.2
PO Box 92/Jkt
Jakarta 10340
INDONESIA

Telephone No: (21) 327860, 333554
Telex No: 61460 AUDIT IA
Fax No: (21) 334083

Patrick O'Donoghue
Oliver Freaney & Company
43/45 Northumberland Road
Ballsbridge
Dublin 4
REPUBLIC OF IRELAND

Telephone No: (01) 688644
Telex No: 30593 OFCO EI
Fax No: (01) 689755

Nigel Rotheroe
Crossleys
PO Box 1
Portland House
Station Road
Ballasalla
ISLE OF MAN

Telephone No: 0624 822 816
Fax No: 0624 824 570

Attilio Arietti
Consulaudit S a s-Arietti & Co
3 Via XX Settembre
10121 Turin
ITALY

Telephone No: (011) 561 2722, 561 1369
Fax No: (11) 553286

Eiten Inamura
Actus Audit Corporation
Samon Eleven Building
3-1 Samon-Cho
Shinjuku-Ku
Tokyo 160
JAPAN

Telephone No: (03) 3352 7600
Fax No: (03) 3353 0080

Charles Gitau
Carr Stanyer Gitau & Co
Longonot Place
Kijabe Street
PO Box 40647
Nairobi
KENYA

Telephone No: (2) 338092/3/4, 214929, 216240/1
Fax No: (2) 338095

Byong Kim
Samduk Accounting Corporation
12th Floor
Seohung Building
68 Deonji-Dong Jongro-Ku
Seoul
KOREA

Telephone No: (02) 735 0241
Fax No: (02) 730 9559

Dr Aiad Ellafi Younis
PO Box 1633
Benghazi
LIBYA

Telephone No: 061 90462

Jean L Faber
Fiduciaire d'Organisation et de
    Révision Fernand Faber
15 Boulevard Roosevelt
33 Rue Notre-Dame
2450 Luxembourg
LUXEMBOURG

Telephone No: 225626
Telegrams: FIDUFALUX LUXEMBOURG
Fax No: 462019, 465310

Robert Teo
Robert Teo, Kuan & Co
171-175 Jalan Maharajalela
50150 Kuala Lumpur
MALAYSIA

Telephone No: (03) 2483700
Fax No: (03) 2426466, 2442880

Martin H Said
Mizzi Scerri Said & Co
Fifth Floor
Airways House
6-10 High Street
Sliema
MALTA

Telephone No: 341857, 341858
Fax No: 336296

A S Hajee Abdoula
Hajee Abdoula & Ramtoola
7th Floor
Moorgate House
29 Sir William Newton Street
Port Louis
MAURITIUS

Telephone No: (203) 212 9477/87
Fax No: (230) 212 9473

Carlos Casares Gonzáles
Gossler SC
Av Alvaro Obregón No.56
Colonia Jardin
87330 Matamoros
Tamps
MEXICO

Telephone No: (891) 6 61 04, 6 61 06
Fax No: (891) 6 61 81
International Mailing:
PO Box 2009
Brownsville
Texas 78522
USA

Mohamed Ouedghiri
Ouedghiri Laraki & Associes
3 rue El Kadi Iass
Maarif
31100 Cassablanca
BP 5039
MOROCCO

Telephone No: (2) 257014/254858/257425
Fax No: (2) 232736

Eppo H Horlings
Horlings Brouwer & Horlings
Koningslaan 30
1075 AD Amsterdam
NETHERLANDS

Telephone No: (020) 6769955
Fax No: (020) 6764478

Owen Pierce
Spicer & Oppenheim
7th-8th-9th Floors
Westpac Tower
120 Albert Street
PO Box 2219
Auckland 1
NEW ZEALAND

Telephone No: 09 379 2950
Fax No: 09 303 2830

I A Eniola
Sulaimon & Co
52 Airport Road
PO Box 1223
Kano
NIGERIA

Telephone No: 064 624517, 645998, 627812
Telex: 77330 KAN NG 0066

Irfan Rehman Malik
S M Masood & Co
Empire Centre
Main Boulevard
Gulberg - II
Lahore 54660
PAKISTAN

Telephone No: (42) 872818, 5712557,
5712558
Telegrams: BALSHEET
Fax No: (42) 872556, 5712556

Jerzy Pawilno-Pacewicz
Multiexpert Sp z o o
Al Jerozolimside 42/139
00-024 Warsaw
POLAND

Telephone No: 39 120 292
Fax No: 39 120 292

Lisboa Afonso
INTERAUDIT-Auditores
Internacionais Lda
Rua Tomas Ribeiro 50-1
1000 Lisbon
PORTUGAL

Telephone No: (1) 54 37 70/52 76 67
Telex No: 63146 CTEAM P
Fax No: (1) 53 53 24

Usamah Ali Tabbarah
Usamah Ali Tabbarah
PO Box 4702
Riyadh 11412
SAUDI ARABIA

Telephone No: (1) 4059928, 4059969,
4053836, 4041765, 4044324
Telex No: 401542 TABARA SJ
Cable: TABARA
Fax No: (1) 4044532

Abdourahmane Kounta
Societé Africaine d'Audit et
d'Expertise
Comptable (SAAEC)
97 rue Mousse Diop
Dakar
SENEGAL
*(Correspondence via Alain
Penanguer, Paris, France)*

Telephone No: 22 01 30
Fax No: 22 59 86

Foong Daw Ching
Teo Foong + Wong
15 Beach Road 03-10
Beach Centre
Singapore 0718
SINGAPORE

Telephone No: 336 2828
Telex No: RS 34033 PACRES
Fax No: 339 0438

Donato Moreno
Audihispana S A
Avenida Pau Casals 13-15 8°
08021 Barcelona
SPAIN

Telephone No: (3) 414 47 76
Fax No: (3) 202 17 23

N S C De Silva
B R De Silva & Co
70 1/1 Chatham Street
Colombo 1
SRI LANKA

Telephone No: (01) 25724/20415/ 422466
Fax No: (01) 25905

A Baha Edden Abdeen
Bahasa Street. PO Box 521
Damascus
SYRIA

Telephone No: 338677
Telex No: AGBAR 41 91 24 SY

Somporn Vechpanich
DIA International Auditing
316/32 Sukhumvit 22 (Sainumthip)
Sukhumvit Road
Klongton Prakanong
Bangkok 10110
THAILAND

Telephone No: (2) 2582799, 25953000-2,
2607481, 2598847-8
Fax No: (2) 260 1553

Ali Ì Şanver
Güreli Aşiroğlu Şanver
Şakayikli Sokak 14
Levent lç 80620
Istanbul
TURKEY

Telephone No: (1) 269 65,
278 96 20, 278 95 58, 268 03 40
Fax No: (1) 278 04 35

Sam Dunn
Spicer and Pegler
Dubai World Trade Centre Level 31
PO Box 9252
Dubai
UNITED ARAB EMIRATES

Telephone No: (4) 3313399, 313389, 313323
Telex No: 47297 MTGCO
Fax No: (4) 313631

Kim Hurst
Neville Russell,
246 Bishopsgate
London EC2M 4PB
UNITED KINGDOM

Telephone No: (071) 377 1000
Telegrams: NEVRUSS G
Fax No: (071) 377 8931

James C Beien
Clifton Gunderson & Co
1211 West Twenty Second Street
Suite 408, East Tower
Oak Brook, Illinois 60521
UNITED STATES OF AMERICA

Telephone No: (708) 573 8600
Fax No: (708) 573 0798

Glossary of Accounting Terms

ENGLISH	GERMAN
Balance Sheet	**Bilanz**
Assets	Aktiva
Long term assets	**Langfristige Aktiva**
Property, plant and equipment	Sachanlagen
Land and buildings	Grundstücke mit Bauten
Plant and equipment	Maschinen und maschinelle Anlagen
Other	Sonstige Sachanlagen
Accumulated depreciation	Aufgelaufene Abschreibungen
Other	**Sonstiges Anlagevermogen**
Long term investments	Langfristige Beteiligungen
Investments in subsidiaries	Mehrheitsbeteiligungen
Investments in associated companies	Beteiligungen
Other investments (market value)	Sonstige Beteiligungen (Börsenwert)
Long term receivables	Langfristige Forderungen
Accounts and notes receivable	Forderungen aus Warenliefergungen
- trade	und-leistungen
Receivables from directors	Forderungen an Vorstandsmitglieder
Intercompany receivables	Forderungen an verbudene Unternehmen
Associated company receivables	Forderungen an nahestehende Gesellschaften
Other	Andere Foderungen
Goodwill	Geschäftswert
Patents, trademarks and similar assets	Patente, gewerbliche Schutzrechte und ähnliche Rechte
Expenditure carried forward	Rechnungsabgrenzung
Current assets	**Umlaufvermögen**
Cash and bank balances	Bankguthaben und Kassenbestand
Marketable securities	Börsenfähige Wertpapiere
Receivables (detail as for long-term receivables)	Forderungen
Inventories/stocks	Vorräte

FRENCH	DUTCH
Bilan	**Balans**
Actif	**Aktiva**
Actif immobilisé	**Vaste aktiva**
Immobilisations corporelles	Materiele vaste aktiva
Terrains et constructions	Bedrijfsgebouwen en-terreinen
Matérial et outillage	Machines en installaties
Autres	Andere vaste bedrijfsmiddelen
Amortissements cumulés	Cumulatieve afschrijvingen
Autres valeurs immobilisées	**Andere vaste aktiva**
Titres de participation -	Deelnemingen
dans des filiales	Deelnemingen in
	groepsmaatschappijen
dans des sociétés apparentées	Deelnemingen in
	verbonden vennootschappen
autres (valuer en bourse)	Overige deelnemingen
	(marktwaarde)
Valeurs realisables à long terme	Vorderingen op lange termijn
Clients et effets à recevoir	Handelsdebiteuren en te inner
Prêts et avances aux	wissels
administrateurs	Vorderingen op bestuurders en
	commissarissen
Créances intersociétés	Vorderingen op
	groepsmaatshcappijen
Créances sur des sociétés	Vorderingen op verbonden
apparentées	vennootschappen
Autres	Overige voerderingen
Fonds de commerce	Goodwill
Brevets, marques et autres actifs	Concessies en vergunningen,
similaires	intellectuele eigendom
Charges à repartir sur plusieurs	Vooruitbetaald op immateriele aktiva
exercises	
Valeurs disponibles	**Vlottende aktiva**
Trésorerie Caisse et comptes auprès des	Liquide middelen
banques	
Tires de placement	Effekten
Créances	Vorderingen
Valeurs d'exploitation/stocks	Voorraden

ENGLISH	GERMAN
Liabilities	**Passiva**

Long term liabilities	**Langfristige Verbindlichkeiten**
Secured loans	Abgesicherte Darlehen
Unsecured loans	Darlehen ohne Sicherung
Intercompany loans	Darlehen von verbudenen Unternehr
Loans from associated companies	Darlehen von nahestehenden Gesellschaften
Current liabilities	**Kurzfristige Verbindlichkeiten**
Bank loans and overdrafts	Bankschulden und Überziehungen
Current portion of long term liabilities	Kurzfristig fällige Teile der langfristigen Verbindlichkeiten
Payables	Verbindlichkeiten
Accounts and notes payable - trade	Verbindlichkeiten aus Warenlieferungen und-leistungen
Payable to directors	Verbindlichkeiten gegenüber Vorstandsmitgliedern
Intercompany payables	Verbindlichkeiten gegenüber verbundenen Unternehmen
Associated company payables	Verbindlichkeiten gegenüber nahestehenden Gesellschaften
Taxes on income	Ertragssteurverbindlichkeiten
Dividends payable	Dividendenverbindlichkeiten
Other payables and accrued expenses	Sonstige Verbindlichkeiten und Rechnungsabgrenzung
Other liabilities and provisions	**Sonstige Verbindlichkeiten und Rückstellungen**

Shareholders' Interest	**Eigenkapital**
Share capital	**Grundkapital (AG's)** **Stammkapital (GmbH's)**
Authorised shares	Genhmigtes Kapital
Issued shares	Ausgegebenes Kapital
Outstanding shares	Ausstehendes Kapital
Capital not yet paid in	Noch nicht eingezahltes Kapital
Par value per share	Nennwert je Anteil
Movement in share capital	Veränderung des Grund- [Stamm-]kapitals

Note: the above terminology follows principally that used in Accounting Standard No. 5

FRENCH	DUTCH
Passif	**Passiva**
Dettes à long terme	**Langlopende schulden**
Emprunts assortis de garantie	Leningen met zekerheid
Emprunts sans garantie	Leningen zonder zekerheid
Empruntes intersociétés	Schulden aan nahestehenden groepsmaatschappijen
Emprunts aupres des sociétés apparentées	Schulden van verbonden vennootschappen
Dettes à court terme	**Kortlopende schulden**
Prêts et découverts bancaires	Schulden aan kredietinstellingen
Partie à moins d'un an des dette à long terme	Lopende afflossingsverplichtingen
Dettes Fournisseurs et effets à payer	Schulden Schulden aan leveranciers en handelskredieten, te betalen wissels
Comptes courants des administrateurs	Schulden aan bestuurders en commissarissen
Comptes courants intersociétés	Schulden aan groepsmaatschappijen
Comptes courants des sociétés apparentées	Schulden aan verbonden vennootschappen
Impôts sur les bénéfices	Vennootschapsbelasting
Dividendes à payer	Te betalen dividenden
Autres créanciers et charges à payer	Overige schulden en overlopende passiva
Provisions et autres dettes	**Andere schulden en verplichtingen**
Capitaux propres	**Eigen Vermogen**
Capital social	**Aandelenkapitaal**
Capital souscrit	Maatschappelijk kapitaal
Capital souscrit-appelé versé	Geplaatst kapitaal
Capital souscrit-non appelé	Niet geplaatst kapitaal
Capital souscrit appelé non versé	Niet volgestort kapitaal
Valeur nominale des actions	Nominale waarde per aandeel
Modifications du capital social	Mutatites in het aandelenkapitaal

ENGLISH	GERMAN
Rights, preferences and restrictions on dividends and repayments	Rechte, Vorzugsrechte und Einschränkungen bezüglich der Dividendenausschüttung und der Rückzahlung von Kapital
Cumulative preferred dividends in arrears	Kumulative Vorzugsdividende soweit die Zahlungen rückständig
Reacquired shares	Zurückerworbene Kapitalanteile
Shares reserved for future issuance under options	Aktien, die fur eiene zukunftige Ausgabe bestimmt oder zur Ausübung eienes Optionsrecht
Other equity	**Sonstiges Eigenkapital**
Capital paid in excess of par value (share premium)	Über den Nennwert eingezahltes Kapital
Revaluation surplus	Gewinn aus Neubewertung
Reserves	Rücklagen
Retained earnings	Bilanzgewinn (nicht ausgeschütteter Gewinn)
Income Statement/Profit and Loss Account	**Gewinn-und Verlustrechnung**
Sales or other operating revenue	Umsatz oder sonstige betnebliche Erlose
Depreciation	Abschreibungen
Interest income	Zinserträge
Income from investments	Erträge aus Beteiligungen
Interest expense	Zinsaufwendungen
Taxes on income	Ertragsteuern
Unusual charges	Ausserordentliche Aufwendungen
Unusual credits	Ausserordentliche Erträge
Signficant intercompany transations	Bedeutende Transaktionen zwischen verbunden Gesellschaften
Net income	Reingewinn

FRENCH	DUTCH
Droits, priorités et restrictions affectant la distribution des dividendes et le remboursement du capital	Rechten, preferenties en beperkingen ten aanzien van terugbetaling van kapitaal
L'arrière dû sur les dividendes cumulatifs	Achterstallige dividenden op cumullatief preferente aandelen
Actions rachetées	Ingekochte eigen aandelen
Actions reservées pour des émissions futures dans le cadre d'options	Aandelen bestemd voor toekomstige uitgiftewaarvoor een optie is gegeven
Autres fonds propres	**Overig eigen vermogen**
Prime d'emission, prime d'apport ou de fusion	Agioreserve
Réserve de réévaluation reglementée	Herwaarderingsreserve
Réserves	Reserves
Report à nouveau	Onverdeelde winst
Compte de pertes et profits	**Winst - en Verliesrekening**
Chiffre d'affaires	Netto omzet
Dotation aux comptes d'amortissements	Afschrijvingen
Produits financiers	Ontvangen interest
Revenus sur titres de participation ou de placement	Resultaat deelnemingen
Intéréts payés	Rentelasten
Impôts sur les bénéfices	Belasting naar de winst
Pertes exceptionnelles	Buitengewone lasten
Profits exceptionnels	Buitengewone baten
Transactions significatives Intersociétés	Belangrijke intra-groepstransacties
Bénéfice net	Resultaat na belastingen

ENGLISH	SPANISH
Balance sheet	**Balance**
Assets	Activo

Long term assets	**Activo a largo plazo**
Property, plant and equipment	Inmovilizado material
Land and buildings	Terrenos y edificios
Plant and equipment	Maquinaria y instalaciones
Other	Otro inmovilizado material
Accumulated depreciation	Amortización acumulada
Other	**Immovilizado inmaterial**
Long term investments	Inversiones a largo plazo
Investments in subsidiaries	Inversiones en subsidiarias
Investments in associated companies	Inversiones en compañias associada
Other investments (market value)	Otras inversiones financieras (valor de mercado)
Long term receivables	Deudas a largo plazo
Accounts and notes receivable - trade	Deudores por operaciones de trafico a largo plazo
Receivables from directors	Deudas de administradores
Intercompany receivables	Deudas empresas del grupo
Associated company receivables	Deudas sociedades asociadas
Other	Otras cuentas deudoras
Goodwill	Fondo de comercio
Patents, trademarks and similar assets	Patentes, marcas (de fábrica y comercial)
Expenditure carried forward	Gastos amortizables
Current assets	**Activo circulante**
Cash and bank balances	Caja y bancos
Marketable securities	Valore mobiliarios
Receivables (detail as for long-term receivables)	Clientes
Inventories/stocks	Existencias

ITALIAN

Stato Patriomoniale
Attivo

Immobilizzazioni

Immobilizzazioni materiali

    Terreni e fabbricati
    Impianti, e macchinari
    Altre
    Fondi di ammortamento

Altre immobilizzazioni immateriali

Partecipazioni
    Partecipazioni in controllate
    Partecipazioni in collegate

    Altre partecipazioni (valore di
    mercato)

Crediti a lungo termine

    Clienti ed effetti attivi
    (da operazionii commerciali)
    Prestiti ed anticipi a dirigenti

    Crediti verso società del gruppo

    Crediti verso società collegate

    Altri crediti

Valore di avviamento
Brevetti, marchi di fabbricazione ed
    altre attività simili
Costi capitalizzati

Attività correnti

Danaro in cassa e presso le banche
Titoli negoziabili
Crediti

Rimanenze di magazzino

SWEDISH

Balansräkning
Tillgångar

Långfristiga tillgångar

Fastigheter, maskiner och inventarier

    Mark och byggnader
    Maskiner och inventarier
    Övriga
    Ackumulerad värdeminskning

Andra tillgångar

Langfristiga investeringar
    Aktier i dotterbolag
    Aktier i närstaende bolag

    Övriga aktier och andelar

Langfristiga fordringar

    Kundfordringar och växelfordringar

    Fordringar hos styrelseledamöter m fl

    Fordringar hos koncernföretag

    Fordringar hos närstaende bolag

    Övrigar fordringar

Goodwill
Patent, varumärken och liknande
    tillgångar
Balanseradeorganisationskostnader

Omsättningstillgångar

Kassa och bank
Börsnoterade värdepapper
Fordringar

Varulager

ENGLISH	SPANISH
Liabilities	**Passivo**

Long term liabilities	**Passivo exigible a largo plazo**
Secured loans	Préstamos con garantia
Unsecured loans	Préstamos sin garantia
Intercompany loans	Préstamos empresas del grupo
Loans from associated companies	Préstamos compañias asociadas

Current liabilities	**Passivo exigible a corto plazo**
Bank loans and overdrafts	Créditos bancarios y sobregiros
Current portion of long term liabilities	Créditos a largo plazo con vencimiento a corto
Payables	Acreedores
Accounts and notes payable - trade	Proveedores
Payable to directors	Administradores
Intercompany payables	Expresas del grupo
Associated company payables	Compañias asociados
Taxes on income	Impuesto sobre sociedades
Dividends payable	Dividendo activo a pagar
Other payables and accrued expenses	Pagos diferidos

Other liabilities and provisions	**Otros acreedores y previsiones**
Shareholders' Interests	**Capital y Reservas**

Share capital	**Capital Social**
Authorised shares	Acciones autorizades
Issued shares	Acciones emitidas
Outstanding shares	Acciones pendientes
Capital not yet paid in	Capital sin desembolsar
Par value per share	Capital nominal
Movement in share capital	Movimiento en capital social
Rights, preferences and restrictions of dividends and repayments	Derechos, preferencias y restricciones sobre dividendos
Cumulative preferred dividends in arrears	Dividendos preferentes accumulados
Reacquired shares	Acciones recompradas por la empresa

ITALIAN

Passivitá

Passivitá a lungo termine

Mutui con garanzie reali
Muti senza garanzie reali
Prestiti da società del gruppo
Prestiti da società collegate

Passivitá correnti

Prestiti e scoperti di banca
Parte correntie di debiti a lungo termine

Altri debiti
    Fornitori ed effetti passivi (da
      operazioni commerciali)
    Debiti verso dirigenti

    Debiti infragruppo
    Debiti verso società collegate

Imposte sul reddito
Dividendi da pagare
Altri debiti e ratei passivi

Altre passivite ed accantonamenti

Patrimonio Netto

Capitale Sociale

Azioni autorizzate
Azioni emesse
Azioni sottoscritte
Capitale non ancora liberato
Valore nominale delle azioni
Varazioni intervenute nel capitale
    sociale
Diritti, prioritá e limitazioni alla
    distribuzione di dividendi ed al
    rimborso del capitale
Dividendi privilegiati dovuti per
    esercizi precedenti

Azioni proprie riacquistate

SWEDISH

Skulder

Långfristiga skulder

Lan mot säkerhet
Lan utan säkerhet
Laneskulder till koncernbolag
Laneskulder till närstaende bolag

Kortfristiga skulder

Banklan och krediter
Kortfristig del av langfristiga lan

Skulder
    Leverantorrskulder och
      växelskulder
    Skulder till styrelseledamöter m fl

    Skulder till koncernbolag
    Skulder till närstaende bolag

Bolagets skatteskuld
Skuld för utdelningar
Andra skulder och upplupna kostnader

Andra skulder och reserveringar

Eget Kapital

Aktiekapital

Övre aktiekapitalgräns
Inbetalda aktier
Utestaende aktier
Obetalt aktiekapital
Nominellte värde
Förändringar i aktiekapitalet

Rattigheter, företräden och restriktioner
    i utdelningar och aterbetalningar

Ackumulerad utdelning pa
    preferensaktier

Aterlösta aktier

ENGLISH	SPANISH
Shares reserved for future issuance under options	Acciones reservadas para futura emisión opcional
Other equity	**Otras reservas**
Capital paid in excess of par value (share premium)	Reservas por prima de emisión
Revaluation surplus	Fondo de regulanrizacion
Reserves	Reservas
Retained earnings	Remanente de ejercicios antenores
Income Statement/Profit and Loss Account	**Cuenta de perdidas y ganancias**
Sales or other operating revenue	Ventas y otros ingresos
Depreciation	Amortizaciones
Interest income	Intereses recibidos
Income from investments	Ingresos financieros
Interest expense	Intereses pagados
Taxes on income	Impuesto de sociedades
Unusual charges	Gastos extraordinarios
Unusual credits	Ingresos extraordinarios
Significant intercompany transactions	Transacciones intergrupos
Net income	Beneficio neto

ITALIAN

Azioni riservate sulle future emissioni
in base ad opzioni

Attri mezzi

Riserva di emmisione

Fondi di rivalutazione
Riserve
Utili non distribuiti

Conto economico

Vendite ed altri ricavi
Ammortamenti
Interessi attivi
Proventi finanziari
Interessi passivi
Imposte sul reddito
Costi straordinari
Proventi straordinari
Operazioni significative con società del
   gruppo
Utile netto

SWEDISH

Aktier reserverade för framtida
   utgivning under villkor

Ovrigt kapital

Inbetald överkurs pa aktier

Uppskrivningsfond
Fonder
Balanserade vinstemedel

Resultaträkning

Fakturerad försaljning
Avskrivningar
Ränteintäkter
Utdelningar
Räntekostnad
Skatt
Extraordinära kostnader
Extraordinära intakter
Väsentliga koncernmellanhavenden

Nettoresultat